Praise for

ROCKS

"A mini-masterpiece . . . Just as the preeminent Stones book was an autobiography from its guitarist, Aerosmith ax man Joe Perry has now given us the best book on [Aerosmith]. . . . The meat of the book proves to be the relationship between Perry and frontman Steven Tyler, a rock 'n' roll partnership with all of the carnage, love, backbiting, separations, and reunions you'd expect. Perry's anecdotes could have been flown in from some ace rock 'n' roll–centric novel, and do more than amuse; the best enlighten, not just about this band and the partnership at the core of it, but the very nature of creativity itself."

—The Boston Globe

"An excellent read . . . There are times when Perry's descriptions of Tyler's interactions with himself and others are laced with near-hatred and disgust . . . but there are also the moments when you realize that if Shakespeare had ever written a play about rock 'n' roll blood brothers, the two male leads would've been Joe Perry and Steven Tyler."

—Guitar World

"Thrilling . . . An intimate narrative . . . This is the raw Aerosmith . . . Perry discusses every detail of the creative process . . . [and] takes you through every developmental stage of his journey in becoming the guitar legend he is today."

—Rebeat magazine

"A story of friendship and love. Since the Aerosmith chronicles have already been brought to vivid life in the band's *Walk This Way*, it left Perry room to contemplate things from a deeper core inside of himself. . . . What *Rocks* gives to his fans is a rare look into the psyche of a man who always heard the music and let the music do the talking."

—*Glide* magazine

"Riveting . . . Eye-opening . . . An engaging read."

—*The Patriot Ledger*

"Joe Perry has been the AxeMeister longer than some of you have been alive. He's been there, and done that. He has been the consummate six-string gunslinger for a band that has always done things their own way. Joe never went Hollywood. Joe never looked over his shoulder to see who was running behind him. Ever the gentleman rocker, Joe sits high atop of rock royalty. Admit it. You're jealous. When I grow up, I want to be Joe Perry."

—Gene Simmons

"An insightful and harrowing roller-coaster ride through the career of one of rock and roll's greatest guitarists. Strap yourself in."

—Slash

"Rockin' Joe Perry 'rocks' again!"

—Jimmy Page

"One might guess that I, Perry Farrell, would admire Joe Perry because he is a legendary guitar ripper, and you'd easily be right on the button—however, what you wouldn't have guessed is that I admire, respect, and have looked up to Joe Perry for years because he is a mad passionate, devoted husband and loving daddy who rocks. Viva familia, Joe!"

—Perry Farrell

"Joe Perry describes with amazing detail and passion the virtual odyssey of his life as the quintessential rock star in America's most famous rock band of all time. Like his riffs, his story is inspired, crisp, and packs a punch. Joe Perry has done for rock and roll what the human genome project and stem cell technology have done for medicine—broken it wide open to inspire and shape our music for many decades to come. I could not stop reading this book!"

—Rudolph Tanzi, professor of neurology at Harvard Medical School and coauthor (with Deepak Chopra) of *Super Brain*

"Evocative . . . Perry's book will strike gold with every Aerosmith fan."

—*Publishers Weekly*

ROCKS

MY LIFE IN AND OUT OF **AEROSMITH**

JOE PERRY

with David Ritz

SIMON & SCHUSTER PAPERBACKS

NEW YORK   LONDON   TORONTO   SYDNEY   NEW DELHI

Simon & Schuster Paperbacks
An Imprint of Simon & Schuster, Inc.
1230 Avenue of the Americas
New York, NY 10020

First Simon & Schuster paperback edition October 2015

Simon & Schuster and colophon are registered trademarks of Simon & Schuster, Inc.

For information about special discounts for bulk purchases,
please contact Simon & Schuster Paperback Special Sales at
1-866-506-1949 or business@simonandschuster.com.

The Simon & Schuster Speakers Bureau can bring authors to
your live event. For more information or to book an event, contact the
Simon & Schuster Speakers Bureau at 1-866-248-3049
or visit our website at www.simonspeakers.com.

Interior design by Ruth Lee-Mui

Manufactured in the United States of America

10 9 8 7 6 5 4 3 2

Library of Congress Cataloging-in-Publication Data for the hardcover edition is as follows:
Perry, Joe, 1950– author.
  Rocks : my life in and out of Aerosmith / Joe Perry with David Ritz.
     pages cm
  1. Perry, Joe, 1950– 2. Aerosmith (Musical group) 3. Rock musicians—
United States—Biography. I. Ritz, David, author. II. Title.
  ML419.P4823A3 2014
  782.42166092—dc23
  [B]
                              2014030144

ISBN 978-1-4767-1459-2
ISBN 978-1-4767-1460-8 (ebook)

I would like to dedicate this book to Billie, my soul mate and wife, without whose help and support I never would have made it this far. And to our amazing boys, Aaron, Adrian, Tony, and Roman, whose understanding and support of this lifestyle has been a blessing. I love you all.

In loving memory of Tony and Mary Perry

CONTENTS

FOREWORD

by Johnny Depp

As I sit here before a most cacophonous piece of blank onion skin, which I ever so delicately stuffed into my sturdy Olympia typewriter, and which surely deserves a more appreciative and well-balanced operator, but alas, such is its lamentable fate to be clubbed by my inept and clumsy digits, the paper screams for me to make the first move.

My thoughts are charged with the challenge of writing a few words on a man. An artist. A significant, nay, eminent artist, not only for me but for many others. A guitarist extraordinaire. A hero whose immeasurable ability has sent him high onto every Greatest Guitar Player list going ever since he sliced through some of the most tasteful and raging notes to be unleashed on an unwitting world. A hero who I've been given the honor to call both friend and brother.

Pondering him—the man, the mentor—the flood of imagery is astounding. I am swarmed by visions, swept away, almost, happily catapulted backward into fond memories of a fucked-up youth, with everything and nothing to look forward to. Did I delve into all those clichéd Things That I Shouldn't Have as a kid? Indeed, I fucking did. With great passion, pure ignorance, and fucking gusto. For a good while there, life for me was an endless, rickety, and dangerous train wreck just waiting to happen. But no self-medication, no booze or chemical what-have-you, has ever done what a solitary sliver of music could do. Not even close.

You see, this middle-aged fuck-up was once that fucked-up kid. Aged twelve, or thereabouts. Sitting in the backseat of my folks' car. We were caught up in traffic outside the Publix supermarket and Eckerd drugstore, where there was some local to-do occurring in the parking lot. A band was playing. As we hit the stoplight, I watched the colors change around the musicians in silhouette with rapt attention. I was captivated. Wholly. And as the sound and vision imposed themselves upon the provincial, compact folds of that spun-out little brain, I knew. Suddenly, everything was in order. The song they were playing was "Dream On." Never more had I needed that moment, that song, or that bat-shit realization, clarifying the very reason for my existence and what I needed to do in order to stay sane and alive: I needed a guitar . . . and quick!

With hard green cash never having bothered my pocket before, I managed to wrangle twenty-five bucks from my mom to pick up a Decca electric. The first Aerosmith record and a Mel Bay chord book had to be stuffed down my trousers and jacket. (Desperate measures and all that.) I played that record and studied the chord book as if it were some holy language. Puberty went by almost unnoticed. I shut myself off from the world, holed up in my little room, practicing, practicing, and practicing again. . . . I had to be note perfect.

And thus my life began.

Now, for me, as a shy, scruffy teen, the name Joe Perry would invoke a reverence for a species I had never known, especially in those early years when all teacher types, no matter how hard they tried, could not penetrate my brain enough to command any respect. Nothing in the world existed aside from the guitar and those who had mastered it as the ultimate form of expression . . . the perfect medium for a reclusive twelve-year-old to vent some serious spleen.

Joe Perry was one of the very few names back then—aside from everyone's ultimate music maestro, Keith Richards—who could inspire any sense of genuine awe into my adolescent mind, galvanizing body and spirit into actually giving a fuck. They were of an ilk never before encountered. The idea of meeting these untouchable heroes in real life was absurd—akin to ordering government-approved marijuana and having it delivered to your door personally by Mr. Obama. Unlikely . . .

But every tinder needs its flint, after all, and in this case, the genius of Joe was able to fully bloom when fused with another musical genius, that of the profoundly fervent, nigh-evangelical showman Steven Tyler, who just so happened to harbor one of the finest, most soulful set of pipes ever to have existed, all accompanied and brought to the fore by the brilliant musicianship of Brad Whitford, Tom Hamilton, and Joey Kramer. One other, sometimes unspoken member of the band that I would like to salute is the legendary producer and all-around wonderful human being Jack Douglas, who sat at the helm for those early records, guiding them, directing them. No doubt his input proved to be beyond integral to their incredible success. Over the years, the band has suffered its ups and downs, as you will read much of here, but all in all they've outlasted the vast majority of their peers and are still going strong today, having survived and ultimately surpassed the many brief epochs and trends tended to far lesser entities than themselves.

Cut to 2010. Hollywood, California. Swing House Recording Studios, just off Sunset Boulevard. Steven Tyler prowls about the room like a high-octane jungle cat. He had kindly invited a friend and me to watch the band record a few tracks for the new album. And there is Joe Perry. Right there, in the corner, just visible in the dark. He called me over and we sat there, he indulging me, discussing guitars and showing me the effects he was using for what would eventually become *Music from Another Dimension!* It was a huge moment for me, to sit there in a room full of idols, with this particular idol paying me any attention whatsoever, let alone confiding in me. And since then, that impossible afternoon, I've experienced the immeasurable pleasure of playing the Hollywood Bowl, among other stages, with Joe, Steven, and the boys. Although the night that holds the most special place in my heart was when that formerly toxic twosome came and played music with my son, Jack, for his birthday party a few years ago. He and I were like a couple of fans—in total awe! I was that little kid again, nearly the same age as my son.

A poetic life was Joe's fate. He was born with a style. He may have gleaned from the greats before him, as everyone must, but he transformed all that learning into his own signature sound. The way he uses musical notes is as personal and unique as any conversation you could ever have with the man. It's how he communicates. He is a master of feel, and with guitar in hand, his muscular, rhythmic tones soar effortlessly, seizing all those in earshot, reflecting the inherent unpretentiousness of his ability. There is something primordial in the nature of his grooves that just flat-out fuckin' rocks, inviting everyone to witness and experience. There's no elitist guest list here. No VIPs. No backstage pass is needed.

If you're holding this book in your hands then, aside from the music itself, you have all that you will ever need. The heart and soul of the man himself, hurled faithfully at the page. The wise, silent one finally speaks! You'll note the sagacious nature of a wholly sapient man. No bullshit. Devoid of it. Plain and simple. All the shyness, the honesty, the love, sweat, tears, and humility of this mysterious creature awaits you, friends, from his beginnings all the way to the here and now . . . and whatever might still be to come.

This book is a gift. A sacred tome, even. A hitherto secret slice of life, beamed in directly from one of the greatest guitar gods to have ever walked the earth, or stepped on a stage, or raged inside the mind of a young soul searching for what the fuck it all means.

Before I leave you I have one final thought that I feel impelled to convey. While I was reading this tale I could not help but continually hear, as if on a loop, the last lines of William Saroyan's brilliant preface to his play *The Time of Your Life*. Saroyan's words beautifully sum up Joe the husband, the father, the man: "In the time of your life, live—so that in that wondrous time you shall not add to the misery and sorrow of the world, but shall smile to the infinite delight and mystery of it."

—Johnny Depp
Boston, Massachusetts
June 6, 2014

ROCKS

In July of 1959, a young mother is standing on the shore of Lake Sunapee in the mountainous terrain of New Hampshire. The sky is cloudless and almost blindingly blue. The day is peaceful but the woman is not. Her heart is beating like crazy. Her mouth is dry. With every passing second, she grows increasingly afraid. Her son has disappeared deep into the lake, and she fears he may be drowning. She's afraid that this time she has let him go too far.

Early that morning he had shown her his makeshift diving rig with a homemade mask, tubes, pulleys, ropes, and cement blocks that would anchor him to the bottom of the lake and allow him to explore the fish life he finds so fascinating. Because she is a gym teacher and swimming instructor, she encourages his physical activities. She knows that, given his shy nature, he is more comfortable under rather than above water. She knows that he is an ingenious child. She likes how he wants to explore. But now this venture has taken an alarming turn. She knows that her son could stay underwater for three to four minutes. But now it's minute five. With her own swimming mask in hand, she takes action. Not about to let her kid drown, she's going after him. She's positioned to take the dive when suddenly he surfaces. He's breathing heavily, but he's breathing. She sees exhaustion in his eyes but a smile on his face.

"It works great, Mom. I can stay down long enough that the fish come out of hiding. Soon as I catch my breath I'm going back down."

A lifetime later, I'm puzzled by that story of Mom and me. I wonder how that nine-year-old kid, whose burning passion in life was to become a marine biologist and whose idol was Jacques Cousteau, turned into a guitarist. I'm puzzled by how someone who grew up in the upper-middle-class New England suburbs—born into a family with virtually no interest in music or art—wound up riding the tidal wave of rock and roll. I'm also puzzled by how I survived that tidal wave and lived to tell the story.

GESTATION

PART I

GESTATION

THE WATER AND THE WOODS

In the essential dream of my childhood I'm in the water or the woods. I'm swimming through an ocean of startling clarity. I'm seeing a thousand varieties of fish; I'm feeling like a fish myself, aware that at any moment a bigger fish might swim my way—a shark or a barracuda. The thought is more exhilarating than frightening. I'm not scared of the possibility of danger. I almost welcome the encounter. I welcome surprise. Nature is nothing *but* surprise, a world of water whose vastness allows me to disappear into pure beauty.

The lure of the woods is its primitive beauty. My dream life in the woods has me lost in a grove of ancient trees. If I keep walking long enough I'll find my way out, but I'm not sure I want out. Being lost in the wilds has a certain comfort. There is no destination, no home. I don't know what's around the bend—a wolf, a wildcat, a venomous snake. I like not knowing. I like the dense undergrowth, the sharp smells of the forest, the songs of the birds, the ever-changing weather, the dark clouds, the quickening of my heartbeat as I suddenly realize that I and I alone am responsible for my survival. For the rest of my life I will stare into the unknown.

In the water and the woods I face danger and discovery. In my real life, as a boy born on September 10, 1950, and raised in the small, quiet town of Hopedale, Massachusetts, I keep going back to the water and the woods. That's where I seek anonymity. It's where I can disappear into wordless, endless wonder.

I'm not saying that I'm able to completely disappear from the emotional ups and downs that characterize every childhood. I'm saying that I want to. My earliest memories all involve being drawn deep into nature, where I welcome, rather than fear, getting lost. I welcome the mysteries that lurk at the bottom of the sea and live inside the dark forest of night.

My parents were good and honorable people. They cared for their two children—my younger sister, Anne, and myself—with loving concern. My mother, Mary, was a graduate of Boston University with a master's degree. She taught physical education in the public schools. Her mind was both curious and brilliant. She was always reading about everything from the earth's chakras to the metaphysics of quantum theory to John Steinbeck's *Travels with Charley*. She wore her hair short and exuded great confidence. As a strong and proud working mom of the 1950s, she was a woman of the future—a liberated woman decades before the movement began.

My father, Tony, was equally upstanding. He had gone to Kent State and graduated from Boston's Northeastern University with a major in accounting. He had grown up in Lowell, Massachusetts, where his dad, a Portuguese immigrant from the island of Madeira off the coast of Morocco, worked in the factories and later owned a funky little grocery store. My dad was born in Lowell and when he was two the family moved back to Madeira where my dad spent his childhood before moving back to the States. After serving in the U.S. Army Air Forces at the end of World War II, Dad graduated from college and began working as an accountant, taking his first steps toward self-reinvention. The family name—Pereira—was shortened to Perry by his father. And rather than stay in Lowell, Dad moved to Hopedale, some thirty miles outside Boston, where the American dream had been set out in the form of suburban perfection. Hopedale was where my father entered the upper middle class.

Founded in 1842, Hopedale was one of the country's first utopian communities. It began as a picture-perfect Norman Rockwell village of industrious dreams. In the 1850s the Draper Corporation, manufacturer of power looms for the textile industry, took over the town. In the 1950s my dad went to work for Draper as a cost accountant. He and Mom bought a duplex in Bancroft Park and rented out the other side.

Mom's parents, the Ursillos, hailed from Naples, Italy, and would have loved to see their daughter enter a nunnery. She rejected most of their old-world notions about womanhood, but she accepted their Catholicism—at least to the point of attending Sunday mass and making sure that her husband and children did the same.

In our household there were few if any remnants of my parents' Italian and Portuguese backgrounds. Only English was spoken. No philosophy but American pragmatism was practiced. Do what works. Adapt to reality. Improve your circumstances by applying yourself. I was raised inside the solid ethos of the Eisenhower 1950s. My mother's child-raising bible was Dr. Spock's *Common Sense Book of Baby and Child Care*. The Perrys were all about common sense. Mom taught generations of children the benefits of exercise. Because of his common sense and sterling reputation, Dad was elected town treasurer. Mary and Tony were a well-respected couple. At home, they spoke to one another fondly. They were affectionate; they hugged; they kissed; they were girlfriend and boyfriend. Together, they comprised a formidable tennis doubles team.

I see them in their whites, out on the court during a fine New England afternoon in May, whacking the ball with studied determination. I am not part of their game but, standing close by, I feel their confidence.

I see them flying high in the cloudless sky in a seaplane that my father is piloting. I am not with them, but from the ground below, I feel their exhilaration as Dad buzzes the local baseball field to get a look at the score. The town officials chastise him for flying too low. He's contrite but I know he doesn't regret his joyride. Straitlaced accountants don't break laws, even minor ones, but I'm glad to see that my dad, whose laces are always super-tight, has some sense of rebellion.

He was the first guy in Hopedale to buy a Volkswagen Bug. Later he bought a BMW before anyone had heard of BMWs. The color, I remember well, was bright orange.

I also remember Dad talking about his buddies and World War II like it had just ended. He told stories about being a waist gunner on a B-17, the heavy-duty bomber, during the last months of the war. I pictured him standing at an open window on the side of a plane tearing through the sky at two hundred miles an hour, thirty-two thousand feet above the ground. The wind's coming at an outside temperature of -32°. Dad's face is covered by an oxygen mask and his chest protected only by a sheepskin jacket as he fires away at enemy aircraft. He realizes that such missions end with a 40 to 50 percent fatality rate. Yet he does what he has to do, a nineteen-year-old with balls of steel.

As a little boy, I would study a tattered black-and-white photo of his crew, amazed that my dad was once so young. He and his fellow soldiers looked into the camera with easy gazes. There was no fear in their eyes. They seemed relaxed about their mission, which, day after day, brought them to death's door.

I saw my father as a man of quiet courage. His goal for his family was simple—a better life. Postwar America was all about optimism and economic mobility. The war had been won and prosperity was at hand. But prosperity had to be earned through skills forged in discipline. It took disci-pline to become a professional accountant. It took hard work for a woman in the 1940s to graduate from college. My parents lived disciplined lives. They were neither doting nor overly affectionate with their children, but they were dutiful and always present. Dinner was served on time. Bills were paid on time. We didn't live beyond our means. We didn't live on borrowed money. Education was valued. Education was seen as the key to greater prosperity.

My education became the first and greatest stumbling block, an-other reason why I longed to lose myself in the water and the woods. Like millions of other kids, I had a learning disability—attention-deficit/

hyperactivity disorder (ADHD)—that was neither understood nor treated. Reading was the only subject at which I excelled. I would much rather be reading James Fenimore Cooper than dealing with participles in French.

My poor school performance was puzzling because my parents saw that I possessed intelligence and curiosity. Marine biology became a passion. When I asked them to drive me to Boston to hear lectures by Jacques Cousteau, my first hero, they were happy to do so. They took me to the Woods Hole Oceanographic Institution on Cape Cod, a paradise for a kid in love with water. I was obsessed with learning from those men who explored the deep. I wanted to go deep. I was told that if I kept up my grades I could come back one summer and intern at Woods Hole.

That never happened.

My grades were below average. That became the great mystery of my childhood: Why was I having such difficulty at school? I was deeply frustrated. I wanted to present my parents with good grades. I sensed their ambition for themselves and for me—and I wanted to realize those ambitions. I wanted to please them. The fact that I scored high on IQ tests only made things worse. I didn't understand why I wasn't doing better, and neither did they. They hired tutors but the tutors didn't help. I read things three or four times without retaining a word. I was always told to try and focus, but that never worked. At school, I felt like I was living under a cloud.

That cloud extended to another area of my childhood: my dad's health. The chronology is vague and the memories blurred, but the specter of cancer entered my childhood at an early date. Somewhere in my young years my father went to the hospital. He was gone for an extended time. The man who returned had a dark beard, and I didn't recognize him. When I realized the stranger was my father, I burst into tears. The ugly scar across his back where they had reached in to remove his cancerous kidney frightened me even more.

Relief from my own struggles at school came from a dreamlike body of water set inside the woodsy landscape of western New Hampshire. Three hours north of Hopedale, Sunapee is a pure glacial lake, a natural wonder of luminous clarity and pristine beauty. The first time I faced the lake, my heart sang. I was a quiet kid, often shy, and not given to outward bursts of enthusiasm. But Lake Sunapee broke down my reserve and had me jumping for joy. To my young eyes, it was an undiscovered world to enter and explore. From the outside it was magnificent, but from the inside—diving under and skiing over its mountain-clear waters—it became even more miraculous. Sunapee became a refuge, a friend, a different and exciting second home, a place that turned my mundane world magical. Its magic turned my life around. Even now, writing from afar, I long to see it sparkling under the summer sun or frozen solid under a white winter moon. Eight miles long and a couple of miles wide, the lake is dotted with eight islands and a shoreline that extends some seventy miles. There are small peninsulas and little lake fingers and sandy beaches wherever you look. The outlying forest is dense with vegetation and animal life. On a night in fall, breathing in the crisp, cool air, you look up into a sky crowded with a hundred thousand stars. In the morning, with the rising sun, you see a hundred thousand trees whose leaves are shimmering gold.

Coming to Sunapee as a child, I fell deeply and permanently in love. My love for the water and the woods never diminished. Later in life, I moved away, but I kept coming back. I couldn't stay away from the place where, for the first and only time, everything made sense. Everything was right—the sky, the lake, the forest, the sense of calm, the feeling of natural order.

My parents began talking about buying lakefront property to build a cabin. They proceeded with the usual Perry MO: Save until the money is there; do not buy on credit; do not live above your means. After carefully surveying the region, they chose a prime piece of property—it featured a hundred feet of lake frontage, in an undeveloped area. It provided one of the best views on the lake. A foundation was poured. A shell was built. Because my grandfather also did some building, my dad used his tools to do a lot of the work himself. My parents were young and athletic and skilled at manual labor. My mom did the painting. It became a family project, and within a year or two we were living in the cabin. Because there was no water or heat, it served us only during the warm months. We closed it up during winter. But eventually we winterized it—a complicated operation that required running a pipe thirty feet out to the lake. The pipe had to be buried four feet down, below the frost line. I helped Dad dig the ditch with a pick and shovel, a job I usually hated, but I loved this one. I loved anything that would enable us to spend more time at Sunapee and work alongside my dad.

As a resort area, Lake Sunapee had a rich history. There had been many ups and downs. When I was old enough to hang out, I saw the remnants of the forties and fifties. Those were the old hotels that were bustling during and just after World War II—the days when Benny Goodman's and Glenn Miller's big bands stopped off to play on their way from New York to Montreal. When I was a kid, those same resorts, in various stages of decay, were still around. There was a decrepit theater, an old skating rink, a variety of old buildings rotting away. At the same time, there was a feeling of excitement from a new generation of kids who hung out at the harbor. The hot spot was an ice cream parlor/burger joint packed wall-to-wall with teenagers, their hot rods parked outside. Some old-money kids cruised up in their parents' classic Chris-Craft speedboats. The yacht club was still up and running and a focal point for Sunapee's high society.

My mother, an instructor for the Red Cross, taught me to swim. I took to it immediately. It makes sense that water meant security, because Mom taught water safety and had certified most of the kids in our cove as open-water swimmers.

Water-ski shows in the harbor attracted big crowds. In trying to imitate the fancy tricks, most times I'd wind up on my ass with a nose full of water, but I would keep trying until I mastered it. I was able to pull off most every trick in the water-ski manual—from two skis to one ski to no skis at all. Driving the boat as her son tried mastering these tricks, my mother demonstrated limitless patience. I saw water as the source of endless amusement. And then came that dark day when water became linked with death.

Friends and I were watching a water-ski show filled with the kind of danger and daring that I loved. It was a weekend when my relatives had come to the lake for a family barbecue. The proceedings were interrupted by a loudspeaker announcement: *"There has been an accident. A doctor is needed. Will a doctor please come to the dock immediately?"* I didn't think much of it. No one in the show had suffered a fall. The accident must have happened somewhere else on the lake. After the show had ended, my sister and I went back to our cabin, where we saw a police car in our driveway. The atmosphere was quiet, cold. A crowd of people was down by the waterfront talking to my family—my parents plus cousins, aunts, and uncles. Dad quickly took Anne and me aside.

"Kids," he said, "something awful has happened."

I didn't want to ask. I didn't want to know. I stayed silent.

"Your grandfather had an accident. He fell from his boat. We're afraid he's drowned."

I remember asking the ridiculous question "Is he all right?" and feeling stupid afterward. But the words had come out and I couldn't take them back.

"I'm afraid not," said Dad with what felt like emotional detachment, a quality I inherited from him. "We can't find your grandfather. He's gone."

I wanted to ask where he had gone, but I knew. Gone meant dead. Drowned meant dead. Later I heard how, in spite of the rough water, my grandfather had insisted on going fishing in a canoe. Someone said he'd been drinking. Patrol boats went looking for him. It was two weeks before his body turned up.

For the first time I faced the fact that a person can be here one min-ute and gone the next. My dad's dad was a strong presence, a man who did nothing to hide his immigrant demeanor. He wore big black work boots, heavy jackets, and frayed shirts. He spoke with a thick accent. The father of eleven children, he lived the life of a workman. As I got older, I heard stories about how he was actually an alcoholic who could turn violent against his wife and kids.

Yet the water in which he drowned continued to call to me. Maybe it was a way of daring or defying death, but in the aftermath of what happened to my grandfather I plunged deeper into Lake Sunapee. Water was my ele-ment. I didn't want to come up. I wanted to stay submerged in silence.

Back in Hopedale, the woods close to our house held another kind of silence. No human talk, just rustling and chirping and scampering over leaves. I stalked through the bushes with my BB gun, a gift from my par-ents, a lever-action copy of a Winchester. I loved that gun. I loved my dog, a trusty beagle. I loved hunting chipmunks and squirrels and birds. I loved honing my skills as a junior woodsman. I couldn't articulate the term, but I had visceral knowledge of what it meant to be self-reliant. I hadn't yet read the New England writers and thinkers who had turned their dialogues with nature into philosophies, but their thoughts were in my blood. As a solitary creature in a forest where my problems in school didn't matter, I felt at home. Wild animals lived in these woods. And so did I.

SOUNDS

There was the sound of my father playing "Turkey in the Straw" on his harmonica. There was the sound of my great-uncle strumming his Portuguese ukulele. The instrument, a small guitar with four strings, had a delicate and beautiful shape. They called it a cavaquinho. Later I'd learn that its history went back to the Grecian lyres that were supposedly gifts from the gods. The mythology cut deep. The sound caught my ear, held my attention, and excited my imagination. I leaned in to listen. I wanted to touch the instrument and see how the strings worked. I wanted to get right up next to the source of the sounds.

The most compelling source of music, though, came from the family who rented the other side of our duplex. They had two teenage boys who were sixteen or seventeen when I was six or seven. The sound of their electric guitars pierced through the common wall that joined our homes and entered my heart. The sound spoke to me in much the same way as the water and the woods. The sound said, *Come here. Come closer. I have what you want.*

Sometimes I'd sneak over and watch the guys play. To a little kid like me, their slicked-down James Dean/Elvis Presley black-leather-jacket look was exotic. Their guitars had the futuristic shapes of moon rockets or the fins of an El Dorado. One of their friends, another greaser, beat out a rhythm on a snare drum. They played Buddy Holly's "That'll Be the Day," the Everly Brothers' "All I Have to Do Is Dream," and Bill Haley & the Comets' "Rock Around the Clock." I can't say whether they played and sang in tune, but to me they sounded good. All I can say is that hearing them rearranged my heart. As a young boy, my heart sought solitude. Now, suddenly, my heart sought companionship in the form of music. The idea that three souls sitting around a room could create this kind of conversation without saying a word was not simply appealing, but overwhelming. I yearned to do exactly what they were doing.

It wasn't entirely the music, and it wasn't entirely their look. It was both. They went together. The music they played and the outfits they wore were not designed to please their parents. Both their image and their sound had sharp edges of defiance. They were cocky enough to take on the garb of the rebel without a cause. "I'm gonna rock around the clock" meant *I don't give a shit about doing my homework.* "All I have to do is dream" meant *Fuck mowing the lawn and taking out the trash.*

I saw that it would not be difficult to adopt this look. It was just a matter of a white T-shirt, jeans, and gel for my hair. I also felt that the music, even as it captivated my heart, did not intimidate my mind. It seemed pretty simple and even possible that, were I to pick up a guitar, I might be able to start making similar sounds. In short, at this preteen age, I had a feeling that I could both walk the walk and talk the talk. I just had to try.

I approached the tasks—to adopt the look and learn the sound—in stages. It was relatively easy to convince my mom to let me wear jeans rather than khakis and a white T-shirt instead of a plaid shirt. But in these early years I saw that I had some unexplained interest in flair. I wanted to make a fashion statement of my own.

It wasn't anger at unreasonable parents or an uprising against an unjust world. I didn't harbor resentments. But I was beginning to realize that I had little interest in fulfilling the expectations of the world into which I was born. For example, when my Italian grandfather put me in the barber's chair to cut my hair, I said, "I need sideburns like Elvis."

"Joey, you're not old enough for sideboard," which is what he called them.

"Well, give me sideburns anyway."

My grandpa chuckled, but I didn't see it as a laughing matter. I didn't get the sideburns and hated the buzz cut that my parents insisted upon. Those sideburns were important to me. So was clothing. I had to have a peacoat. When my parents said no, I remained adamant. They wanted to know why I had to have a peacoat. I couldn't say, but it was a look that I needed. I hated wearing the uniform of button-down shirts and neatly pressed trousers. My clothes had to represent my spirit, and my spirit, now excited by music, was curious and unsettled.

The music in my house was the usual middle-class fare of the fifties—the sound track from *South Pacific* and *Carousel*, the pop tunes of Patti Page, background music with sweet little melodies, flaccid rhythms, and harmless messages. Easy listening, though, was not easy for me. I wanted something harder and stronger. When my parents saw that my initial encounter with the Portuguese cavaquinho had led to my interest in the guitar, they suggested the piano instead.

There was a spinet in our living room and I was encouraged to take lessons. Nothing interested me less. The piano was safe, the guitar dangerous. I wanted the guitar. I had heard other kids practicing scales and dealing with sheet music. I wanted nothing to do with notations on a page. I had no interest in memorizing scales. That felt like torture. I was looking for thrills. Thrills came from a guitar. I wanted the guitar—and that deep, unfettered music. Rock and roll hit me below the belt before I knew what below the belt meant.

I didn't get a guitar for a long while, but music kept calling me, especially the music I heard at dance parties. As I sat in the corner and watched, I saw the effect that the rhythms and rhymes were having on my peers. I loved rock and roll the most but noticed how ballads affected the girls. They were a perfect excuse for close dancing.

I got a Heathkit radio that made me hunger for a guitar even more. At the end of the fifties, when I was approaching ten, I searched for and found the songs that got me going. I heard "Hound Dog" on the radio and saw Elvis on television. When his songs came on the air, I heard girls whispering and giggling. I knew that his sound was thrilling them. Elvis was daring and dangerous. His mystique was magnified by the fact that our parents found him unacceptable. Elvis's music was great, but I didn't find it transformative. The music that really rocked my world came from Chuck Berry.

As a grown man who has come to appreciate good books, I look back at this period and consider Chuck Berry the Ernest Hemingway of rock and roll. He was strong, simple, and manly—a force of nature who created a musical lexicon all his own. He broke it down to the most essential elements. He had two voices—his singing voice and the voice of his guitar. His singing voice was insistent and compelling, the storytelling voice that let you know that Johnny B. Goode never learned to read or write so well but he could play a guitar like ringing a bell. Well, I wasn't the best student at school and I sure as hell wanted to play a guitar like ringing a bell. The guitar voice was the voice of his heart, his rhythm voice, the fuel that made the song blistering hot.

One month I was a kid fantasizing about being Jacques Cousteau and the next I was a kid dreaming of being Johnny B. Goode. It was an easy transition because they had something in common: They were mysterious strangers, gunslingers who stood outside conventional society. They had places to go and stories to tell. I had wanted to follow Paladin, the gunslinger in the TV show *Have Gun—Will Travel*, as he chased down the bad guys with his sharp wit, wisdom, and, of course, a six-gun. Now I wanted to follow along with Chuck Berry as he led me into rock-and-roll music, any old time you use it, with a backbeat you can't lose it. He was the pied piper luring the kids with something far more seductive than a flute. He had his rough-and-ready guitar; he had the rockin' pneumonia; he needed a shot of rhythm and blues; he said, "Roll over, Beethoven, and tell Tchaikovsky the news."

As the fifties turned into the sixties, I was knee-deep in rock and roll and rhythm and blues. Just the sound of those words was enough to get me going, running back to the Heathkit to get a load of Chuck Berry's playing and Roy Orbison's singing. At the same time, my BB gun let me pretend that I was Paladin. Now I had to have a guitar of my own so I could become Johnny B. Goode.

My parents wanted me to take dance lessons where the waltz and the fox-trot were still being taught. Dance class was hell—the boys on one side of the room, the girls on the other. Awkwardness ruled. My hands sweaty, my heart heavy, my eyes fixed on the floor, I hated every minute but was determined to stick with it because it was a chance to meet girls.

My parents urged me to choose an instrument for the school band. The school band bored me and so did the instrument I was given—the clarinet. I later learned that the clarinet was the high-pitched voice of my parents' generation of music. Jimmy Dorsey and Benny Goodman played the clarinet. I didn't give a shit about the clarinet. After a few weeks I turned in the instrument and went back to begging.

"Get me a guitar—please. I need a guitar."

My parents finally relented. One blessed day a guitar arrived. The box came from Sears. I knew by the shape that it contained a guitar. My heart beat like crazy. I pulled out the instrument. The first thing I did was look for the cord that would let me plug it in. There was no cord. My heart sank. I knew it wasn't electric, but the fact that it was a guitar—an actual guitar!— was reason enough to celebrate.

Yet I still wanted electricity; I wanted volume; I wanted to try to make the sounds I heard on records by Bo Diddley. When I looked in the window of the record store and studied Bo Diddley's album *Bo Diddley Is a Gunslinger*, he was dressed in a black cowboy hat, black cowboy shirt, black boots, and double-holster pistols. He was standing in a corral. A horse stood nearby. In front of Bo was a streamlined electric guitar. Right then and there I saw the connection between rock and roll and the outlaw life.

The even bigger revelation, though, was the noise I could make with my first guitar. Getting even close to hearing the sounds in my head was more exciting than putting on a cowboy hat or leather jacket. The sounds coming from these six strings made me grateful to my parents for putting this instrument in my hands.

The instrument was a $12.95 Silvertone student model that came packaged as part of a complete kit. I took the box up to my room. In addition to the guitar there was a red, white, and blue strap, a small illustrated manual, a 45-rpm instructional record, and a plectrum, commonly known as a pick. Where to start?

Even watching my teenage neighbors play guitar, I never paid attention to which hand was doing what. So being left-handed, I naturally took the neck in my right hand and strummed with my left. It didn't sound like anything. When I put on the record, I was instructed to do the opposite—put the neck in my left hand and the pick in my right. That's what I did. After a quick lesson in tuning, I began fingering the strings. My fingers quickly grew sore, but I kept on. Something was sounding like chords. It didn't matter how sore my skin was—the sound of chords was enough to keep me going for hours.

A lifetime later, people are always asking me why, as a lefty, I play right-handed. My answer goes back to my first guitar. Playing those first chords, I was naively following that instructional record. Little did I know that I was playing backward—and would do so for the rest of my life. I ask myself today: *What kind of guitarist would I be if I had not conformed to a method designed for right-handers?* I have no idea.

All I know is that, backward or not, I was learning some basic chord changes. I could start playing along with pop songs. Then came the unfortunate day that I leaned the Silvertone against the wall. I was playing tag with my younger sister and accidentally knocked it over, breaking off the headstock. Bummed out, I put the pieces in a box and the box in the closet. There it stayed for close to a year until . . .

The Beatles!

The Beatles exploded in 1963. When I first saw their name in print, an adult told me that their name was incorrectly spelled. That made it even better. They represented a new kind of show business. We were used to seeing Topo Gigio on *The Ed Sullivan Show*, but the Beatles rocked the TV set off the living room floor. The Beatles were raucous and exciting. They were unfettered energy. When the Beatles appeared on *Sullivan*, it was like a national holiday. The Beatles represented the start of the British Invasion, and smashed down a door through which I was ready to walk. There was an undercurrent of sexuality that felt primal in its rhythms and hit me—a thirteen-year-old—right in the groin. In a subtle but powerful way, this band completed the picture. What I had heard at those teen parties started making more sense to me. With every song I heard, the connection between sex and music was becoming clearer.

My parents might have admonished me with "Turn that down!" when I blasted "She Loves You" on my 45 record player, but they never forbade me from listening. Hell, for all I know, they may have liked it. Much later on my mom told me that my dad's favorite Beatles song was "Hey Jude." They never told me to stop as I tried to work out every last Beatles song on my guitar. I was the diligent student, strumming to "I Saw Her Standing There" while my sister, Anne, and I sang the lyrics.

It was the Beatles who caused me to ask my father to epoxy my broken guitar back together. When he was able to do it, I was off and running. By then I had been rubbing elbows with other friends who had guitars. That gave me the chance to play on higher-quality instruments. The difference was remarkable. Now I needed a better guitar—and an argument to get my parents to buy me one.

When my parents had wanted me to play clarinet, they had made me take lessons. The same was true when they urged me to play piano. So when I presented my case for a better guitar, my promise to take lessons broke the ice. Mom and I went to Constantino's, a music store owned by her cousin in Lawrence, where she bought me a decent acoustic. Naturally I still wanted an electric, but I was glad to get my hands on any upgrade.

My parents were trying to protect me from the rising teen culture that, more and more, was defined by screaming electric guitars. The culture of motorcycles, tattoos, deviants, and delinquents was abhorrent to upwardly mobile people like the Perrys. Our town prided itself on being clean and white. Rock and roll was seen as dirty and black. Our town put a premium on conformity. Rock and roll was about rebellion. It was the sound track of the upcoming political, social, and sexual revolution. It was going to have the power of a tidal wave—and no one saw it coming.

In the early sixties we moved to a single-family home in a more rural part of town. I loved that it was surrounded by four acres of dense forest. It was also a ten-minute walk to the first tee of the golf course that my dad and mom, along with other fanatical golfers, had built with their own hands. It was in that house on Mill Street that I got increasingly obsessed with procuring an electric guitar.

At every birthday and Christmas I looked for the one gift my parents knew I wanted above all others. It was never there. How could I get one? Pray? Not really. I wasn't the praying kind. Even though we attended the neighborhood Catholic church as a family, we were hardly devoted believers. We went to Sunday services because that was what a good upstanding American family did. Neither God nor Jesus nor Mother Mary nor the holy saints spoke to me. I didn't seek or feel their spirits. I felt bored. I also felt the imposition of a certain moral code. I didn't know how to fight it, so I absorbed it. That code, which insisted that premarital sex was wrong, led to a whole battery of weighty emotions.

Strange, but even a kid like me who didn't take his Catholicism seriously was seriously impacted by it. As my body began awakening to sexual feelings, I thought those feelings were wrong or negative or even evil. I was confused about what it would mean to act on those feelings. I did know, of course, that Catholicism requires you to confess your sins. Masturbation is seen as a sin. To confess it is to wipe the slate clean, even if you have to do time in purgatory. Well, I have heavy time to do in purgatory.

The line separating the sanitized white-bread culture of Hopedale and the funky rock-and-roll culture of the wider world was blurred. I loved my parents. My parents loved me. I loved music. And my parents, despite their doubts, allowed me to listen to all the music I wanted to. Driving over those two-lane highways to Lake Sunapee, my parents let me play the guitar in the backseat to my heart's content. If I wanted to figure out the guitar licks to Chuck Berry's "School Days," they didn't stop me. And if I sang lyrics about dropping coins in slots and hearing something hot, lyrics about hail hail rock and roll that will deliver me from the days of old, I wasn't restrained. My sister, Anne, smiled and sang along. My mom and dad continued discussing their upcoming tennis match or dad's golf handicap. The guitar was not taken from me—not once, not ever—and became, like my dog and my BB rifle, my constant companion.

Aiming to keep my promise about lessons, I took down the name of an elderly gentleman that my folks knew. He lived around the corner and played flamenco guitar—whatever that was—and was willing to teach me. The man was kind and patient. I was fascinated to watch his fingers move over the frets. In our first lesson, he showed me some basic positions. He mentioned scales. As he and I played a few notes together, I was thrilled by the richness of his tone. It was strong and true and satisfying to the ear.

"I know you like that rock and roll," he said, "and that's fine, but let's first learn the fundamentals. Once you get the basics down, you can take it wherever you like."

I didn't like the way this was going. It reminded me of piano and clarinet lessons. I had no interest in spending years learning songs that I didn't like. I wanted to get to the heart of rock and roll. But I had made a commitment to my parents and was determined to stick with it. Forty-five minutes a week was a small price to pay for my new guitar.

The following week's lesson was on a Tuesday. The school bus that brought me home passed by my guitar teacher's house. I had brought my guitar to school and, anxious to get to my lesson, I asked the driver to drop me off at my teacher's house. When the bus pulled up, I saw that a hearse was parked out front. It didn't take long to learn that the hearse had come for my teacher. He had suffered a fatal heart attack the night before. There was no more talk about guitar lessons after that.

The Lake Sunapee summers became a staple of my childhood. It was just me and Mom and Anne in our cabin all week until Dad drove up from Hopedale for the weekend. Waiting for him to arrive on those Friday nights, it was always an anxious time for me. I kept playing my guitar, but the guitar didn't make me less nervous. Dad should have arrived by eight, but now it was nine, now it was ten, and I grew afraid. I was scared that Dad wouldn't come, scared that, as it had his father and my teacher, death would snatch him away. A car wreck would kill him. So when he finally arrived, at midnight, I ran to the door and hugged him with all my might.

Those summers were all about the water, the woods, and the guitar. I lived inside the lake, every day diving deeper, my imagination absorbed by the underwater life swimming around me. I bought scuba-diving magazines and fantasized about adventuring to the Great Barrier Reef in a sea of coral splendor off the coast of Australia. My BB shot improved considerably. I stalked through the bushes, pretending to be living in an earlier period of history when man hunted his food and survived on his ability to deal with the wild.

At summer's end, I felt a certain dread. I didn't want to leave Sunapee.

Hopedale meant school and school meant misery. My performance hadn't improved. I liked reading, but reading about diving gear. I liked flipping the pages of music magazines and stopping at every ad for every guitar. My own playing had advanced to the point that I could play most of the pop songs of the day. In terms of the instrument itself, I focused on what I wanted: a semi-hollow solid-body Gibson cutaway. I liked the full shape. I had seen Chuck Berry play variations on classic Gibsons. I loved the sexy shape of those models. Looking back, I realize it's probably due to my Italian DNA. A full-body Gibson 335 brought to mind a picture of the full-bodied Sophia Loren, my voluptuously curved, big-breasted dream woman, the one who kept adding time to my future debt in purgatory and confessing to the priest every Saturday, "Father, this week I saw a woman on TV . . ."

Chuck Berry continued to be my imaginary mentor. Of course, Elvis made an impression. Along with a hundred million other kids, I had loved "Hound Dog" and "Blue Suede Shoes" and "Jailhouse Rock." Elvis was cool. There was nothing about him that I didn't like, but it wasn't until later in life that I came to appreciate him fully. As a kid, Chuck was the first musician whom I saw in a heroic light. His language, both in his lyrics and riffs, made sense. Whenever he was on television, I ran to our Sylvania console. As a performer, he had the looks and the moves. He had the duck walk. He had the attitude, the swag, the internal combustion. He sang as well as he played. He also had the brand of guitar—a Gibson—that I wanted.

"If you want it bad enough, you'll work for it," said Dad, who, unhappy with my poor grades, seemed to be distancing himself from me. Because he had done well in school and advanced himself in the professional world, he expected me to do the same. He couldn't deny that I was a good kid. I wasn't a bully, I didn't get in trouble, and I did as I was told. Yet despite my best efforts, I couldn't be the kid he wanted—the kid who made all A's. Instead I was a kid who kept bugging him for an electric guitar. And in his mind, that meant a switchblade in your right pocket and a greasy comb in your left.

I wanted the electric guitar so badly that I set out to do something I hated—mow lawns—to save up money. It was only the image of the Gibson that got me through the monotony of mowing. I sweated through the work, Chuck Berry's "Almost Grown" playing inside my head. I sweated each day at school, never knowing when I'd be called to the principal's office, where I'd be chastised for inferior grades and told that I needed tutoring and extra time in study hall.

When I turned fourteen in 1964, the major event in my life was the Beatles' *Hard Day's Night*. I was already obsessed with the band's music, but the film ignited my obsession. I loved every minute of that movie—four rebels running from the stage to the hotel while being chased by hordes of screaming girls; four outsiders bonded by their music, their humor, and their determination to live life on their own terms. That was what I wanted. I left the theater with one thought: *I need to have a band, I need to play in a band, I need to find some guys who love music as much as me and form a band.*

That band would require electricity. In spite of my odd jobs—mowing lawns, shoveling snow, selling greeting cards, throwing newspapers—I still hadn't put away enough money for the electric guitar. Meanwhile, I was intrigued that the Rolling Stones' first album, out that same year, was practically all covers of blues and rhythm-and-blues songs. They did Chuck Berry's "Carol" and Jimmy Reed's "Honest I Do." Unlike the Beatles, the Stones, like the bluesmen before them, sang about how they lived on the edge. Compared to other groups coming out of England like the Dave Clark Five, the Stones were painting a picture that was darker, wilder, and more dangerous. Musically, their original song lyrics spoke to issues of the time that still hold up today.

I began playing along with these records and, still without an electric guitar, I formed my first band, Chimes of Freedom. The name came from a lyric by Bob Dylan, another artist I had recently discovered. Dylan caught my ear because his voice was unconventional. I heard his voice as conversational—he seemed to be talking as much as he was singing. He felt authentic. I liked when he went from guitar to harmonica. Most important was his message. Every time I heard their lyrics I would discover something new and different, like the Rolling Stones. I took their words as poetry that didn't have to rhyme. I also learned that you didn't have to have a Paul Anka or Barbra Streisand voice to make great music. You could grunt, growl, or talk your way through a song.

The drive to play music at any cost became the central force in my life. Once I put together my first band, that urge never diminished. Ironically, that drive came from my father, who preached, *If you want something badly and work hard enough, you can get it.* Talent was never mentioned as part of that equation. Looking back, I know I had a modicum of talent, but hard work was the key.

I never dreamt of becoming a big star and playing in front of tens of thousands of people. I never dreamt of glory, or fame, or even fortune. I just dreamt of playing music and, more specifically, playing in a group. It was the group feeling that I loved so much. It was the group miracle that I sought—the sheer thrill of three or four or five musicians conducting a raucous conversation with their instruments.

My cohorts were Dave Meade, playing his big brother's bass; John Alden on drums; and sometimes Bill Wright on tambourine and guitar. We covered the Byrds, the Beatles, Dylan, and Chuck. We had no real gigs. Our repertoire consisted of just a few songs. We found the courage to set up in a distant corner at some living room party. Even that made me nervous, but it also gave me comfort; I knew that I wouldn't have to dance. You could say that it was at those parties that I lost my musical virginity years before I lost my sexual virginity. To play out loud before a group of partygoers, even if they were only thirteen-year-old girls, was an act of courage. It took additional courage to play the guitar and sing, because I didn't think that I was very good. Yet I learned the songs off the records and was able to create a rough facsimile of what I heard. None of the girls laughed or booed. None of them made fun of me. They appreciated my willingness to get up there and play for them. Their appreciation added to my courage.

Dave Meade's big brother had a record collection that widened my world. He was a college student with advanced taste in music. In his collection were five albums that changed my life: John Mayall's *Blues Breakers with Eric Clapton*; *Having a Rave Up with the Yardbirds*; *Chuck Berry Is on Top*; the Kinks' first live record; and a "best of" John Lee Hooker album.

When I borrowed the Mayall album and brought it home, my father happened to glance at the cover. Four guys were sitting in front of a concrete wall with some slight graffiti. You couldn't call their hair long—just a little shaggy. One of the four guys—Clapton—was reading a *Beano* comic book. They were dressed in ordinary-looking jeans.

"Why would young men want to look like that?" was my dad's only comment.

I had no answer. I didn't bother to tell him that Mayall and Clapton, along with the Yardbirds, had cracked open my head and heart to an English-confected blues-based music that was changing my life. I didn't say that the sounds they made actually gave me a physical charge of energy. I didn't explain how Clapton's guitar made more sense to me than any book I had read, in or out of school. I didn't say how I listened to those records with unrestrained joy and insatiable curiosity.

I saw that those sources and songs were all American—Muddy Waters and Little Walter, Sonny Boy Williamson and Howlin' Wolf, Freddie King and Otis Rush, Ray Charles and Robert Johnson. And because my main man Chuck Berry was the ultimate American rocker, I clearly saw—and felt—that the bottom line was black American blues.

As much as I loved listening to the blues masters, it was the English rockers who caught my attention. They played these old songs with the explosive energy of young men with something to prove. The English students of American blues became my teachers and role models. Because they were white and only a few years older than me, I related. I looked up to them as hip older brothers. Like them, I was searching for the Holy Grail hidden deep inside black blues.

I felt that the line between hard rock and up-tempo blues was blurry. To my ears, excitement and sexuality lurked behind every backbeat and chord change of both styles.

John Alden, my friend who was a drummer, added to my musical education. Because Dave Clark was a drummer, John related to the Dave Clark Five, one of the most important bands in the British Invasion. John and I went to a show—the Caravan of Stars—at the Boston Armory. I didn't know it at the time, but I was witnessing history. The Beatles had stopped touring, as had the Stones. I had missed them both. So to catch the Dave Clark Five as the last touring act of the first wave of the British Invasion was lucky timing. The place was half empty, but, man, I felt an excitement I'd never felt before. When the show was over, I knew that I couldn't live life without having a band.

At fourteen or fifteen, I was a loner, yet music kept me from feeling lonely. I was an outsider, and yet music put me on the inside. I was not into team sports. I spent most of my time after school walking the woods with my dog and BB gun or sitting on my bed practicing guitar.

Mom being a girls' gym teacher gave me special access to the fair sex. When she coached the girls' basketball or field hockey teams, I'd go along as her assistant. Early on I developed friendships with girls, most of them older. They didn't look twice when I walked through the locker room to have a word with Mom. They were comfortable with me, and I felt safe in their presence.

This was a huge advantage. At a time when other guys were objectifying women, I saw them as equals—and as friends. When they saw me coming to their games with a guitar under my arm, they saw it as a sign of coolness. Unlike today, not everyone had a guitar then. The guitar was a great conversation starter. But that conversation usually ended up with me singing a Bob Dylan song, as opposed to a hot encounter under the bleachers.

I definitely wanted a girlfriend, but I wanted an electric guitar even more. Every Christmas morning I'd run downstairs hoping to find the object of my dreams. On my fourteenth Christmas, I saw an enormous box waiting for me. It didn't have the shape of a guitar, but maybe it contained one anyway. It didn't. It was a Wollensak stereo reel-to-reel tape recorder. I liked it; I liked mechanics and especially mechanics related to music. But I was also bewildered. What the hell was this? The recorder had to have cost as much as an electric guitar. Knowing how desperately I wanted the guitar, why would Mom and Dad get me a recorder instead? Maybe it was their way of telling me, *Here's a way to record your electric guitar.* Maybe my main gift—the electric guitar—was hidden in a closet or under my bed. I immediately set out and searched every corner of the house, but it wasn't there.

"You look disappointed," my mom said. "We thought you'd love the recorder."

"The recorder's great," I said, "but it's not a guitar."

"You have a guitar."

"It's not electric."

"*It's a guitar*," my dad said emphatically. "Be grateful for what you have."

There was no arguing with that, so I kept quiet. I didn't want to seem ungrateful, especially in light of having received this high-tech tape recorder. But, damn it, I wanted what I wanted.

A year later my dream finally came true. I had saved enough lawn-mowing money to convince my parents to throw in the rest. Mom took me back to Constantino's music store in Lawrence. There among the accordions, mandolins, and violins was a small selection of electric guitars. There was one Gibson, a 335, the model used by Chuck Berry—just what I wanted. But it was fifty dollars more than a Guild Starfire IV.

"Please, Mom," I begged.

"The Guild looks fine," she said, "and the Guild costs less. We'll take the Guild."

I took it, held it, stroked it, and came to terms with the compromise. I was overjoyed that, at long last, I could realize those high, piercing sounds that I had yearned to make. Once I got home and plugged it into my small amp, I played for hours on end. The sound made my family crazy but I didn't care. By then I was gone.

Soon I found another guy who gave lessons, Steve Rose, considered the best guitarist around. He was probably nineteen and had a band called the Wild Cats. I'm not sure I knew the word *avant-garde* then, but that's how I saw Steve. He was ahead of his time. His hair was a lot longer than anyone else's, he had a decided swagger, and, most importantly, he could play. His licks were smoothed-out and self-assured. When I later learned something about the blues and listened to masters like Freddie King, I saw where Steve was coming from. At the time I met him, though, I simply saw him as someone a lot further down the road than I was. His siblings and parents were musical. In fact, the family home was set up like a music store. They were a dealership for several instrument makers. Besides taking lessons there, you could buy a piano or saxophone. You could also hire the family to play at your bar mitzvah or wedding. Steve Rose was the first businessman/musician to come into my life.

He taught me the names of chords and walked me through the Beatles fake book. He kept saying that his main job was to teach me to teach myself.

"All you need is a different guitar," he said.

"Which one?"

"This is the one." And with that he pulled out a Fender catalogue and pointed to a Stratocaster, the wildest guitar I had ever seen. But given its price tag, he might as well have told me to buy a Bentley.

One Friday night I went to see Steve's band. It was inspiring to hear guys I knew playing the hits of the day. During a break, Steven took me backstage and showed me his latest acquisition.

"It's handmade," said Steve.

When he opened the case and I saw the instrument, I felt the stirrings of a hard-on. The smell—the heady aroma of new wood mixed with plush felt lining—was as stimulating as the instrument.

"Isn't that what George Harrison plays?" I asked.

"It is," said Steve. "A Gretsch Country Gentleman. Double-cutaway hollow body. What do you think?"

"I think I'm in love," I said.

I left Steve's with extreme guitar envy, realizing that not only did I love the instrument in its many configurations, I actually *lusted* for guitars. It was a lust, unlike the lust for sex, that carried no guilt, no mixed feelings, no fear, and no confusion. It was a lust that has strengthened over the decades and even now, a half century later, burns with the same flaming heat that engulfed me as a boy.

PREP

I was a high school sophomore with no interest in high school. My grades weren't getting any better. I took advantage of all the extra help the school had to offer. Because my parents were so conscientious, I had been given every sort of test—academic, physical, and psychological. I had been given tutors. I had taken preparation courses to help me with college entrance tests. Yet nothing seemed to help. That's when my parents decided that I needed more hands-on attention. If I were to get into college, I'd need a prep school, a boarding school, a place where I could finally realize my intellectual potential.

I wasn't happy about leaving my friends and my family. It took me a while to get over it. My parents made it clear I had no choice in the matter. At the same time, the idea of skipping out of Hopedale and living in a dorm free of my parents' supervision was appealing.

The shift was seismic. Vermont Academy, in Saxtons River, was considered an excellent all-boys prep school with a fine faculty and high academic standards. Unfortunately, neither the faculty nor the standards interested me. I was drawn to the misfits like myself.

The misfits were many. For the first time in my life, I was in the middle of a multiethnic mix. There were Jews, blacks, Latinos, WASPs, and budding hippies. There were kids who took their studies seriously and kids who ran wild. There were spoiled kids from rich families who'd drifted from prep school to prep school. They were also wise guys who, because of my ethnic looks, liked to call me Kike Catholic. Never having been exposed to prejudice before, I laughed. It rolled right off my back. And when they saw it had no effect on me, they stopped the taunting. I got along with everyone.

My parents proved to be right about prep school. I would learn all kinds of new things, but not the things that my mother and father had in mind. For example, a kid from New York City brought the *Village Voice*, with long articles about a musical group called the Velvet Underground. Another kid from New Jersey had the Underground's first album. A kid from California had a joint and gave me my first hit. I didn't love it or hate it. I was more interested in how it helped me hear a radical East Village rock band called the Fugs.

There was a dress code at Vermont Academy—chinos and corduroys, blazers and loafers. In defiance, I wore my shirt outside my trousers and made sure that my shoes were scruffy.

I didn't become the super student that my parents were hoping for, but I did encounter books—like *On the Road*—that spoke to me. I couldn't explain why Jack Kerouac's writing seemed to have nothing and yet everything to do with the lyrics of Chuck Berry and Bob Dylan. My connection with Kerouac was Dad's brother Uncle Bing, who had lived on the same street in Lowell with him and had known him since childhood.

I met other guys who turned me on to the Young Rascals. A white kid from Colorado was listening to James Brown's "Papa's Got a Brand New Bag." A black kid from Harlem was listening to the Four Seasons' "Rag Doll."

Vermont Academy was where I learned to party. There was one time an older kid indoctrinated me into his ritual of getting high—or low—on Robitussin, the cough syrup laced with codeine. One Saturday afternoon I followed him around from dorm room to dorm room, where he'd finagle underclassmen into giving us their cough syrup. Given Vermont's cold climate, everyone suffered from coughs and everyone had Robitussin. By the end of the day, we had an ample supply. The Saturday night football game became a lot more interesting.

Sports were mandatory. I joined the ski team. We had our own slope on campus. I was good enough to compete but always messed up the time trials on purpose so I wouldn't have to race. I got all the benefits of being on the ski team, including trips to Okemo Mountain, one of the great ski areas in Vermont.

As a sophomore, I found myself hanging out almost exclusively with the outsider seniors, the ones who smoked and drank and listened to loud rock. They pointed me in the direction of the best band put together by Vermont Academy students—Just Us. Seeing that I was a passable guitarist with enough chops to play some lead, I was admitted. If their version of "Twist and Shout" was closer to the Isley Brothers' original than the Beatles' cover—the version I had learned—I quickly adapted. The band gave me a certain status among the deviant population.

Back home over the holidays, my parents asked me, as parents do, about my new life at Vermont Academy.

"What do you have to say about your new school?" asked Mom.

"It's okay."

"Well, are you liking it?"

"Liking it okay."

"How you getting on with the other kids?"

"Okay."

"How about your teachers?"

"They're okay."

"Joe," said Dad, showing some frustration, "can you give us a little better idea of what's going on up there other than one-word answers?"

I couldn't. I didn't. When it came to discussing things, I resorted to the stock teen jargon of monosyllabic responses. I knew that the real excitement I had discovered at prep school—the turn-on to the radical new music coming out of London, New York, and Los Angeles—wasn't anything they wanted to hear about. They wanted to hear that I had fallen into a good-grade groove, that I was passing tests with flying colors and finally fulfilling my potential as a student.

I wish I could have explained to them what was happening inside my mind, but I couldn't even come close. I cloaked it all with an "it's okay" or "everything's fine" or "there's nothing to worry about." How could I say that the one thing that kept me from the boredom of school was this new band called the Jimi Hendrix Experience and their new single called "Hey Joe," which had me wandering around in a daze, amazed at what this guy was doing with a guitar. Hendrix thrilled me and motivated me but mainly obsessed me and convinced me that this instrument was at once the simplest and most complicated source of wild creative pleasure that I could ever imagine. When I listened to Cream's "I Feel Free," it made me feel free.

Sex, of course, was the other pleasure that I had in mind. Wasn't it time that I lost the burden of my virginity? As the other guys in school boasted about their exploits, I could only sit in silence. I wasn't interested in boasting—boasting was never my style—but I was horny and hungry for experience. At seventeen, I remained unconfident in that area, and my seduction skills were nonexistent. Being in an all-boys school further lessened my chances.

Vermont Academy required that we each adopt a hobby. I chose photography. I liked it not only for its artistic and mechanical properties but because it fulfilled the requirement of belonging to a club. It also allowed me to maintain my loner status. I took photography seriously and learned how to develop my own prints in the darkroom and even roll my own 35-mm cartridges. Best of all, it gave me an excuse to wander the woods.

Fall in Vermont is paradise on earth. The natural world takes on a startling radiance. Each tree becomes a wondrous piece of sculpture. With camera in hand, I never tired of walking through the woods and snapping pictures. No matter how much film I brought, it was never enough. I wanted to photograph everything I saw. And then I saw her.

She was one of the few girls who lived in Saxtons River, and I was fortunate to meet her. There were precious few girls in this all-boys environment. It turned out she went to an all-girls prep school and was on a break. She had long, chestnut-colored hair and light brown eyes. Her faded blue jeans fit her snugly. I couldn't deny that she was looking at me as I passed by her small woodsy house. She was raking leaves off the lawn. I wanted to say something but, as usual, words failed me.

"You go to school at the academy?" she asked.

"Yeah," I said.

"I'm Betsy."

"I'm Joe."

"I think I've seen you on my way home from school."

"Oh," was all I could manage.

"You taking pictures of the birds?"

"I'm taking pictures of everything."

"Does that include people?"

"Well . . ."

Seeing that I was shy, she said, "I'm just messing with you."

"I'd like to take a picture of you," I said. "I really would."

"You don't have to take a picture of me, but if you're interested in nature photography I can show you some cool spots. I grew up in these woods."

"I'd love that."

As we walked along the hidden trails, she spoke more than I did. That was fine with me. Every now and then we'd stop so I could take a picture. She was in every single one. As much as I loved the sight of the distant mountain covered with snow, I loved the sight of her face even more.

Our encounters went on for some time. They almost always involved walks through the woods. I would have gladly gone all the way had Betsy allowed me, but just having a female friend was a precious gift.

Summertime at Sunapee continued to be the highlight of the year, not only because I could return to the lake and the land that I loved so deeply, but because the area was alive with music. I got a job at the Anchorage, the local burger joint, where the jukebox, one of those great old monstrosities from the fifties, was always rocking great music. There was something about jukebox speakers that gave music an extra buzz. Maybe it was the blinking lights; maybe it was the robotics of the eager arm grabbing the disc; maybe it was the needle pouncing on the vinyl. Whatever it was, the jukebox was beautiful. Because I worked there, my boss would give me a fistful of quarters. Every week after the jukebox guy put in the latest 45s, I became the de facto DJ at the Anchorage. It was one job I didn't mind. I couldn't go wrong: the Mamas & the Papas' "Monday Monday" or "California Dreaming," The Troggs' "Wild Thing," the Beach Boys' "Good Vibrations," the Beatles' "Paperback Writer," the Stones' "Paint It Black," the Lovin' Spoonful's "Summer in the City." The music made my kitchen chores tolerable and gave them a rhythm. The French fries fried quicker to Donovan's "Sunshine Superman" and the cheeseburgers grilled greasier to the Temptations' "Ain't Too Proud to Beg."

I did everything at the Anchorage from sweeping the floors to unloading ice cream off the delivery trucks. Most of my work was in the kitchen. I had a little window where I'd place freshly washed dishes and bus up the dirty ones. That window was perfectly placed, giving me not only a great view of all the goings-on in the Anchorage but also a clear view of Lake Sunapee harbor. I can still smell that intoxicating brew of motorboat exhaust and fried clams.

Everyone came through the Anchorage, including a kid a few years younger than me who stopped by the window to strike up a conversation. His name was David Scott, but he was called Pudge, despite his skinniness. His dad was the commodore of the yacht club.

"You play guitar, right?" he asked.

"Right," I answered.

"I play drums."

"Cool. I wanna put a band together."

"I'm in. I also know another guy who plays guitar. He teaches tennis at the yacht club."

"Bring him by."

That kid was Tom Hamilton, who grew up in New London, one of the towns bordering Lake Sunapee. He had a wry sense of humor, was smart, and liked to party. Most importantly, we dug the same music. Tom and I became fast friends.

I started hanging out with Pudge and Tom. With a case of beer and the radio blasting, we'd chug off into the middle of the lake. We also started jamming in Pudge's basement. Often his parents were out of town. But even when they were there they'd let us play long into the night. Because I had a few more notches on my guitar, Tom switched to bass and the Jam Band was born: Tom, Pudge, and I.

Tom also had a winter band, Plastic Glass, that included a hard-core blues lover, John McGuire. John was a harp player who refused to wear shoes and worshipped black blues. Like Eric Clapton, he held the attitude that the blues should never be corrupted. I didn't argue, because I loved the blues, but I also loved loud, guitar-based rock, whether it wandered away from the blues or not. And since the blues was an impure form itself—I saw the blues as a beautiful mongrel—how could anyone make the case that the blues should be pure? These were the discussions in which we engaged, young fledgling musicians in half-formed bands, our heads exploding from Pudge's parents' whisky or the newly discovered Romilar cough syrup that took us to a place of woozy reflection.

Sometimes John would share lead vocals with me in the Jam Band. Sometimes he'd play harp. It didn't take long for us to develop a set list of rocking songs. In no time we were playing actual gigs. One of the early ones was at the Barn, the Sunapee music venue owned by John Conrad, the first gay man I ever encountered. John was also a stone-cold alcoholic who woke every day at noon and began drinking Chablis out of a gallon jug. He sat cross-legged in the Barn's kitchen, where he held court in the hallowed space that back in the forties had attracted the big bands of Count Basie and Gene Krupa. As John spoke, his favorite employee, Louise, an eighty-year-old woman who was strong as an ox, scrubbed the floors and washed the windows. You could also rent a room at the adjacent hotel, the Conrad Manor, and, if you were so inclined, come to Sunapee during one of John's gala gay weekends. In these months, just before the Stonewall Riots helped launch gay liberation from Greenwich Village, John, high on wine, was already liberated. He couldn't have cared less if some tourists recoiled at the sight of men in satin short shorts.

Beyond the Barn, we played boathouse parties, backyard parties—hell, we'd play anywhere. Pay was nice but not essential. For many summers the Jam Band was *the* house band of Sunapee. I remember one late September night when we played on a flatbed truck illuminated by the beams of car headlights. It was so cold that it actually snowed. But we didn't give a shit. Long live rock and roll!

On a clear summer's day, looking out at the Lake, Tom Hamilton and I would sit under the shade of a great oak tree and talk about the future. The future concerned music and music alone. Fantasies of being onstage in front of a mountain of Marshall amps. Fantasies of traveling to the Fillmore in San Francisco to see bands with names like Jefferson Airplane and Quicksilver Messenger Service. Fantasies of fleeing our home lives, our parents, our schools, our provincial New England prison.

I got a glimpse of what lay beyond those borders in 1967 when I found myself in a little theater in Boston watching a movie called *Blow-Up*. I didn't know anything about Michelangelo Antonioni. All I knew was that the Yardbirds were in the film playing a version of "The Train Kept a-Rollin'," rewritten for the movie. Even more amazing was the short-lived lineup of guitarists Jimmy Page and Jeff Beck. The movie was a strange and startling portrait of a London fashion photographer in which mystery, sex, rock, and rebellion all came together. I had read about the ultrahip Flash scene and now, seated in this art-house cinema, I was watching the scene come alive before my eyes. My ears were even more thrilled when Page and Beck appeared at a critical moment and took over. I'd never heard guitar sounds like that before. Those few minutes of film showed me how to mesh two searing guitars in the same band. Little did I know that I was watching proto-Aerosmith.

Even though I had come to see *Blow-Up* because of the Yardbirds, I wound up loving the movie just as much. Cutting-edge music, cutting-edge cinema.

I loved this Flash art/music scene coming out of England—the energy of cockney East London clashing with the art school dandies, Keith Moon's bass drum bombs, the mock mod attitude of Kenny Jones in Small Faces. Beyond London, though, I loved this era of lightning-fast changes and quirky metamorphoses. I loved the psychedelic drones, the massive feedback fed by bass-bottomed R&B, the sight of Hendrix praying at the fiery altar of his flaming Stratocaster at Monterey.

There was a revolution happening right outside my door, and it all seemed connected in a disconnected way—the Kennedy assassinations, MLK, the Vietnam War, Timothy Leary, civil rights marches, and sexual freedom. All I knew was that the music of Jeff Beck and Jimi Hendrix and Jimmy Page's Led Zeppelin captured all that confusion. It was the call of rock and roll—a call I had to answer.

Everything was changing in the world, but nothing was changing at Vermont Academy. My grades got worse as my musicianship got better and my hair got longer. Having heard Jeff Beck and Jimmy Page, I concentrated on my guitar with a new ferocity. In my junior year I took over Just Us, the prep school band, as both lead guitarist and singer. I was making good musical progress, even as I was making no progress in school. My parents protested.

"What's wrong?" asked Mom, calling from home.

"Nothing."

"What can we do to help you?"

"Nothing."

"When are we going to be seeing some improvement on your report cards?"

"I don't know."

Dad called and said the school didn't like the length of my hair. "They wrote us and said it was too long."

"I want it longer," I admitted.

"Why?"

"I don't know."

"I want you to cut it, Joe."

"I won't."

"You have to. Are you listening to me? Will you cut it?"

"I won't."

I didn't.

My contempt for the conventions that required boring dress codes grew. And so did my hair.

That summer a kid from California came through Sunapee with some purple mescaline tablets that, at five dollars a pop, provided a gateway to still another territory. Tom Hamilton and I got high together. I can't report that I saw God or stepped out of my ego like a baby chick stepping out of its egg, but during a walk through the woods the leaves spoke to the wind and the grass had a greenness that nearly blinded me.

Style was always under discussion. John McGuire, the champion for uncontaminated blues, was still around. He was in Tom's band in the winter and a part-time Jam Bander.

"I think it matters what we wear onstage," I said.

"What matters is the blues," said John. "True bluesmen don't give a shit what they wear. You really wanna wear funny white shoes and play through Marshall amps?"

"Are you kidding? Of course. Fuck yes," Tom and I said, laughing.

Steven Tallarico, a local rocker, had been coming up to Sunapee for years. His parents had a family connection with one of the resorts, Trow-Rico. Every summer he'd blow in from Greenwich Village with a different band to do two- or three-week runs at the Barn. In most of these bands he was the drummer who sang. His drumming always blew me away. A lot of bands passed through, but Tallarico's were always the best, especially the Strangeurs. They covered Beatles, Stones, and Byrds songs note for note. Everyone looked forward to seeing the Strangeurs, who actually had a song on the Anchorage's jukebox, "The Sun." The tune was professional sounding but too poppy for me. Still, I was impressed that these guys had actually been in a recording studio.

The first time I encountered one of Tallarico's bands in person, I was not left with a positive impression. They came into the Anchorage acting like they owned the place. Big fish in a small pond. They were wearing super-glam rock star clothes in the middle of the day when everyone else was in T-shirts and shorts. They took over a booth and stayed for hours. Loud and obnoxious, they ran most of the other customers out of the place. From time to time, Steven would break out in a fake English accent. Their meal culminated in a food fight. Whipped cream was flying everywhere. They left a mess that I had to clean up. I wasn't happy, but

I had no choice. I guessed that was how obnoxious rock stars from New York acted. Little did I know. . . .

Her typical pose was to position herself in front of the pinball machine at the Anchorage so that sunlight caught the luster of her dark hair. She was beautiful. She wore edgy clothes. She attacked the machine with a certain confidence and aggression not typical of a teenage girl. While she played, I'd sneak peeks from the kitchen. I liked to watch her manipulate the flippers. She was focused. She rocked the machine hard yet instinctively knew how to prevent a tilt. She maintained the game's high score, frustrating the most determined men. The ceaseless bells and whistles and pings, celebrating her skill at keeping the pinball in play, became the sexy sound track to her little drama.

The drama continued when she moved over to the jukebox. She stood there casually puffing on a cigarette, surveying her choices. Her choices were inevitably hip and usually English. She favored the same groups I did. When she first spoke to me, it was about music.

"You play guitar, don't you?" she asked.

"How'd you know?"

"I usually hear about anything that has to do with music. I love music. My dad teaches music at Cambridge High. He plays in a band."

"What kind of music?"

"He can play any kind. He started out playing jazz. Ever hear of Billie Holiday?"

I hadn't.

"Well, he played with her and Dizzy Gillespie. And my uncle's a famous musician. Ever hear the theme song from *Batman*?"

I had.

"He wrote it. His name is Neal Hefti."

"What's your name?"

"Elyssa."

"I'm Joe."

"When can I hear you play?"

"Any time. I'm always playing."

I didn't know it at the time, but Elyssa was also part of a cultural circuitry that included Steven Tallarico. They had known each other since they were little kids. Their parents were friends. Steven's dad, like Elyssa's, was a highly trained musician who taught high school music and, in their earlier days, played in jazz bands together. Elyssa even knew that Steven had started out as a drummer.

"Is he your boyfriend?" I asked.

"Oh, no, he's too crazy to be my boyfriend. He's more like a cousin."

"Do you like him?"

"Steven's cool."

Elyssa went on to say that Steven had spent a year or two at the public school in Sunapee. He moved in with his uncle and aunt because his parents felt that he needed to get away from his big high school that was close to New York City. Their hope was that Sunapee would calm him down. Apparently, though, the plan didn't work.

"He's loud and arrogant," said Elyssa, "but he's also a great showman. He goes around saying he's going to be a rock star in a way that's kind of obnoxious. But when you hear him play the drums and sing, you believe him."

It was hard to know what to think of Steven Tallarico, so I didn't think much about him at all. He was in his world, I was in mine, and I just didn't see those worlds colliding.

POST-PREP

I recently looked up the meaning of "stoicism." One definition talks about indifference, passiveness, and endurance. Another mentions "a firmly restraining response to pain." Was there a stoic part of my personality that, in my late teens, unexpectedly strengthened? Maybe. Looking back some forty-five years to this earlier moment in my life, the description feels right: *firmly restraining response to pain*.

The pain was caused by my failure as a student. In spite of my accepting help from tutors and counselors, my schoolwork continued to suffer. I felt like I was beating my head against the wall. When it came to my grades, my father had given up even mentioning the subject. I felt like he had given up on me. He and I drifted apart.

"Joe is exhibiting passive-aggressive behavior," one of my teachers wrote my parents. "The fact that he refuses to trim his hair, in accordance with our health and appearance code, is unacceptable."

Two wars were raging at once. The first, the macro war, was the 1968 culture war in which long hair was a symbol of rebellion against the previous generation of hopeless conformists. The second war, the micro war, was more subtle—the war within me. I felt like a caterpillar half in and half out of the cocoon. I saw the enemy as school and school regulations, but not my parents. They were more confused by my behavior than adamant about keeping me away from the counterculture. My desire to make my parents proud never dissipated: I always wanted to please them, but not being able to—especially in the one area, academics, that they valued most—caused me inner grief. I wanted to escape the whole messy swamp of confused feelings but didn't know how.

After spring break of my senior year, I went back to Vermont Academy feeling sick at heart. I didn't want to be there. In my mind, I was back at the Boston Tea Party, the synagogue converted into a psychedelic club on Berkeley Street, where I had seen the Jeff Beck Group with Rod Stewart singing and Nicky Hopkins on piano. Seeing Beck's guitar reignited my obsession with getting just what he had—a Gibson Les Paul. My electric Guild felt wrong. I didn't see how much longer I could keep playing it, not after hearing what Beck did with his Gibson. After the show I waited around the stage door. I just wanted to shake his hand. These were the early days of his slow-growing fame, when he was playing clubs that might be half-empty, and I was the only fan hanging around backstage.

"You're great, Jeff," was all I managed to say when he finally made his exit.

"Thanks, man."

He expressed no interest in further conversation, which was fine, since I had nothing more to say. He seemed very moody, very distant, very mod—all the things I admired most about the mysterious blues cats from London. Their passion for their masters, all Americans, had helped get their masters gigs at the same Boston Tea Party, where I saw Muddy Waters with Otis Spann. It's also where Buddy Guy made his dramatic entrance using a long cord that went all the way to the street, a trick he had learned from *his* master, Guitar Slim. I was learning by listening, learning by watching, learning by studying even the smallest gestures made by these guys, English and American, black and white, who had taught their guitars to talk in a secret language that seemed as easy as a conversation and as inscrutable as a riddle.

Vermont Academy, which actually had ivy growing up its walls, had me climbing the walls because those walls were so far away from the Boston Tea Party. I didn't relate to the teachers, except for one—an English instructor, who invited me to his home, where he lived with his wife and young kids. He had longish hair—not hippie long, but longer than his colleagues'. He also had open-minded attitudes. He was interested in the younger writers and poets associated with the antiwar movement. He knew I played music and liked to hear my opinions about certain bands. We'd discuss Dylan, the Stones, Pink Floyd, and the Byrds. I was also intrigued that he had a pistol license. I was surprised that a liberal teacher was also a gun owner. When he talked about his feelings about the Second Amendment and the weighty responsibility that comes with owning a gun, I listened carefully. He became a mentor.

As winter turned to spring, my hair grew longer. It was now below my shoulders. In April I came down with a bad case of the flu and was sent to the infirmary, where I stayed for over a week. A couple of friends came by to visit.

"Once you get out of here," said one, "they're gonna make you cut your hair."

"When you go to sleep," said another, "keep one eye open. They may cut your hair in the middle of the night."

We all laughed.

I knew the guys were right to warn me. For a long time I had ignored the mandate. Not only had my parents been put on notice, I'd been called to the headmaster's office at least four times.

After a week or so, I was back on my feet. I was in no mood for prep school lectures. And yet that's exactly what was waiting for me.

I went back to my dorm room and sat there, doing nothing for the next three or four hours. A few of my friends dropped by to see what I was going to do. I considered the situation. The school had rules. Vermont Academy had traditions to uphold.

I had been vocal in my defiance of those traditions—at least when it came to cutting my hair. After I left the infirmary, my first class was history, and the teacher let it be known that he would not allow me in the room if I had not cut my hair. The man served as one of the dorm masters. He

41

wasn't a bad guy. He had even helped tutor me. I didn't dislike him. At the same time, I had no intention of obeying him. If going to his class with long, uncut hair meant a showdown, then it was time for the showdown.

I followed my fellow students through the door of the history classroom and sat down.

"Mr. Perry," he said, looking directly at me, "I hope you're feeling better."

"Yes, sir, I am."

"That's good. But I notice that you have not cut your hair."

"No, sir."

"I don't have to remind you of the rules. You either cut your hair or you leave my classroom."

This script had been playing inside my head ever since I left the infirmary. The outcome was a foregone conclusion.

After several long seconds of dead silence, I gathered my books and walked out. Back in my dorm room, a couple of my friends came by.

"What are you going to do?" asked one.

"I guess I'll be leaving Vermont Academy," I said.

At the end of the day I called my mother.

"Would you mind picking me up and bringing me home?" I asked.

"What's wrong?"

"Nothing."

"Joe, something is obviously wrong if you're leaving school."

"They won't let me in class if I won't cut my hair."

"And you aren't going to cut it?"

"No."

"Why not?"

"Because I don't want to."

"Graduation is just around the corner, Joe. Are you sure you want to do this?"

"I'm not sure of anything."

"Then wait it out."

"They won't let me."

"They will if you get a haircut."

"I can't do that."

"You can't or you won't?"

"I won't."

The next day Mom drove up. I packed my stuff, told a few friends goodbye, and left.

Thus began a difficult period that cast a shadow over my future and my soul. Much to their credit, my parents didn't give me a hard time. They realized that I was suffering and, lacking a remedy, left me alone. I fell into a loneliness I had never felt before. It wasn't a physical loneliness, because I was back in my boyhood bedroom with my mother and father and sister, Anne, around. It was a spiritual loneliness.

I missed Vermont Academy—missed my friends, missed the Just Us band, missed the photography, missed walking in the woods with Betsy. The reality of having left school sank in. And even though I felt uncertainty about the future, I also felt free. My destiny was now in my own hands. I was excited to see what would happen next.

Determined to get my degree, I planned to finish out my senior year at Hopedale High. My dad set up a meeting with the principal.

"No worries," said the man. "Your credits from Vermont Academy are transferable. As soon as you pass all your final semester courses here, you'll graduate on time."

"Thank you," I said with great relief.

"No need to thank me, son," he said. "The only thing you need to do is run out and get a haircut."

"And if I don't?"

The half smile on his face gave me his answer. I walked out of his office and never saw the man again.

Just like that, I literally walked a half a mile from the principal's office through town to the employment office of Draper Corporation. I'd had jobs since I was a kid, from shoveling snow to working in a restaurant. So at this point I was ready for anything.

"Anything" meant any job that I could get at Draper, the only major employer in town. Draper Corporation, a manufacturer of textile looms, had been bought out by Rockwell, the huge firm that now ran the factory—a million square feet worth of machinery. The factory was the town's lifeblood. Since I was in need of a transfusion, I went to work at the factory. But when I applied for a job, I made it clear to the employment office that I didn't want my dad to know. I didn't want to use his executive influence to get me a better position. I wanted to take whatever job they would give to any other high school dropout. That meant working on the assembly line.

When my parents found out, they had to adjust to the idea. After all, children of Hopedale's upper middle class usually did not take several steps down to work in the factory. The idea was to step up. My question, though, was—*step up to what?* Once I realized that my undiagnosed ADHD would keep me from going to college and becoming a marine biologist, music and music alone became my focus. My plan was to form a band that could support me, but until then I'd have to find some plausible source of income. And since I had no skills other than the guitar, the factory looked like my best bet.

I tell you now that the factory did me good. I tell you now that it made me stronger and put me in touch with a side of life I needed to know about. I tell you now that it gave me a tougher skin. At the time, though, I would have told you none of that. I would have said that the experience was maddening. It was brutal and dirty. I was down there in the pits. I told the foreman that I could read and write, hoping it might lead to better job and pay, but it didn't. Sometimes I thought of my friends at prep school who were on their way to Dartmouth and Harvard. But it was my choice to be here and it was where I stayed. I punched the clock. I did what I was told to do. I worked with hot metal parts coming off a conveyor belt. My coworkers weren't any more tolerant of my long hair than the headmaster or principal. They called me a hippie and a faggot. At the end of the day my hands were scarred and my hair filthy with the sand from the blast furnace. It wasn't fun. The other guys had ethnic backgrounds similar to mine—there were Portuguese and Italian workers—but we were in different worlds culturally. I was listening to the Doors singing "Strange Days." They were listening to Glen Campbell singing "Wichita Lineman." And after being there for a while, when I talked about how I wanted to trade in my mom's Chevy Nova station wagon for an MGB, you wouldn't believe the grief I got from the other workers. Foreign cars were looked on as un-American.

There was also the question of the draft. My high school deferment was no longer applicable, and I was suddenly 1-A. At the same time, my parents were concerned about my mental condition. They couldn't understand why, so close to graduation, I had dropped out. They sent me to a psychologist for a short period of time. Without my asking, the psychologist apparently wrote my draft board. Just like that, I was reclassified 4-F.

I'd make my musical escapes on the weekends. Going to the Boston Tea Party in the city's South End, I got the only schooling that mattered to me. This was a blessed time for music lovers. Because there were few sold-out shows, you could get close to the band and drink it all in.

On these musical sojourns I was sometimes accompanied by Elyssa Jerret. She was working at a boutique in Boston, where concert promoters gave her free tickets and backstage passes. It was Elyssa who got me close to the dressing room to catch a glimpse of the performers. One night it was Peter Green, the Fleetwood Mac founder and guitarist, whose blues chops equaled or surpassed Clapton or Page. His instrument, I noted, was a 1959 Gibson Les Paul. His "Rattlesnake Shake" had me out of my mind. When it wasn't Fleetwood Mac, it was Spirit or the Who or Ten Years After. Then Monday morning it was back to the factory.

At night I still sought out musicians and sometimes found myself in Milford, the town that sat on Hopedale's northern border. It was through one of my musician friends that I met a girl described as a "free spirit." I took that to mean that she might sleep with me. She did. I was grateful to finally lose the label of virgin. After all, I was eighteen. It was high time. But the experience was hardly transformational. We did it—that's about all I can say. It was rote. She was somewhat more familiar with the exercise than me. She offered neither compliments nor complaints. We had a few more dates and that was it. Romance was not even remotely present. The pleasure was limited, not only by a hurry-up tension but by my own lingering Catholic guilt. The discovery of sexual ecstasy was still some years away. At this point ecstasy had more to do with music. Yet I also realized that my mother's Chevy Nova station wagon, which I'd bought from her for two hundred dollars, had its advantages, especially when it came to fitting a sleeping bag in the back.

In my late teens, the notion that I could actually make a living from music was still more dream than reality. I had been raised on the premise of practicality. You do what's possible, achieve what's possible, and discipline yourself accordingly. Working in the factory was my way of endorsing this ethos. I hated it, but what the fuck: I did the best I could. I didn't like it when I saw guys cutting corners and slacking off. My parents had taught me better. But in working the assembly line day in and day out, the monotony got to me. The grit and the grime, the grind and heat and endless boredom had me down. I definitely got the blues.

My only cure for the blues was to play the blues. I became a factory worker by day and a blues rocker by night. I reconnected with my friends from Hopedale High and formed a band that I called Flash. Dave Meade was my bass buddy and on drums was either John Alden or Dave Carchio, depending on who was free.

Dave Meade's big brother went to Amherst and asked us to play at a party his frat was throwing. This was our first real gig, and the first time we'd be performing for more than five people who weren't our friends. When I learned that we'd be paid five dollars each, I couldn't believe it. Up until this point I had never seriously connected rock and roll with money— just pure joy. I never dreamed of playing on the same stages as my idols, much less living their lifestyles.

At 8 P.M. sharp, when the keg was cracked and the beer started flowing, we hit it hard. Earlier I was a little nervous, but after a few beers we got the groove grinding with a blues. When the dance floor filled up, my anxiety eased. I felt like I was one with the audience. And because the blues seemed to facilitate their grinding on the girls, the boys kept requesting that same blues. This went on for hours.

After our last set a few of the frat boys came up to me. Because they were drunk, I worried that they might get belligerent. Did they think we had been flirting with their girls? Was this gonna get ugly? But I was surprised to learn that, instead of being confrontational, they were simply inquisitive. They wanted to know all about the music.

What was the name of the blues we'd been playing?

Had we written the songs?

What were the names of the records we listened to?

Which bands did we like?

Would we come back and play their next dance and be sure and play that same blues?

In short, they were into everything we were doing. They had never heard the magic before. Like us, they were looking for knowledge about the magic. They were, in fact, my earliest fans and an indication of the keen interest shared by a whole generation of college kids. We left that gig feeling that we were not alone in our passion for rock blues. Though I was only at the very start of my own path of discovery—a path I still follow today—it felt great to be carrying on the tradition, and also to get paid. I'd moved from playing acoustic with Chimes of Freedom to lead guitar for Vermont Academy's Just Us to playing lead in a decent band that could knock out basic blues. Slowly but surely, I was finding my voice.

We had our share of beer that night, but beer wasn't all that interesting to me. On the other hand, when listening to the Yardbirds do "Smokestack Lightning" and hearing someone say, "Man, those guys are stoned on fucking speed," I began to develop a romantic view of the relationship between drugs and music. I hadn't quite entered that relationship, but it wouldn't be long. The interest was already there.

My biggest desire was to keep playing. On a semi-regular basis we found work. Dave went down to the Hopedale Town Hall and, for two hundred dollars, rented a large room in the old building that included a wooden dance floor. I imagined big bands from the swing era playing there. I drew up posters that we plastered around town. We hired a friend to work the door, where tickets were $1.50. We actually wound up making a little money.

We also found a friend who played organ. With that came a bigger sound, and it wouldn't be long before we were playing songs like "Hush" and "Gimme Some Lovin'." I hooked up a trailer to my station wagon, which allowed me to load up the Hammond B-3, the Leslie tone cabinet, and a mash-up of amps, PAs, and electronic odds and ends. At the gigs we'd concentrate on the blues and keep the tempo right on the edge. We could take a four-minute song and extend it for twenty minutes. Our hormone-crazed ears heard the sexual drive of the music we were making—and we kept driving 'em home. If the people giving the parties had let us, we would have played all night long.

I was a serious introvert, but the formula of booze-before-music broke down the barrier, especially when I knew we'd be playing a song like "Happy Jack," which I'd just learned off the new Who album. The fraternity crowd probably didn't know it, because it wasn't a Top Ten tune, but I didn't care. I'd slip it into our repertoire anyway. I paid close attention to records by Blue Cheer and Ten Years After, listening for songs that not only moved me but challenged me. I was always working on my chops.

In the fall of 1969, something happened that I thought might change my life and jump-start my musical career. I met some guys who invited me to Block Island, where they were putting together a band and renting a house. Their plan was to get together a repertoire, rehearse, and aggressively go after gigs.

Block Island is Rhode Island's version of Martha's Vineyard. It sits in the Atlantic some thirteen miles offshore. No more than a thousand people live on ten square miles. It's a small paradise, certainly a more attractive destination than the assembly line. I decided to take a chance and go.

I took the hour-long ferry ride and arrived on a picture-perfect afternoon. The weather was mild, the flowers in bloom, the pastures a deep and lush green. With my guitar, suitcase, and amps in tow, I hitched from the pier to the country road where my friends had rented a rambling old house with four or five bedrooms. They were glad to see me. I didn't know them all that well, but because they had heard of me and my playing, they made me feel at home. There was a bass player, a drummer, and a lead singer/guitarist who acted like a quasi leader. More or less, though, the band ran like a democracy.

"Hey, man," said the drummer as we shook hands. "Hope you don't mind sharing a room."

"Not at all."

When he took me upstairs and introduced me to my roommate, I was taken aback. My roommate was a cute little brunette, a hippie chick with long hair and tinted granny glasses and bib overalls that were tight enough to reveal a beautiful body.

"I'm Joe," was all I could manage to say,

"I'm Sally."

I looked around the room and saw that there was only one place to sleep—a double mattress that sat on the floor.

"Well, while you guys get acquainted, I'm gonna do some errands," said the drummer.

I stood there for a while feeling awkward before Sally finally broke the silence.

"I'll help you unpack," she said. "I took the bottom two drawers in the dresser and saved the top two for you."

"Thank you," I said, "but I don't mind unpacking." I did so quickly. Then the awkwardness returned.

"Wanna go for a walk?" asked Sally. "The island's really outta sight."

"Sure."

I was grateful that, like me, Sally didn't do a lot of talking. She knew a nature path—actually, the whole island was one big nature path—that led to an expansive meadow covered with yellow daisies.

"I like to lie down and just watch the clouds," she said.

I lay next to her. I was excited by her presence and, for that matter, this new chapter in my life. The big puffy clouds were pushed along by a gentle breeze. My imagination was pushed along by the joint we shared. There was no hurry, no problems, no factory job, no parental pressures. Just me and Sally in a field of daisies on Block Island. What could be better?

Back at the house, both the bassist and the drummer had girlfriends who, along with Sally, did the cooking. There was hot soup and homemade bread and a fresh-baked cherry pie. After dinner the guys brought out four huge bricks of tightly wrapped hash.

"It's enough to last us all winter," said the drummer.

The dope was strong and, when Sally and I went to our room, so was the lovemaking. It was my first real lovemaking, the first time I was with a woman who was truly free with her body. She had no inhibitions. She enjoyed it as much as I did. She acted like a blow job was the most natural thing in the world—and with Sally, it was.

The next day I awoke with a slight hash hangover. I looked for the drummer and the bassist but they were walking the nature paths with their girlfriends. When they got back, I suggested we break out our instruments and play.

"After dinner," they said.

After dinner the hash came out again, and we got high again, and the high led me and Sally back to our bedroom, where the sex was even better than the night before.

The next day I told the guys, "Hey, we need to rehearse."

We did. We worked our way through the standard fare, from Chuck Berry to the Stones. I could see that, with practice, we could get good enough to gig.

"Are there any gigs on the island?" I asked.

"No, but there are gigs in Providence."

"How are we gonna get those gigs?" I wanted to know.

"No problem, man. We have friends. And the ferry runs to the mainland four times a day. Let's get high."

When I got high, I wanted to play even more. When these guys got high, they stopped playing. So a pattern set in. Sally and I went to the field of daisies every afternoon, the girls cooked for us every night, after dinner the hash mellowed us out, and then Sally and I fucked ourselves to sleep. This might sound like a pretty good definition of paradise, but for me it wasn't.

I wanted to rehearse more. The guys didn't. I wanted to know more about their contact in Providence who could get us gigs. But I couldn't get any answers. Work wasn't their top priority.

"You stress too much, Joe," they said. "Just be cool."

But as each day went by, I was realizing that, when it came to music, these guys were only half-serious. They liked music but they didn't love it—not the way I did. They loved the do-nothing lifestyle of Block Island. I loved that too. It reminded me of the lazy days at Sunapee. I loved that Sally was a great lover and a sweet chick. I loved that the hash was good. I loved the wildflowers and the low-hanging clouds and the breezes coming off the ocean. I loved it all, but I needed more. I needed to know that the music was going someplace. And it wasn't.

After a couple of weeks I realized that I needed to get out. When I told Sally I was leaving, she was a little sad but hardly devastated. She was a free-loving chick and would find another free soul to love. The guys were disappointed but they knew I wanted more than them. They didn't argue. I hired a couple of local kids to help me carry my guitar, suitcase, and amps down to the ferry. I got on the boat on an unseasonably cold and overcast day. Looking at the island slipping off into the distance, it was still a beautiful sight. It was a short chapter but a good one. For the first time, I had tasted real sex and loved it. And just as importantly I had learned that, no matter how intense the physical pleasures of lovemaking and doping, I needed more. I needed to find guys who shared my drive to play rock and roll.

After Block Island I went back to the factory and Flash. But as spring turned to summer, I quit my job and moved up to the lake, which was by now a tradition. Renewed by the water and the woods, I was revived by my musical friendship with the Jam Band—me, Tom Hamilton, and Pudge Scott. We knew this would probably be one of our last summers to hang out.

Elyssa was back in the middle of the mix. In fact, she was the one who brought Steven Tallarico to one of our gigs at the Barn. I didn't know he was there until after the fact. Even if I had known, it wouldn't have made a difference. The Jam Band's jams were just that—experimental excursions through Hendrix's "Red House," a glimpse of MC5's "Ramblin' Rose," or a taste of Beck's "Rice Pudding." John sang, I sang, I played guitar, Tom played bass, Pudge kept us moving along. At that point I was so deep in my learning groove that I had little self-awareness. My concentration had been on the musical and physical moves of Pete Townshend and Jimi Hendrix. In the only area where I had consistently been a good student, I had paid strict attention to how these men articulated their instruments. I had also borrowed whatever grand gesticulations—Pete Townshend's sweeping windmills, for example—that were critical to their style. Early on I saw that the entertainment element of rock guitar was essential. Chuck Berry played to please. He put on a show. And if his show hadn't been as spectacular as it was, he never would have captivated me so completely.

"**S**teven Tallarico likes your playing," Elyssa told me a few days later. "He thinks you're the real deal."

I was happy to hear it. I considered Steven the real deal. His bands were always professional sounding. I loved the raw emotion of his singing voice. Something was drawing us together.

Not much time passed before Henry Smith, Led Zeppelin's drum roadie and Steven's close friend, asked us to make an audition tape backing Steven, who was trying out for Jeff Beck. By then Steven's many bands—the Strangeurs, Chain Reaction, Fox Chase, William Proud—had split up. He was looking for a gig.

We all gathered at the Barn, where the owner, John Conrad, always a true supporter, let us do the taping. It was Tom, Pudge, and me backing up Steven.

Before we started, he and I had a chance to talk. It was the first time we had a chance to say more than hello to each other. We had a few laughs and discussed the song we were going to play. Steven was witty, animated, and all about the music. He lived and breathed the stuff. His energy was manic. He believed in himself. I sensed that he had the same strong self-confidence and drive that I did. At this point I took his manic energy to be part of his drive, like mine.

Time to get started. Henry ran the tape recorder. We played before just a few of our friends, including the always-present Elyssa. After rehearsing, Henry rolled tape and before long we got a good rock demo of the Beatles' "I'm Down."

We cracked a few beers to celebrate and then decided to play some more—just for the hell of it, this time with Steven on drums. I had never heard him jam before. He really cut loose. He was by far the best I'd ever played with. I'm so rhythm-oriented myself that finding someone whose grooves were so right was thrilling. The interplay between us was something I'd never experienced with another musician. We each had different vocabularies, but we spoke the same musical language. We played songs that we knew in common and blasted through a couple that we didn't.

He had soul and grit and an astounding range. Before the jam, I was a little concerned that Steven might be too pop for me. But when we got together on "Train Kept a-Rollin'," Yardbirds style, I knew that Steven was no stranger to the blues—or at least the English version of the American blues.

"We gotta do this again sometime," he said after it was over.

"Anytime," I agreed.

We talked a little longer about all the bands he'd been in and why he was fed up with the business.

"These bands keep falling apart," he told me. "I'm getting tired of trying to keep it together. The music business is fucked up. Man, I'm seriously thinking of quitting."

I told him that I was impressed when I saw that the Strangeurs actually had a single, "The Sun," on the Anchorage jukebox.

"That record didn't go anywhere," he said. "It didn't make us a dime."

"So what are you going to do now?" I asked.

"Not really sure. I think I'm going to stay up here for the winter."

In jamming with Steven, I began to see him in a different light. I liked his energy; I was blown away by the connection we shared during the jam; but I also detected deep insecurity. I began to see that his nonstop stream of talking was a way of covering up. He'd have to keep telling you how good his bands were and how good he was—not to convince you, but to convince himself.

The Jam Band continued jamming that summer. We even found a girl singer who played keyboards and joined us for several gigs. The Jam Band was always solid, but the Jam Band wasn't enough.

Tom Hamilton and I returned to the shade of the oak tree, where we had another discussion about the future. We got high and went into a fantasy about getting our act together and breaking into the music business. It was that recurring fantasy about forming a band that actually had a shot to go big-time.

I'd been through Chimes of Freedom, Flash, Just Us, the Jam Band,

and the crazy cats on Block Island. I wanted more. And I wanted to achieve it with Tom. Over these past summers, we'd become brothers.

I put it to Tom plainly: "I think we should move to Boston, rent an apartment, and start a band. I think we should just go for it."

"I'm with you, man," he said. "I'm with you all the way. The only problem is that I have another year of high school. I don't want to miss my senior year. Besides, my parents would flip out if I quit."

I wasn't happy, but I understood. I couldn't see going to Boston by myself, not without my buddy Tom. I agreed to wait. That meant spending another winter at the factory in Hopedale.

That winter was one of the longest of my life. Even though I had a little seniority and better pay, I hated the work more than ever. Those dark months went by slowly. The conveyor belt moved slowly. Time stopped. At $2.40 an hour I was still putting away money, but my savings were adding up slowly. The overheated tedium of the conveyor belt got to me. So did the constant harassment from the workers about my faggot hair and my hippie looks. I kept to myself. I stayed sullen. I made up the courses required to get my high school degree. Not that I planned to go to college, but I still wanted to please my parents, who remained baffled over my life as a factory worker.

I sold my station-wagon-and-trailer vehicle that we had used to lug our gear around. Instead I took my savings and finally bought a used MGB. That sports car represented a break in my thinking. I no longer saw myself as someone who wanted to haul around band gear. I wanted something better. And I didn't want to wait. I drove down to Boston to hear Jeff Beck make blues magic on a Les Paul. That next week I was out shopping for my own Les Paul.

I saw less and less of my parents. They were as understanding as they could be. They were steady, they were strong, but at that point my dad had become a virtual stranger. The long winter got to me. Handling the red-hot metal got to me. Breathing the factory's toxic fumes got to me. The sunless days and freezing cold nights got to me. In the middle of that frozen winter, I broke down. Approaching twenty years old, I felt like I had lost it.

The grit and the grime, the grind and heat and endless boredom had me half out of my mind until one day I called up my supervisor and said I

ROCKS

54

was sick. I called it the flu, but it wasn't the flu. It was the blues—the low-down, can't-get-my-ass-outta-bed blues that had me in my room for two straight weeks, not waking up till four in the afternoon and doing nothing but making model rockets.

My mom and dad looked in on me, but they were as confused as I was. I had a feeling they thought I was a hopeless cause. I thought the same.

I broke down completely, only to start slowly building back up. I'm not sure where the motivation came from. It probably had a lot to do with the weather. That gray New England winter sky can definitely get to you. When the cold weather started to thaw, I got it together enough to return to the factory, where my boss seemed glad to see me. The boss was always appreciative of my hard work. I counted the days until summertime. As soon as the warm weather hit, I was off to Sunapee, where the Jam Band would reconvene and Tom and I could solidify our plans to finally get the fuck out of Dodge.

The summer of 1970.

Here comes Mark Lehman, rolling into Sunapee in his hippie-ized step van—a UPS-style truck. Mark pictured himself as R. Crumb's Mr. Natural. He was Mr. Laid-Back, Mr. Cool, Mr. Right on Time. I loved the guy. A couple of years older than us, Mark literally became our way out of town. But he was much more than that. He was a happy spirit. His mood was always upbeat. He dug pot and beer. When he drifted into town and heard the music that Tom and I were making, he decided to stop drifting and hook up with us. He joined our pirate gang. The minute he heard Tom and me talking about moving to Boston and starting a band, he said, "Count me in, brothers. I want to help any way I can." It turned out that Mark helped in every way possible.

The plan was for Tom and me to move to Boston and find an apartment big enough to house a band. The hardest part was telling Pudge—the third member of the Jam Band—that we were leaving, but Pudge, still in high school and not about to quit, understood.

I approached Mom, rather than Dad, because, well, Dad and I still hadn't learned to speak to each other.

"How are you going to support yourselves?" she asked.

"We'll all get part-time jobs until the band starts making money."

"Apartments are expensive. Part-time jobs don't pay much. And I imagine it'll take whatever band you form a while to start making money. Are you sure you have enough savings to get an apartment?"

"I have some, but not enough. I need to borrow some."

"How much?"

"A thousand dollars."

"Well, Joe," she said, "I need to discuss it with your father."

At that point I was convinced that Dad had given up on me, but I was wrong. The next day Mom said they'd loan me the money. I was deeply grateful.

Excited by the prospect of moving, Tom and I took a couple of trips to Boston in August to look for places. The idea was to move in September, when the college kids returned and the city became alive with parties and music.

Until we left, John Conrad let me live in a deserted old farmhouse next to the Barn. In exchange for helping clean up the Barn, Tom and I could also rehearse there for free. In our pre-Boston life, the Barn was our last stop, John our dear drunk uncle sheltering us during our last days. In fact, I even got free food at the Barn if I could get to the kitchen before noon. Louise, the beloved old lady who really ran the place, would cook me a big breakfast of bacon and eggs that I'd devour in a hurry so I could be gone before John showed up. John's early-afternoon hangovers were brutal and his behavior less than civilized. Steven Tallarico and Henry Smith once dosed John with acid, thinking that LSD might give John a new outlook on life. But when he came down from the trip he was still the same irascible John.

This was the same summer that a Sunapee friend named Guy Williams and I had something of a Tom Sawyer/Huck Finn moment. We sneaked through a barbed-wire fence into a farmer's field, where the corn was plentiful. We low-crawled through the dirt, stuffed our shirts with ears of corn, and stealthily made our way out. Just when we thought we were free, we heard the farmer shouting.

"I got my twelve-gauge loaded with rock salt," shouted the farmer. "And I ain't scared to using it. Get off my fuckin' land!"

Boom! An ear-shattering blast.

We managed to escape unharmed and that night we cooked up the corn and went to bed on full bellies.

All that summer the musical excitement had been building. There was a definite buzz when, sometime in early September, Elyssa showed up at Sunapee after spending a month abroad, where she had found her way into the center of rock-and-roll London. We all gathered around to hear her Jimmy Page and Jeff Beck stories. She also showed up with a boyfriend, a tall lanky Chicago blues guitarist who called himself Joe Jammer and was signed to Led Zeppelin's manager. If Elyssa had been the coolest chick in Sunapee before, now she was the coolest chick in all New England.

With summer coming to a close, the countdown had started. In a few weeks we'd be on our way to Boston and a new life. In the deserted house where I was staying, horses roamed freely around the grounds. They made strange sounds—whinnies and screeches—that kept me up at night.

One night Tom came over with some beer and weak LSD. We climbed onto the roof of the place where I was staying and, flat on our backs, took in the moonscape. The stars were smiling, the sky was laughing, the breeze off the lake sang a song about our future. We were almost there, the fantasy almost realized. After knocking off a six-pack, we heard rock music. It wasn't imaginary. It echoed up the valley from John Conrad's Barn. It was one of Steven Tallarico's last bands playing at the club. They were playing so well you'd swear you were hearing the original record of the latest Beatles hit.

The countdown to departure day continued. It was a strange, restless summer. Sometimes I was up, sometimes down. One night the gang came over to the deserted house by the Barn to announce that they were going to the sandpits to party. We'd build a bonfire. We'd smoke dope and drink beer. We'd jump off the cliffs and act like crazy fools. On this particular night, though, I just wasn't in the mood.

"You guys go ahead," I said. "We'll talk tomorrow."

"You've got to come," said Elyssa. "It's going to the biggest blast of the summer."

"I think I'll just stay here."

Tom, Pudge, and the others tried to convince me otherwise, but I wasn't moving. I was feeling blue. As the night went on, the blue mood turned even darker. I was used to the blues. They were part of my personality—and always would be. But on this particular night, it was more than that; it was feeling that I needed to be alone. I just wanted to have a few beers and go to bed.

Next morning the phone rang off the wall. It was my friends saying the cops busted them at the sandpits party. A few of the kids managed to run away, but the cops hauled most everyone off to the station and called their parents to post bail. It was one mess I was able to avoid. Now, more than ever, I couldn't wait to get to Boston.

The countdown continued.

During my last week in Sunapee I was driving my MGB by Trow-Rico and happened to see Steven mowing the lawn. I stopped to say hi.

"Hey, man, how's it going?" I asked.

"Mowing up a storm, brother."

"What about the music thing? You still down on the business?"

"Don't have any plans," he said.

"We got a gig on the *Mount Sunapee*." That was the largest boat on the lake that made daily cruises filled with tourists while the captain pointed out historical sights. The night cruises included music. "You can come hear us if you want," I added. "It's a booze cruise. It'll be a blast."

"I don't think so. I'm just lying low. You going back home in September?" asked Steven.

"Actually, Tom and I are moving to Boston. We're looking to start a band."

"Cool."

"What would you think about hooking up with us?"

"Sounds interesting. Lemme think about it."

"Okay. See you around, Steven."

"Take it easy, Joe."

A few weeks later, Tom and I piled all our stuff into Mark Lehman's step van, which smelled of skunk weed and stale beer.

"You guys ready?" asked Mark.

"Ready."

He gunned the engine, the van belched like it was about to explode, and we were off.

PART 2

THE BIRTH

THE COMMONWEALTH

In September, the college kids came to Boston in droves. Each fall there were nearly three hundred thousand new faces. Tom, Mark, and I arrived with them—not college kids but rock kids prepared to do whatever the fuck it took to make it. Boston might not have the big-time status of New York or L.A., but Boston was practical, Boston was close by, and Boston was happening.

The month we hit town I turned twenty. That same month Jimi Hendrix died and a few weeks after that Janis Joplin was gone. Confusion was in the air. So was excitement. The week we arrived, Tricky Dick was the prez. His goofball vice prez, Spiro Agnew, was screaming against the evils of the very rock aesthetic we embraced. We mourned the death of our heroes, but these were the culture wars. Then there was the real war in Vietnam. All of these things pointed to the reality that rock and roll was not a career you aspired to if you expected any longevity. To me it was day-to-day survival and a test of will, an attitude that said nothing would stop us from starting a band and getting paying gigs. We were too young and naive to do anything besides play hard.

If, like nearly every other rock-and-roll band, we were on the outskirts of acceptable society, that didn't mean that we lacked social and economic drive. In the world in which we placed ourselves—call it an antisociety—we yearned for recognition and sustenance. We were determined not to have real jobs. We wanted to keep the party going. In this particular moment in time—a year after the breakup of the Beatles and the disaster at Altamont—rock culture was in turmoil. But then again, I viewed rock and roll as the sound track to what was happening in society. The songs were the anthems to our rebellion. If a tornado was heading our way, so much the better. Hadn't I been thrilled to see Jeff Beck destroy his guitar in *Blow-Up*? Didn't that feel right to me? The insane energy of the music made musicians do insane things. Culturally, I was down with free love. But I can't say that I was a card-carrying hippie.

We found a pad in the center of the student ghetto called Allston-Brighton. Our place was on the main drag at 1325 Commonwealth. Undergraduates would catch the trolley that ran from downtown to Boston College right in front of our building.

To get to the second-floor apartment you could take the rickety stairs or an elevator the size of a small cage. I took the big room in front—supposedly a living room—and turned it into my bedroom. It had lots of windows. The trade-off was that we could use it as the party room because it had the biggest couch. Soon, though, every room turned into a party room. My sense of interior decor had me hanging a parachute from the ceiling. Tom took the dining room as his place to sleep. He liked it because an upright piano sat in the corner. Mark Lehman took the bedroom next to mine. In the back of the apartment was a kitchen, another bedroom, still vacant, and, at the end of the hallway, the only bathroom. Because the hallway was used to store our amps and equipment you'd have to walk sideways to enter the bathroom. At this point, our lives were all about twists and turns.

Our first priority was to round out our band. I was on guitar, Tom on bass, but what would the rest of the lineup look like? Did we want a trio? A four-piece band or a five-piece band? And what would those pieces be? We decided not to decide. Better to choose the cats based on the quality of their playing rather than on a preconceived idea of the band's final configuration. No matter what that configuration, though, we'd need a drummer. You can't stand in front of a mountain of Marshall amps and play loud rock and roll without a kick-ass drummer. At the same time, the seeds of the kind of band I wanted had been planted in my mind. That's because I'd been lucky enough to see some of the best live bands in the world at their peak.

Through a friend of a friend we met a kid named Joey Kramer. He came from Yonkers, New York, and was a student at the Berklee College of Music, but was considering dropping out. His current gig was with an all-black R&B band whose members called him their white soul brother. He said he was interested in auditioning, so we set up a time at the student union at Standish Hall at Boston University. Playing behind Tom and me, Joey seemed comfortable. I immediately heard how his R&B chops would give a rock band a unique funky punch. Musically, we meshed. But Joey was on the fence about leaving school. Tom and I loved his feel but we made no decision. After all, he was the first cat we'd auditioned. It was still an open oyster.

A few weeks later—this was after Labor Day—we trucked back to Sunapee in Mark's hippie van for a party that Pudge was throwing at his parents' lake house. The first person I ran into was Steven.

"What's up, man?" I asked.

"I'm living in a boathouse on the lake. I may spend the winter up here. You guys find a place in Boston?"

"A big place."

"Where?"

"Commonwealth."

"And you're working?"

"Not yet. Just trying to get it together. We started auditioning drummers. But the slot's still open. You interested?"

"Yeah, that would be cool. It would be great to play together, but I just wanna sing."

"That's what I'm thinking," I said. "A singing drummer. I remember you singing from your drum set and it was great."

"I just wanna stand up front and sing. I love the drums but I don't wanna fuck with 'em anymore. Wanna concentrate on being a front man."

"Well, we auditioned a drummer who plays kick-ass R&B and could fit the bill. If you wanna just sing, he could fill the drum spot."

"It's something to think about," said Steven. "You have room in your apartment?"

"Lots of room. Three bedrooms."

"All right, cool. I'll come down. Sounds like more fun than winter-izing the cabin."

I had thought about asking Steven if he wanted to hook up with us. He definitely had the chops, whether on drums or vocals. Plus he had been doing this for a while and had more experience. But the fact was, as good as his four or five bands were, they weren't able to keep it together and make it to the next level. They always broke up. He even left his musical partner of at least four years behind. But I figured if there was something off about him, I could deal with it. It would be worth it to have him in our band. Bottom line, there was something about him I liked. It was like meeting a long-lost brother. Looking back, I can certainly put my finger on it, but back then it was just a vibe. So I asked him to join the band and Tom was all for it.

Back in Boston I called Joey and said he had the gig. I told him we had a lead singer.

"Who?" he asked.

"Steven Tallarico."

"He's from Yonkers," said Joey. "We went to the same high school. We were in Battle of the Bands together. I love that guy. He's one of the best fuckin' singers around. This band's gonna be outta sight. Man, if Tallarico is in, count me in too."

When I told Tom about the conversation with Joey, he was into it. Things were coming together.

Next morning the phone rang. It was Steven.

"I was thinking, man, that if I'm gonna join your band I gotta bring along my bass player."

"That won't work," I said. "You're looking to join a band that Tom and I have already started. And Tom's the bass player. That's nonnegotiable."

"Well, if I can't have my bass player, I want to bring in my friend Ray Tabano to play guitar."

"We already have a guitarist," I said. "Me."

"Ray can play rhythm guitar. If you get to keep your bass player, it's only fair that I get to keep my guitarist."

I thought about the idea of a second guitarist. Some of my favorite and best-sounding live bands, like Fleetwood Mac and the Yardbirds, had two guitarists. Might be interesting to try it. Although I hadn't met Raymond or heard him play, he figured to be good. Steven's bands always had great players.

"Okay, man," I said. "We've got a deal. I just need to hear Raymond play."

I could hear in his voice that Steven was serious about joining. I was certainly serious. He said he was ready to go but needed a couple of weeks to go back to Yonkers and get his stuff.

Steven announced his arrival with a loud knock on the door. When I opened it, he was all smiles. "I'm here, you motherfuckers," he said, "and this band is about to burn!"

I liked hearing that. I liked that his ambition matched ours. He dug the apartment. It was quickly decided that he and Joey, the boys from Yonkers, would share the bedroom in the back. We were ready to roll except for the fact that I hadn't met Steven's friend Raymond Tabano, the guitarist about to join our band.

"You'll meet him tomorrow," said Steven. "He and his old lady just opened a leather shop right here in Boston. We'll drop by there tomorrow. They're custom-making a bag for me."

The shop, the Yellow Cow, was on Newbury Street, Boston's hip equivalent of Cambridge's Harvard Square on the other side of the Charles River. Raymond was a big guy, over six feet, with thick brown hair down to his waist. He was into a Southwest look. Lots of turquoise. Like Steven,

Raymond was older than me. He seemed to have his shit together. Also like Steven, he was a ball of energy.

I liked his place, not only because of the heady smell of leather but because the leather goods themselves—the jackets, pants, and wallets—were artfully designed to attract those counterculture consumers with the money to buy the hippest merchandise on the street. The fringed bag they made for Steven was especially cool.

Raymond was friendly while his wife was withdrawn. The shop was just getting started, and I'm sure she was afraid that the band would take up all his time. From the opposite side, I had the same apprehension. Would he put the shop before the band?

"The band comes first," he told me. "Count on me, man. I'm with you all the way."

I was eager to hear Raymond play. We were all eager to start rehearsals. That meant finding the right place. Mark and his Keep On Truckin' step van was our chief mode of surveying the city. We spent a lot of time rambling around town, meeting girls in front of the dorms, and, when we were lucky, bringing them back to the apartment. Mark was always cruising up and down Comm Avenue and Beacon Street. He liked picking up hitchhikers on their way to or from BU. Some of those hitchhikers became regulars and would chip in with a buck or two for gas. Mark was always making a new friend who could help us. His makeshift taxi service became a metaphor for the band. We picked up money wherever we could.

I signed up with an employment agency that put me in touch with a Catholic Italian family who ran a maintenance company. They hired me to clean a synagogue in Brookline. Three times a week I swept the floors and washed the windows. During the Jewish High Holy Days, I helped set up extra chairs and hang decorations. The work wasn't exciting, but it was dependable. I did it for a year. Steven found work at a bagel shop but he didn't last long.

After searching for a place to rehearse, we finally made a connection at the West Campus dorm of BU. The dorm master said we could use the basement if we agreed to play a few live shows on campus. We said sure. Rather than lug our stuff back and forth from the apartment, we left our equipment in a closet in the basement under lock and key. This got to be a hassle when the college kids started setting off fire alarms in the middle of the night. We'd have to throw all our shit in the closet, lock it up, and head up to the street and wait for the all-clear. Sometimes this happened two or three times in the same night. Musical coitus interruptus.

In these early days, Elyssa Jerret was living with her parents in Brookline, the next town over. When I visited her the first time I was surprised to see that the Jerrets lived in a rented apartment, a perfectly nice place, but nothing that matched the high-society image they conveyed to the world.

Still platonic friends, Elyssa and I once spent the night together in that West Dorm basement. Rather than take the time to load up all our equipment in the closet, one of the band members would volunteer to sleep on a blanket on the floor and guard the stuff. On the night I volunteered, Elyssa stayed with me. I couldn't help but hope it was her way of turning our friendship from platonic to physical. I was wrong. She held back on the big prize. And naturally, that made me want it even more.

The initial rehearsals in that BU basement were rough. We spent half the time getting to know each other and the other half learning how to play the songs. Except for Steven, who's always something of a bull in the china shop, we were walking on eggshells, learning how to communicate. Working with Steven was frustrating. He was a perfectionist to the point of madness. He would scrutinize the smallest part of a song to death. He liked to go on and on, discussing a chord change or a transitional riff, and then demand that we play it for a half hour. It was clear that he was used to being a leader—but so was I. I was starting to get a vision of what this band could be, and that didn't include sounding like robots. When you play in a rote manner, it can kill the spontaneity that leads to magic energy.

I'd heard stories about how, at Steven's insistence, his former band partner Don Solomon would endlessly repeat a pattern to the point that Don wound up taking his bass to the bathroom, where he'd sit on the toilet, thus achieving a musical version of multitasking.

Repetition is all well and good when you're learning scales and techniques, but it does nothing to get the creative juices flowing. My idea of a rehearsal was to play a song front to back a bunch of times, letting everyone throw in different ideas. Not only does this allow the band to learn the song, but sometimes, with new ideas kicking in, a new song is born.

Yet often at our rehearsals we'd never get to play a song all the way through. Steven would stop every few seconds because, in his mind, someone made a mistake. No doubt, Steven's scrutinizing helped bring the band along on a technical level. But it drove me crazy. I'd have ideas in my head that, given the stop-and-start methodology, would get lost. I knew Steven had a lot to teach us, but my instincts about rock and roll carried as much weight. Between the two of us this would soon give Aerosmith its unique sound.

Then there was Steven's volatile relationship with Joey. Because Steven was a great drummer himself, he didn't hesitate to obsessively criticize Joey. Much of this was good. But much of it was painful for Joey. It was really tough to watch this. The son of an abusive father, Joey was facing another kind of abuse. Steven could be more than demanding in his attempts to school Joey; he could be emotionally brutal.

This was our early dilemma: We didn't want to be a cover band but we had to play covers, not only because we had no inventory of originals but because getting work meant playing familiar songs the kids could dance to. We would put our own touches on these songs and make them as unique as we could. The competition was stiff. There were bands everywhere playing every kind of music. I wanted us to stand out. I wanted us to come up with something new. I was convinced that the diverse musical backgrounds of everyone in our band could create something original. But that would take time.

There were early indications of strong musical chemistry between Steven and me. Back at 1325, apart from the other guys, we started jamming as a duo. We worked by feel, not talk, and when it got good we kept it going. We had a little mic and tape recorder. Because my riffs tend to be melodic, Steven would scat along with them. At the beginning of our collaboration he stayed off the piano—that would come later—and concentrated on percussion and vocal.

The first song Steven and I wrote together was on Mark's water bed. I had my guitar and Steven played percussion on his thighs. His rhythms inspired my riffs. My riffs inspired his vocal lines. The result was "Movin' Out," which bears the traits of many Joe-Steven songs to come. The guitar lays down the lines; the licks are thick; and in a sudden burst the singer starts telling the story in unison with the instrumental drive. From the start of our partnership, the assumption was that I'd provide the musical foundation and Steven would write the lyrics. Because he was the singer, and a highly verbal guy, it seemed logical. He had to act those songs; he had to believe the script; so who better to write the script than Steven?

Steven was—and remains—a painfully slow lyricist. He's super glib as a conversationalist, but when he has to fashion words to fit a melody, it takes him forever. The more we worked together, the slower he became. Early on I saw that it was something I'd have to get used to. I never did. I write in a rush. I don't over-critique what I write. I usually just let it rip.

The beginning of my relationship with Steven involved more than music. We became buddies. There was the obvious cultural bond. We were both rebels with a reckless streak. He had a greater affinity for sugary pop. I was glad to see that he had left most of that in Yonkers. I had a greater affinity for roughhewn rock. We both loved the Yardbirds. We both loved the blues. We both loved the look coming out of London. We both loved wandering through the woods back in Sunapee and water-skiing on the lake. Like me, Steven was deeply drawn to nature and felt at home in the wild. And unlike me, he was familiar with the wilds of New York City and was the first guy to show me around Greenwich Village.

We went one weekend—just the two of us.

"Ever been to New York?" asked Steven.

"Not since I was a little kid," I said.

"The first thing I do is head to the Oyster Bar in Grand Central Station and drink Guinness. So that's what we're gonna do."

That's what we did. That same night we walked through Greenwich Village. I'd finally arrived in that fabled Land of What's Happening.

"I'll show you where I buy my espadrilles," said Steven.

We went to an incense-burning Indian store, where we bought roped sandals. I wanted to go to Max's Kansas City and hear the Velvet Underground, but they weren't performing that night. Steven started talking about all the times he had heard the Underground before. In fact, Steven had been talking since we left Boston. Steven never stopped talking. There was a propulsive energy and a manic charm to Steven's talking. In some basic way, Steven *is* his talking. His talking fills in all the gaps and can actually make it easy to be with him—mainly because you just kick back and listen. That's usually what I did. His talking can be brilliant. His verbal riffs, like musical riffs, are adventures in extravagant storytelling. His talking has a rhythm and rhyme all its own. But in the end his talking wears your ass out. He sucks up all your energy. Yet his insights are original and his language bombastic. Many times I would say, "Write that stuff down. It would make a great lyric." He never would. I heard many songs slip through our fingers. Mostly his talking was entertaining. But holy shit, when will he ever shut the fuck up?

One afternoon the band came home from a rehearsal to be greeted by a mountain of a man sitting on the stoop in front of 1325. I mean, this guy was three hundred pounds of pure mean. If he were a dog, he'd have been part pit bull, part Rottweiler, with a Budweiser sign painted on his side.

"Where the fuck do you hippies think you're going?"

"We live here," I said. "We have a place on the second floor."

"I run this building," he said. "I'm the superintendent. If you're some kind of a weird commune, you can move out. I hate hippies."

"We're a band," I said.

"What kind?"

"Hard rock."

He thought about that for a second. Then he asked, "How do you feel about James Brown?"

"We love him," I said.

"James Brown's the best. I got every James Brown record ever made."

Turned out that the super's name was Gary Cabozzi, a thirtysomething ex-marine back from Vietnam with greasy black hair, a big mouth missing a few key teeth, and a take-no-prisoners personality. He was wearing a white wife-beater. Old-school tattoos ran up and down his arms.

As a gesture of peace, I offered him a beer from the six-pack I'd just bought. He accepted the beer and invited us downstairs to his basement apartment, where he lived with his wife, his dad, and his twelve-year-old son. The setup included a damp atmospheric man cave with a beat-up club-size pool table and a fridge stocked with beer. He had more neon bar signs than you'd see in Kenmore Square. The place smelled the way a musty, dusty, damp, smoky barroom should smell. His secondhand stereo sounded great, especially when he blasted James Brown records. His James Brown obsession seemed strange because he was not only partial to the *n*-word but displayed all the basic prejudices of your classic Boston redneck.

After this first meeting he understood that, rather than peace-and-love hippies, we were basically hard rockers who liked R&B as much as he did. That was our bond. In practically no time, Cabozzi became our biggest booster. We had an open invitation to use his basement to rehearse. Gary became our muscle and our in-house watchdog.

We soon began hearing Cabozzi stories. As a one-man vigilante, he had reportedly deterred all sorts of burglaries in the building. He was famous for scaring off bad guys. Legend had it that he'd been shot in the arm, only to chase the shooter down the street. He caught the assailant and, with his belt, beat him with his good arm to within an inch of the guy's life.

There were times when life at 1325 looked like a TV comedy—a gang of skinny kids looking to break into the big time. Steven was the chatterbox extrovert, jumping on tabletops to command attention. Tom was the nice guy in the corner, diligently practicing his bass. Joey was the hard-hitting but insecure drummer looking to win our approval. Raymond was the outside cat, the leather-goods merchant doubling as a guitarist. Mark was the facilitator, the driver, the roadie, the folkie and loyal friend. I was the sullen and silent one in the front room, spending all my time looking for the lost chord.

Mark might have been looking for that chord one night when we were all in Tom's room smoking cigarettes and pot and drinking beer. Mark was fooling around with folk songs on his guitar.

"Anyone smell anything strange?" asked Tom.

"Yeah," said Joey. "Pot smoke. Cigarette smoke."

Joey was right, but so was Tom. The smell was something stronger.

The haze of smoke was darker than usual. Then came a crackling sound. And then the distinct odor of something burning. That's when Steven popped in and said, "Smoke's coming out of Joe's room."

I ran to my room, where I saw my coffee table engulfed in flames, inches from the parachute hanging from the ceiling. I yelled for help and within seconds the guys were running back and forth from the kitchen, pouring pitchers of water onto the parachute. Amazingly, we extinguished the fire before it hit the highly flammable parachute and engulfed the whole building in flames. It was another instance of our guardian angel being right on time.

We spent a lot of time reading R. Crumb comics and watching old Three Stooges movies. We might have been cracking up to Moe, Larry, and Curly—or Moe, Larry, and Shemp—one day when Steven came running in, talking a mile a minute about how on his way up the stairs he peeked into the basement apartment and saw this chick sitting on a couch. According to Steven, her legs were spread apart, her eyes were shut closed, and she was masturbating. Like many tales told by Steven, we took this one with a grain of salt.

In the annals of these funky formative years, there is the famous story of the suitcase found outside the building. This story has been told many times. I can only report it from my point of view. The details were blurry to me back then and remain blurry now.

One fine day a suitcase was found in front of 1325. Depending on whom you believe, it was retrieved by either Joey or Steven or both. Depending on whom you believe, the suitcase contained only dirty clothes or a little pot or a lot of pot or a little money or a lot of money. Depending on whom you believe, no one touched the money that was never there.

I was ignorant of all this intrigue when one night came a loud knock on the door. When we opened it, three street thugs appeared, one of whom had a gun pointed right at us.

"Give us our fuckin' money," he said.

"What money?" asked Steven.

"The money you stole from the suitcase."

"There wasn't any money, just some nasty clothes and a little pot."

"There was a *lot* of fuckin' money," the gun-toting gangster insisted. "There was two thousand bucks. And you took it."

"I didn't."

"Look, you hippie asshole, lying is as good as dying. I'd as soon kill you as look at you. Keep lying and you're dead."

The dialogue heated up. The gangster kept pressing, Steven kept insisting on his innocence. I was thinking, *This shit could really end badly*, when suddenly the back door crashed open and Gary Cabozzi came running through the apartment wielding an enormous sword. Seeing what was coming at him, the second gangster pulled out his gun. The gun was aimed at Cabozzi's head.

"You got two seconds to shoot me," said Gary, his eyes shining with murderous rage, "before I'm on you like stink on shit. You better fuck me up before I fuck you up—and do it quick, 'cause the cops are on their way."

The gangsters backed down. Cabozzi won the day. He said that twenty years later he learned that it was Steven who took the money.

Cabozzi and his basement bar often involved drama. We were rehearsing there late one night when his son ran in shouting, "Call the police! Call the police!" The son's friend had jumped off the roof. The boys had been huffing—breathing hair spray from a balloon to get high—and the kid thought he could fly. We ran out to see neighbors standing around a body that had landed in the alley between two buildings. It was a shocking sight: Under the harsh streetlights, the boy's head was twisted in an obscene way. The police arrived, the ambulance arrived, but it was too late. The boy was dead. We went back to Cabozzi's basement and tried to reconvene the rehearsal, but on that dark night, at that dark moment, none of us had the heart to play another note.

What's in a name? We weren't all that concerned, but we had to call ourselves something. This went on for months. In the meantime, we implemented the only plan we had for finding work: Steven and I contacted all our previous connections from our previous bands. Whenever we played back in my home territory, we were Flash, Joe Perry's new band. Whenever we played in Steven's home territory, we were Steven's new band or whatever his last band was called. Whenever we played in new territory, we used whatever name was popular with us that week. We knew we needed something to stick with.

In high school Joey had had a band called Arrowsmith. How about that for a name? Tom thought he was referring to the Sinclair Lewis novel *Arrowsmith*, mandatory reading back then. Steven and I liked the name but, given our fascination with flying, thought it would be cooler with an aerodynamic spelling. In the final analysis Aerosmith was the only name no one objected to. So we kept it.

Our first gig as Aerosmith was in my part of the state, in Hopkinton, where the Boston Marathon starts, at Nipmuc Regional High. The set was all covers—and sometimes covers of covers, like covering the Stones' cover of Chuck Berry's cover of Bobby Troup's original "Route 66." We did "Great Balls of Fire," "Train Kept a-Rollin'," "Rattlesnake Shake"—all the stuff we'd been practicing.

That night at Nipmuc High, the crowd appeared mildly amused but hardly enthusiastic. Sparks flew, but they didn't come from the audience. They came from a nasty confrontation between Steven and me.

He kept screaming for me to lower the volume on my guitar. Well, if you're playing with Marshall amps, as we were, they aren't effective until they reach a certain volume. That volume is fuckin' loud—but, hell, rock and roll is fuckin' loud. I wasn't cranking the volume to antagonize Steven; I was doing it to achieve the right rock-and-roll balance. We were using the same amps that the bands we admired used in similar-size venues. Sometimes I think Steven looked at this volume thing as an ego competition. My point, though, was always the same: *Why be in a rock band if you don't want to play loud?*

"My ears are bleeding," Steven would complain after a show.

"Let 'em bleed."

"Next time, you're gonna turn that shit down!" Steven screamed.

I didn't respond. I didn't have to. I knew there was no way in hell to lower the volume and keep the band on the edge. Plus I had to keep my guitar loud enough to hear over the drums. I was going to keep the volume where it needed to be. And I did. Besides, if Steven cared so much about his voice—as he often claimed—why was he always abusing it by screaming after the shows?

That first gig, like the suitcase incident, revealed Steven's inclination to grab things that weren't his. That night he stole a Nipmuc High T-shirt out of a student's locker.

"Why would you want to go and do some dumb shit like that?" I asked him.

"Why not?" he asked. "It's just a souvenir."

We had the same problem at another one of our early gigs. We were hired by the Officers' Club at the Navy Yard at Charlestown, Massachusetts, to play on Tuesday nights, a good time because it didn't get in the way of our weekend engagements. They asked us to play a couple of songs they could slow-dance to. The pay was our usual rate, plus they gave us a three-course meal and two kinds of wine. We were scheduled to play there for three straight months. After one night, Steven and Raymond were on their way to the office to get paid when they spotted a slide projector by the door. When no one was looking, they stole it. A week later the Officers' Club called to say that our services were no longer required. This was a blow, because we badly needed the work.

We managed to find some out-of-town gigs. There were a number of famous small to midsize rock clubs that booked groups like the Allman Brothers as well as up-and-coming bands like us. In this era these clubs were always rocking, packed to the rafters with young kids the same age as the musicians they were cheering.

One of these shows was at the fabled Alex Cooley's Electric Ballroom in Atlanta. When we got to our dressing room, the groupies were waiting, already stark naked and ready to romp. These were full-service ladies eager to give it up in a variety of ways. One of the chicks approached me. I shook her off. I didn't demur out of prudery, but only because the rock version of a Roman orgy held no interest for me. I went off by myself with a bottle of Rebel Yell and watched the backstage show. A few minutes later, when I was walking out, I saw something that cracked me up: Standing over a wastebasket, Raymond Tabano was pouring Jack Daniel's over his Mr. Important.

"I'm cleaning it real good," he said, "'cause I don't want to bring anything home."

When we came off the road with a little money, I applied a portion of it to my new hobby—mixed drinks: piña coladas, black Russians, and Irish coffee for that first morning jolt. I bought an inexpensive blender and a bartending book. I developed a certain expertise. It became part of my domestic life at 1325.

Usually I'd eat giant fast-food burgers, but there were times when Mark would whip up great hippie feasts. His years of communal living taught him the art of good simple cooking. He showed us how to roast brown rice before boiling it.

Steven also knew something about communal life. This was hardly his first experience of sharing a home with a band. His thing was food labeling. Every can of mustard and container of yogurt bore the name of its owner. Kitchen duty was always a high priority for Steven—who did what and when. Serious weekly discussions were held about who had been negligent about leaving dirty dishes in the sink. Then there was the monthly ritual of Steven and Joey cleaning their back bedroom. They'd empty it out completely and scrub it from floor to ceiling.

Even though I didn't share their mania for cleanliness, it was understandable. The apartment was hardly hospital-sterile. In fact, one of our weekly activities was roach hunting. We'd turn out the lights in the kitchen, wait ten minutes, and then, armed with Raid, fly swatters, and squirt guns filled with bleach, ruthlessly attack the creepy buggers until we got 'em all. Naturally, the next night they'd be back in even greater numbers.

From the start, our strategy for survival was simple: Operate on two tracks. The first track was local. That meant take any gig you could get—any local high school or college dance, any gig that might pay us a few hundred bucks. Do that as long as you need to do it. Don't turn down anything. Just keep playing.

On the second track, keep looking for a break. Maybe an agent or a manager would notice us and get us a deal. Maybe a promoter would spot us and book us into some big venue.

So here came Zunk Buker, a friend of ours from Sunapee who used to hang out at the lake. A couple of years our senior, Zunk had become a well-established pot dealer. He was always crisscrossing the country in campers and vans, buying and selling premium product in considerable quantity on both coasts. He did this for several years, making good money. After making his first million, he and his business partner settled in La Jolla, California, where they decided to go into concert promotion and produce rock shows in San Diego. He had recently promoted a Steve Miller concert in San Diego.

"Hey, Joe," he said one day on the phone, "I hear you guys have a band. Come out here so my guys can meet you. I want you to check out our setup."

Next thing I knew I was heading west. This was my first long plane trip and my first taste of California. Zunk met me in San Diego, where he had just concluded some business. His spread in La Jolla blew my mind. Palm trees out front. An ocean view out back. In the driveway of his glass-and-steel house was an array of hot rods and custom choppers. Parading around the pool was a lineup of suntanned blondes in short shorts and bikinis.

"The real fun starts tonight," said Zunk. "There's a surprise coming."

The messenger arrived in the late evening looking like Raquel Welch. She was greeted as a conquering hero. When she reached into her purse and pulled out a giant condom, I understood why. The condom was stuffed with cocaine.

"This isn't street shit," said Zunk. "This is primo. This is high-octane. This is a rocket ship to the moon."

He took out a buck knife and cut down the length of the condom. The blow spilled out on a coffee table, around which everyone gathered while Zunk prepared the lines. Before long, the lines were gone, and I was enjoying life on the moon.

Later that night there was talk of promoting a concert for us, but I can't remember the details. This was a new high for me, and my cognitive skills were definitely diminished. I did, however, get the idea that Zunk was eager to promote our band. He had the money and the means.

The next morning I woke up and, for the first time, suffered a bloody nose. That's one of the many downsides of potent blow. When I went to the bathroom I saw Zunk opening the hallway closet, whose every shelf was lined with cash. That was the upside of selling potent blow.

They fixed me with a going-away present—a footlocker holding a pound of grass and case of Coors, which back then was unavailable on the East Coast. We said goodbye and I flew home, convinced that Zunk and his partners would soon be booking us in major California venues. When I reported the good news to the guys in Boston, they were as excited as I was. Because we never wanted to think of ourselves as strictly a Boston band—in those days the only Boston band to break out was J. Geils—we liked the idea of jumping to the West Coast.

"How long do you think it'll be?" asked Steven.

"You know Zunk," I said. "He moves fast."

The cops moved even faster. The week after I left La Jolla, Zunk was busted. They raided the house and hauled off the whole crew. If I had stayed over, I would have wound up in prison. That's the real side of selling potent blow.

We were back on the first track, the local grind, where our next challenge became Raymond. The guy had the right look. He wore handmade colorful headbands, leather pants, and an elaborate Indian breastplate. He played rhythm guitar in the classic style. He had also made an important contact at WBCN, Boston's hip FM station. He got their best DJ, Maxanne Sartori, to play one of our two-track demos over the air. Those were the days when DJs could play whatever they wanted. Maxanne put us in her mix and became a key supporter.

Raymond had his strengths, but he also had his problems. The biggest was that he was either chronically late to rehearsals or didn't show at all.

His wife would call us at rehearsals wanting to speak with him.

"He isn't here," I'd say. "Isn't he at the shop?"

"No. He told me he was with you guys."

His pattern of playing both ends against the middle went on for months. Clearly he wasn't spending time practicing his guitar, and he sure as hell wasn't rehearsing with the band. The band was far from his top priority. After a few of these incidents, I knew that we'd have to replace him. But because Raymond was a big guy with a reputation as a brawler, he was intimidating, and no one wanted to tell him that he was out.

To secure his position, Raymond had always relied on his long relationship with Steven. At the same time, he realized that I, more than anyone, could no longer support him. So he tried to charm me over to his side. He invited me to his house, where he cooked up a hippie meal of tofu and brown rice. After dinner he broke out his best hash. The talk turned to how he and I should take a firmer hand in running the band. *Me and Raymond?* No way. I rebuffed his ploy.

Instead he formed an alliance with Joey. But when Raymond called a band meeting to inform Steven, Tom, and me that he and Joey had decided to take a greater leadership role, Joey demurred. Feeling our instant antagonism to the plan, Joey just sat there, acting as if he didn't know what Raymond was talking about. From there, things got worse.

I was the strongest voice to call for his dismissal. I had the least to lose, because my attitude has always been *I'll do what I think is right for the band and I don't give a damn about pleasing everyone.* My passion was for improving the band. Tom and Joey certainly knew I was right. Steven couldn't argue the fact. The bottom line was that Raymond was an adequate rhythm player who never improved beyond that. So it was decided. It seemed only fair that, given the fact that Raymond was Steven's longtime bandmate and close friend, Steven be the one tell him.

"I can't," said Steven.

"Then who?"

Tom, Joey, and Steven all pointed at me.

"You tell him," said Steven.

Steven used to talk about how Raymond was a gang leader in high school. In fact, Steven was one of the guys Raymond used to bully. By recruiting Raymond in his bands, Steven felt like he had neutralized his adversary.

His adversary had become his ally and protector, another reason Steven had been so reluctant to fire him and insistent that I do the dirty work.

I'd fired people a number of times in my bands, and it was never easy for me. I decided to do it over dinner at Ken's, a steak joint on the corner. I tried to be diplomatic. I said it wasn't anything that he'd done wrong. We were moving in different musical directions. I needed a different kind of guitarist. But Raymond didn't take it well.

"This is your doing," he said. "Not Steven's. Steven would never let me go."

"The group's a democracy," I said. "We took a vote. We all agreed. We need to make this change."

"Steven didn't agree," said Raymond. "He's always been loyal. He'd never drop me."

"It looks like he has."

"Bullshit. I'm going to him directly."

"Go."

Raymond went. Given the complex but powerful psychology that had bonded Steven and Raymond, I was afraid that Steven might cave. He didn't. Like me, he had a vision of our musical future. Raymond wasn't part of that vision. We needed a guitarist who could fuckin' play.

We found that guitarist in Sunapee the first summer after we'd moved to Boston. We'd gone back to the lake in the hopes of keeping the old tradition alive. We played some parties and a few gigs at the Barn. We ran into Brad Whitford, who was a friend of Twitty's, a guitarist in one of Steven's bands. Brad started hanging out and jamming with us. He fit right in. It felt like he had been there from the beginning. He loved the same music we did, had seen Jimi Hendrix live, and liked to party.

I learned that Brad had grown up in Reading, a suburb of Boston, and was going to the Berklee College of Music. He was a talented player with a deep appreciation of what I was going for. He knew we were a serious band with serious ambitions. He also didn't have the kind of ego that would drive him to try and outdo anyone. He was content to let me take the lead. He knew how to complement that lead. Brad was also a strong lead player himself. And as the years went on that proved to be a big part of Aerosmith's sound. We clicked and, just like that, the lineup was locked in. Brad moved into 1325. That was a big deal. Raymond had never lived with us. Now, for the first time, all the members of Aerosmith were living under one roof. That did a lot to solidify the band.

Brad and I became fast friends. He loved beer as much as I did. But beer always took second place to the music. When it was time to work, we worked. We had an unusual way of developing our parts. We rarely if ever talked about what our parts would be. We just listened to each other and played what felt right. It still works today.

One weekend I went home to visit my parents, and the topic of work arose. I was telling my dad about the band and some of the parties we'd been playing.

"You aren't drinking too much, are you, Joe?" he asked.

I knew that he was haunted by his father's drinking—and the way his dad had drowned.

"You don't have to worry," I said. "We work really hard. I'll have a few beers, but I never let drinking get in the way of work."

When he asked me about pot, I could tell him the truth—that I didn't like it very much and never bought it. Hard drugs were not yet part of our scene. Someone might have a little coke or a few pills, but alcohol was basically my only recreational tonic.

During that encounter with Dad, I noticed that he lacked his usual energy. He looked a little pale. I wanted to say something, but I didn't. My father was the strong, silent type and I knew that if anything was wrong, he didn't want to be questioned about it.

My fears were validated when my mother called me in Boston a few weeks later. A phone call from Mom was rare. I usually kept my parents abreast of my activities with a postcard or a letter, a tradition I'd started in prep school. A call usually meant bad news.

After a few pleasantries, Mom told me why she was calling: "Your father's cancer has come back."

"That's terrible," were the only words I could manage.

"He fought it off once," she said, "and he'll fight it off again." Besides, cancer treatment had improved dramatically. "We're hoping for full remission."

I was shaken but responded in probably the same way Dad did. I shut down my emotions. I put them in some hidden compartment of my mind and double-locked the door. I carried on.

Girls were always a good diversion when it came to avoiding my deeper and darker emotions. But when it came to courting, I wasn't a player and still suffered from a negative self-image. I still saw myself as the skinny guy in the corner. But I was starting to realize that some girls liked the skinny guy in the corner, especially if he played guitar. I found a few girls to spend the night with me, but none with whom I'd want a long-term relationship.

Judy Nylon was different. I met her on Newbury Street, where she worked as a hair stylist in a shop that had a big Harley-Davidson sitting in the window. These were the days when men and women were going to the same places to get their shags styled. Gender-bending was the order of the day. Judy was very worldly, a cut above most of the other girls I'd met. I was attracted to her style and knew she had things to teach me. So I found myself hanging out at the shop on a regular basis. On an average day, after taking care of band business at 1325, I'd stop off at the liquor store for a bottle of cheap wine and wander down to Judy's shop and watch her work. The owner, a young Italian guy who became my friend as well, liked having me around. At day's end Judy and I would go to her loft, which was filled with art books, underground magazines, and novels. She had great taste in literature and a special fondness for Jack Kerouac. Reading more of his work, I felt a tremendous bond with the Beats.

The Newbury and Charles Street scene was another kind of adventure. It was where Judy and her crowd gave me a glimpse into fashion. The whole band had a fascination with clothes. Other bands might not give a second thought to what they wore onstage. Not us. The British Invasion had marked us sartorially as well as musically. Going back to the day I first viewed *Blow-Up*, I was excited by the relationship between rock and fashion. In some sense, rock *was* fashion, almost as though you played your clothes and wore your music. I remember being given a pair of custom-made white boots from Carnaby Street. They were covered with embroidered flowers and seemed to say everything I needed to say about art. I didn't take them off for two years.

Flowing silk shirts, flowing velvet scarves, bell-bottom pants—I was always on a search for clothing that supplemented the freedom I was feeling in the music. I felt that having a look that separated us from the audience heightened the experience. Sometimes that meant dressing down by performing without our shirts. Because we were thin and devoid of well-defined musculature, we fit the mold of what real rockers were supposed to look like in the early seventies.

There were several strange interludes to our musical journey that didn't involve music at all. The first involved advanced psychology. Tom's sister, Cecily, went to a fancy girls' school, where she was able to get us a gig. One of Cecily's closest friends at school had a father who was a renowned Harvard professor. When the prof heard about this struggling rock band, he thought we'd be great subjects for his study on motivation. He offered us ten dollars a day and said it would take a couple of weeks. Were we game?

Why not? We were looking for any connection we could find. Harvard and Cambridge weren't exactly our stomping grounds, but maybe we'd find some gigs over there. Besides, ten dollars a day could help pay our beer bill. We signed up and found ourselves taking every kind of test known to man—Rorschach, IQ, oral tests, essay tests, the whole gamut. They even filmed us sitting there working up our answers.

In terms of analyzing our motivation, I didn't see any great mystery. Our motivation was music first and money second. One fed the other. Without music there was no money, and without money it was hard to make music. I still don't quite understand why the good professor needed two weeks to see something that could be explained in two seconds. I didn't mind, though. I liked being able to say that, although our tenure was short, Aerosmith went to Harvard. (By the way, we were never shown the results of the tests. I'd give anything to see them now.)

Another strange side trip: A group of college-age gay guys wanted to make a student film about us. Their intentions seemed purely artistic, and, again, hoping that the release of the movie might help spread our nonexistent fame, we went along with it. The boys filmed us rehearsing and performing. At their suggestion, they shot us working out in a gym, hardly our natural habitat. They had us wearing exercise outfits as we huffed and puffed on stationary bikes. We felt like we were re-creating a scene from the *Monkees* TV show. The film, like the Harvard study, remains locked away in an unmarked vault.

I was sure that Mark Lehman would be with us for the long run. He was the sixth member of the band, the guy who did everything with us but play onstage. When it came to keeping the enterprise on course, Mark was the man. He did more than his fair share of the heavy lifting, including carrying Marshall amps that weighed a ton. We all pitched in, but Mark did the lion's share of the work. In his Keep On Truckin' R. Crumb–decorated step van he literally drove us to where we wanted to go—bigger and better gigs.

Mark suffered from mood swings, but his awareness of those swings seemed to be his salvation. Occasionally he would lose it and fall into anger or frustration. Usually, though, he saw these episodes coming and, to protect us from his emotional imbalance, he'd spend a couple of days locked up in his room. If there happened to be a gig during a dark mood, we knew to stay out of his way. We could almost see the cloud over his head.

Steven was not an easy person to live with. Every day we were learning more about his peculiarities. When it came to telling people what he thought of them, he had no filter. When it came to hurting people's feelings, he had no restraint. I suppose that a confrontation between Mark and Steven was inevitable, but until it happened I really didn't see it coming.

Mark had cooked up one of his brown rice and vegetable specials, a meal we all loved. We were especially grateful because we saw that, though he was struggling through one of his dark episodes, he still cared enough for us to prepare dinner. It was during dinner when Steven got up to go to the fridge to look for something. That's when he exploded.

"Goddammit," Steven shouted, "how many times have I told you assholes that you have to label your shit? There's a bottle of juice that's not labeled, and that fuckin' pisses me off."

As Steven spoke, he gave Mark a look of vicious suspicion. That's when Mark lost it. He jumped to his feet, knocking over his chair. He pounded the table so hard that the glasses and bottles and plates went flying. Then he grabbed his huge cooking knife and threw it into the floor with such force that it drove into the wood, inches from Steven's foot. He stormed out of the kitchen, screaming, "I quit!" before slamming the door to his bedroom so violently that it came off its hinges. Without another word, he packed his bag and was gone the next day. We were shocked. We've never heard from him again. To this day I mourn his absence and regret that, on this crazy path we were following, our friend Mark Lehman became Aerosmith's first roadkill.

Not only did we miss Mark as a brother-in-arms, we also missed his arms. We had to take up the slack in the heavy-lifting department. On more than one occasion, I downed a couple of speedy diet pills in the morning before heading out to rent a U-Haul. Then came the long ordeal of loading up our shit, driving seven or eight hours to some gig in New Hampshire where we played a three-hour show in a high school, only to reload and drive back to Boston, still buzzed on speed. By the time we finally made it to 1325, the sun would be rising. When it came to transportation, we needed a better solution than the U-Haul.

The solution came in the form of a band of West Coast hippies riding around in a Ken Kesey–style Prankstermobile, a fire-engine-red converted school bus that they were eager to sell. Totally retooled to accommodate this traveling circus, the thing was jerry-rigged to run on propane as well as gasoline. All seventy-two seats had been removed and a few benches installed, leaving lots of room for our amps. In the back was a little kitchen and propane stove. The bus turned out to be a white elephant, but at the time it seemed perfect. The only problem was—where to get the money to buy it?

I went back to Mom. When it came to the band, my parents had been our angels. Throughout the years, they'd come to all our gigs when we played within thirty or forty miles of Hopedale. Once they saw how deadly serious I was, they supported me without reservation. They realized that I hadn't given up on my music career and never would.

"The gigs are out there, Mom," I said, "and renting a U-Haul truck is expensive."

"So it all comes down to transportation?"

"That's it. Would you please cosign for a loan?"

"How much do you need?"

"They're asking twenty-five hundred dollars for the bus."

"And it actually runs?" she asked.

"Runs great. We had it checked out."

"I'll talk to Dad and let you know, Joe."

Once again, my parents came through. I met them at the bank and we took out the loan. Unfortunately, they had to pay off the loan. We couldn't make the payments.

The bus turned into a nightmare. We'd have to drive around Comm Ave. for over an hour to find a place to park—and that was the least of our problems. Because it had been refurbished by nonmechanics, the wiring was a mess and the engine put together with spare parts. The breakdowns were nonstop. Were it not for Gary Cabozzi, the bus would have been a total loss. It turned out that, among his other talents, Cabozzi was a trained mechanic. He took it upon himself to keep the thing running.

Imagine this: Freezing winter night in Boston. Blizzard blowing in. Wind and snow and icy streets. Cabozzi under the hood of the bus, trying to get it going.

"Fuck these motherfuckers who fucked up this engine," he told me. "They didn't know their ass from their elbows."

"You better come in, Gary," I said. "You'll get sick if you stay out here."

"I'm not even feeling the cold."

"Man, how's that possible?"

"I just fried up some chili peppers in olive oil, made a sandwich out of 'em, and washed 'em down with a couple of cold beers."

The recipe worked. Cabozzi stayed out there for two more hours until he was able to turn over the engine.

Cabozzi became an integral part of our operation, taking over Mark's role—and then some. He not only helped us load and unload the amps, he became security. During a gig at Boston University, his participation expanded even more—much to our shock.

There must have been three hundred students at the show. We were rocking out when we broke into James Brown's "Mother Popcorn." That's when Cabozzi exploded. Pushing people out of the way, he ran to the front of the bandstand and went into a crazed James Brown dance routine. After thirty seconds, he actually jumped onstage and did every split and twirl in the James Brown catalogue. It was a bizarre sight: This three-hundred-pound giant with missing teeth and greasy hair, giving himself over to unrestrained contortions. The kids gave him a thunderous ovation. He was ecstatic. And so were we . . . at least that first time. When he broke into his James Brown routine at the very next gig, we had to take him aside and say, "Hey, Gary, the first time was fun. But enough's enough." He understood and cooled it.

Big excitement: In the winter of 1971 we got a call from the assistant to Steve Paul, the man who managed Johnny and Edgar Winter and owned Blue Sky Records. He wanted to see us play live. He was putting us on a bill with Humble Pie and Edgar's White Trash at the Academy of Music in New York City, a two-night stand with two sets each night. As the third band, we'd open the show with a fifteen-minute set. This was heady stuff. Steve Paul had connections. Steve Paul could take us to the next level.

The pay was only a couple of hundred bucks, but it was worth it just to see our name on the marquee. Rick Derringer was in Edgar's band and Steve Marriott was in Humble Pie, who were still at the top of the heap on the strength of their latest live record, despite Peter Frampton's leaving for a solo career. This was our first chance to rub elbows with the guys we wanted to be. The only problem was that Tom's bass amp was in the shop and we didn't have time to get it out. We were told that the crew would get us one.

They gave us a short sound check, but when we asked the stage manager about a bass amp he said he couldn't find one. In cold-blooded New York, no one was willing to give us a hand. We were forced to plug Tom's bass into a guitar amp that turned his notes into farts. Two hours before showtime, we started to panic. Something had to be done.

Steven asked a friend to run up to Yonkers to find us an amp but didn't know if he could get back in time. Frazzled, we really hadn't given much thought to the show. We were also distracted by meeting all these famous cats. Rumors were flying that Johnny Winter himself, one of my guitar heroes, might be playing with his brother. Johnny had been off the scene for nearly a year and had just gotten out of "rehab," a term I was hearing for the first time.

But where was our goddamn bass amp?

We kept looking at our watches until, minutes before we had to open the show in front of five thousand hard-core rock fans, the thing finally showed up.

We slammed into our first song, "Make It," and got the crowd going. At one point we did a tune we called "Major Barbara," for which Steven, on harp, and I, on lap steel, sat side by side. After our fifth number, our time was up. We got a polite hand from the fans and walked off into the wings.

"What the fuck were you guys doing sittin' down in the middle of your set?" screamed Steve Paul. Before we could respond, he raged on, "Who do you think you are? No one knows your name. No one knows your songs. You only had fifteen goddamn minutes to get the house rocking. What the hell were you doing?" Before we could defend ourselves Paul was off to see about Edgar.

We were lucky enough to catch Edgar's set when, right in the middle, his brother Johnny stepped out. The crowd exploded. Johnny ripped into "Rock and Roll, Hoochie Koo" and we were in blues rock heaven.

By the end of the gig we'd won the respect of the crew and our fellow musicians. We got some nice compliments, even from Steve Paul.

"I got to admit," he said, "you aren't bad for a baby band. Call me in six months."

We never did. By then we'd found a manager of our own, a character unlike anyone I've met before or since.

SHOT IN THE DARK

The Fenway Theatre, with its large stage, was one of those old refurbished theaters in the Back Bay on Massachusetts Avenue. It held about sixteen hundred people and was just the kind of venue we'd been lusting for. The place had seen better days, and because of that, someone said maybe we could rehearse there for free. We went over to the meet the manager.

"Nothing's free around here," said the man, whose name was John O'Toole. He was in his early thirties, a rough, broken-nosed Irishman who had recently been released from jail. "It'll cost you fifty bucks a day."

He might as well have said five hundred. We had started to leave when, just like that, O'Toole changed his mind. Maybe he saw the drive in our eyes.

"On second thought," he said, "it wouldn't hurt to give you a listen. Could be we could work something out. The theater's gonna be dark next week, so let's see what you got. But don't expect us to turn on the heat. And you better come during the day, because at night we ain't turning on the lights."

We jumped at the chance. We needed the experience of playing in a real concert hall. We showed up the next day in our overcoats. I wore a pair of woolen gloves with no fingers. The place was fuckin' freezing but we took advantage of all the time we could. They kept the curtains closed so the heat from the few illuminated stage lights made it bearable.

"You guys ain't half-bad," said O'Toole. "I'll let you rehearse but you're gonna have to open for some of the shows we'll be putting on here. You get to rehearse for free but then you have to play for free."

We took the deal. After a couple of days we got the idea that John was becoming a fan. He was hanging around while we rehearsed and nodding his head to the music. That weekend we were to open for Cactus, a band made up of former Vanilla Fudge members. When a hellacious snowstorm hit, Cactus canceled and a desperate O'Toole asked us to substitute and play a long set. We were ready.

The storm meant that the audience would be small. To play before a few hundred people in a sixteen-hundred-person venue is usually a drag. But to us it was a privilege. We played our asses off. O'Toole was moved. He thanked us again and said he wanted us to meet his boss, Frank Connelly.

At that point I hadn't heard of Connelly, but Brad Whitford had. Brad still had his concert tickets from the sixties that said "Frank Connelly Presents Jimi Hendrix." Connelly was also the owner of the Carousel, a big club in Framingham. He was the man who had brought the Beatles to Boston. At the time, Connelly was the biggest promoter in the area.

"Come back Monday afternoon," said O'Toole, "and play a set like you played tonight. I'll make sure Connelly is here."

Monday came around and at the appointed time we were standing onstage behind the closed curtains, wondering what was going to happen next. Finally John showed and said, "When I give the word, the curtains will open. Just play like you did during the snowstorm. Play for a half hour."

We were surprised that we still hadn't met Connelly, but it was clear that he was sitting out there because we saw the glow of a huge cigar in the vast darkness. The thought of playing for a one-man audience—especially a man as powerful as Frank Connelly—put us on edge.

A voice rang out: "All right, open 'em up."

The curtain parted, the stage lights went on—that added to the drama—and we hit it. We cut loose with all guns blazing. There was no stopping between songs, not a second of silence until the last number, after which the curtains closed and the only sound in the theater was the hum of our amps. Then we waited for the verdict.

It came a few minutes later when John bounded through the stage door. The smile on his face said it all.

"Frank liked you. He wants you to meet me here tomorrow."

"What for?" we wanted to know.

"You'll see tomorrow."

We headed back to our fort to unwind, but that was impossible. The rent was due and we were flat broke. Panic set in, but at least we had tomorrow's meeting. Maybe that meeting would lead to money.

After a night of tossing and turning, we showed up at the theater the following afternoon. John was waiting for us in the office with a stack of papers.

"This is your lucky day," he said. "Frank has decided to manage you. I don't have to tell you what this can mean. So all I will tell you is to sign these management contracts. They're completely standard. Take 'em home, look 'em over, and bring 'em back to me tomorrow. Signed."

"If we do," I said, "can you help us out with some immediate cash?"

"No problem," said John. "Just sign the contacts."

Amazed and excited, we went back to 1325.

"Someone just pasted something on your door," said one of our fellow tenants as we were climbing the stairs.

It was an eviction notice—not a warning but a third notice that said pay up or we'll throw your shit out on the street.

The irony was not lost on me: In one hand I was holding an eviction notice and in the other I was holding management contracts. I knew that the smart move would be to call an attorney. We required good legal advice. But I also knew that we'd been living week to week. Gigs were hard to find. Our pockets were empty. Our stomachs were empty. Hunger trumped reason. We also knew that Connelly was the best bet we had of getting somewhere, and we didn't want to piss him off.

So we signed, John gave us the cash to pay the rent, and we were all set to meet the man himself.

O'Toole told us come to Giro's, an old-school steakhouse in the North End, where Frank Connelly held court at a round table in the back. Everyone knew him there, and most everyone looked connected. It was a wiseguy-friendly establishment. Frank was a big stocky Irishman in his early forties with a shock of white hair and piercing blue eyes. He was dressed richly, in a blue blazer with gold buttons, a silk ascot warming his neck. He spoke in a thick Boston accent. I don't think he knew how to pronounce the letter r. He also spoke like a poet. He peppered his speech with hyperbole and metaphors. He told stories in great gusts of enthusiasm. He was the first genuine mogul I had ever met, a wholly original character whose Irish blarney carried enormous charm. He was quick to smile and quick to laugh. We couldn't resist him, especially since his praise of our music was unrestrained.

"The Beatles have their place," he told us as he ordered a second or third round of double whiskeys before dinner. When it came to drinking good bourbon, Frank showed us the way. "The Stones have their place as well. Jimi Hendrix was an innovator and I would say the same was true of Janis Joplin. When I booked Simon and Garfunkel to open for the Lovin' Spoonful at my Carousel Theater, I realized that Paul and Art had distinct voices and distinct talents. I was delighted to help promote their fledgling career. But lean in and listen to me closely, boys, when I tell you that these names, as grand as they may be, need not intimidate you. Your very art defies intimidation. Your art, your musical genius, will stand on its own. You will, in short, create your place. It won't be long—I'm talking about a few years, not decades—before Aerosmith is viewed as a cultural phenomenon. I realize that so many of your heroes, those musicians who appear so intimidating, are Englishmen cloaked in the modish fashions of the day and celebrated for their incomparable artistry. But you know better than I that these clever Brits have simply rerouted music born in America and none too subtly resculpted the sound. The sound is our native sound and you boys are our native sons. When I hear you, I hear that sound expressed in a form whose direct passion outstrips any band out there on the world stage today. Note that I say 'world,' because the world is your market. They will love you as passionately in Paris as they will in New York. London will embrace you, just as they embraced Hendrix. When the curtains opened and I heard you for the first time, all I could think of was a huge tribe of Indians chasing me over a hill. You gave me more excitement than I can handle. Now I want to share that excitement with the rest of the world. In the meantime, you will learn to drink as gentlemen. Where's our lovely waitress? Our glasses are empty and the night is young."

While he was talking, I was thinking, *This man is great. This man is paying our rent and buying us dinner plus all the drinks we want. Most of all, he's got vision and faith in us. This man is the answer to our prayers.*

Naturally, we hung on Frank Connelly's every word. In short order, he became not only our manager but our surrogate parent. We took to calling him Father Frank. In turn, he rechristened each of us. Steven was "LM" (for loudmouth), Tom "Low Gear," Brad "Light Horse," Joey "Soitanly" (after Curley of the Three Stooges' pronunciation of the word *certainly*), and I was "Flash." Since Frank had no idea that one of my first bands had been called Flash, I chalked this up to his uncanny insight.

Frank came to many of our gigs and, before we went onstage, he loved to say, "Remember why we're here. We come to play!"

Connelly saw us as a band but also as individuals. He spent private time with each of us. Because we were young, hungry, and impressionable, we were convinced that he was our savior, our key to fortune and fame, the man who would take us from our lowly status as a struggling baby band to big-time success. After our first meeting, not a day passed before he called to say that he had something lined up. Could we be at his office the next morning?

We were there, ready to rock.

"Where are we headed?"

"Just out to the parking lot. O'Toole will tell you what to do."

It turned that O'Toole needed us follow him to a warehouse, where we were to unload a truck. The truck was filled with a theatrical set that been used for a one-man play in which E. G. Marshall had portrayed H. L. Mencken. Frank, who was also bringing *Jesus Christ Superstar* to Boston, had produced the Mencken play. He paid us each ten bucks to dismantle the scenery and schlep it into storage.

I found most everything about Frank intriguing. One day he might use us as moving men, but a week later he'd have us to dinner at his home, where he'd regale us with stories.

"Did I tell you about the unfortunate incident involving my driver and Brian Epstein?" he asked.

"Brian Epstein, the Beatles' manager?" I asked.

"The same. A charming chap. He flew into Boston a month before the Beatles were to arrive to work out the final details for the concert I was promoting. I had my driver meet him at the airport and bring him to my office. I don't know how the subject came up, but during the ride my driver made known his views on homosexuality. I believed he used the unfortunate term 'faggot' more than once. He did not know that Mr. Epstein was gay. Incensed, Epstein forced the driver out of the car. At the time, they were in the tunnel beneath Boston Harbor. The next thing I knew, Epstein was calling me from his hotel, saying that he had no intention of doing business with heathens. Naturally, I offered my deepest apologies and assured him that my driver's attitudes did not reflect mine. That evening over cocktails I tried my best to remedy the situation. I painted Boston as a most liberal and open-minded metropolis. I salvaged the date, and the Beatles came, but they were here and gone within twelve hours. Epstein, ever the erudite Englishman, still believed that we Bostonians are heathens."

Another time I was riding with Father Frank in his oversize Olds Delta 88 when the car broke down in the middle of Copley Square. I got out and saw pieces of engine hanging from below the car. Taxis and buses and cars were blasting their horns at us. We'd caused a major traffic jam.

"How's it look?" asked Frank.

"This car is screwed up," I said. "We're not going anywhere."

"Yes we are," he said. "We're going to have a drink."

Unperturbed, he left the car where it sat and led me to a wood-paneled bar in a swanky hotel nearby. It was the middle of the afternoon, but not too early to enjoy the best bourbon in the house. Frank called the bartender by his first name and acted as though this had been our intended destination all along. When I asked what he was going to do about his car, he said he'd instructed the bartender to make a call. No worries. It was a good chance for us to get to know each other better. Frank always began our conversations by asking about my family. He had fine manners. From there the talk usually moved on to women. He wanted to know if I understood the nature of romance?

I confessed that my experiences were limited. I briefly mentioned the episode on Block Island. The story amused Frank, but, if I didn't mind, he wanted to offer me some paternal advice. I didn't mind at all.

"Women are delicate creatures," he said, "whose aesthetic sensitivities are far greater than ours—far more artistic, far more subtle, far more romantic. When you encounter a young woman who is drawn to you—and I have no doubt, dear Joe, that many are passionately so drawn—I would suggest not merely a date to a theater, a concert, or a movie, but rather a weekend."

"A weekend?" I asked.

"Precisely. A weekend that begins with a long train ride from Boston to Montreal. Ideally, the trip takes place in winter, when the landscape is covered in a freshly fallen snow. You go first class, of course, and enjoy a fabulous four-course meal in the dining car. Upon arrival, the awaiting limousine takes you to a quaint bed-and-breakfast where the proprietor speaks only French. You don't want to go to a large convention hotel, such as this one. A small and intimate lodging is far more conducive to the kind of mood you wish to establish. You'll request the attic room with the exposed-beam ceiling and wood-burning fireplace, the coziest of all their accommodations. That night, with the flames roaring and the logs crackling, she will surrender to your every desire. The next day you will devote to shopping—shopping for her, not for you. You'll survey the small boutiques in the old quarter of the city. In one such charming shop you'll help her select a pair of thigh-high fur-lined boots fashioned in Russia. You'll tell her how the rich bronze hue of the leather brings out the radiance in her skin. Then, after a quiet dinner of paté, roasted quail, and French champagne, it's back to your attic paradise and even deeper erotic pleasures. In the morning, you'll take the train back to Boston, her head resting on your shoulder as you gaze out the window, your heart filled with wonder and gratitude. You'll know that you've made a memory that will never fade."

By the end of this story, Frank and I had polished off a fifth of bourbon. He was roaring drunk. I was silently drunk. When he went to the bathroom,

I could see he was having a little trouble walking. But no matter how much he drank he was able to carry it off with aplomb. He never lost control. When we did manage to get up and make it through the lobby and out the door, a brand-new Olds 88 was waiting at the curb, along with a driver.

"After you, dear boy," said Frank, motioning me into the car. "Just tell my man where you need to be dropped off."

I wanted to ask how all this had been so quickly arranged, but I didn't. My mind was reeling with thoughts of midnight train rides to Montreal.

"It's all a beautiful mystery, isn't it?" asked Frank as he surveyed the busy streets of the Back Bay.

I didn't know what he was referring to, but it didn't matter. I repeated his words. "Yes," I said, "it's all a beautiful mystery."

It's no mystery how we up-graded our rehearsal situation. Through Frank's theatrical connections, he hooked us up with the Charles Playhouse in downtown Boston. On the weekends we'd play clubs and high schools, and during the week we'd rehearse all night at the Charles. They gave us the key to the theater so we could come and go as we pleased. We loved it because we didn't have to break down our gear after each rehearsal. When we arrived, we turned on the stage lights and marveled at how great our equipment was starting to look. Brad and I had managed to get some mid-sixties vintage Marshall amps that had the kind of sharp, gutsy sound we'd been searching for. At the end of our session, our only responsibility was to cut off the main circuit breaker, leave our stuff onstage, and split. We were certain our equipment was safe.

We loved coming into the theater every afternoon, turning on the lights, and digging the look of the stage that was filled with our equipment. It was a moment of pride. Every dime we had was invested in this gear. So you can imagine what it felt like to arrive one day and, after switching on the circuit breaker, see nothing but a completely empty stage. It was a kick in the gut. We were wiped out. Every last piece of equipment—every mic, every one of Joey's drums, every one of those precious Marshall amps—all gone. It was worse than someone stealing your girlfriend. Aerosmith without our equipment was like a race car driver without his car. Our whole identity was in the coolness of the gear we had assembled—the way it looked and the way it sounded. This was a devastating blow.

We never figured out how the thieves got in or out. We called the cops but the equipment never turned up. Frank fronted us the money to replace it. The new amps, though, sounded nothing like the old ones. We mourned the loss for months.

But we kept working our asses off and no doubt kept getting better. Knowing that we had a major promoter like Frank Connelly behind us motivated us even more. At the same time, the scene at 1325 got wilder. We had cultivated a small but loyal fan base. Those who knew us best knew that we liked to get high. They knew they'd be especially welcome if they arrived with pot or beer.

Casey, one of our favorite dealers, was a 1325 regular. He'd roll up in his tricked-out 1947 Ford (called the Blue Diamond because of the blue costume-jewelry diamond glued on the dashboard) or his 500-cc Kawasaki and deliver the goods. One time I jumped on the back of the Kawasaki and accompanied him on a run. We were zipping through the intersection of Memorial Drive and Longfellow Bridge in Cambridge when Casey realized that the two-pound brick of good stuff inside his jacket had slipped out and fallen on the street. No problem. He simply executed a quick U. I jumped off the bike and stopped traffic while he scooped up the pot.

Things didn't always go that smoothly. After spending a couple of nights at Judy Nylon's loft, I thought I'd better check in with the guys at 1325. Because it was a beautiful day, I walked halfway from downtown and took the train the rest of the way. But the bright day turned dark when I saw that the door to our apartment was off its hinges. The place had been turned upside down. It looked like a tornado had ripped through. I soon learned that the night before Brad and Tom had been sitting on the couch, peacefully passing a joint, when the cops broke the door down and tore up the place, expecting to find mountains of drugs. All they found was half a smoked joint. They hauled Brad off to jail. We posted bail and he was later released and the charges dropped. It turned out that the cops had been looking for me. One of our dealers had been busted and, dropping a dime on us, had given up our address as a drug house. Because my name was on the lease, I was the object of the police pursuit. Rather than take a chance, I figured I'd lie low. I sure as hell wasn't going to give myself up for some bullshit charge. I spent the rest of the week in Cabozzi's basement drinking beer and playing guitar. When I resurfaced I knew we had to tighten up our act at 1325. No more open-door policy. In the meantime, we had to pool our money for a new door.

There was also the ongoing transportation challenge. I had traded in my broken-down MGB for a Saab, a geeky but reliable ride that couldn't go faster than sixty miles an hour. I hadn't had it for two weeks when the engine blew up. Band transportation was equally challenging. Despite the diligent work of Gary Cabozzi, the red bus was always busted. The only way to heat it was to leave its oven door open. Frank came to the rescue when he bought us a used Delta 88 hardtop. The car was both a blessing and a curse. It was great to have a vehicle that actually worked, but because we took turns using it for private purposes it caused friction. We were always fighting over who got to use it next.

Frank Connelly impressed me not only with his faith in the band, but his drinking. As much as he knocked 'em back, I never saw him get sick. The closest he came was an evening when he drove us to a gig at a club out on Route 9. After the show we started pounding 'em down pretty good. Frank's speech was slightly slurred, the only hint that the booze was taking effect. When it was time to leave, his usual elegant attire was still perfectly in place, although his walk was a little off-balance.

"Want me to drive?" I asked.

"I'm fine, Joe," he said. "Never been better."

We hit the highway, and after fifteen minutes, he finally admitted that he was tired.

"I think I better get a room," he said.

Given his erratic driving, we were relieved. He drove us all to a nice motel. The second he opened the car door and tried to get out, he fell to his knees. We helped him inside, where he never lost his presence of mind.

"Take out my wallet, boys," he said, "and register me quickly. Get me the best room they have."

The clerk looked at us suspiciously. We'd just played a gig. We were half-drunk ourselves, a pirate gang of sweaty rockers. The clerk probably thought we were ripping Frank off.

"Do not look askance at these gentlemen," Frank told the clerk, sensing the vibe. "They are artists. They work for me. And now, in an unusual turn of events, I have placed myself in their care."

We got the key, helped Frank to his room, and put him peacefully to sleep. The next day he called to express his appreciation.

"How are you, Frank?" I asked him.

"Never been better."

Frank understood that our band needed tough-minded help. That's why he made John O'Toole our road manager. This was fine with us. Raised in the rough section of Dorchester, John had emerged from his time in prison as a no-nonsense businessman with great loyalty to Frank. The only serious problem arose when, for the first time, John encountered Gary Cabozzi.

We were playing K-K-K-Katy's, the big rock club in Boston's Kenmore Square. Before the show, Cabozzi had taken his usual position: An imposing figure, he stood guard in front of our dressing room, his massive arms folded in front of him. No one could get past him. Gary was the bulldog who liked to scare people away.

Up came John O'Toole, who, ignoring the bulldog, reached for the door and started to walk into the dressing room.

"Where the fuck do you think you're going?" said Cabozzi.

"To see my band," said O'Toole.

"Your band! Who the fuck are you kidding?"

O'Toole ignored him and kept going. At the very moment Cabozzi put his hand on O'Toole's chest, I happened to be passing by. I saw what was happening. Blood was about to be spilled.

"It's okay, Gary," I said. "This guy's cool. This is John O'Toole. He's helping us out."

Cabozzi backed off, but the tension between him and O'Toole only increased with time. Gary sensed that in the management regime headed by Frank Connelly, his role as our protector would be diminished—and he didn't like it.

From the get-go, Frank said that we'd have to showcase in New York.

"I am not an immodest man," he said, "and, as you already know, I am a presence to be reckoned with in the environs of greater Boston. I can help establish you boys as the biggest band in New England. But while that in and of itself is no mean feat, it is far from your goal. Your goal is world domination. Because I want to help you realize that goal, I must admit to my limitations. The powerful record executives are in New York. These are the deal makers. I know them by name and I've tangentially dealt with a few of these gentlemen, but I lack the clout that would bring them to a showcase, say, in Manhattan. On the other hand, I know managers with that clout and I'm recommending two of them—Steve Leber and David Krebs."

"Do you trust them?" I asked.

"I know they left William Morris to go out on their own, and they're smart and crafty."

"But do you trust them?" I repeated.

"In this business, I trust no one. But I do trust their ambition. And I trust the fact that, among all the managers in New York, they were the first ones to spot and manage the New York Dolls. You've heard of the Dolls, haven't you?"

I had. Friends who'd seen them in New York described them as the edgiest rock band to emerge in years. They were being called the new Stones. Connelly introduced us to their management team, Leber-Krebs. They struck me as nothing more than two business guys looking to make a buck. They said the right things and had the right contacts, but there was no emotional connection. They seemed to have no affinity for music. But, according to Frank, most managers didn't.

"They don't have to understand you artistically," Frank said. "They have to understand you commercially. These guys understand musical merchandise. They were involved in producing *Jesus Christ Superstar* before me and made a fuckin' fortune. These guys can smell out money."

I'm not sure what Leber-Krebs saw in the New York Dolls, but I was crazy about the band. So were the New York critics. In 1972, the year we did our showcases, the Dolls were the shit. I heard them as straight-out rock and roll, the essence of what I loved. They were also hilarious. They understood how to marry performance art and rock. They just did whatever the fuck they wanted to do. When they showed up at our sound check for our first showcase at Max's Kansas City, I was excited to meet them. David Johansen, the lead singer, was wearing his spandex suit and spiked high heels. Johnny Thunders wore a black leather jacket and skintight red jeans. Coming from provincial Boston, we didn't know if they were camp or gay or cross-dressing weirdos. We played a few songs and they watched us intently. Afterward, they complimented us generously. Quickly I saw that they were as straight as we were. David and Johnny knew their shit. Underneath the glitter, I saw them as street punks trying to make it. We had lots in common.

The Dolls' big advantage over us, though, was that they lived in New York. Their fashion sense was steeped in kitsch. Arthur "Killer" Kane came out wearing a tutu and knee-high leopard boots. They also understood the fine art of attracting the media. The press adored their outrageous outfits. Following the English, Steven and I had begun wearing some makeup, but we weren't prepared to take it as far as the Dolls. We were hardly the product of an underground glam scene, but we—or at least I—could dig that scene as funny and fun and gutsy. They pushed the boundaries of androgyny but were as macho as marines. When I got hold of that early stuff by the Dolls, I played it all the time. Steven, Tom, Brad, and Joey didn't share my enthusiasm. They understood the crazy appeal of their stage packaging but thought the music was too crude. Yet the crudeness was what I found alluring. They didn't care about musical nuance. They didn't care about anything. They just wanted to kick ass.

We apparently had not kicked ass during our first appearance at Max's, because we got no offers. Back in Boston, Frank was his usual reassuring self.

"One time means nothing, boys," he said. "My belief in you is stronger than ever. In baseball, if you have a lifetime average of .333, meaning you fail two-thirds of the time, you go to the Hall of Fame. The average successful record executive is batting no better than .200. That means he's wrong four out of five times. To be rejected by such a corporate animal—one ruled by caution, trepidation, and fear—is simply business as usual. I am certain that an enlightened executive will emerge who will, like me, possess the acumen to understand that Aerosmith is not merely a merry band of brilliant musicians, but the next mega-band that will light arenas and stadiums the world over. Trust me, boys, there is no cause for discouragement. It is more than a faint glow that you see at the end of the tunnel. It's a spotlight a thousand watts strong. It's triumph, it's victory, it's a vindication of everything you've been working so hard to achieve. That's why I'm convinced the preparation for the next showcase should be supercharged. I'm booking you back in the Sheraton in Manchester for two solid weeks. Two solid weeks of woodshedding will do you nothing but good. To eliminate all distractions you might encounter at home, I've booked you at the hotel so it will be a time of nothing but music, music, music."

We moved up to New Hampshire and did as Frank instructed. The Sheraton wasn't terrible. Brad and I would start the day with a couple of double martinis, followed by a free lunch buffet, followed by a few hours of rehearsals. In the evenings we'd play the nightclub, where the crowd was older than we were used to. No matter. We got them dancing. I also managed a short-term fling with an especially hot waitress.

After the two-week live-in/warm-up at the Sheraton, we returned to New York with a vengeance. It was either the second or third trip to Max's Kansas City—I can't remember which—when Steven noticed a few limos lined up outside the club. He thought it meant the moguls had come out in force to see us. He also imagined that John Lennon or Mick Jagger or David Bowie would show up. Steven was always seeing stars. For my part, I was convinced that I needed some extra energy. We'd been up for hours preparing our set. We knew that this was going to be a make-it-or-break-it show. To give myself a little more fire, I took a couple of Crossroads, a diet pill form of speed that was popular in the early seventies. I'm not sure if the drug helped or hurt my performance. I was too busy playing to notice. But it did get me past the nervousness.

After our six- or seven-song set was over, I saw Steven huddling with

Leber and Krebs and another man I didn't know. Afterward Steven said, "That was Clive Davis."

"Tell me who he is again," I said. I'd heard his name but hadn't connected the dots.

"He runs Columbia. He discovered Janis Joplin. He made her a star."

"Wasn't it her music that made her a star?" I asked.

"You know what I mean," said Steven. "Anyway, he loves us. He said *I'm* gonna be a star."

A few minutes later Leber and Krebs brought over the man to meet me. He was immaculately dressed and said all the right things.

"I like your band," said Clive Davis. "I want to sign you to Columbia."

"That's great," I said. "Thank you."

There was more small talk, but within a few minutes Davis was gone.

It took us ten long years to learn that Clive actually signed Leber-Krebs to a production deal. We, in turn, were signed to Leber-Krebs as hired hands. At the time, we were certain that we were a Columbia act, not understanding that Leber-Krebs had the power to fire any one of us at any time.

Back at the Gramercy Park Hotel, I was still buzzing from the speed and grateful that New York television, unlike Boston television, was an all-night affair. The flickering images helped me process my jumbled thoughts.

Naturally I was a little dazed, but to be honest, I was also a little disappointed. I had hoped we'd sign to Atlantic or one of their subsidiaries, like Atco. Atlantic had the hard rock bands we liked—Cream, Zeppelin, the Stones. Atlantic also had a louder and richer sound than the other labels—the exact sound our music called for. On the other hand, I couldn't complain about being on the same label as Bob Dylan. As dawn broke and I finally managed to drift off to sleep, I felt relieved and satisfied that we finally had a deal. Columbia was cool.

"Columbia is great," said Frank when we got back to Boston. "Columbia is international. They've got the best distribution of any label. Leber-Krebs will know how to deal with Columbia. The signing advance will take care of you for a while, but not for long. You'll make a great record, but even if it sells, royalties take forever to come your way. When you're done recording you're going to have to get on the road and stay on the road. Record sales are great, but you can't count on them alone. The only thing you can count on is your ability to put on a killer show. Listen to me, boys, when I tell you that you can only count on yourselves. Remember our motto—'We come to play.' That motto's the key to everything."

Frank was right. One thing would never change: The five of us were going to live or die as a band based on our relationship with our fans. Our fans were everything, and our shows were the best way to get them to love our band.

As Frank gave us more personal counseling, he became less involved in our actual business. Leber-Krebs were taking over. We heard that Frank had sold them a 50 percent interest in us but never knew the details. My view of Leber-Krebs came down to one word—*skeptical.* On the other hand, I couldn't deny that it was Leber-Krebs who got Clive Davis to our showcase and cut our deal with Columbia. Soon they'd be booking us as an opening act for major artists. All this was great, but in my heart I wished it had been Frank, not Leber-Krebs.

Over the next several months it became clear why Frank could no longer pull those strings. He was growing physically weak. He looked frail. He avoided the topic of his health until it became too obvious to ignore.

"Boys," he said, "I need to undergo treatment and won't be able to attend your shows for a while."

Then he said the word none of us wanted to hear—*cancer.* Because my dad had been battling cancer since the first year I moved to Boston, cancer was much on my mind. The news about Frank devastated me. The thought of losing these men—so important to my development as a human being—was overwhelming. I'm not sure how or where I stuffed my fear, but I did. I soldiered on.

Dad had been in and out of the hospital for some time. I didn't know about the drama—Mom would tell me years later—but before my father had been diagnosed with cancer he and his secretary had been having an affair. He had actually left my mother and moved in with the woman, although he and my mother continued to date during this separation. It was only when he got sick that he returned home with the support and understanding of my mom. Emotionally and otherwise, he required my mother's care. Yet his strong streak of independence had not diminished. He insisted on driving himself back and forth to his cancer treatments. After one such session, he got into a minor car accident. After that, my mother took over the driving. For a while it looked as though the cancer was in remission and that, once again, he had survived the dreaded disease and continued to live at home.

Like my father, Frank did not want to go into detail about his cancer. All I knew was that he was not as active as before. At the same time, he continued to do us great favors.

It was Frank who arranged for us to rehearse in the visitors' locker room at Boston Garden. The original Garden, built in the twenties, was sacred ground. It was essentially a boxing arena where the Bruins and the Celtics won their trophies. It was the most electric spot in the city, where all the holy wars were waged. As we prepared to go into the studio we found ourselves in the bowels of the building that housed the arena that was used for wrestling matches during the summer. While we were struggling to put together the songs that would turn up on our first album, Haystacks Calhoun, Killer Kowalski, or Andre the Giant would come limping from the whirlpool to the massage table.

Then came the week that the wrestling matches gave way to the Rolling Stones. I was a fan, but I didn't have Steven's holy reverence for the group. The last time the Stones were in town I was standing outside the Tea Party when a friend from Sunapee came driving by, saying that he had a free ticket.

"Get in," he said. "They'll blow your mind."

"I think I'll pass."

"Are you crazy?"

"No. The Stones are great. I'd just rather see Fleetwood Mac."

This time I went to see the Stones with Steven. It turned out to be one of the most famous shows in rock history. Earlier that summer they'd released the blistering two-LP *Exile on Main Street*. The huge crowd at the Boston Garden couldn't wait to hear them play those songs live. The air was thick with pot. The buzz was tremendous, everyone sky-high on anticipation. But then came the delays—hour after hour, we were kept waiting. Salvation came in the form of Boston mayor Kevin White, who, looking like a regular Stones fan with his jacket off and his shirtsleeves rolled up, had the cool to explain what was happening. Bad weather had forced the Stones' plane to land in Providence, Rhode Island, where they got into a scuffle with a photographer. Keith and Mick had been thrown in jail. They'd gotten out quickly but then had to make the drive to Boston, where the crowd was restless. The mayor, fearing a riot, got us to calm down. He said he was lifting the train curfew so public transportation would be running no matter what time the show ended. Then he threw out a couple of footballs and told us to stay loose because, one way or another, the Stones were gonna rock the house tonight.

And man, did they ever. When the Stones finally took the stage they looked like wrecks. They looked the way the Stones are supposed to look. The crowd went nuts. The Stones transcended the boundaries of normal rock and roll. That night they earned the title of the greatest rock-and-roll band in the world. Later I'd come to believe that at on any given night, any band can earn that title. But back in the summer of 1972, the Stones wore the crown.

The next day when we returned to the Garden to rehearse in the locker room, Steven and I first walked out into the arena. All of the Stones' equipment was gone. We climbed up onstage and lay on our backs for a few minutes, side by side. Looking up into that cavernous arena, we said the same words at practically the same time: "One day . . ."

TWINGES OF LOVE

The months before the fall of 1972, when we actually started recording our first album, were wild. I had my first and only affair with an older woman who, in many ways, turned me out. It began in the improbable town of Framingham, a big suburb twenty miles outside Boston, where Frank had a friend who owned an upstairs restaurant that was temporarily closed. We were allowed to rehearse there. Downstairs was a club where the locals liked to hang. Among them were musicians and actors performing at Caesar's Monticello, a dinner theater just down the street. Among the regulars was Judy Carne, famous for her stint on Rowan & Martin's *Laugh-In*, the national TV show. She was the English bombshell who delivered the "sock it to me" line. She was doing a summer run of *Cabaret* at Caesar's.

Judy was far more attractive in person than on TV. Off TV, her language was salty and provocative. Her body was alluring. She had a thin frame, big brown eyes, full lips, and an upturned nose. I saw her as a super-seductive pixie who dressed in the latest Carnaby Street fashions.

She traveled with an entourage whose aura was pure sex. Her bosom buddy was her makeup girl and confidante, a gorgeous curvaceous redhead who gave the guys the idea that she couldn't wait to get out of her clothes. It was a hot scene. The sexual tension was thick, like a stick of sweet incense. Once word got around that a Hollywood star like Judy was a nightly regular, the place was packed. No live music but loud rock and roll blasting over the sound system. It was the perfect hang for us, a band on the make. In the afternoon we'd rehearse upstairs, then head to the bar downstairs. We had the run of the place because the owner was a friend of Frank's. He'd go around telling everyone that we were the recently-signed-to-Columbia hot new band. He also ran a betting pool built upon what lucky guy could get to Judy's super-sexy assistant first.

The real prize, though, was Judy, who held court at her table. It was fun watching the rock-and-roll guys parading around like peacocks and sending drinks over to Judy's table, battling for her attention. Ms. Carne regarded all this coolly. She just sat back, drank, and watched. We'd been told that she liked good coke, which explained her frequent trips to the women's room. On her way back from one such trip she stopped at our table. The club owner had introduced us a few nights earlier, when only a few pleasantries had been exchanged. This time she walked right over to me. Someone scrambled to get her a chair. She sat down and, in her charming English accent, said, "How you doing, mate?" Before I could reply she reached over for my vodka gimlet and took a long, slow draw. "Hmm," she said. "This is really fabulous. May I have one?"

Naturally, I ordered her a drink. I was shocked that, in this crowded club of guys dying to approach her, she had approached me. At the same time, I wasn't shocked enough to pass up the opportunity to get to know her. We started chatting, the drinks kept coming, we moved closer to each other, our conversation grew more intimate, and soon the rest of the club seemed to disappear. By evening's end she asked me to drive her home in her Cadillac. We went to her luxurious house. That night we got little sleep.

Judy took me to a new dimension of hedonism. She had a doctor's bag filled with high-quality cocaine, one variety more potent than the next—bottles, pills, powders, syringes, everything 99 percent legal. She had managed to get prescriptions for everything, even the coke. She always looked her best, walking around the house in an X-rated version of the R-rated lingerie she wore in her show. She got a kick out of telling me that her voluptuous redheaded makeup girl—the chick that the men at the club were pining for—was really her makeup boy. Judy loved to laugh. She had a voracious appetite for life's pleasures. At thirty-three, she had earned her PhD in sex and drugs. At twenty-one, I was her willing pupil.

One evening near end of her run in Monticello I was driving her back from Boston when I got into a minor accident, causing her to sprain her ankle. The ER doctor recommended that she stay off her feet for two weeks. She liked the plan, checked us into the Copley Square Hotel, and freely shared her pain medicine with me. We supplemented those pills with goodies from the doctor's bag. When that supply ran low, she knew who to call. She had made connections with local dealers with products far above my pay grade.

Judy had no pretense about love and romance. She told me that her boyfriend was in Africa making a movie. After her engagements on the East Coast, she'd be heading back to L.A. to be with him. They had an open relationship.

My relationship with the band was a little strained by this episode. While living with Judy at the Copley Square, I had to curtail rehearsal time with Aerosmith. Judy required all my tender loving care. Steven kept calling, wanting to know if he could come over. On several occasions before the car accident, Judy had hung out with the band and was extremely generous with her stash. I now sensed that Steven wanted to get into her doctor's bag—and maybe get into something else. I never invited him over. Forced to stay off her feet, Judy was naked most of the time and didn't want company. I had no interest in a threesome and neither did she. We just wanted to be alone.

One night she felt strong enough to go out on the town. Her friend Bette Midler was playing Lennie's On-the-Turnpike, a jazz club on Route One in Peabody. This was the year that Midler's first album, *The Divine Miss M*, had been released. Barry Manilow was her musical director and the show was as campy as campy gets. I dug it. Afterward we went to her dressing room and Judy introduced me as her friend.

x

Bette slowly looked me up and down before saying, "Well, I can certainly see *why*."

I may or may not have blushed, but I certainly felt strange. Never before had a woman described me as an object of erotic appeal. Such moments do wonders for a guy's confidence. It gave me a boost, as it would any kid from the suburbs.

The other major change in my life had to do with Commonwealth. After two years, we decided to close up shop at 1325. By then the guys had gravitated to their girlfriends—Brad with Laurie, Tom with Terry, and Joey with Nina. Steven and I moved into a three-bedroom basement apartment on Kent Street in Brookline that had been smartly refurbished by our friend Henry Smith, with whom we shared the place. The move happened during the end of Judy's two-week recovery at the Copley Square. Once I was settled in, I went off with Judy on her last East Coat gig—a ten-day engagement in Philly. The band wasn't happy, because I'd be missing more rehearsals. But this was the end of my time with Judy and I wanted to enjoy it as long as I could.

One night before I left for Philly, Steven and I were alone in the Kent Street apartment. He wanted to show me how to shoot coke.

"Have you ever done it?" he asked.

"Never," I said. "You actually put a needle in your arm, like with heroin?"

"Yeah, it's the ultimate high. You gotta try it."

I hated needles. The whole shooting-up thing turned my stomach. But after Steven's selling job, I was up for it.

"You're gonna love it," he said. "Watch me first."

I sat and observed. He was fastidious about the process. He painstakingly sterilized the needle and spoon. He placed a tiny amount of coke in the spoon and, as a final precaution, heated it up before injecting me. Within twenty seconds, the top of my head turned into a blinding light. The rush of euphoria was far too intense. My heart felt like Man O' War's hoofs galloping across the finish line. I started to grit my teeth. Steven saw that I wasn't having fun.

"Maybe I gave you too much," he said.

A few days later I was in Philly with Judy. I went to her cabaret shows every night, but after the third or fourth performance I got a little bored. Judy was onstage and I was alone in her dressing room when I noticed a vial containing a few grams of pure coke. The stuff looked like ice crystals. I glanced down at her trusty doctor's bag and noticed some opened syringes. The devil on my shoulder whispered, "Give it a try. This time you'll love it." I heeded the devil and went through all the motions Steven had taught me, taking care with each step. I don't know whether it was my needle phobia or injection inexperience, but I somehow turned myself into a blood donor. Blood was spurting everywhere—my clothes, the counter, the floor. I made one horrible goddamn bloody mess.

When Judy arrived, her first concern was for me. "Did you hurt yourself?"

When I told her what I had tried, for the first and only time she raised her voice at me.

"Why the fuck would you do that?" she yelled.

She quickly saw that I didn't need to be told that I'd made a mistake. She apologized for her outburst and helped me clean up the mess. That was it for shooting up. I never shot up again, in spite of the fact that people thought you needed needles to do heroin. Needles and I don't mix.

My last days with Judy were bittersweet. After her engagement in Philly, we drove back to Kent Street, where she stayed with me for a few days. I asked if she could stay a few days longer. I was feeling twinges of love.

"Come on, Joe," she said, "I have my career and my boyfriend. You've known about that from that start. Besides, what do you expect me to do— live in your funky apartment and have babies?"

It seemed a little harsh. My heart was a little broken. The lease on her Caddy wasn't up, so I had the use of her fancy car to console me. After dropping her at the airport, I drove up the back ramp of the Boston Garden to meet the band. I hadn't been to rehearsals for weeks. I'd been on a grand adventure. The thought of all that stimulation—sexual and chemical—had me in a deeply reflective state of mind. I had aged at least ten years. When I got to the rehearsal space I figured the guys would be glad to see me, but all I got were dirty looks.

Before Judy, I had embraced only two of the three pillars of the un-holy trinity of sex, drugs, and rock and roll. Judy provided the sex part with such intensity that I felt like I'd made up for lost time. Many men—myself included—harbor fantasies of such affairs. A free-spirited woman with an affinity for unabashed sex and good coke may be seen as a gift from the heavens. The Judy Carne chapter was short but powerful. Soon after she left, another woman took her place and stayed. That surprised me, de-lighted me, and ultimately drove me to the brink. It was the start of a new chapter, one in which massive success and spectacular failure fought for center stage.

MAKE IT

In many ways, moving to Kent Street marked the start of a new chapter. For the first time, Steven and I were living together alone. This allowed us to become closer friends. Using old barn wood, Henry Smith transformed what otherwise would have been a dreary basement apartment into a work of art. In addition to the bedrooms there was a hangout room, where we'd throw small parties, and a kitchen with floor-to-ceiling windows for fresh air and lots of natural light. Ever resourceful, Henry even found a way to jerry-rig the fuse box so we never got an electricity bill. Our across-the-alley neighbors were navy guys whose ship had been dry-docked. With plenty of time on their hands, they'd come over and party with us.

In contrast to 1325, with its open-door policy, Kent Street was a lower-key scene. Tucked away in that basement, it didn't even have a number on the door. It was an out-of-the-way hideaway that not everyone knew about. Kent Street was where everything changed between me and Elyssa, after years of maintaining a platonic friendship.

Steven and Elyssa had their own friendship and connection from childhood, a kind of kissing-cousin playful rapport. For my part, I had always desired her while respecting the friends-only boundary she had established from the start. When she broke up with Joe Jammer, her guitar-playing boyfriend, I renewed my hopes that she might turn my way. But it didn't happen. I was just glad that we were friends. Besides, given the fact that Boston is a hot college town, I was not lacking in female companionship.

Then came the night when, after a local Aerosmith gig, she came back to Kent Street with Steven and me. All three of us were surprised when we woke up the next morning with the realization that during the night things had been radically altered. Elyssa had come to my room and slept in my bed. We became lovers. For me this represented a dream come true. Elyssa was both a cool chick and a hot pistol, a woman beautiful enough to find work as a model. She also possessed a quick wit. With her acid tongue, she had no reservations about saying anything to anyone. When she was on, she could be really funny.

From then on we were a couple. Three or four nights a week she'd come to Kent and spend the night. On one of those nights Steven had to bang on the thin wall that separated his bedroom from mine and yell, "Keep it down in there." Three months later, Elyssa and I moved into an apartment on Beacon Street. Later we moved to a larger place in Brookline where, incidentally, Maxanne Sartori, the DJ who'd proved so critical to our career, lived next door. It was there that I turned the extra bedroom into a practice room with a little four-track recorder.

In 1972, Aerosmith cut our first record—a learning experience. I'd never been in a recording studio before, and this little one at the far end of Newbury Street—Intermedia—had probably just been converted from eight to sixteen tracks. My main concern was getting the sound right. I wanted our stuff to sound real—live and loud. I wasn't interested in fancy. We were, after all, a garage band, and I wanted a garage band vibe. What I quickly learned, though, was that a recording studio can be cruel: It spits out exactly what you put in.

Columbia told us that our producer was Adrian Barber. He had a good reputation because of his work on the early Cream records. In some ways this was the easiest record we made and in other ways the hardest—easiest because we were playing songs we'd been rehearsing and performing for two years; hardest because we didn't know what we were doing. I figured that Barber would push a few buttons and that what we played would come out sounding like a record. Wrong. Our playing was tight, yet too tight. We sounded neither spontaneous nor explosive, two of our best qualities. My attempts to explain this to Barber went in one ear and out the other. It wasn't entirely his fault. I didn't have the right technical vocabulary to say what needed to be said. In the end, Barber and his assistants simply set up mics, got an acceptable take, and moved on. After each take, Steven and I sat behind the board, trying to learn as much as we could, but Adrian had no interest in conducting a class in recording.

The songs were in place. Steven had been banging those chords to "Dream On" for well over a year. He played them over and again on the piano until we knew them as well as he did. Brad and I transposed the guitar parts from his piano licks. I didn't know the least thing about voicing. I just winged it. I wasn't crazy about the song—mainly because it was slow. My attitude was simple: The only good slow song is a slow blues. "Dream On" was hardly a blues. It was a slow song in a genre that didn't excite me. The five of us worked that song to the point where it became a live show-stopper with the right dynamics. So it fit in with the rest of the record.

Tom and I turned Steven on to an album by a band called Blodwyn Pig, formed by the original guitarist from Jethro Tull. Steven had the lyrics and, inspired by that album, finished "Mama Kin." "Mama Kin" was always around. We all liked it. We knew the material like the back of our hands: "Movin' Out," "Make It," "Somebody," "Write Me," "Walkin' the Dog." But in recording the songs, something got lost. Steven treated the sessions as if they were rehearsals, going for perfection rather than letting the band cut loose like a live gig. That undercut our spontaneity. It would take us years to understand the vital role of spontaneity in recording.

But Steven wasn't alone. We were all grappling with our technical demons. None of us knew the mysterious relationship between music and machines.

Our producer was practically useless. He had little input. When I heard the playback, I kept thinking, *We're better than this. We should sound better than this. We're being recorded wrong. We sound fuckin' flat.* But because I lacked the studio chops to prescribe a remedy, I kept quiet. It pained me, though, that my guitar voice was not cutting through.

Steven's singing voice wasn't either. I was surprised that he was so nervous. After all, he'd recorded before. But that didn't ease his discomfort. His insecurity was forcing him into a different persona. He overdid it and, compared to his natural singing voice, his voice on the record sounded affected.

Don't get me wrong. I love this first record. There's magic on it, but just not the magic I had envisioned. It's an accurate snapshot of who we were at the time—young, hungry, and determined to make our mark.

Unfortunately the packaging was lame. We didn't even see the cover until the first printing. It was something that Columbia just threw together. We saw that "Walking the Dog" was listed as "Walking the *Dig.*" The whole thing was sloppy. It marked the start of our education in dealing with labels. Moreover, this particular label had little interest in promoting us compared to Bruce Springsteen, whose debut album came out the same week as ours. Unlike Aerosmith, Springsteen was tailor-made for Columbia. He came out of the Dylan tradition. The label publicists had a field day promoting him. The public was ready for a rock hero with Bruce's look and sound. We got the idea that Columbia didn't think the public was ready for us.

If the release of a record is the birth of a band, ours was a stillbirth. We kept running to the newsstand to pick up *Rolling Stone* and read a review. But *Rolling Stone* never ran one. It's one thing to have your debut criticized; it's even worse to have your debut ignored. We were pissed.

But we knew that we were onto something, because every time we played a new town the audience went wild. And we were always asked back. When we played a venue we had played before, the crowds were bigger. The evidence was right in front of our faces. Fans were digging us.

It was Frank who booked us in Revere, Massachusetts, back then a tough beach town where bank robbers and assorted felons felt right at home. For a time we were the house band at

Scarborough Fair, a big rock club partly owned by Frank, where we played two or three times a week. Connected to the club was a bar used as a hangout for local gangsters. During the bleak winter season, Revere became a haven for bikers looking to smash heads.

At one of our shows Steven, not famous for restraint of tongue, had words with one of the biker chicks coming out of the ladies' room. I don't know the exact lead-up to the line, but when he said, "Honey, your string is hanging," I knew trouble was brewing. Her boyfriend was the leader of a murderous biker gang. When she told her honey about the insult, word quickly got back that not just Steven but all of Aerosmith were going to be dealt with.

Frank flew into action. "Boys," he said, "we must flee, and flee at once."

First he put out the word that we would be leaving through the rear exit. Then, recruiting his gangster friends from the connecting bar to help, he had us leave through the front door, where a car sped us out of harm's way. Once again, Frank saved our asses.

Frank had to save our asses still another time. Ironically, our adversary was our friend Gary Cabozzi. We loved Gary. His out-of-his-mind James Brown gyrations to our music will forever be part of Aerosmith folklore. He had been our protector. But as time went on, his protective tactics proved too crude. Frank felt it best that Gary be replaced by John O'Toole. Near as I can recall, I was recruited to tell Gary the bad news. I decided not to do it in person. I knew Gary would flip out and lose it. Better to do it by phone.

"Hey, man," I said. "It isn't that we don't love you, because we do. And it isn't that we don't appreciate everything you've done for us, because we do. You were there in the beginning and we'll never forget that."

"What the fuck are you trying to say, Joe?"

"All I'm saying is that things have changed and Frank wants to streamline our operation. Frank thinks it's better for everyone if John O'Toole does our road management."

"I like John," said Gary. "I've been working with him. I'll keep working with him. What's the problem?"

"That's just the point, Gary. There is no problem. We just want to keep working with John and Frank and, well, it doesn't look like your job is necessary."

"Not necessary? What the fuck do you mean? Is that what John and Frank said? If they did, I know you guys told them to go straight to hell, right?"

"Not exactly. Actually, we agree with John and Frank."

"You're firing me?"

"You don't have to look at it that way. You can just see it as a change. Things are changing for us."

"I tell you what's gonna change," said Gary. "Your life's gonna change. Or let me put it another way—your life's gonna end. And not just yours, Joe, but Steven's and Tom's and the whole lot of you miserable assholes. I don't need to hear this shit, after what I've done for your band. I've sweated blood for you guys. And now I'm getting that blood back. I'm grabbing my shotgun and I'm coming after each of you lousy motherfuckers and I'm blowing your fuckin' brains out."

Given Gary's nature, I didn't doubt him. I immediately called Frank, who urged that we all get out of town. With Frank behind the wheel, we escaped to the Sheraton off the Mass Pike, the hotel known to locals as the Castle. We settled in a large suite and sat around debating the seriousness of Gary's threat. In my heart I did not believe that Cabozzi would murder us in cold blood. But it was Frank's sense of drama, not my sense of Gary, that led the way. After a couple of hours and a lot of scotches, Frank decided we should go to Giro's and see John O'Toole.

At Giro's, the North End steakhouse where we'd met Frank the first time, Connelly was king. He always received a celebrity welcome. Before long the bourbon was flowing and none of us was feeling any pain. An hour later, John O'Toole arrived.

"My good man, John," said Frank. "Did you remember to bring the hardware?"

I watched O'Toole slip Frank a chrome-plated .44 Magnum. This was no Saturday night special, but the kind of outsize pistol favored by Roy Rogers. Frank stuffed the huge weapon in his belt. As the evening went on, the drinking intensified. With every shot of bourbon, thoughts of Gary Cabozzi faded. We felt safe.

"Look who just came in," shouted Frank. "My dear friend Ricardo Montalban. You must meet him."

With that, Frank got up and escorted us to Montalban's table. As we made our way over, however, the .44 Magnum slipped out of Frank's belt and fell to the floor. All action stopped. Every head turned. But Frank was cool. He picked up the gun, gracefully placed it back in his belt, and greeted the actor with great warmth.

"These are my boys," he told Montalban, "the rock-and-roll band that will soon be conquering the civilized world."

No one mentioned the gun, Montalban bought us drinks, and at evening's end we were all drunk and convinced that the threat from Cabozzi was over. Fortunately, that proved true. Gary's love for us overwhelmed his rage. Our friendship was eventually renewed.

Our hope was that Leber-Krebs would convince Columbia to put money behind our album. But hope isn't muscle, and the truth is that, for all their bragging, our managers lacked muscle. The label, deeply in love with Springsteen, saw us as a throwaway. Later I'd learn they almost dropped us, but we were such a low priority they didn't even bother doing that.

Back in Boston, Frank kept our spirits high. "Boys," he said, "the battle has just begun. It's going to be a long campaign and it can only be won on the road. Treat every city, every market, every performance like a battle. This is hand-to-hand combat, gentlemen. This is trench warfare. So eat hearty. Drink hearty. Fortify yourself. Sharpen your swords and steel your determination. There is no going back. There is only forward motion. Victory will not be easy, but victory—bloody and hard-won—will be yours."

We took these words to heart. The battle plan came down to one thing—the road. If they paid us to play, we'd play. And we vowed to play anywhere, everywhere, all the time, every night, all night, no matter how long it took to get played on the radio, no matter how long it took get people to start buying our record.

Normally we'd go on the road from one to three weeks at a time. Sometimes we drove ourselves—just the five of us. On longer stretches

John O'Toole would come along. As 1972 turned to 1973, this was still the era when every city had its version of the Fillmore, old theaters that had been converted to rock clubs that held anywhere from five hundred to three thousand fans. These were fabled venues that excited our imaginations, given that we were rock fans ourselves—the big Masonic Temple in Detroit; the rock palaces of Pittsburgh, Philly, Toronto, and St. Louis. Night after night we played the shit out of our first album. Our live performances were ten times better than the record. The musical energy was high, we were high, the fans were high.

The groupie phenomenon was still in full swing, but given my relationship with Elyssa, I was even less interested than before. If a chick was willing to jump into my bed, that only meant she had jumped into the bed of another musician the night before. Contracting the clap was as common as a hangover. I wasn't looking to score chicks. I was looking to score fans. I wanted every last person who came to our show to remember us. After the shows, we'd sit in our dressing room and listen to the crowd leaving the venue. If we didn't hear much noise, we were disappointed. But if we heard fans screaming with excitement—shouting out our lyrics over the sound of breaking bottles—we knew it was a good fuckin' night.

On a rainy weekend afternoon on our way to a gig, our hearts started hammering when a cop pulled us over in New Jersey. The state trooper didn't look much older than us. We thought he might give us a break. No such luck.

"Get out of the car," he said before calling for backup.

The second we stepped out, the rain turned into a torrential downpour. While we stood there getting soaked, I remembered that back in Boston a friend had slipped me a joint that I'd stuffed into my pocket. My plan had been to give it to Brad, who loved weed. As it turned out, Brad had stuck two ounces of his own pot down his pants. When the second trooper arrived, they searched me, but not Brad, and discovered my joint. That gave them cause to haul us down to the local station, where we were lined up and chained by our hands to a wall. After a few minutes one of the troopers started shouting something about a Black Panthers riot in Newark. Just like that, cops were swarming everywhere, grabbing their shotguns, and heading out the door.

In the midst of the excitement, Steven whispered to Brad, "Give me your pot."

"Why?"

"Just give it to me, goddammit."

Because Steven was next to an open door, he was able to free his hands and throw the two bags of weed into the next room. In all the commotion, no one saw him to do it. We were relieved until we were unchained and escorted one at a time into that very room—the interrogation room—to be fingerprinted. When I got into the room I saw that the two bags of pot had landed on the corner of a table in full view. Somehow the troopers searching us didn't see the pot, or maybe they figured it was evidence from another case. Who knows? Who cares? In the end, all they had was my one rain-soaked joint. A court date was set. The day we came back for the hearing, we were huddled around the motel TV watching the Watergate hearings. I said, "And you think we have problems!" Our problem was over quickly. Frank's lawyer got the charges dropped. There was only a small fine to pay.

It was also Frank who found a pair of brothers with a couple of limos to take us on a three-week run through Ohio, playing every club in the state. Frank also replaced O'Toole with Robert "Kelly" Keller, whose stomach was the size of a small continent. Kelly consumed beer like elephants consume peanuts.

Steven wasn't really a beer guy—his main things were Tuinals and shooting cocaine whenever cocaine was around—but Steven was competitive. Skinny Steven wanted to go toe-to-toe with fat Kelly. One night after a gig they got into it.

After twelve or more beers, Steven was gone. We put him to bed so he could sleep it off before we went to another one of our rooms to see how much damage could be done in ten minutes. The idea of wrecking a hotel room was a rite of passage. We'd heard that Led Zeppelin had done it and felt obligated to uphold the tradition. On this particular night beds were overturned. Sinks were pulled from the wall. Televisions, chairs, and desks were destroyed. Mission accomplished, we took off in our limo for the next gig. Tyler woke up the morning after to find two state policemen at his door. They weren't going to let him leave until the damage—caused by us—was paid for. This was never our intention. We were going to send a limo back to pick up Steven and drive him to the venue. He said he climbed down a rainspout and hitchhiked, but with Steven, you never know. I have a feeling he slept off his hangover in the back of the limo like we had planned. He showed up at the gig and sang his ass off.

When you're a baby band looking to open for a more prominent act, you can't be choosy. Your hope is that their audience will become your audience. It's a way to expand your fan base. But in the instance of our first tour with a name band, that didn't happen. Our managers had us opening for the Mahavishnu Orchestra, whose sophisticated audience had no interest in what we were playing.

John McLaughlin, Mr. Mahavishnu, was an incredible guitarist of world stature, a virtuoso who had helped lead Miles Davis into fusion, a wildly creative meeting ground between rock and jazz. His cohorts—Billy Cobham on drums, Jan Hammer on keys, Rick Laird on bass, and Jerry Goodman on violin—were tremendous technicians. The band bordered on genius. They lit incense and burned candles and, dressed in white, looked like monks. Seeing them live was almost a religious experience. Not that they weren't loud. McLaughlin had a mountain of Marshalls and let loose a sound you could hear three states away. Their music held nothing for me, but I appreciated their skill. And, unfortunately, their audience didn't appreciate us. Their audience had come to hear musical masters, not some up-and-coming garage band.

Mahavishnu's fans would boo us or call out "Vishnoo, Vishnoo, Vishnoo" during the middle of our set. I understood their frustration. But we still put on the best show we could. When we got through and the Mahavishnu men came out, they asked for a moment of silence, as if to purify the air that we had polluted with our rock-and-roll chaos. They then sounded a gong, whose echo was followed by an explosion of their amazing music. Instantly, their crowd forgot that we had even played.

When we finally found ourselves opening for a more suitable act—the

Kinks—it hardly helped our confidence. That's because Ray Davies gave us no respect. He was known for treating his support acts like shit and proved true to form. Usually the headliner has no problem allowing the opening band a sound check. Not Davies. We had to go out there cold. No matter, crowd-wise it was a step up from Mahavishnu. Kinks fans heard what we were doing and liked it.

We had no real fans in the press. Most of the reviews—whether of our record or our live shows—made the Rolling Stones analogy. Mick had big lips and so did Steven. Standing right next to him was the dark, brooding lead guitarist. Only a very few writers took us seriously. Even fewer actually listened to us. The *Point*, a hippie paper in Providence, put Steven on the cover and wrote that we played like our lives depended on it. And *Creem*, the Detroit-based rock magazine who'd been hip to the Dolls before anyone, completely got us. They called us the real deal.

At the time of our emergence I wasn't interested in defining our place in the musical landscape. We just wanted to play for the people. We wanted to work. But looking back, I have a different perspective. I see us as one of the first American bands to grow out of the heady concoction of blues-based English rock that had dominated the previous decade. Like everyone, we knew the Beatles' and Stones' stuff, and, like everyone, we absorbed it. But I really cut my teeth on Ten Years After, Peter Green's Fleetwood Mac, and the Yardbirds. These bands had the live energy that I wanted. Because these groups had either dissipated or moved to the sidelines, I saw a vacancy that Aerosmith could fill. We could put a new slant on the blues rock tradition and start a new fire to dance around. The critics didn't get that, but fuck the critics. We were playing for the fans and they were getting it in a big way.

Despite Steven's extroverted nature, in these early years he was reluctant to talk to the audience. I'm not sure why. Offstage, he couldn't stop talking. Onstage, something else happened. Before the first record came out, he'd trimmed his name from Tallarico to Tyler, making it easier to remember. He wanted to be remembered. We all did. But facing an audience, he was deeply insecure about addressing them. Because he would whip the mic stand around, the crew would use strips of cloth to hold it together. As time went on, the cloth got longer. Steven added his scarves. That's how the scarf thing began. Tying a bunch of colorful scarves to the mic stand gave him something to hide behind. Fiddling with the scarves during a guitar solo gave him something to do with his hands. He was still working out his stage schtick.

It was a strange paradox—chatty on the street, reticent onstage. A crowd wants to be acknowledged and engaged. If we were playing, say, in Detroit and the Tigers or the Lions had just won a big game, they want to hear "How 'bout those Tigers!" or "How 'bout those Lions!" They want to hear *something* from the lead singer. But Steven was reluctant to say a word. Once he opened his mouth to sing he was great. But when it came to ingratiating himself with a few simple words to the fans, he balked.

When I questioned him about it, he bristled. He said he didn't want to mouth a bunch of clichés. I said it didn't have to be clichéd. It was just a way of welcoming the crowd. If it was so important, he said, why didn't I do it?

"Okay, Steven, I will." That's the last thing he wanted—me engaging the crowd. His ego couldn't handle that. The argument continued . . .

"The mic is for singing, not talking," he said.

"I'm not talking about a lot of talking. Just a little. Just enough for you to acknowledge the fans and loosen them up."

"The music does that."

"A little foreplay wouldn't hurt."

"I'm not into foreplay, I'm into fucking."

Detroit is a gutsy city, a working-class blues roots and rock kind of place. Detroit is Motown. Detroit's a hardworking metropolis, and Detroiters recognize a hardworking band. Before us, Boston's J. Geils, one of the great live bands, owned Detroit. So when Detroit heard about a new up-and-coming band from Boston, their attitude was, "Okay, boys, let's see what you got." Knowing that Detroit liked balls-to-the-wall rock, we hit it especially hard. During our run at the Michigan Palace, we won over the city. From then on Detroit became an Aerosmith stronghold. Even during our worst slumps, we could count on Detroit. For that matter, all those struggling cities where the factories were closing and the suburbs had stolen their thunder—Cincy and Dayton, Cleveland and Toledo—responded to a struggling band. They needed our energy and we needed theirs.

We made it through the cold Midwestern winter of '73 and went back to Boston, hoping to reconnect with the hometown crowd on something called Summerthing, a series of big outdoor concerts on the Common, right in the middle of the city, a perfect place to make a splash and remind the local fans that we had a record in the stores. J. Geils, James Taylor, Bonnie Raitt, and Loudon Wainwright III were all considered, like us, Boston-based acts. They were all scheduled to perform. Wouldn't we be the perfect addition?

"That's precisely what I said," said Frank. "I told the promoters they cannot possibly do this concert series without you. But unfortunately, boys, the promoters didn't see it that way."

"What did they see?" I asked.

"They see you as a band whose first album has failed."

"We can't even get an opening slot?"

"I'm afraid not, Joe. I'm afraid that once again we're facing impresarios with limited vision. But be not discouraged. The vision will hold because the vision is true. Be brave, be strong, be not distracted, and you will not be defeated."

During down times Frank was always there for us. Frank was there to take us out for big steak dinners in fancy restaurants with red leather booths and old-school bartenders. Frank brought the blarney. My fervent wish was that Frank, and not Leber-Krebs, could have been our frontline manager as we navigated the tricky waters of those early tours. But Frank was fading. Like my father's, his struggles with cancer were intensifying.

However, there was one bright light that showed us our fan base in Boston was growing. We played a show at Suffolk Downs with Sha Na Na headlining. They had become national headliners but most of the band was from Boston. The show was sold out and it was obvious that a large part of the audience was there to see us. In fact, at the end of our set, they threw their empty beer cans in unison straight up in the air. It darkened the sky. It took us by surprise but it made us realize Boston was taking us to their hearts. Steven and I hitchhiked home from that show. Were we so excited and wanted to get home to celebrate.

On one of those rare occasions when I made the forty-five-minute drive from Boston to Hopedale to visit Dad in the hospital, he said he was better but his appearance told me that he was not out of the woods.

I brought him the first Columbia album we had just received. It represented the most success I had ever realized.

"Is it selling?" Dad asked. "Are they playing it on the radio?"

"It's doing great."

"Are you tired of touring?" he asked.

"No, touring's fun."

"I suppose," said Dad, "that the idea is if you keep touring the records will start selling."

"That's the idea," I said. "The music business is rough and we're not making a lot, but we're making progress. As a matter of fact the band and I finally saved enough to pay you back the money you loaned us for our bus."

It felt great to hand my father a check. I could see that he was surprised and pleased. I waited for Dad to say words of approval. I wanted him to say, *I'm proud of you. This is a real record from a real record company. You've come a long way since those days when you were begging us for an electric guitar. You've really stuck with something. I admire you, son. I'm proud of you, son. I love you, son.*

I sensed he had those feelings but couldn't express them. He couldn't say anything. He was emotionally consumed by the fact that his cancer had returned.

"I gotta go," I said. "I love you, Dad. See you soon," and with a hug I left and headed back to Boston.

When we learned that Leber-Krebs were coming to Boston to get us to re-sign their management contract, I called a band meeting. I wanted us to hire a lawyer. The only person I felt connected with was Laura Kaufman, the publicist in Leber-Krebs's office who was devoted to Aerosmith. She had a beautiful spirit and a huge heart and genuinely loved us. But I still had enormous trust issues with both Steve Leber and David Krebs. I knew we needed a lawyer.

"What for?" asked Steven.

"We have no way of knowing whether Leber-Krebs are screwing us."

"Leber-Krebs are all we have."

"That doesn't mean we shouldn't have some kind of checks and balance."

"They don't want us looking over their shoulders."

"I don't care what they want," I said. "They need to be accountable. We need an outside counselor."

My argument got nowhere. My bandmates were reluctant to challenge our management.

"Besides," said Steven, "Columbia's letting us do a second album. Leber-Krebs are close to Columbia. Now's not the time to rock the boat."

"I don't care," I said. "I'm bringing my own lawyer."

Elyssa's cousin was not an entertainment lawyer, but he was a lawyer nonetheless, with a small practice in Somerville. When he accompanied me to the management meeting, the band was annoyed, and Leber and Krebs were somewhat shocked. Quickly realizing he had no experience with music contracts, Leber and Krebs took him into another room, where they reassured him they were presenting us with a standard management contract. The rest of the band signed with no questions. On the advice of my lawyer, I signed with lots of questions, which basically were never answered.

We wanted back in the studio. I myself was eager to see if we could capture the sound that had eluded us the first time. Leber-Krebs definitely earned their keep by convincing Columbia to give us a second shot with another record, but it was Frank who kept us alive long enough to get those showcases at Max's Kansas City. Frank was the true believer.

It was also Frank who told Leber-Krebs that if we were to cut a second record, the band better move back in together and concentrate on writing. The idea was to dislodge us from all distractions—like women and partying—and get us to focus. We got an apartment in Brookline and rehearsal space in the dungeon-like basement of a store called Drummer's Image on Newbury Street.

Tiger, Joey's Great Dane, who was big as a small pony, became the beloved band dog and joined us in our Beacon Street apartment. He had a frisky temperament and would jump on you the second you walked through the door. With his paws on your shoulders, he'd look down at you while giving you a face full of tongue.

Though girlfriends were prohibited, I made an exception for Elyssa, who was over practically every night. Soon all of the other guys followed suit and invited their women as well.

Steven and I fell into a writing routine. Sometimes we'd work at home, where we set up a drum kit for Steven and an amp for me. That's where we wrote "Same Old Song and Dance" and I came up with the riff to "SOS," a song for which Steven already had lyrics.

The Perry/Tyler team was not a fully formed unit. But then again, it never would be. For the most part, we were playing our club set. "Train Kept a-Rollin'," for example, recorded by Tiny Bradshaw during the swing era, Johnny Burnette in the fifties, and revised by the Yardbirds and Led Zeppelin in the sixties, had long been part of our show and thus became part of our second record.

Back at the Drummer's Image, the whole band worked as a unit to hone material for the new album. We'd jam for five or six hours at a time, stopping to run back to the apartment to catch reruns of *The Three Stooges*. The TV was in Brad's room, where all five of us religiously watched the episodes, no matter how many times we had seen them before. The Marx Brothers may be wittier, and Chaplin and Keaton are geniuses, but my heart is with the Stooges—then, now, and forever.

On one of those afternoons when we arrived back at the Beacon Street apartment, we opened the door expecting to be pounced on by Tiger. Instead we found the dog spread out on the floor. We panicked and were about to rush him to the vet when we realized that Tiger had gotten to the plate of pot brownies left atop the fridge. Clearly he had scarfed them down. That night he was the only one partying.

Columbia said they wanted us to cut the record in a "real studio," which in their mind meant a place in New York. They also insisted that Bob Ezrin, who had worked with Alice Cooper, produce the album. We were impressed by his credentials but weren't all that happy to learn that, before agreeing to work with us, he'd have to come to Boston to hear us play. Couldn't he just listen to our first album and figure out whether we met his criteria? No matter—he came, he liked us, and he signed on. We drove down to New York, checked into the Ramada Inn on Forty-Eighth Street, and headed over to the Record Plant, a famous facility most recently used by Little Feat. Back in the sixties it was where Hendrix had cut *Electric Ladyland*. This was our first time recording in a state-of-the-art studio.

When we arrived, Ezrin introduced us to Jack Douglas, his engineer. For all practical purposes, Jack became our producer. Ezrin might have shown up three or four times, but only to make suggestions, like that of bringing in additional musicians to augment our sound. We were okay with using top-flight horn men like trumpeter Randy Brecker and his brother Michael on tenor. We had, after all, already set the precedent for horns on the first album. Moreover, our policy was "Let's try anything."

At times I was easy to work with. And then there were times when I wasn't. These were the days when I was building up a definite arrogance. During one session, for example, we were sitting out in the studio wearing headphones when the feedback blasted my years. I reacted impulsively, without thinking.

"What the hell is wrong with you motherfuckers?" I barked. "Can't you get anything right?"

Jack got up from the board, left the control room, and came over to my chair.

"Look, Joe, if you have a complaint, I'm happy to hear it. But if you talk that way again to us, I'm coming out and busting you in the fuckin' mouth."

I saw his point and apologized. From that moment on, Jack and I became friends. Within a year or two he would become our main producer and a man critically important to the rise of our band. At this point, I saw Jack as a no-nonsense New Yorker with a tough attitude, deep knowledge of the studio, and a great East Coast sense of humor.

An example: One night after we'd gone home, Jack and Jay, our engineer, brought in a bunch of live crabs and affixed them to the ceiling of the studio with superglue and fishing line. Fortunately, we weren't the first people to arrive the next morning. The first guy in was a hippie who worked in the office. He had to make his way in total darkness through the studio to find the light switch. The fact that he was tripping on acid didn't help his ability to adjust to the dangling crabs. His freak-out lasted for days.

I've never freaked in the studio. I see the studio as a sanctuary, a place—like the ocean floor—to explore. The exploration of sound is endlessly fascinating to me. In this early phase I faced great frustration. I wanted to know more than I knew. I wanted to play more than I was capable of playing. And I wanted to realize a sound that eluded me. Jack Douglas helped enormously. He became a great teacher. But Jack could only work with what we gave him. And I wanted to give him more.

We all did. We all put in endless hours, fueled by whatever substances were available. When we finally ran out of gas, we reluctantly left the studio. As the first light of dawn was turning night to day, we walked down the middle of Eighth Avenue to our hotel. We were carrying our guitars and didn't want to get mugged. In those days the center of Manhattan was a seedy place. You could smell its decay. We probably didn't smell much better. After fourteen or fifteen hours of playing, we didn't have a lot to say to each other.

On one hand, it was satisfying to say that we were in New York City cutting a second album, but on the other hand, I knew that the album, in spite of a few bright spots, still didn't capture the power of the band. We were better than the record we were making. And yet I didn't know how to get there. I didn't know how to get from good to great.

My frustration intensified after someone stole my black Stratocaster from the studio. Losing a guitar is like losing a friend. That fucked me up for months.

We pressed on. We cut "Seasons of Wither," another ballad. I still didn't love ballads, out of general principle, but this one had a haunting feeling that I dug. It turned out that, with all our work, we were still one song short. That's when we took a riff and lyrics left over from one of Steven's earlier bands and, with the five of us in one room, fashioned a new song.

In an all-night lock-up session in Studio C, we knocked out "Lord of the Thighs"—a nod to the novel *Lord of the Flies* that reflected the seedy side of New York we kept seeing on our walks up Eighth Avenue.

A̲ll this happened in the fall of 1973. Meanwhile, Columbia rereleased "Dream On"—the ballad from our first album—as a single. To make it more commercial, they put an orchestra over the original track without our involvement or approval. I had mixed feelings because I didn't see the song as emblematic of the band. It was soft and we were hard. Yet the song hit the pop charts and started moving up. Give credit to Maxanne Sartori at WBCN in Boston. Maxanne played the hell out of it. As one of the first female DJs, she was a pioneer and one of our greatest champions. At a time when our critics were calling us too derivative, Maxanne called us originals and never wavered in her support.

Even though "Dream On" eventually became a classic, for years Steven was outraged at the A&R people for messing with it without his consultation. I understood his rage. That's like an art dealer taking a painting by, say, Picasso and adding a few lines here and there to make it sell quicker. I don't mean to imply that we were Picasso, but we were damn serious about our music. We should have at least been consulted. We couldn't complain, however, about the results.

I would have been happier if our first hit had been hard-core rock and roll, but a hit is a hit. A hit meant we'd have a better shot at survival. With our second album coming out, "Dream On" pushed our debut album onto the charts, although it didn't get very high. But that was okay. We were on our way.

As "Dream On" was building, we were headlining small clubs. The more "Dream On" airplay, the bigger the crowds. When we got back to Boston, it was like a light switch had been turned on, and we saw something we had never seen before. It happened at a high school auditorium in Shrewsbury. Frank had booked the gig. The place was packed with twenty-five hundred fans. There was an excitement that was entirely new. The fans knew all our lyrics. They wouldn't let us off the stage until we played three, four, five encores. They were out of their minds for our music.

After that night, Frank spoke to us in the dressing room.

"You know, boys," he said, "Sinatra had his day at the Paramount back in the forties. Elvis had his day in Memphis in the fifties, and the Beatles had their day on *Ed Sullivan* in the sixties. Well, today is such a day for you. And if you have any doubts, here's the proof."

From his briefcase he pulled out the fattest wad of money I had ever seen.

"This represents only a part of tonight's receipts," he said. "From now on, gentlemen, you can put your money problems behind you. Your future is not only rosy, it is as green as the greenest Irish pasture."

I knew we still had a long way to go, but gone were the days when we spent hours phoning our friends, pleading with them to come to the club so we could show the owner that we actually had a few fans. This was a moment I'd never forget, and certainly one of the most exciting in the history of our band. The thrill hasn't been matched by anything since.

I got further confirmation of our rising popularity when, a few days later, we played the field house at Boston College. The frenzy over our music turned into a riot. Fans who couldn't get in used railroad ties to smash in the doors. Shattered glass showered us as we huddled in the dressing room. The riot was ongoing. When we got to a brand-new Boston nightspot called the Box—where the old Psychedelic Supermarket had stood in the sixties—fans were lined up around the block. With over twenty-five hundred screaming music fans crammed together and hundreds more beating on the doors to get in, the police revoked the Box's license and closed the place down. I was told that the band posed a danger to civil decency—a statement that was music to my ears.

When your record comes out, you have high hopes. You've worked your ass off, you've heard the stuff a million times, the mixes are swimming around your brain, and you're convinced there are least three or four hits on the album. Your girlfriend—in my case, Elyssa—is telling you how great it is. When you play it for your friends, they say the same thing. You've sold yourself big-time and anything less than a smash will be a disappointment.

Get Your Wings came out in the first quarter of 1974, complete with an image of our new winged logo on the cover. We'd worked the road before and played every gig like it was our last. But now we were playing bigger venues before bigger crowds.

The touring never stopped. We never stopped playing Detroit, never stopped playing Columbus, Fort Wayne, Cincinnati, Cleveland. We felt like if we could win the heart of America, the rest of the country would follow. Back in Boston, the tables finally turned and instead of opening as a baby band we got booked into the Orpheum as headliners. Blue Öyster Cult opened for us.

But other than those theaters in Boston and Detroit, we were still an opening act. Name 'em and we opened for 'em: REO Speedwagon, Argent, Suzi Quatro, in our never-ending search for new fans in new parts of the country.

Our first full-tilt rock-and-roll tour had us as the openers, followed by the New York Dolls in the middle slot and then the headliners Mott the Hoople, hot with their huge hit "All the Young Dudes."

Until now, the English groups hadn't given us much respect. They tended to be arrogant, distant, and downright hostile. Mott was different. They were great guys, a solid rock band that blew me away the first time I saw them at the Tea Party in Boston. As arena rock performers, they showed us the tricks of the trade.

By then David Johansen, the charismatic lead singer of the New York Dolls, and I were buddies, and Elyssa had become friends with David's wife Cyrinda Foxe, a glamorous woman who, as part of the underground world of Andy Warhol, had appeared in Warhol's *Bad*. David and I had spent time together running the streets of his ultrahip New York, visiting art dealers, drug dealers, and performance artists of every ilk. David was a pioneer, an early rock anarchist.

On this tour, the Dolls clung to that New York arrogance that had served them so well in the Big Apple but nowhere else. There was also resentment. By then we thought we were a better band. But because they were press darlings, we had to open for them. The Dolls, who acted like the headliners, also resented opening for Mott. They demanded cases of champagne, went on late, and often didn't bother to show up at all.

This was my first time seeing how hard drugs could stop a band in its tracks. I knew that on their first trip to England in 1972 their first drummer, Billy Murcia, had died a drug-related death. Back then, they were already on the highway to hell. They were on that highway when, at the Holiday Inn in Florida, I looked out the window and there in the hot summer sun I saw their bass player, Killer Kane, stagger by the pool in the stage clothes he had worn the night before—thigh-high furry platform boots, torn leotard, a stained and ripped leather jacket. His face was covered in sweat, his makeup running, his lipstick smeared. He could barely walk as he screamed out, "Where's the nearest liquor store?" He needed to get his morning bottle of blackberry brandy that, even at his young age, was the only thing his stomach could handle. He was clearly killing himself.

My heart went out to Johansen, who was trying to keep it together. Yet, seeing that the Midwestern and Southern audiences didn't relate to his band, David was consumed by bitterness and left the tour halfway through.

I couldn't help but draw comparisons between the Dolls and Aerosmith. After all, we were going after the same audience. Yet there were big differences between us. We had our makeup and our scarves and our attention-grabbing stage outfits, but we avoided the gender bending. That just wasn't us. For the most part, our fans were college kids or working guys who liked to party to hard rock and roll. We wrote, recorded, and played to please that audience. So, unlike the Dolls, we didn't run the risk of coming on like elitists. We also thought we knew our limits when it came to drugs and drinking. This, of course, would prove to be a lie, but it was a lie that, at the time, I believed. I'd get high but not fall-down high. I'd get loaded but not to where I couldn't play. In fact—at least in this beginning stage—you could argue that the booze and the blow could not only be felt in the music but amplified the character of the music. I'm convinced that later on, when we got better drugs, the music got better as well.

If you're an addict—and Aerosmith would eventually prove to be a band of addicts—the drugs will take you out. Ultimately the drugs have to be put down. Either you kill them or they kill you. But for a twenty-two-year-old like me, it took a very long time to come to that realization. It was the easiest thing in the world for me to look at the dying Dolls and say "That'll never happen to us. We're too professional to put on a sloppy show. We're too concerned about our fans to disappoint them. We give them our best every night. We're rocking harder than ever, and all the drugs are doing are putting more fuel in our tank. The drugs aren't killing our motivation; they're adding to it; it's all working together. Besides, waving a bottle of Jack Daniel's guarantees us a huge response from our fans."

This was the same period when I had a front-row seat at both the death of the Dolls and the birth of Kiss. Kiss, whose first album had just come out, was slated to open for us in Marion, Ohio. It was a weird venue. The promoter put us in a dinner theater setting. Even though he had removed the chairs and tables, you could still smell the baked fish from the buffet.

I was always curious to hear a new band, figuring I could learn something from the competition. And I usually did. The guys in Kiss were wearing tight pants, leather jackets, and the kind of seven-inch black platform boots you could buy in the Village. The big thing, of course, was how they painted their faces. In comparison to the Dolls, though, who wore tutus and dresses, that was hardly shocking.

While it was true that Kiss's road crew and ours didn't get along—there was at least one nasty backstage fight—I had no problems with Gene, Paul, Ace, or Peter. I liked them. All of their tunes were good basic rock and roll. Even more importantly, they were pushing the envelope when it came to putting on a show. Their drum riser moved up and down, something of a novelty. Gene was also either breathing fire or eating fire—I can't remember which. Rockets had not yet started firing off of Ace's guitar, but even at this low-tech starting point, the audience loved the gimmicks. You couldn't deny that Kiss was introducing something novel to rock and roll.

Most musicians were competitive about their bands. I know we were, but I never took it personally. Hearing Kiss for the first time, I was quick to judge. Obviously, unlike us, they didn't come from Fleetwood Mac–rooted blues rock. They didn't come from the Yardbirds or Led Zeppelin. Kiss saw rock as extreme theater. It wasn't the Dolls' theater—the theater of ironic high camp—but a far more popular theater, the Saturday afternoon movie theater of cartoons and horror films. Kiss married rock to comic book superheroes. Brilliant!

Even though we headlined, Kiss got twice the response we did. The crowd, lukewarm for us, went nuts for them. After watching all this, I hit the roof. I went back to the dressing room and freaked out. I was pissed.

First, the Dolls get all this press love without even knowing how to tune their guitars, and now Kiss is getting all this fan love by putting on a circus show. Meanwhile, we're busting our asses trying to write songs and play them right. What the fuck!! We're banging our heads against the wall. What do we have to do to make it—paint ourselves blue and have monkeys flying out our asses? Isn't it supposed to be about the music?

As years went on and I crossed paths with Kiss many more times, we all became really good friends, especially Gene, and my attitude changed. In a certain way, Aerosmith and Kiss grew up together. There's a definite link between their audience and ours. A lot of critics attacked them—and still do—for being too gimmicky. But I came to see them as genuine innovators who understood the only thing that really matters: satisfying the fans. Through their showmanship, they turned on millions of young kids to rock and roll. For that fact alone, they deserve to be in the Rock and Roll Hall of Fame. I write them in on the ballot every year. It pisses me off that—until this year—the self-appointed gatekeepers who control entrance to the Hall have locked them out. Those gatekeepers are part of the same critical elite that looked down on us in our early (and later) years. I can understand why snobbery is part of the world of classical music or ballet or opera or even jazz. But rock and roll? Hell, when Chuck Berry said, "Roll over, Beethoven, and tell Tchaikovsky the news," wasn't he telling the snobs to fuck off? Wasn't he saying that rock and roll was busting down the doors and letting everybody in? And Cheap Trick, one of the best and hardest-working rock-and-roll bands in the land, aren't even on these people's radar.

In recent presidential elections, you see candidates pouring all their money into Ohio, the most critical swing state. Well, back in 1974 our agents must have been thinking the same way: Crack Ohio and you'll crack the rest of the country. It was a campaign to break us out as a national band. We thought we might be making some progress when *Rolling Stone* saw fit to mention our second album, saying that we were playing with "pent-up fury" and that we "maintained an agile balance between Yardbirds and Who-styled rock and seventies heavy metal." I especially liked this line: "They think 1966 and play 1974."

We played the outdoor Schaefer Music Festival in Central Park—fifty thousand people strong—where Rory Gallagher opened for us. He was a hard-drinking Irishman with his own brand of blues rock that captivated the crowd. In between songs, he'd belt down another Irish lightning that seemed to add to his energy. He kept playing and playing, way beyond his cutoff time. Afraid of inciting a riot, the promoters let him go on—at our expense. When he finally left the stage, the crowd, wanting more Rory, started throwing cans and bottles. We set up among the flying debris. The debris kept flying during our set. Brad got hit and a broken bottle cut Joey's arm, but in defiance, we held our ground and played, only to be cut off by the curfew. I remember it as the only time that we were blown off fair and square in true rock-and-roll style. That night Rory Gallagher was just too good to stop.

In our own camp, the friction between Steven and me never stopped. After every show, the dressing room became the battleground. Tom, Joey, and Brad would watch as we went at it—Steven the perfectionist versus Joe the anarchist. Ironically, our contrary energies gave Aerosmith the edge over many other bands. But that knowledge didn't take the sting out of the fights. Steven would often start off by coughing so hard that he was able to spit out pinkish phlegm. "It's blood!" he'd cry. "I'm coughing up blood for this band!" My answer was, "That wouldn't have anything to do with that sandpaper version of coke that you snorted up before the show, would it?"

Listening to these arguments, outsiders might have thought that we were on the verge of murdering each other. They also might also have thought that the band was about to break up. But the opposite was true. This was a period when we were motivated beyond reason. Come hell or high water, we were going all the way.

PART 3

THE CLASSIC ALBUMS

TOYS

Experimenting with alcohol—and then drugs—was a minor distraction in the first years of Aerosmith. Even earlier, substances were incidental to what I was doing as a teen—struggling at school, working at the factory, learning the guitar, and forming baby bands. I used drink and drugs to get me past points of shyness and reticence. They afforded me certain comforts. I could hide behind them or I could stand in front of them. I considered them a friendly, useful tool. Because I was shy and never liked crowds, I faced this paradox: I possessed an iron confidence in my talent but had a bit of a complex about showing it off. Later I'd learn the term *performance anxiety*. At the time, I just called it nerves. All the way back to my days with Flash, I'd count on a shot of Jack Daniel's to both loosen me up and calm my shakes. It always worked to the point where I was never without a pint in my guitar case. It was always one shot—no more, no less.

As the age of hedonism hardened in the seventies, drugs became more prominent—and so did our skepticism about the government's view of them. Pot was called a "gateway" drug, while we knew from experience that it did little more than mellow you out. In contrast, legal alcohol fueled all sorts of violence and deadly crashes. We didn't believe anything the government said about drugs.

As Aerosmith spent our first three or four years on the road, establishing ourselves as rockers to be reckoned with, each of us became connoisseurs of the drugs of our choice. This was particularly true of Steven and me. We looked at the more exotic drugs the way wine cognoscenti viewed vintages of Beaujolais or pinot noir. I liked coke. I had a couple of dealers who once in a while would bring me excellent stuff, which would be quickly consumed. Then I'd be cool until the next shipment hit town. I'd compare it to going to a party expecting to drink beer and having someone walk in with a bottle of twelve-year-old single malt. You have a few hits and then it's gone. You don't wrap your life around it; you enjoy it in the moment and then let the moment go.

Once in a great while I'd save a line of coke if I knew I'd be writing. But if the coke wasn't there, I'd write anyway. I wrote what has become my most famous riff—"Walk This Way"—totally straight. The goal was always to access that place and spirit where riffs flew off my guitar. I had tried it Steven's way—grinding away at an idea, beating it to death, going over it again and again. But for me that killed the magic. I sought spontaneous inspiration. At certain times, certain drugs could trigger that inspiration. Truth be told, at least for a while, the drugs worked. I could write both stoned and straight, yet I'd be lying if I said that a couple of beers or a couple of lines didn't lubricate the process.

Writing was on our minds as we began our third album, *Toys in the Attic*. When I think of the toys, I think of guitars and the all the cool and ever-improving paraphernalia that goes along with the instrument. At the time, I was deep into Strats, and like all Strat fanatics, I faced the problem of what happens when you get crazy with the whammy bar that creates vibrato: The instrument goes out of tune. (Just listen to Hendrix's live recordings.) I got the idea that I could correct the situation by designing a bridge-and-nut combination on the bar that would control the vibrato and keep the guitar in tune. With scraps of wood, a neck from a broken guitar, disparate spare parts, and a battery of hacksaws, files, and electric drills, I went to work. After toiling deep into the night for weeks at a time, I finally put together a bulletproof whammy bar and actually got the thing to work. It was so jerry-rigged, though, that I was unable to mount it on a real guitar. For that, I needed the expertise of a machinist or engineer. Realizing that I should be writing rather than re-designing, I abandoned the project. Ironically, a few years later Floyd Rose, using the same principles I was toying with, manufactured the first locking vibrato arm.

My lifelong obsession with guitars reached a new level when, in this same period, I acquired my first '59 Les Paul. The Les Pauls that Gibson produced that year are the greatest vintage crop the instrument has ever known. I wasn't into collecting guitars—that would come later—as much as I was looking for the instrument that expressed what I was hearing in my head. Brad Whitford and I shared this passion for the right sound and listened closely to figure out how we could most effectively complement one another. Since Aerosmith was and will always be primarily a live band, it was the live interaction between two guitars that interested me most.

Three-piece groups—like Hendrix, Cream, and Jeff Beck—sounded great on record because, in many instances, they would overdub other instruments. But live—at least to my ears—they could sound somewhat empty. To honor the song, which is always the goal, we wanted the fullest sound possible. That's what Brad and I were going for. It wasn't an ironclad rule, but we generally concluded that if one of us was playing a Strat, the other should be on a Gibson. In my heart, I'll always be a Les Paul guy, but as I moved into the middle seventies, I also couldn't resist the Strat and the creative flexibility of the whammy bar.

Together, Brad and I fooled with dozens of pickups, pedals, and amps in an attempt to broaden our tone. Through his technical training at Berklee, Brad had developed a sophisticated musical vocabulary. I definitely learned from him, carefully listening to his progressions and closely watching his fingers. At the same time, he gave me all the space I needed for those riffs that jumped off my guitar out of pure instinct rather than premeditated design.

All this experimentation came to fruition on *Toys*. Our first two al-bums were basically comprised of songs we'd been playing for years live in the clubs. With *Toys*, we started from scratch. It was our first album that was written from the ground up. Making this record, we learned to be recording artists and write songs on a deadline. In the process, we began to see just what Aerosmith could accomplish. With everyone throwing in ideas, *Toys* was our breakthrough.

That breakthrough was facilitated by Jack Douglas. In the studio, he moved into the slot of the sixth member of the band. Just as the Beatles had George Martin, we had Jack. Jack was funny, loose, hip, tough, and New York. He was perfectly suited to our musical sensibility. We loved him. Just as we knew how to play our instruments, Jack knew how to play the studio. Together, we made magic.

One of Jack's gifts was simple encouragement. He did this by being present during the incubation stage. We rented a house and jammed in a converted barn in Ashland, Massachusetts, where isolation helped us focus. On many of those early days it was just a matter of Jack listening to us riff and letting us know when we hit on something strong.

One day at the end of a session, Steven, Jack, and I were standing around discussing the next day's agenda. Jack said we really needed a kick-ass up-tempo rocker. Demonstrating, he started tapping out a beat on his thighs. I picked up my '55 Les Paul Junior that I'd just gotten from Johnny Thunders and, without thinking, picked up on Jack's groove and played the riffs of a song that would eventually be called "Toys in the Attic."

"Don't know where this is coming from," I said to Steven, "but is this something you can sing to?"

"I think so," he said. "I can use the melody from the riff. Just try and throw in a few more chords."

Jack helped arrange it and, within minutes, the song was written. When it came time to record it, the band threw in their own stuff and even-tually Steven came up with lyrics. The experience reconfirmed that self-editing and unbridled spontaneity were the keys to my writing.

From Ashland we went to the Record Plant in midtown Manhattan, where we set up camp in a hotel close to the studio. Some of us brought along our girlfriends; others didn't. I mentioned "Walk This Way," one of the enduring hits off this record. I'd actually started the song months earlier at a sound check in Honolulu. I'd just replaced my stolen Strat with a new one and was starting to get to know it. Every time I pick up an unfamiliar guitar, old riffs sound new and inspire me to write. At the same time, I'd been listening to the Meters' "Hey Pocky A-Way," one of my favorite grooves. A great New Orleans band headed by singer/keyboardist Art Neville and anchored by guitarist Leo Nocentelli, drummer Zigaboo Modeliste, and bassist George Porter Jr., the Meters were cranking out the funkiest shit to come along since James Brown. (The Stones, who had them open their 1975 tour, felt the same.) Their "Cissy Strut" became an anthem for me. Other funksters seemed calculated or over-the-top. But the Meters were naturals, as evidenced especially in their bass and guitar lines. I was looking for a feel-good funk-drenched natural riff of my own.

As I wrung out this new Strat, I was making sounds that echoed the Meters. I thought it'd be cool to incorporate that kind of funk with some Aerosmith power behind it. At the Honolulu sound check, I turned to Joey and said, "Gimme something funky, like you used to play with your old R&B bands. Just lay it down." I beat out the tempo I was hearing in my head and Joey did the rest. This was his meat and potatoes. The riff flew out. I knew it needed another section—plus a chord change—that would differentiate it from the usual 1-4-5. So I just got out of my own way and started to play. The music wrote itself.

That was the music we recorded at the Record Plant. Steven scatted a few lyrics but nothing substantial. Given the power of this music, he was looking for something special. Hours passed, and still no story emerged. Jack suggested we take a break. The guys went to see Mel Brooks's *Young Frankenstein.* Having already seen and loved it, I passed and went up on the roof to chill. Later that night the guys came back, still laughing from the film. Everyone was throwing lines back and forth. Jack did a killer imitation of Marty Feldman saying, "Walk this way," the old Marx Brothers line.

"That's what we should call the song," said Tom.

"Give me a couple of minutes," said Steven, grabbing his pen and yellow pad. "I'll be right back."

When he returned, he was all smiles. "I've got it," he said. The lyrics are a great example of Steven's knack for the double entendre, something he learned from the blues tradition. The original lyrics, by the way, were written on the wall by the fire escape where Steven sat and composed them. When the record of "Walk This Way" came out, David Johansen told me, "That's the nastiest song I've ever heard on the radio."

By building an album from the ground up, we were also reshaping the sound of Aerosmith. New instruments can create new sounds. So with the first money I was starting to make, I bought a few guitars, including a six-string bass. Ever since I'd seen Peter Green play the instrument years earlier, I'd wanted one. They were fairly rare back in the mid-seventies, but I was able to find a decent one. Every instrument has secret sounds buried within it. My job was to find those sounds. This bass turned out to have "Back in the Saddle" hidden inside, but I wouldn't find it until our next record.

While working on *Toys in the Attic,* I started experimenting with open tuning. I learned that by listening to the old blues greats who, I discovered, tuned their guitars to various chords for various reasons. Driven by spontaneity, they bent or broke the rules to suit whatever was going through their heads. In this spirit, I started fooling with an open-E tuning that led to "No More No More." But when we got through arranging it, we had a problem: Our structure called for a solo in standard tuning. To solve that, we arranged the song with a breakdown near the end, allowing me to play the bulk of the song with the E-tuned guitar before switching, in the blink of an eye, to a totally different guitar to take the song out.

"Sweet Emotion," another tune from *Toys* that became a classic, was born out of a Tom Hamilton bass riff that Jack heard and encouraged Tom to expand. When Steven got around to writing the lyrics, he later said they were about his disdain for Elyssa. He was convinced that she was cutting me off from the rest of the band and threatening our future. At the time, I didn't see it that way. As far as I was concerned, the band was going full steam ahead. The truth was that Elyssa never cut me off from the band. I was playing and writing better than ever. I never missed a rehearsal or a show. It was just that the band couldn't stomach Elyssa's high school antics. And I couldn't blame them.

Frank called me out to his new house in the Boston burbs. This turned out to be one of the last times I saw him.

"I miss you, Joe," he said. "I just wanna spend a little time with you. Come out. Have dinner. And if you wind up having one too many, you can stay overnight in the guest room."

That's just what happened. Despite his physical ailments, Frank's spirit was in fine form. The first thing he did was ask about my family. I told him that my dad had been undergoing some medical tests and that I was worried. He also wanted to know how I was getting along with Steven. More than anyone, Frank knew that my relationship to Steven was the key to the band's success. And he encouraged me, for the sake of the group, to be patient.

After dinner we got to drinking. That was the night he introduced me to the lethal combination of sambuca and coffee. Frank and I kept drinking till five in the morning, at which point he excused himself to go bed. But I couldn't sleep. The sambuca had me drunk but the coffee had me wired. It was not a pleasant high. The high was further damaged by my realization that this might be the last time I'd ever get to hang out with Frank.

In the long and troubled four-decade history of Aerosmith, many men have come along to take their turns as managers. I respected Frank Connelly above all of them. He was far from perfect. His links to the underworld could have had disastrous effects. Apparently he had gone to a shady character who had loaned him a small amount of money to help us through a dry period. A few of them showed up at one of our first Boston Garden shows. They threatened to break the legs of our lead singer if we didn't give them a piece of the band. Leber-Krebs spent most of the show in the room with these guys. Somehow things got worked out peacefully. I'm sure money changed hands. Maybe it was Frank's strange but powerful karma that protected us. But one thing's for sure: Leber-Krebs proved they had the right stuff that night.

When he died a few years later, I kept picturing him in better days—with his hip shades, his ascot, his wild white hair, and his winning smile. His sister contacted me and said, "You know, Joe, Frank spoke of you often, and I'd think he'd like you to have this." She gave me Frank's silver and turquoise ring, the one he wore all the time. That meant the world to me. To this day I keep that ring on my desk along with a photo of Frank. His spirit continues to help me through hard times.

Back at the Record Plant, we still hadn't built enough toys to fill the attic. We decided to cover a song sent to us by Zunk Buker, our friend who'd gone to La Jolla. Zunk was a devotee of Dr. Demento, the über-hip DJ. That's where Zunk heard "Big Ten Inch," recorded in the early fifties by R&B powerhouse Bull Moose Jackson, who sang that when he wanted to heat up his girl, he'd whip out his big ten-inch . . . record.

The minute we heard "Big Ten Inch," we knew we had to record it. The lyrics fit right in with Steven's fondness for double entendres. Beyond that, we liked the idea of going back to an earlier era and borrowing from another genre. We didn't want to be categorized as a heavy metal band. In fact, we didn't want to be categorized at all. We were too eager to discover what was over the next musical hill to confine ourselves to one style. That both helped and hurt us. It helped because it kept our music fresh, but it hurt because record companies tend to pigeonhole acts. One exec said to me, "What am I supposed to tell the stores? Do they put Aerosmith under heavy metal—or blues—or pop?" I didn't know. That wasn't my problem. My problem was making good music. And if mixing pop ballads and old R&B with heavy rock was puzzling, maybe it's okay to be puzzled.

The great thing about working with Jack Douglas was his sense of song. He knew that "Big Ten Inch," a period piece, required a boogie-woogie piano. It was swing before swing had its resurgence in the early nineties. Jack had the good taste to recruit Scott Cushnie, who had played in the Hawks, the seminal Ronnie Hawkins band. Scott was so good that when we went on tour later that year he came along and became an honorary Aerosmithsonian, playing piano and singing harmony vocals.

When you're finished recording an album, there is a moment when you scrutinize it and have to decide whether it measures up. Well, I'm as scrutinizing as they come. Listening to *Toys in the Attic*, I felt good.

Whatever had eluded us in the first albums had finally been realized. The studio had not only captured our essence but expanded it. I was certain that we had cut an incendiary record. I wasn't waiting for validation from the record company or the critics. I was betting on our fans. All that counts are the fans.

I wasn't surprised when *Toys* went crazy, but the industry was. No one else was expecting it. The record flew out the door and, in the middle of post-Watergate America, turned Aerosmith into a supergroup. Starting in the spring of 1975, we toured like demons. Not only was *Toys* a huge hit, its success spilled over onto our first two records. In an astoundingly short period of time we were looking at three gold records. With that wind in our sails, we were excited to hit the road and do live versions of the material from *Toys*. We were ready to tear it up.

Leber-Krebs were basically running our show, booking the gigs and putting their new act, Ted Nugent, as our opener. Ted was far more interesting as a character than as an artist. He had a good lead singer—Derek St. Holmes—and a couple of decent rock songs. It was his persona, though, that won over the fans. He was the wildest wild man since Jerry Lee Lewis. You never knew what he was going to do. He'd come out in a loincloth, looking like Tarzan with a beard and crazy curly hair down to his waist. When you weren't looking, he'd pull out his bow and start shooting flaming arrows across the stage. You'd think he was a drinker but he wasn't. After the show he'd down a quart of chocolate milk to recharge his batteries so he could service the groupies lined up outside his motel room door.

I remember the time he'd flown all night from Africa, where he'd gone on a safari, barely arriving on time to open for us. Wearing buckskin covered with dried blood, he came to our dressing room. "Guys," he said, "you gotta look at this." He opened a blood-soaked handkerchief containing the claws of a lion he had killed the day before. Then he went out onstage and let loose that wild man from the woods. (In the eighties, he invited Steven and me to his preserve outside Detroit. I've never seen a hunter with such finely tuned instincts. He also had a strict policy—if you ain't gonna grill it, don't kill it. Ted has a deep respect for wildlife and embodies a primitive relationship—man versus beast—that is something to behold. Few Westerners in the twenty-first century could survive in the middle of the deepest darkest primeval forest. Ted is one of them.)

Even though we'd become headliners whose ticket sales were rivaling those of Jethro Tull, Led Zeppelin, and Alice Cooper, at times we were still opening. In Cleveland we opened for Rod Stewart, in front of a crowd that exceeded eighty thousand—the most fans that we'd ever faced. Maybe they were there to see Rod, but you couldn't tell by their reaction to our set. They wouldn't let us off the stage.

This was the same tour when, for the first time, we saw the formation of the Blue Army. It happened in Toledo during one of the shows that Nugent was opening. When our limo pulled up to the gig, the line of fans snaked around the huge stadium. We were told that, hoping for good tickets, they'd been there since the night before. It seemed like every last one of them was wearing blue—blue denim jackets and blue jeans. Most of them had long hair and reddened eyes. Their dedication amazed me. "Well," I told Tom, "there's our Blue Army."

The name stuck. The Grateful Dead had their Deadheads; now we had our Blue Army. At first glance the crowd looked mostly male, but we could see plenty of females out there. In those days of general admission, the guys muscled their way to the stage. The screams of the women, though, let us know we had a big following among the ladies—and they were all wearing blue.

The Blue Army was crazed to the point where promoters had to start building fences between them and the stage to hold them in check. I had a feeling they wanted to carry us off on their shoulders and parade us around the town square.

The mystical connection between us and our fans was reinforced forever one night in Grand Rapids, Michigan. A no-smoking policy had been passed just before our arrival, in an attempt to prevent pot smoking. The Blue Army defiantly lit up the moment the lights went down. A couple of dozen guys were handcuffed and hauled off. Infuriated, we sent our tour accountant to the police station with a briefcase full of cash. We bailed out everyone. Word quickly spread around the country: Aerosmith looked out for their Blue Army.

When we came home and sold out the Boston Garden on two straight nights, we were elated. Only a couple of years earlier Steven and I had lain on our backs and daydreamed of doing that very thing. To us the Garden was the Taj Mahal, the Colosseum, and the Vatican all rolled into one.

And yet in the midst of this frenzy, my bandmates were deeply unhappy with me because of the way Elyssa was causing trouble. She couldn't let a week go by without instigating some kind of he-said/she-said gossip. Her wisecracks were often brutal and offensive, her skill at pushing buttons uncanny. So I found myself in the middle: determined to be loyal to my girlfriend yet equally loyal to my band.

Elyssa had worthy adversaries. Tom Hamilton's wife, Terry, whom I admired, was, like Elyssa, witty, pretty, and tough. Terry wouldn't take shit from anyone. When Elyssa pushed, Terry pushed back. Of course the same was true with Steven, whose push-and-pull relationship with Elyssa went back to childhood. In a strange way, Steven was both the brother I never had and the brother Elyssa loved to tease. The verbal jostling was further fueled by the drugs we were consuming. The stronger the stuff, the less civilized the exchanges.

If I sided with the band and accused Elyssa of making trouble—as I did on many occasions—it would turn our household into a nightlong nightmare. Our most dramatic fight happened when I told her that she couldn't come on the road for a ten-day run of shows. By then her relationship with the band had turned poisonous. After the tour, Elyssa was still enraged about not accompanying me. We started arguing all over again, but when she pulled me over for a kiss, I thought the fight was over. Instead, she bit my lower lip. I felt a slight pinch and put my hand up to my mouth. I tasted blood. She'd bitten completely through my lip. "You're fucking crazy," was all I could say before calling a cab to take me to the hospital. When I got home all stitched up, she was sweetness and light. Knowing she had crossed a line, she'd turned into Mother Teresa. With the help of pain pills and a couple of shots of Jack Daniel's, I passed out. When I woke up the next morning, we reconciled.

For all the turmoil between us, the original infatuation I had for

Elyssa still held. The bottom line was that I loved her—at least according to my understanding of love as a twenty-five-year-old man. Like a heroine in a fifties film noir—the female character known as the black widow—Elyssa was crafty and maddening . . . and always ready to twist the knife.

It was a sunny day in L.A. The band was there to do a TV show and Dad happened to be there on business. I was eager to see him and invited him to lunch. I was ensconced in my favorite bungalow at the famous Beverly Hills Hotel. Dad brought along a business associate. We ate eggs Benedict on an outdoor patio with palm trees and lush foliage all around us. He was proud to show me off to his friend. Given Dad's courageous battle with cancer, I was proud of him. A few months earlier he had had a lung removed—yet there he was in suit and tie, trying to look strong, forging ahead, making plans for the future. I didn't detect fear in his eyes, only determination. Our conversation was upbeat. He wanted to know all about the band—the new album, the tour, our growing popularity. Given all the bad report cards I'd presented to him during my childhood, it felt good to give him a good report about my career. We didn't say the words—that wasn't our style—but we sensed the powerful love that we felt for one another. It was a good moment in the sun. I saw him as a successful businessman. He saw me as a successful artist. We had done one another proud. What I didn't know, though, was that this would be the last time I'd see him in good health.

It was later that same summer when he took a turn for the worse. Mom called to say that this time the prognosis was alarming. And yet he was there, along with Mom, to witness one of the weirdest moments in my life. It was like a scene out of a movie.

MARRIAGE AT THE RITZ

August 5, 1975: In a city famous for snobbery, the Ritz hotel was the snobbiest of all. If I hadn't been the one getting married, the Boston Brahmins who ran the place would have thrown me out. Come to think of it, they tried to do just that. As I made my way to the front door of the stately hotel overlooking the Public Garden and Boston Common, I reflected on what it had taken to get me here.

I'd gotten along famously with Nick Jerret, Elyssa's dad. Besides being a teacher, he was a working musician, always rushing off to a gig. I respected his work ethic and he respected mine. So it made sense that Elyssa and her mom, Marsha, dispatched him to argue the case for our marriage.

"You've been living with Elyssa for a long time, Joe," he said. "Don't you think it's time you made an honest woman of her?"

I didn't have a good answer. Part of me wanted to say, *No, I really think it's time to get out of the relationship altogether.* I wasn't entirely happy with Elyssa for many reasons. I'd wanted a child—especially a son—only to be told that she wasn't ready for children. I'd wanted her to make peace with the band, only to watch her make more trouble. I had tried leaving her before, but it created more distress than I could handle. I'd reconciled myself to thinking that our union was my fate. There was also the heartbreaking fact that my father was dying. Before he left this earth I needed to show him that I had settled into a stable relationship and had a somewhat normal life. The main reason I went along with the marriage was that I wanted to see my dad at my wedding.

If there were ever a time I needed a mentor to discuss my decision to marry, it was now. But Frank Connelly was gone and my dad was in no frame of mind to be objective. I was feeling alone in the world.

I left all the wedding plans to Elyssa and her mom. That's how we wound up at the Ritz. My first dilemma was deciding who would be my best man—Tom Hamilton or Steven Tyler. Elyssa solved that problem when, as a result of an argument, she disinvited Terry Hamilton, meaning that her husband, Tom, would not be attending. That got me plenty upset, but at least Steven would be there. I regretted that because of Elyssa, my relationship with Tom had suffered.

I arrived in full rock-and-roll regalia—a flowing scarf and fancy fedora. No wonder the Ritz didn't think I belonged. I managed to get through the front door, but security wouldn't let me into the private suite where the ceremony was to take place.

"I'm the groom," I explained.

The security guy was incredulous. "Wait here," he said, and called his supervisor.

After getting the word, he shook his head. "You're clear."

I didn't want to be clear. I wanted to be high and, while there was some heavy drinking before the ceremony, drinks weren't what I had in mind. The ceremony itself was strange. The cultural divide could not have been sharper. Our rocker friends were dressed to the teeth in rock-and-roll finery; our families were dressed just the opposite, in Ritz-Carlton acceptability. When the minister asked Elyssa, "Do you take Anthony Joseph Perry to be your lawfully wedded husband?" her mom, feeling no pain, yelled out, "Who the hell is this Anthony guy anyway?"

The minute the ceremony was over, Steven turned to me with his let's-go-to-another-room look. I nodded my head and, with Elyssa and

Steven's date in tow, we quickly escaped to an empty suite. Steven poured out a gram of light brown powder on the coffee table and split it into four lines.

"Your wedding present," he said. "To a long life and lots of love and happiness."

We snorted up the high-grade heroin and then gave hugs all around. For all the triangular Joe-Steven-Elyssa drama that had preceded this day, I felt that Steven was genuinely glad to be at our wedding.

We returned for the cake cutting. My mother embraced me and my dad shook my hand. I looked in his eyes and saw that he was in pain. In these few months since I had seen him in L.A., he had lost weight and looked extremely weak. I told him how much it meant that he had come to my wedding. "I wouldn't have missed it for the world," he said. "I know you'll understand if we leave early, Joe, but I've gotta get a little rest." He managed a smile and so did I. As Nick Jerret, my new father-in-law, played a medley of show tunes on a grand piano, I walked my parents to the door. My heart was heavy. I was losing my father.

There was no honeymoon, only another Aerosmith tour. In fact, we had changed our wedding date several times to accommodate the band schedule. And while I would face heavy criticism that my relationship to Elyssa was injurious to the band's welfare, our marriage had been timed to make sure that I didn't miss a single gig. My devotion to the band was as great as my devotion to Elyssa. In time, it would prove even greater.

When we were based out of Boston or not touring I would visit my dad, who was back at the Beth Israel Deaconess Medical Center in Boston. Not once did Elyssa come along; she claimed she couldn't handle hospitals. I brought along the gold album that we'd been awarded for our first album. I wanted him to have it on his wall to remind him of our success. He was medicated and his treatments had taken an awful toll. But he was still sharp enough to speak about me about practicalities.

"I know you're making good money, Joe," he said, "but are you saving any? Are you taking care of business?"

I assured him that I was. I wanted to say much more to him. I wanted to say that I needed his guidance and support. I wanted to say that my life was complicated, that I had this difficult wife, that I had this difficult relationship with the band, that I was taking a lot of drugs and that the drugs were making me feel great—maybe too great. But I said nothing. The last thing in the world I wanted to do was worry him in his condition.

"Thanks for coming by, Joe," said Dad. "Next time you'll see me I should be back home."

"Great, Dad," I said, but I knew that he would never leave the hospital. I visited him there three or four more times, watching his steady decline. Then came the day when, with my hand on his shoulder, he passed away. I thought I was prepared but I wasn't. I don't think a son can ever be prepared for the loss of his father. When it happened, I could feel my heart break in two. A sadness washed over me unlike any I had ever experienced. It wasn't that my father and I had enjoyed the closest of relationships. For a good portion of my life we struggled to communicate. For years we had lived in different worlds. But the unspoken love between us was powerful. And maybe because it was unspoken, it carried an even greater weight.

He was honored with a military burial and seven-gun salute in his hometown of Lowell. I was presented with the flag that had been draped over the coffin. Steven was a pillar of strength and support for me. He rode with my family and me in the limo; he stood beside me and helped me carry the casket. That day, like many others, he was the brother I never had. My mother, stoic throughout, gave me Dad's college ring from Northeastern University. I put it on a gold chain, and as I write these words, it still hangs around my neck.

Mom's strength never wavered. Her life continued, her intellectual curiosity grew, but I felt the loneliness she endured. She told me how proud my dad had been of my success, how he spoke of that success to all his relatives and friends, how he'd boast about me. That was the first time I heard about his boasting. That made me miss him more.

I look back and think of my father, Tony Perry, as an honest man. He cared for his children. He learned a profession. He served the people he worked for and the larger community as well. He rose from the working class to the upper rungs of the middle class, no mean feat in America. And though I moved into a rock-and-roll culture that was foreign to him, he, along with Mom, supported me at every key turning point. I was blessed to have such a good dad.

My new marriage to Elyssa suffered even more when she refused to attend my father's funeral. She had never made the effort to bond with either of my parents. Now, with dad gone, there was no love lost between Elyssa and Mom. My mother had her number, and Elyssa knew it.

It also didn't help our marriage that we got lost in possessions. Elyssa's interest was in improving our lifestyle, and I went along with the upgrade. It was Elyssa who taught me about Rolex watches and fine china. It wouldn't be long before we moved from our apartment to a Tudor-styled house on Waban Hill Road in Newton, a mini Italian villa built in the twenties by heirs of the Sears fortune and then owned by a woman who called herself a countess. It was elegant, even aristocratic, with intricate woodwork and a huge stained-glass window in the two-story living room. It suited Elyssa so well that our roadies called it Villa Elyssa. To me it was the perfect party house, with a stereo the size of a small PA system and a suit of armor in the front hall.

I gladly turned over the decoration of our house to Elyssa and her mom. My thing was music—and as soon as we moved into the house I built a small demo studio in the basement. Dick "Rabbit" Hansen, my guitar tech, and Nick Spiegel, one of Aerosmith's longtime techs, and I covered the walls with scraps of carpets and the windows with packing materials. Once we soundproofed the space, I put in a Scully eight-track tape machine and an Audiotronics mixing board. I wanted real drums, but it was Saturday night when we were finished wiring it up and the stores were closed. So impatience got the best of me: I made a drum kit out of empty boxes. Steven came over and showed me some basic drum licks. I was soon laying tracks. The first of those tracks—"Get It Up"—wound up on a future Aerosmith album.

I liked my new home and studio, and there were a lot of good times and parties. David Johansen and his wife, Cyrinda Foxe, would come up to

Boston to visit us. David and I started writing together and discussed the idea of my producing his first solo record.

My home was comfortable, but, in truth, I saw my real home as the road. The road had a momentum and excitement of its own. The road was where we kept our music razor sharp. The road was where we encountered our colleagues who inspired us to perform at even higher levels. The road was where we got to gig and make friends with all the great bands of the day.

As we continued touring behind *Toys*, we started hearing "Sweet Emotion" on the radio—our first Top 40 pop hit—and then in early 1976 "Dream On" was rereleased for the second time and became our first Top Ten hit. We were firing on all cylinders. But Steven and I were also firing at each other. There were always the fights over volume. He never stopped complaining that we played too loudly, but we never got any complaints from the fans. Steven's volatility, an ongoing issue, was turning into rage-aholism. One minute he'd be patiently signing autographs and posing for pictures with every last fan; the next he'd be screaming bloody murder on the phone. You could (and still can) hear him through the hotel room walls.

Adding to the neurotic mix, Raymond Tabano, our former guitarist and former leather clothier, was back on the scene. He'd remained tight with Tyler and convinced us he that could increase our income by taking over the merchandise. Tabano became the T-shirt man. He signed a deal with Leber-Krebs and then reinforced his position by finding us a warehouse—a big, long corrugated steel building so large that we could park all our cars inside—just outside Boston in Waltham. For years this was our playpen. We built a makeshift stage downstairs and used it for rehearsals. Upstairs there were game rooms and offices. We named it the Wherehouse and kicked off our residency with a Halloween party where we hired hostesses dressed up as French maids. We invited a gang of friends, mainly from the Boston music scene, and jammed the night away—playing, singing, smoking, and coking.

In the aftermath of the triumph of *Toys*, our next job was to come up with something better. Steven had bought a house on Lake Sunapee, where we started working on new material. Elyssa and I went up there in the dead of freezing winter and stayed in his guesthouse. The small town had only one gas station and one restaurant, run by our friend John Andrews, who also tended bar in this establishment.

One snowy night we were sitting at a secluded table at John's place, where, over the course of the evening, Steven and I slowly got plastered. Except for us, the place was empty. John was happy to hear stories of our successful tour behind *Toys*. He said that New Englanders were proud that the Bad Boys of Boston had made good.

Interrupting the serenity of a quiet evening, a couple of guys walked into the bar like cowboys swaggering into a saloon. Except these cowboys were really English roadies. They spoke in thick cockney accents.

"Hey, mate, you have any British ale, not that bloody fuckin' piss that passes for beer here in the States?"

John couldn't oblige the guy. The second roadie was even coarser, furious that John's inventory of scotch didn't include the brand he was looking for.

From complaining about America's bad booze, they began trumpeting the wonders of America's greatest band—the E Street. Turned out they were roadies for Springsteen taking off a few days to go skiing.

"None of the bloody fuckin' rock and rollers around here can hold a candle to Bruce," said the first one.

"They can all kiss my ass," said the second. "The only thing worse than the music around here is your pissy beer."

"I gotta tell you gentlemen," said John, looking at us out of the corner of his eye, "you've wandered into Aerosmith territory. They're our local heroes."

"Did you say *Aerosmith*?" said the louder of the roadies, laughing. "Is that the shit that passes for music around here? Well, I give 'em another year and they'll be sitting on top of the rock-and-roll trash heap with the rest of the forgotten bands. Aerosmith's a bloody fuckin' joke."

In a rare moment of restraint, Steven kept quiet. Neither of us was inclined to tell the bloats who we were. Just let them rave on. After finishing off a couple of inferior American brews, one asked John for the location of the nearest gas station. They were nearly out of fuel and some thirty miles from their hotel. There was one such station around the corner that stayed open late.

Without missing a beat, John said, "Nearest station is forty miles down the road." He gave them precise directions, careful to steer them clear of the station less than an eighth of a mile away.

"Hope you guys make it," Steven shouted out as the roadies took their leave. "If you get stuck, you can always call Bruce to tow your ass in."

ROCKS

Finally off the road from *Toys*, Steven and I had started writing songs for the album that would be issued in the spring of 1976 under a title I had thought of—*Rocks*. Diamonds are called rocks, and nothing is harder than a diamond. I wanted the hardest-rocking record imaginable.

For *Rocks*, we did much of our preproduction experimentation at the Wherehouse, which provided us a great sound. The room had a warm, alive feel. That gave Jack Douglas the brilliant idea of parking the Record Plant mobile truck inside the Wherehouse. Thus the creation of Record Plant North. We could seamlessly move from rehearsal to recording without breaking stride. There had always been an element of tension in our previous recording sessions. Getting used to a rented studio with all its quirks was never easy or quick. But this time was different. This time we could simply cut loose and relax. This time we were home. That sense of comfort and confidence is why, to my ears, *Rocks* became our best-sounding and hardest-hitting record.

I'd written a bunch of riffs that were fun to play, but that's all they were—riffs. So, in one instance, I started writing some lyrics and was toying with singing the song myself. This was touchy because singing was Steven's jealously guarded territory. Being in a band with one of the best singers in the world set up an inevitable comparison. In that comparison, I ain't gonna look too good. But what the fuck. I couldn't let that stop me. As the great blues prophet John Lee Hooker once said, "If it's in him, it's gotta come out."

Beyond that, anytime the spotlight shone on me I detected a bit of jealousy from the other guys. After a while, though, the band came around and supported me, as long as I sang the song as a semi-duet with Steven. I called it "Combination" and, to this day, remain surprised how often I'm asked to play it live.

The words to "Combination" are:

The street is cold, the dawn is gray
My heart says no but my head says stay
My work is finished, or so I've been told
Can't part the three of us, once we got a hold
I forgot the name
I took a shot on the chin
I'm rearranging my game
Tell by the shape I'm in
In the line of fire, you know what to say
They gave us no choices, just one shade of gray
My legs keep moving, I don't seem to stray
But I know each step we take, they're one step away
I found the secret, the key to the vault
We walked in darkness, kept hittin' the walls
I took the time, to feel for the door
I found the secret, the key to it all
I got the nouveau riche
And dragged it home to bed
I traded you for me
I took it all and said
I find my own fun, sometimes for free
I got to pay it to come looking for me

Walking on Gucci, wearin' Yves Saint Laurent
Barely stay on, 'cause I'm so goddamn gaunt

When I wrote the music for the kickoff song on *Rocks*—"Back in the Saddle"— I was in my bedroom, flat on my back, fucked up on heroin, playing my six-string bass. The music flew out of me—all the parts, all the riffs. It came in one special-delivery package. I was still in the stage when the drugs were opening doors to my imagination. And I was lucky enough to have a connection that got me heroin as close to pure as I would ever see.

Rocks represented not only the first time that Aerosmith was listed as coproducer (along with Jack Douglas), but the first time the Perry/Tyler team wrote as many as four songs on the record. As usual, Steven went through his agonizingly long gestation period before he found the words to "Back in the Saddle," "Rats in the Cellar," "Get the Lead Out," and "Lick and a Promise." In some sense all these songs were about movement. "Saddle" has us riding back out there on the rock-and-roll range. "Rats in the Cellar," of course, is Steven's witty contrast to "Toys in the Attic." Both he and I were intent on getting down to the grit and grime of the basement. "Get the Lead Out" is a straight-up exhortation to get up and dance.

At the Record Plant in New York, Tom wrote the riff on guitar for "Sick as a Dog." We recorded him on guitar, me on bass, and everyone else in their usual places. Then, with the tape still rolling, at the breakdown I gave the bass to Steven and picked up my guitar to play the solo. Looking like the Keystone Cops, we did this three or four times before we figured out who was going to run where and through which door. It took a while, but we ended up with a great live take. Brad also wrote some strong songs with Steven—"Last Child" and "Nobody's Fault."

Looking back at *Rocks*, I see its one-word theme as *party*. Its one driving purpose was to reidentify us as America's ultimate garage band, with blistering guitars, blistering vocals, balls-to-the-wall smash-your-eardrums production. When it came out in May 1976, the cover showed five diamonds, one for each of us. We saw the record as a jewel, the culmination of all our angst and anger and excitement and joy as go-for-broke rock and rollers. *Rocks* was the ultimate sound track to the party we were throwing for our fans at every one of our live shows.

In 1976, the reality of the music business was somewhat unreal. On the soft rock side of the fence, Elton John, Frampton, and the Eagles were flying high. On the hard side, Aerosmith, Kiss, and ZZ Top were setting the world on fire. Sales were so unprecedented that the industry even invented a new category—platinum—to recognize a million-plus units sold. It didn't take long for *Rocks* to reach that mark.

We started the *Rocks* tour big—and it only got bigger from there. Detroit had always been ground zero for us, but no one was sure we could sell eighty thousand seats at the Pontiac Silverdome. We did. We had a couple of days off before the next gig—Madison Square Garden, our first time in that venue. Elyssa and I went back to Boston for a little R&R. On the day we were to fly on the band plane to New York, we snorted up a fresh crop of cocaine and downed a fistful of Tuinals. We crashed in bed. Because I had mentioned that Elyssa and I might fly out to New York earlier to do some shopping, the band left without us. But when they got to New York and we were nowhere to be found, the alarm went off, along with my alarm clock, which we slept through. Elyssa's mom was alerted. She came over but even her shouts didn't rouse us. We were sleeping the sleep of the dead. She got some guys to break down the locked door to our bedroom. Only then did I realize what was happening. I caught the last shuttle out of Logan Airport and miraculously walked onto the stage of Madison Square Garden on time. The after-party was at Rick Derringer's. That's where I met John Belushi, who had just started out on *Saturday Night Live*. He jammed with us till dawn. If there was ever a true rock and roller, it was John.

It was a summer to remember. I could never forget jamming with Jeff Beck on September 10, my twenty-sixth birthday. Elyssa had convinced Jeff, whom she'd met years before in England, to join us onstage doing "Train Kept a-Rollin'." There could be no better gift. Jeff had been opening for us, but it was—and remains—impossible for me to think of Jeff as an opening act. We were merely the band that followed him. As I watched him onstage each night, he gave me a lesson in the fine art of rock guitar.

There were sold-out stadium shows in Chicago; Anaheim, California;

and Seattle. The ever-growing Blue Army was as crazy loyal as they were crazy aggressive. They took to throwing explosives onstage. We were dodging firecrackers. We hated that. How the hell did we become targets? Well, one mad fan said that they were lovingly giving back to us what we were giving to them—the fire they felt in our music. Our music was geared to stimulate them beyond reason. Unreasonably, they were expressing their appreciation by bombing us with pyrotechnics. I didn't buy that explanation, but what could I do? Who were we to demand civilized behavior from our fans when our own behavior defied civility at every turn?

Steven was busted for uncivilized banter during our show in Memphis. The police claimed he violated an anti-profanity ordinance by using the word *fuck*. Obviously Steven had grown more comfortable talking to the audience, especially in the parlance that he and they loved best. The cops roughed him up and threw him into a cell, where he stayed for a few hours until our lawyers bailed him out. When he arrived at the hotel a free man, the band celebrated by flinging TVs into the pool. Such were the activities expected from rock stars.

Our exploding popularity got to the point where even *Rolling Stone* had to put us on the cover—except they didn't. They put Steven on the cover with a sorry photo. The accompanying story was just as sorry. They wrote that "guitarist Joe Perry plugs in his guitar like a grease monkey getting ready to tune a carburetor." They said that Steven Tyler had a voice "that makes Alice Cooper sound like Vic Damone" and that we made "brain damage music." Not then, not now, not ever would we win over the hearts of the New York critical elite. I thought at the time, *Fuck 'em*. The fans were coming in droves. The pact between the Blue Army and us was sacrosanct and growing stronger with every show. In the aftermath of *Toys* and *Rocks*, that shrill chorus of critics calling us a poor man's version of the Stones was being been drowned out by our impassioned supporters. We had accomplished the seemingly impossible. Ignoring the warning signs that come with too many shows, too much success, and too many drugs, we picked up the pace.

I couldn't wait to get to England. I wanted to prove to British fans that we were more than an Americanized version of English rock bands who were themselves Anglicized versions of American blues bands. I wanted to prove that we had our own voice and style. That drive was greater than the drugs I was consuming or the melodramas surrounding me. That drive got me out there onstage every night. I wanted to win over the world. In spite of the petty dramas, we all stood together. It was us against the world.

Ironically, we had to first win over our management. They didn't like the idea of booking us abroad. I personally had been pressuring them for years to introduce us to European audiences, and for years they'd been resisting. Everyone with a modicum of sense understood that rock and roll had become a global business. I wanted Aerosmith in that business. It made no sense that, five years after signing with the biggest label in the world, we had not even started to establish a worldwide presence. Leber-Krebs argued that we had no market over there. I counterargued that we needed to establish a market. Maybe we couldn't get booked into stadiums or arenas, but surely there were prestigious clubs that would have us. Later I'd learn that management was reluctant because, though they enjoyed cozy relationships with U.S. promoters, they lacked those connections in Europe. In other words, they couldn't earn enough money off us in foreign markets to make it worth their while.

Reluctantly, they booked us and we were off. Our first English gig was an outdoor festival in the middle of nowhere. It'd been raining for days. When we met up with my guitar tech Rabbit I asked, "How is it?" He handed me two new pairs of wellies—knee-high rubber boots—one for me and the other for Elyssa. "You're gonna need these," was all he said.

Old-timers on the crew were comparing it to Woodstock. An opportunistic farmer who had placed a wooden board from the band trucks to the stage was charging ten dollars a load to carry the equipment. Given the fact that there were ten bands with enormous piles of equipment, he must have made a fortune that day. In my dressing room, I asked for milk, only to have a stagehand take me outside and point to a goat tied to a fence. They did, however, provide an ample supply of Newcastle Brown Ale, the potent beer we'd heard about from the English cats in America.

Would the Brits dig us? We had some doubts, but not for long. The audience knew our lyrics and sang along. They'd been waiting for us. They fuckin' loved us. During our stay in England we also got to hang out with

Queen, one of my favorite groups. Because we'd started out around the same time, admired each other's music, and were about the same age, there was a natural bond between us. They were a great band. I'd gotten to know the guys when they had played Boston, and it was a treat being with them on their home turf. Of all the members, Freddie Mercury, like most lead singers, was aloof. He was the only Queen cat I never got to know. Other than that, Queen shared none of the anti-American band bias prevalent among other British rockers. England was a blast.

Germany was different. Our first three gigs were, by coincidence, close to U.S. Army bases. The fourth, in Cologne, was canceled due to poor ticket sales. We had committed to a live interview in Cologne and went there anyway. Because no one at the radio station knew English, we were at the mercy of our interpreter. Little mercy was shown when the DJ interviewing us kept hollering accusations in German, allowing the interpreter no time to translate and us no chance to reply. When we finally got him to slow down, we learned he was telling the live audience that we'd come to his country not to entertain Germans but only U.S. troops. That was a lie. Through our hassled interpreter, we heatedly argued back, pointing out that the majority of the audience in our shows had been German. But the DJ cut us off. Pissed as hell, I stormed out and Steven followed. Sweet revenge came the next time we came to Germany. Our Cologne show was sold out. German fans turned out to be among our most devoted.

I was wiped out from nonstop traveling, and yet when I learned that in early 1977 we were booked in Japan for a seven-show tour, I was excited. Asia was a huge rock-and-roll market. I couldn't wait to get there.

Before leaving, between the European and Japanese tours, I managed to squeeze in a five-day vacation in Barbados with Elyssa and my techs Nick and Rabbit. No drugs, but copious amounts of Mount Gay rum. When Elyssa turned in early, my guys and I played chess until we became restless and jumped on one of those jitneys, a golf cart on steroids, and raced through the cane fields, stalks whipping by and snapping back at us at forty miles an hour. We powered up the side of a mountain, where, at midnight, an all-night restaurant and bar served caviar and iced vodka. During the day, an old islander, his dive knife tied around his waist with a rope, took us diving with equipment left from World War II. The snorkeling was sensational. As soon as I hit the water, my hangover was gone. If only I could have lingered longer in Barbados.

But it was on to Tokyo, where the legendary Mr. Udo, the man who brought the Beatles to Japan, treated us like we were the Second Coming. There were no drugs, but there was endless sake. There were unexpectedly enormous crowds who, quite formally, applauded for ten seconds after each song and then abruptly stopped. You could hear a pin drop. We asked our translator if we were doing something wrong. "No," he said. "They stay silent because they don't want to miss anything you say or do between songs." Knowing they were listening that intensely gave us an extra boost.

Money was pouring in. If I wanted anything, I called management and the cash was there—but not so much the accounting. I should have demanded to see the books. Tom, Brad, and Joey bought Ferraris. Among other cars, I bought a couple of Porsches and an old Bentley convertible. We were all putting the pedal to the metal. We'd become a cash cow, selling out major venues around the world. But even as we made it to the top, our management never failed to remind us that there was always another band right behind us, ready to take our place.

Management was cagey. They saw us as their perfect vehicle to break the new baby bands, mostly from Europe, that they had signed and booked as our opening acts. Management was driving us harder than we were driving ourselves. It was like running a race where, the second before we crossed the finish line, management stepped in and pushed the line farther ahead.

After years of nonstop touring and recording, wouldn't common sense demand that the band take off six months or even a year? Wasn't it time to come down to earth and chill? But we were simply too high—high on fame, high on drugs, high on stimulants of every variety. We needed to stop and figure out what was happening. A break would give us a chance to find perspective on our borderline-crazy lives. A break would give us a desperately needed rest.

And yet, instead of resting, we cranked up the engine and drove full-speed into still another all-consuming project that, despite its enormous promise, proved to be the beginning of the end.

ALL TOGETHER AND TOTALLY APART

Management: *You gotta get started on a new record right away. And to ensure your privacy, how'd you like to record in a former nunnery, complete with its own chapel, situated on a hundred acres in the middle of the woods?*

All five of us agreed to go. Our work ethic prevailed. Our mantra hadn't changed—plow ahead and keep working. Yet as Elyssa and I drove to Armonk, New York, in my Porsche Turbo Carrera, I was burnt-out like never before. I was beaten down by five years on the road followed by many weeks down in the basement eight-track studio of our house in Newton, where I'd worked up a bunch of tracks highly influenced by the Sex Pistols and the Ramones. I felt the raw energy that punk was bringing to rock. I loved their attitude. It reminded me of what the proto-punk New York Dolls had expressed years earlier. In response, I wrote "Bright Light Fright," lyrics and all.

As much as I was influenced by the present, I also continued to be inspired by the past. Much of the material I had worked up in my basement eight-track was born out of playing old-school open tuning. I never stopped paying homage to the old blues guys. By then I had a sizable inventory of guitars and never tired of experimenting with them: double-necks, Gibson Les Pauls, Stratocasters, and custom models by master craftsmen Bernado Rico (B.C. Rich) and Bill Lawrence. These were the instruments I used to make the music I was bringing to the nunnery. I put my dozens of ideas on cassette tapes and threw them into a big cookie tin. These demos weren't finished, but they were listenable.

On paper, the plan sounded ideal. Jack Douglas, our trusty producer, had arranged to bring in a battery of the latest and greatest recording equipment. Today it would merely be a matter of a few computers and mics. But back then it was a massive science project. To create a studio meant hauling in thousands of pounds of equipment.

"Get the guys whatever they need," management told Jack, who did just that.

Beyond bringing the best machinery to capture our music on tape, we were given a full staff to cater to our every need—a twenty-four-hour gourmet cook, servers to bring us food, housekeepers to clean up after us. With so much help at our fingertips, what could possibly go wrong?

Try everything.

The truth is that we were all together yet totally apart. We were separated from one another, both physically and emotionally. We were scattered. Our rooms were in distant sections of the estate. Overall, the vibe was mellow. When it came to writing, though, it felt like we were trying to squeeze toothpaste out of an empty tube. Everyone was exhausted from constant touring and recording. I was in a marriage I wanted out of. Adding to the madness of the moment was the fact that we were being fueled by a medicine chest of high-quality drugs. With Manhattan only forty-five miles away, there was a continuous flow of dealer friends from the city.

I woke up each morning to a double black Russian. Right off our room was a huge attic used for storage, where I'd have target practice with my .22 while sipping my morning pick-me-up. Since I was usually the last one up, the popping of the .22 echoed through the halls and let everyone know I was awake. In the afternoons, Joey, who lived for fast cars, would jump into his Ferrari and tear up the back roads. One afternoon when he returned to the Cenacle, as the nunnery was called, he borrowed my .22. He and Steven stretched out on the ground and shot at cymbals they had set up as targets. They took turns, passing the rifle back and forth, until at one point, Joey passed out, the gun resting in his hands.

Joey wasn't the only one knocked out from overdoing everything. We were all in the same condition. We were more into our diversions than our music. Artistically, we were less prepared for this record than we had been for any other. Steven had been hanging in his newly built house in New Hampshire. He had invited us a bunch of times to hang out and write, and I had invited him to Newton for the same reasons—but, in truth, we were living very separate lives. We had separate friends, separate dealers. Our drug-buddy relationship would wax and wane over the years, but at this point, we were off in separate universes.

Jack Douglas also liked getting high, although that never got in the way of his work. When he saw that I was coming to the sessions too loaded to perform at my best, he got pissed. "You look like shit warmed over," he said. He got even angrier when I wasn't able to give him the new music he'd been expecting. That's because I couldn't find the cookie tin where I'd stashed my demos.

Jack's opinion meant a lot to me, and I didn't want to disappoint him. Since *Rocks*, he'd produced Cheap Trick—his discovery—and Patti Smith. Well, I loved Cheap Trick and I loved Patti. I also loved Jack, but at this point I loved drugs more. A year or two ago we had been musicians fooling around with drugs. Now we were druggies fooling around with music.

Adding to the pressure was the great anticipation surrounding this new album. Fans considered *Toys* and *Rocks* masterpieces. They were counting on our next record to be even better. One die-hard fan said, "What the White Album was to the Beatles, the post-*Rocks* album will be to Aerosmith." Instead of our White Album, though, we cut our Blackout Album.

On my end, only once did light break through—when Elyssa found the cookie tin that held my demos. I immediately felt vindicated. Among those tapes was not only the fully realized "Bright Light Fright," but tracks that led to other songs like "I Wanna Know Why," "Get It Up," and "Draw the Line," the title tune. Something I'd started with David Johansen became

"Sight for Sore Eyes." But the lyrics literally took months for Steven to write, and by then we were back at the Record Plant in New York.

Our recording setup at the Cenacle became a sad metaphor for everything that was wrong with the band. It was all about separation. Joey was drumming in the two-hundred-seat chapel. I was in the living room with my amps piled inside a stand-up-size fireplace. Somewhere else in the nunnery Steven was in an isolated booth. Brad and Tom were in other rooms, totally apart. The only eye contact came through crude black-and-white closed-circuit TV monitors. The sound was muddy. There was no connection, no togetherness.

Somehow we pulled the songs together. Steven, Joey, Tom, Brad, and Jack cut some tracks in the chapel, using the confessional as a sound chamber for a snare drum. That became "Kings and Queens." They also did something called "The Hand That Feeds." To fill out of the album, we had to pull out Kokomo Arnold's old "Milk Cow Blues." Elvis had sung it and so had the Kinks. I was doing it way back in the days of the Jam Band. For years Aerosmith had been using it as an encore song. It rocked, and now we were recording it because our creative well had gone dry.

While we were at the Cenacle, Raymond—the guitarist turned merchandiser—would run to New York City to cop blow for Steven. (By that time we all had separate dealers.) On one occasion when Raymond was spending the night at the Cenacle, Steven decided to have some fun. While Raymond was still upstairs, Steven came down to dinner with a smirk on his face.

"In about five minutes," he said, "you'll hear the loudest fuckin' scream you've ever heard in your life. That'll be Raymond. Just wait."

Right on time, we heard this harrowing scream.

"What the hell happened?" I asked.

"I set out two thick lines of coke on my bed stand," said Steven. "I knew Raymond couldn't resist."

"So why's he screaming like somebody tore out his fingernails?"

"Because," said Steven, "it wasn't coke. It only looked like coke. It was plaster I scraped off the ceiling."

Jack also couldn't resist a practical joke. His most successful was perpetuated on Joey. Joey's weakness was chocolate. Put a big chocolate cake in front of him and he'd devour it whole. Joey was also into crazy diets, purging himself of his excesses.

"The most effective diet," Jack explained, "is simple. For a couple of weeks you eat nothing but green apples and drink nothing but water. On the last day you drink a cup of olive oil—and that's it. You'll lose a minimum of ten pounds."

Not realizing that Jack was inventing this diet out of thin air, Joey bought the concept and carried out the plan. Aware of Jack's mischief, Steven, Brad, Tom, and I struggled to keep straight faces. On the last day, after Joey downed the olive oil, the shit literally hit the fan. He spent at least twenty-four hours in the bathroom. When he emerged, realizing he was the brunt of Jack's joke, he went looking for Jack. One of the hardest-hitting drummers in rock, Joey is built like a bull. And he was pissed. Jack had to disappear for a day until Joey calmed down.

The most lasting illustration of our time at the Cenacle can be seen on the cover of the album. We had decided early on to call it *Draw the Line*, and, following the advice of Tom—the only one of us conversant in fine art—we asked Al Hirschfeld, famous for his cartoon sketches of Broadway and showbiz celebrities, to draw us. We were elated when Hirschfeld agreed. When he came to the Cenacle we weren't sure what to expect. This was, after all, our first experience working with an artist of his caliber. He was a friendly older gentleman in a frumpy suit. We discussed music and art. He told us how he liked to ride the New York subways and sketch people by putting his hand in his pocket and, without looking, drawing them on a small pad. After a half hour of fascinating conversation, we asked him what he needed us to do. Should we pose? Did he need to do a sketch?

"Oh, no," he said. "I have everything I need. Give me a week and I'll send you the drawing."

We were amazed. He didn't make a single note or sketch a single line. We were even more amazed when the drawing arrived. Al Hirschfeld caught the essence of each of us. He did exactly what we'd hoped for—he drew the line. The cover was brilliant.

When most of the music for *Draw the Line* was complete, we got tired of waiting for Steven to write the lyrics and decided to split. Before the morning of our departure, we'd been up all night shooting a long promotional video. At daybreak I was having trouble standing up straight. I was nonetheless determined to ride my motorcycle up the ramp into the truck that was hauling my stuff back to Newton. I gunned the bike hard and wound up flying off the ramp into the bushes. The crew ran over, expecting the worst. Other than a slight bruise, I was fine. I gathered my composure and, in my best Frank Connelly voice, said, "I might need to practice that a bit more. But I'm fine, boys. Why don't you take over?" After a good long nap, my head was finally clear enough for me to get in my Porsche to head home. Not far outside Boston, I saw something that hit me in the gut: a black Ferrari mangled in the center guardrail. I immediately recognized it as Joey's. No one was around. There was just the wrecked car with blood all over the seats. My heart hammering, I sped to a pay phone and was finally able to reach Tom.

"The car's totaled," said Tom, "but Joey walked away with just a few stitches."

Relieved, all I could think was that this was a day when our guardian angel had been working overtime.

Even though the album wasn't finished, that summer we were doing gigs here and abroad. Steven and I were running in and out of the Record Plant in New York. He was still writing lyrics and I was still recording overdubs. Back home in Newton, I was speeding in my Corvette when, in passing a car, I crashed into the guardrail and nearly flipped over before the car came to a stop. While waiting for the cops, I had to endure dirty looks from the people I'd zoomed past in the last half mile. I felt pretty damn stupid and vowed to tone down my driving.

"You hurt?" asked the officer who arrived on the scene.

"I think I'm fine."

"Your car's a mess. Sure you're okay?"

I got out of the car, stretched, and felt for broken bones. There were none. I wasn't even sore.

I looked at the cop and said, "I'm okay."

"Given how you fucked up your car, that's amazing."

I agreed. But now what?

My father with his crew near the end of World War II.
He's second from the left, standing.

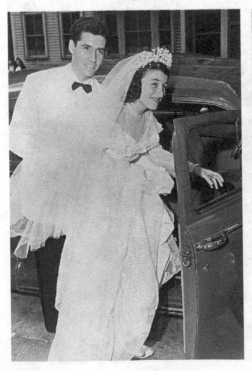

The start of the All-American
Perry family.

My mom and dad, Mary and Tony.
I was the gleam in my dad's eye.

The diving bell
that I made
from junkyard
scraps. Still under
construction.

A collage of my
early days, made
by a fan. Thanks.

Joe Perry

My first band,
Chimes of
Freedom.
Left to right:
Bill Wright,
John Alden,
and me.

My Vermont Academy Prep School band, Just Us.

Everything plugged into one sorry amp. Left to right: Dave Meade on bass, John Alden on drums, and me at the mic.

In the woods with my camera at Vermont Academy.

Dance "Flash" poster I made to promote a show Dave Meade and I did periodically at the Hopedale Town Hall.

The cover I hand-drew for one of four acetates we had pressed of a recording of Jam Band.

The Jam Band performing on the lawn on the side of the New London Inn in New Hampshire, down the road from Lake Sunapee. From left to right: Tom Hamilton, Dave Scott (aka Pudge), and me.

Within the first week of moving into the apartment at
1325 Commonwealth Avenue, Boston, Massachusetts.

The early '70s. Left to right: me and Tom at a sound check.

Ray Tabano at a show in the Boston suburbs.

Below: Backstage at an early show when we were officially Aerosmith with Brad Whitford, with my mom there to cheer us on.

Aerosmith

+

Joe Jammer
from London

Come one
Come All - ha! ha!

The BARN
July 3, 1971

→→

A poster drawn for us by Elyssa Jerret to promote Aerosmith. This was the last summer of the old crew hanging at Lake Sunapee, New Hampshire.

At the Fenway Theater. Left to right: Tom, me, and Brad.

The only picture I have of Father Frank Connelly, given to me by his sister the same day she gave me his ring. I still miss this man. His spirit still runs through the band.

An early photo shoot of the band. Left to right: Brad Whitford, me, Joey Kramer, Steven Tyler, and Tom Hamilton.

Maxanne Sartori at a party. She's the cute blonde to the left who was one of the first female disc jockeys in the country. The top DJ at WBCN Boston, and the first to play "Dream On" as a demo. Thanks to Raymond Tabano for bringing it to her attention.

Me and Elyssa on the road with Aerosmith.

Steven and me at the first Aerosmith show at the Orpheum Theater in Boston.
If you look closely, you can see the cut on my lip.

My family at my wedding reception to Elyssa. Left to right: Dad, maternal
grandpa Ursillo, Mom, Grandpa's wife, and my sister Annie.

Not a happy man. In the background is the Wherehouse, in Waltham, Massachusetts.

Trying out my new meerschaum pipe. It worked.

Steven and me onstage, around 1973.

The first of many dives together with Steven in Maui.
Left to right: me, Nick Spiegel, and Steven.

Early morning hours working on tracks for *Draw the Line* at Air Studios.

David Krebs disembarking the Aerosmith plane somewhere in Europe, during the 1977 tour. I actually think he had a warm spot in his heart for the band.

Somewhere in Manhattan. I just did a blast of something good
and was solving the problems of the world.

David Johansen of the New York Dolls in New Orleans, July 4, 1976. The owner of the club got us onstage to jam for free drinks.

Sailing on a day off in Maui. The two standing shirtless guys are Henry "The Horse" Smith and Nick Spiegel, then, left to right: me, Elyssa, Steve Leiber, and his daughter.

Aerosmith at Texas Jam with Ted Nugent jamming with us.

Near the end of the 1977 European Aerosmith tour. Left to right: Joey, Brad, Tom, Steven, and me.

"Hey," he said. "Aren't you Joe Perry?"

"I am."

"Well, look, I better call an ambulance for you, just to make sure."

"Thanks," I said, "but I'm okay."

"At least let me drop you off. Where do you want to go?"

"Dunkin' Donuts would be good."

That's where we went for a cup of coffee. I called a towing service to haul off the car, and that was it. Thankfully, I didn't get a ticket and avoided injuring myself or anyone else.

But I didn't get off scot-free. The episode drove me deeper into the illusion of being invulnerable. I didn't know it at the time—I wasn't thinking that way; I wasn't thinking at all—but the more invulnerable you think you are, the more vulnerable you really are.

This was the same demented period when Elyssa and I took a private plane, piloted by Zunk Buker's dad, from Logan to New York, where I had work to do at the Record Plant. I'd been up for three days—no eating, no sleeping—at my home studio in a rush to complete material for the still-incomplete *Draw the Line*. Before takeoff, my body checked out, I went blank, and the next thing I knew I was waking up on an EMT gurney surrounded by state police. Elyssa had taken the drugs out of my pocket and put them out of sight. An ambulance rushed me to a hospital, where the doctor said he had never examined a human being with a lower amount of blood sugar. He told me to go home and eat steak. He said that I gave undernourishment a bad name.

Even with the decay of our artistry—as evidenced by *Draw the Line*, an album that didn't hold a candle to *Toys* or *Rocks*—there seemed to be no commercial consequences. In Baltimore we sold out the Civic Center, but the stage monitors crapped out. That's when I enacted my own version of a flip-out. I started pushing monitors into the crowd, pleasing the fans to no end.

Another time, I got carried away again at the climax of a show when I threw an old Les Paul Jr. straight up in the air. This was before I had a wireless rig. It went sailing upward until it reached the end of the patch cord that, acting like an elastic band, whipped it back down. As it hit the floor, the headstock broke off. Fortunately, the repair geniuses at Gruhn Guitars in Nashville did an amazing job. They crafted a mother-of-pearl inlay and had it sounding better than ever.

These incidents became an apt metaphor for my conflicted psyche. I was both arrogant and impulsive. It didn't take much to ignite my anger. At uneven and unpredictable intervals, chemicals were popping off in my brain. At times I acted crazy. I wouldn't go so far as to say that there was a method to my madness, but I never once entertained the notion of cracking up completely. In my out-of-control behavior I was convinced that I could maintain some degree of control. I always felt there was a line that I'd never cross. In fact, I never did. Now, though, I know that much of that was due to good luck.

I have clear images of what had to be the most unclear summer of my life. In fact, management thought it'd be a good idea if two of our security guards spent the summer in a guest room at our home to keep an eye on me. I remember receiving a large shipment of opium that had us swinging on the distant stars for a month or more. I remember being introduced to rare vintage wine and buying it by the case. We drank it like Sprite. I remember my friend from Morocco who made leather suits in whatever color I named. We had the same skinny build so they always fit like a glove, right out of the box. Fresh off the plane, the package would be waiting for me in the backseat of the limo, where I'd slip it on. Knowing that my leather maker liked to include special treats, I'd find a gram or two of premium blow stuffed into one of the secret pockets.

I remember Eurofest '77. Munich in August. It never stopped raining. That's where Steven collapsed onstage. Soon he was spitting up blood. But then, so was I. It was the poor-quality coke. It acts like sandpaper on your throat. I was singing backup and only one song. I can only imagine what it was doing to Steven, singing full-throttle every show. Afterward, we didn't discuss it. It simply happened. He needed some rest. I needed some rest. He needed to take fewer drugs. I needed to take fewer drugs. He took more drugs—and so did I.

Munich was also where I ran out of coke, out of Tuinals, out of everything except the mini-bottles of booze in my room. I turned on the TV and saw a picture of Elvis. It was framed in black. I didn't need to know German to understand that the King was dead. The entire nation of Germany, where he was considered a god, went into mourning. I went into mourning. When we got to Hamburg, the scene of our next show, we came out after the Doobie Brothers. The emcee asked for a moment of silence in honor of Elvis. I looked out into the crowd and couldn't see a dry eye. Grown men were weeping openly. I thought about hearing "Hound Dog" when I was a kid. I wondered about the journey that had led Elvis to such an early death. I didn't want to think about death. I remember thinking, *That's never gonna happen to me.* I've never known any drug addict— including me—to straighten out because of another addict's death. Though I was well past my teen years, I still clung to that foolish sense of teen invincibility. I was a bullfighter putting on a blindfold and charging into a ring while screaming, "Bring it on."

In our determination to complete *Draw the Line*, we booked time in English studios to redo a vocal or add a guitar part. Jack Douglas, who came along on the tour to make sure this album got finished, arranged for us to record at George Martin's famous AIR Studios, where Martin had experimented with sounds for the Beatles.

When *Draw the Line* came out that fall, the album set a Columbia sales record—well over a million copies sold in fewer than six weeks.

Zunk Buker's dad, an air force pilot, was another angel on our shoulder. Not only did he expertly fly Steven's twin-engine Cessna, but he wouldn't let the band charter a plane until he had a chance to painstakingly check it out. Many were the times I heard him tell Leber-Krebs, "I don't care what kind of deal you made, the boys are not getting on this plane." In one such encounter, he saved our lives. He looked at a Convair and firmly put his foot down. "No way," was all he said. A week later, on October 20, 1977, that Convair crashed with Lynyrd Skynyrd on board, one of the worst tragedies in rock history.

More frightening than the precarious planes, though, were the crowds in Philadelphia. We were playing the Spectrum when some asshole lobbed an M-80 onstage. It went off like a bomb right in our faces, searing Steven's cornea and tearing an artery in my right hand. I was bleeding profusely. Another quarter inch in the wrong direction and Steven could have been blinded. We were rushed to the ER, where absolutely no one paid us any immediate attention, so Elyssa started screaming and pushed everything off the nurse's desk. Not a great way to make friends, but it got results. We were hurried back to the examination rooms. As rude as she might have been, Elyssa rose to the occasion, displaying an impassioned loyalty to me, Steven, and the band.

As a result of our injuries, we had to cancel a month's worth of shows.

I had a nasty night in Newton when I ran out of coke and had to go out and score. This was unusual. The best dealers in town gladly made house calls, but for some reason no one was responding to my requests. Elyssa was tired and wanted to stay home. So a friend of mine and I went down to the Paradise, a club where I found a connection. By the time we got back home, I couldn't believe my eyes. A fire had destroyed our house. The second floor was a smoldering ruin. Cops and firemen were everywhere. Elyssa was nowhere to be found. Someone said that, unharmed, she had gone to her mom's. The cause was a faulty electrical outlet.

The important thing was that Elyssa had not been injured. In another piece of good fortune, my guitars remained untouched. Thanks to the Newton Fire Department, the blaze was contained to the master bedroom and second floor.

Of all that I lost in the fire, what I missed most was the gun I had inherited from my dad. I kept it close to my bed and it was gone. Unlike me, my dad wasn't a hunter—he was a golfer—and this one gun, a .22 Saturday night special that was given to him by his father, was his only weapon. It meant a lot to me, and I still regret the loss.

My reaction to the fire was typical. I went on a three-day binge. After hiring armed guards to protect our house, I went to a friend's, where I slept on the kitchen floor. When I woke up, I plied myself with whatever get-high substances he had. I vaguely remember calling Elyssa and talking about what we would do next, but there was no movement on her part or mine to get together. Under normal circumstances I would have gone back to console her. But subconsciously I was feeling that when the house burned down, so did our marriage. Before the fire there had been billboards every two feet, staring me right in the face with words that screamed *YOU ARE IN THE WRONG RELATIONSHIP.* Yet it took the blazing heat to bring that message home.

One night I got a call about a shoot-out at the house. A burglar had tried to break in. One of my armed guards had opened fire. No one was killed but the story made the papers. Then came another call: Two women, who were an alluring combination of movie producers and groupies, wanted me to meet them at a bar in Logan Airport to discuss featuring me in a film. I went, I drank heavily, I half-listened to their plans. Some guy, probably drunk himself, overheard my name and approached the women. "I heard you talking about Joe Perry," he said. "You want to stay away from that guy. They have shoot-outs at his house." The women flew off into the night. I never heard from them again.

I moved into a hotel and Elyssa eventually joined me. We rented a house in Brookline. You'd think we'd have discussed the trauma we had just endured, but practically nothing was said. We made arrangements to have our home repaired, with Elyssa's mother overseeing the project. We went back on the road. Business as usual.

The continual presence of Cyrinda Foxe—Elyssa's friend and David Johansen's wife—only added to our overall estrangement. Sometime earlier, Elyssa had invited Cyrinda on several Aerosmith road trips. Cyrinda was happy to accept and often showed up with an ample supply of drugs to complement our own stash. Of course David knew about these trips and would ask me to keep an eye on his wife. Like most couples, they were having their problems but were still together. The bond between Elyssa and Cyrinda was strong.

That dynamic changed radically, though, when one night at the Beverly Hills Hotel Cyrinda wound up in Steven's bed. I was shocked and dismayed. When the affair turned into a rock-and-roll soap opera, culminating with Cyrinda leaving David for Steven, I felt partially responsible. Elyssa was also pissed. She felt that Cyrinda had used her to get to Steven. I wound up apologizing to David, but there was nothing I could say that really mattered. I felt terrible for my friend.

Rumors floated around insinuating that I had designs on Cyrinda. Nothing could have been further from the truth. Not only was she not my type, she was my friend David's wife. Regardless of hearsay, nothing even remotely inappropriate ever transpired between us.

Tired of running at full speed—partying, touring, recording—I knew I needed a break. I asked Elyssa to find a place in the Caribbean where we could stay for ten days and get away from it all. We needed to chill from our little heroin jones. So we flew down to Montserrat, where we rented a beautiful three-bedroom cottage, complete with original Picassos on the wall, tucked into the side of the mountain overlooking the sea. It was as close to paradise as I was likely to get.

But there was trouble in paradise. I had brought a few hits of dope that let us get through the first days smoothly. When my supply was exhausted, though, my body rebelled. I'd kicked before, but those other times had been while I was on the road, when I was fully occupied with the band. This time there was nothing that intense to distract me, so the withdrawal was rough. But with the help of the local rum, I toughed it out.

My spirits lifted when I learned that George Martin, the famed Beatles producer, was staying at a bed-and-breakfast on the island. I sent word to him. He was happy to see me, and together we surveyed the mountaintop property where he was planning to build a studio. He pointed to a cow in the middle of a pasture and said, "That's where the board will be."

"It'd be great to record here," I said.

"And I'd be honored to host you," said George, ever the English gentleman.

We went back to town, where, in an open-air bar by the beach, we drank rum as George regaled me with Beatles stories. I listened attentively, but my mind began to wander. My body was still hurting.

Over the next days I sought relief through nature. I went into the jungle, wearing my leopard-print swim trunks and brandishing my ten-inch hunting knife. Playing the part of the hunter-gatherer, I feasted on wild bananas and swung on vines like Tarzan.

Feeling increasingly edgy, I went back to our cottage and made the mistake of calling my dealer in Boston. When I had left, he'd complained about the city being dry.

"The situation's changed," he said. "I have an ounce of China white waiting for you."

That was all I needed to hear. Suddenly the Montserrat sun was too hot, the food too bland. There was only one beach, and it was too small. There was no TV. I found every excuse imaginable to cut short our vacation. I kept envisioning that China white. Just like that, I booked the next flight out. Elyssa and I packed in a flash and ran to the airport. It turned out George Martin was on the same flight, and we had another engaging conversation and a few more drinks as we flew through a cloudless sky over the Caribbean.

The second the plane touched down, Elyssa and I raced over to the dealer's house.

"Man," he said, "you just beat the storm."

"What storm?"

"A blizzard's about to hit."

By sheer luck, we'd slipped in just in time. Within hours, the Great Blizzard of February 1978 blanketed Boston. Logan Airport went dark for days. The city was completely shut down. Elyssa and I got home in time to watch the storm outside our living room window. After snorting up a combination of heroin and coke supplied by my man, we were numbed out, impervious to the chaos caused by Mother Nature.

THE RUTS

Later in 1978, George Martin reentered our lives when we were asked to be in *Sgt. Pepper's Lonely Hearts Club Band*, a movie produced by Robert Stigwood, the producer of *Jesus Christ Superstar*, *Grease*, *Tommy*, and *Saturday Night Fever*. The thing was a mess. I believe the Stones wisely turned down the role that was given to us. The cast included Steve Martin, Billy Preston, and Earth, Wind & Fire. Along with Alice Cooper, we were villains. As a matter of fact, we were labeled the Future Villain Band. Peter Frampton was the hero. That made sense since *Frampton Comes Alive* was a huge-selling album and Frampton was up on the charts as a solo artist. Management told us that we'd get to murder both Frampton and the Bee Gees in the movie. We were game. I checked into the Beverly Hills Hotel as "Richard Burton," a good move since room service presumed that Liz Taylor was with me. When I picked up the phone to order a drink, they were at my door before I had time to put the phone down. The Hollywood movie experience was . . . well, Hollywood. Unbelievable waste. Hurry up and wait. Oceans of booze, drugs in the trailers, endless takes and retakes, total confusion about the script. I didn't know if all films were made like this, but we felt at home.

The script was flipped so Frampton would kill Steven. We said no. That seemed wrong. Instead we killed the Bee Gees and it was a character called Strawberry Fields who shoved Steven off the stage and killed him. The Future Villain Band then killed Strawberry Fields. It wasn't exactly *Citizen Kane.*

We realized that our involvement with this could look cheesy, but we looked at it as another adventure. The real hook was being able to work with George Martin on our cover of "Come Together." We flew to New York to work at the Record Plant. Our idea was not to stray too far from the original. We had too much respect for John Lennon's classic to go changing it just for the sake of change. We ran it down and waited for the arrival of George Martin.

When the tall and elegant Mr. Martin arrived, we said quick hellos over the intercom and ran down the song for him. We sat there nervously, waiting for words of wisdom from the genius producer.

"It sounds good, boys. Please proceed."

We were shocked. We figured he'd have a lot to say—either adding or subtracting from our interpretation. But he had no suggestions whatsoever. So we kept playing until we formulated a good basic track.

When we went to the control room to greet him face-to-face, he was the same genial gentleman as ever.

"Keep doing what you're doing, boys, and I shall see you shortly."

And with that he left.

When the movie came out, no one could believe how bad it was. No matter, we had a blast at the premiere. Chevy Chase, sitting directly behind us, kept the wisecracks coming and was more entertaining than the movie itself. *Sgt. Pepper's Lonely Hearts Club Band* went from being a potential blockbuster to a bomb within days of release. The critics started calling it "Stigwood's Folly" because supposedly the budget ballooned from a few million to $30 million.

Before we left L.A., we got dressed up as coal miners, our faces smeared with dirt, for some publicity shots. The shoot took place in front of a cave in the Hollywood Hills, an old location for a thousand and one cowboy flicks and sci-fi shows. At my suggestion, we climbed to the top of a sandpit and rolled down, getting so gritty that it later took hours to wash the sand out of my hair.

"Come Together," the Aerosmith version released as a single, went to number 23 on the pop charts. We were working on *Live! Bootleg*, an album of old shows that we intentionally wanted to sound bootlegged. A couple of those tracks were recorded off the air onto a cassette. It had hiss all over it. We left on the hiss because the hiss was real. But I'm not sure Columbia ever understood our concept. They wanted a clean sound, but we wanted to keep it real. That's the thrill of a real bootleg. Leber-Krebs had us playing the biggest venues in the country. We called it the Bootleg tour.

That was the summer of 1978, the same summer Steven married Cyrinda at Sunapee. In September came word that Keith Moon, one of the great drummers in all rock, had died an alcohol- and drug-related death. I mourned his passing and kept partying. At twenty-eight, I still felt invincible.

The tour went on. We were headquartered at the Whitehall Hotel in Chicago. A Learjet took us to the usual spots where we'd been playing for seven or eight years—Detroit and Toledo, Cincy and Madison, St. Paul and Indianapolis. No band covered more American soil. No band worked the heartland any harder. Other bands might come through once every two or three years, but we were there, in your face, every few months.

It was at the Whitehall that Brad and I borrowed Steven's cassette recorder to fool with some riffs. We went to my room, where Elyssa and Brad's wife, Karen, were also hanging out. As we were playing, they were discussing Steven's lascivious behavior the previous night. He had met a girl at the bar and, in full view of everyone, started making out with her—to the point where they should have gotten a room. As Elyssa and Karen recounted the story, they themselves had a few drinks and didn't hold back on any of the salacious details. Brad and I stuck to our guitars and, when we were through laying down our ideas, returned the recorder to Steven.

The kicker was this: I forgot to take the tape out of the machine. Later that night Cyrinda arrived. I'm not sure who turned on the tape machine, Steven or Cyrinda, but the cassette got played. You could hear Brad and me jamming, but just as clearly you could hear Elyssa and Karen detailing Steven's escapade. Steven and Cyrinda listened to the entire tape. That's when their floor of the Whitehall Hotel exploded.

The two of them came running up to our room. Steven, who thrives on this kind of drama, demanded that the four of us listen to the tape in its entirety. I didn't want to. I couldn't have cared less, but Steven insisted. He listened to it over and again. Cyrinda went batshit. Steven accused Elyssa of spreading evil gossip and trying to destroy his relationship. And while Karen and Elyssa were clearly guilty of gossiping, their facts—the very facts that Steven was looking to deflect—were completely accurate. The madness went on for hours, Cyrinda screaming that Steven was a cheater and liar while Steven screamed that we were the real culprits, whose aim was to undermine his relationship with Cyrinda. Another typical night of Aerosmith fun and games.

Leber-Krebs were managing foreign bands who wanted to make it in the states. They lured these groups with the prospect of opening for Aerosmith while they shopped them a record deal. Most of the bands wound up on Columbia. From a business angle, we didn't give this much thought. But we did get to hear a lot of the up-and-coming new groups. Some were good, others great. None, though, was greater than AC/DC, still one of my favorite bands of all time. During the one summer that AC/DC was on our tour, they pushed us hard. We had to be on our toes.

My hand was still fucked up from the explosion in Philly. I was battle weary and so was Steven. He'd swing the microphone stand around his head and mine like he was going to strike, but I never worried about that. No matter how vicious the animosity between us, a physical altercation was never a threat. The line of civility between us was thin, but it existed. Something powerful kept both of us from crossing it.

That winter Nugent opened for us at Madison Square Garden. Nugent and Aerosmith were also on the same episode of *The Midnight Special*, a TV show featuring top pop and rock acts that came on after Johnny Carson on Friday nights.

The next night we were back in Philly, the first time at the Spectrum since Steven was nearly blinded and I got blasted by the M-80, a firecracker so dangerous that it's now outlawed. We had our doubts, but we felt, why let one crazy fan wreck it for fifteen thousand others? Besides, it was around Thanksgiving, a good time to feel gratitude for all our fans. They had even bought a billboard near the venue apologizing for what happened last time. We hadn't been onstage longer than a half hour, though, when a missile was launched from the crowd—it was either a whiskey or a beer bottle—and landed right in front of Steven and me. Glass shattered everywhere. Steven's face got cut. As we left, he was bleeding profusely. That was it.

Nineteen seventy-nine had to be one of the lowest years of my life. Approaching twenty-nine, I felt disgust on all sorts of levels. I realized that my marriage had hit a dead end but I didn't have the wherewithal to end it. I realized that the band's drugging and drinking—including my own—was out of hand, yet no one felt any compunction to curb it. Musically, the band was on cruise control. We were playing the same shit we'd been playing for years. If Steven and I had found a way to deal with our differences, that would have helped. But we were further apart than ever. He saw Elyssa—and my willingness to lose myself in my relationship with her—as the cause of Aerosmith's problems. The band members never addressed those problems. We never had open and frank discussions about what was wrong. Instead, Elyssa was used as the scapegoat for many Aerosmith issues.

I was never part of the boys' club. I had no fondness for the after-the-show blow-job room. While I liked losing myself in chemicals, losing myself in anonymous sexual mayhem was not my style. I'm a one-woman man.

The insanity of our tour-record-tour-record cycle was going into its eighth year. What was required was creative renewal. We needed fresh energy and new ideas. That's when we started planning the next record.

The struggle was more monumental than ever. The five of us were able to come up with a bunch of song ideas. That happened at the Wherehouse in Waltham. Then when we went to Media Sound in New York to record the tracks, Steven was there to help out with the arrangements and the recording. I thought we cut some of the best tracks we'd ever done. The guitar interplay between me and Brad broke new ground. Everyone was at the top of his game. When it came time for lyrics and vocals, though, Steven began to drift away.

Slowly, progress ground to a halt. I started to get annoyed, then aggravated, and then out-and-out pissed. I'd been working these tracks along with Tom, Brad, and Joey. They were hot. For example, I was switching between a bottleneck to a six-string to a lap steel on something called "Cheesecake." But nothing could be finished without Steven. Weeks went by. Then months.

This was when Leber-Krebs decided to hold one of their rare meetings to review our financial status.

"The band is broke," said Krebs, "and you'll have to do some festivals in between recording your new album."

We had never done that before. When we toured, we toured; when we recorded, we recorded. That was our ironclad ritual. When I objected to changing the long-established routine, David Krebs said we had no choice. Beyond being broke, each of us owed money for our in-room hotel charges from the previous tours.

I wondered how in hell that could be. We'd headlined some of the biggest festivals in the history of rock and roll. We'd been selling out arenas for years. We'd made untold millions. Where did all of it go? And what about the merchandise and publishing money?

Krebs gave a long answer that sounded like double-talk.

"If what you say is true," I said, "at least show us the paperwork that proves your point."

Nothing he had made any sense to me. And it got worse.

"Joe, you personally owe $180,000 in room service charges."

"If we're so broke," I said, "how am I going to get that kind of money?"

"Make a solo album," he suggested.

That thought had never occurred to me before. I had never thought about doing a record on my own any more than I had thought about leaving the band. At this moment, though, I did have one thought: Come hell or high water, I was getting my own lawyer and putting him on the case.

Meanwhile, we still had to finish the album that would be called *Night in the Ruts*. We went to work every day, spending a fortune on hotel bills and studio time with nothing to show for it. We were still waiting for Steven to do his job—write the lyrics and sing them. I couldn't comprehend why Steven was taking so fuckin' long. A fruitless pattern was set: We'd wander into the studio in late afternoon. We'd hope Steven might have completed a song, but he hadn't. So we waited some more. By early evening the dealers would show up, letting us sample their best stuff with the hopes of scoring a big sale. No problem there. We'd get high and the party would start. And still no Steven. Tired of waiting and disgusted with the band's inability to complete the record, I packed up and went back home to Boston.

With the Leber-Krebs money mess in mind, I called a lawyer to intervene on my behalf. I needed my own representative. I needed to know where the money had gone. We had several meetings and my hopes were high. But my hopes were soon dashed when I saw how Leber-Krebs totally overpowered my lawyer. It was the same scenario as when I had introduced Elyssa's attorney cousin into the mix. Given Leber-Krebs' powerful position in the music business, lawyers were easily intimidated. My lawyer stopped discussing an audit, leaving me in the dark about where the money had gone. I still couldn't comprehend being broke.

Back in Boston, Elyssa and other friends encouraged me to go out on my own. What a concept! The notion became more and more appealing. It felt like freedom. I'd be free not to give a shit whether Steven showed or not. The band's dysfunction had come to a junction. Bluesman Robert Johnson might have sold his soul to the devil at the crossroads, but I was feeling like I had no soul left to sell. My soul had been smoked up, snorted up, drugged up, fucked up. My soul was in tatters. I wanted off the road but management said we owed so much money that we couldn't afford to stop doing what we had been doing ever since the start of our musical enterprise. We had to keep playing, keep touring, go back to the Midwest, back to California, back to Texas, playing big venues, big festivals, to big crowds of fans who wanted to see the band.

We had to keep going at any cost. There was no way to stop the machine. There was no way to get off the merry-go-round. But another real problem was that I was addicted to excitement. After all, that was what we had worked for. We were living the dream.

I had to keep going, going, going—until I finally realized, when push came to shove, I could do whatever I wanted. I had a choice. I could just fuckin' quit.

PART 4

THE PROJECT

OUT

I had been harboring an illusion for a long time that I didn't want to shatter. The illusion was that, no matter what, I could put up with the band and the band could put up with me. The illusion was that I could stay with this band while also staying with Elyssa. I was pissed off by her high school antics, but maybe deep down part of me approved of her misbehavior. Whatever my ambivalence, I stood by and watched her verbally attack the guys and their wives and girlfriends. When I talked about leaving the band, Elyssa had no ambivalence about supporting me. She was certain I could make it on my own.

The fact that Steven couldn't finish his lyrics and vocals to complete *Night in the Ruts* frustrated me to no end. I knew it was hard for him, but the drugs were making it worse. And why was I the only guy in the band willing to put the screws to management and demand a detailed explanation on how in hell we could possibly be broke? Something was fucked up. Everything was fucked up.

Then came the infamous episode during the summer tour of 1979 that has fallen into the realm of mythology. The story has been told a hundred times from a hundred points of view. My point of view is vague. I know it happened during a July gig in Cleveland at an outdoor stadium during the World Series of Rock. Nugent and AC/DC were on the bill, and so were Thin Lizzy and Journey, all opening for us. We played our set. At one point someone threw a small vial of powder onstage. Steven picked it up and shot me a glance. He poured some on the mic and we dared each other to go first. I forget who took the first sniff, but we both sampled it. We were laughing pretty hard over the roll of the dice. Turned out to be weak blow.

When we got offstage I learned that there had been a vicious confrontation between Elyssa and Terry, Tom's wife. Terry was a great chick. She spoke her mind. I liked her. I hated hearing that Elyssa had thrown a glass of milk at her. Fortunately no one was physically injured, but the emotional damage was nasty as it could be. Steven ran in and started accusing me. I hadn't even been there when the fight happened, but that wasn't good enough for Steven. He was saying that my inability to keep Elyssa on a short leash was the problem.

"Let's get out of here," was all I said to Elyssa.

That's the night I walked away from Aerosmith. Elyssa and I went back to Boston. I guess it was loyalty that let me stay with Elyssa. She was my wife, and for what it was worth, I still valued our commitment to each other. Part of me probably knew that what had happened in Cleveland was the last straw. For years Elyssa had caused bullshit that put the band members at odds. But the truth is that the band never sat down and talked about our problems. When we would try to confront each other or explain our feelings, we'd wind up screaming. It was the band that broke up the band, not any outsider. None of us was willing to take a hard look at ourselves and our issues. Rather than look in the mirror, it was easier to lay it flat on the table, snort what was on it, and blame someone else.

I stayed put. I stewed. I thought about it long and hard. I had dozens and dozens of demo tapes that had gone nowhere—mainly because Steven never bothered to put lyrics to them. No matter how intense my relationship to drugs, I didn't lose my drive to keep making music. The choice I faced wasn't whether to go on making music or not—it was a foregone conclusion that I would—but whether to make that music with or without Aerosmith. Continuing with Aerosmith meant working with a management team I had not trusted for years. It meant playing with bandmates who had angry resentments against each other. It meant playing with Steven, whose drugged-out ways, though no more extreme than mine, triggered his resentment of me.

The whole operation had become a nightmare. I was tired of the bullshit. I just wanted to get in a van and go play rock and roll. I was willing to play clubs—any clubs. If there were a hundred people, as opposed to a hundred thousand, fine. If there were forty, fine. I'd find a few good musicians and just get out there. No complications, no weird management, no drama. Just music. Just go out there as another rock-and-roll pirate and do what I do.

Because Aerosmith had gotten so crazily complicated, the idea here was to keep it simple. I saw my solo effort as nothing more than a project. Thus the name, the Joe Perry Project, me and a couple of guys. The first guy I thought of was David Hull. I knew him from the old days, when he was with Buddy Miles. Hull was one of the best bass players I'd ever heard. I remembered him as a witty cat and easy to be with. He'd been in a good band called Dirty Angels, and I was convinced he'd fit right into my band. I was right.

I was also right about Ralph Morman, a tremendously soulful singer with a voice that reminded me of Paul Rodgers of Bad Company and Free. I'd met Ralph years earlier when he was with Daddy Warbux, a band once managed by Frank Connelly.

When I saw him again in 1979, he said, "Great to see you, Joe."

"Hey, man, how are you, Ralph?"

"Not all that great. Been doing odd jobs."

"Not singing?"

"Not really. You know anyone who's looking for a singer?"

"Yeah. Me."

After auditioning a few drummers, I settled on Ronnie Stewart, who was working at a music store in Boston. I told him that he'd better keep his day job because there were no guarantees.

I put the guys up at the Holiday Inn and used the Aerosmith

Wherehouse for rehearsals. I figured that since I was a one-fifth owner of the place, why not use it? I'd leave little notes on the blackboard.

"Mind if I use the Wherehouse the rest of the week? You guys aren't using it—even though you could use the practice."

My former bandmates would answer with notes of their own.

"Sure, go ahead and use it. You need to practice a lot more than us."

For all the tense feelings on all sides about my leaving, there was room for good-natured ribbing. The connection remained.

I'd washed my hands of the *Night in the Ruts* album and wasn't there for its completion. Because I was out of the band, I couldn't believe that that all my guitar parts—both leads and rhythm—remained on the record. I was told that when Steven finally did show up to do his vocals he was smoking crack. It certainly didn't sound like that, though. He finally wrote the lyrics and finished the album. This crack thing was something new to me. I didn't know anything about it. It was just coming onto the scene.

On the cover of the *Ruts* record they used that photo of us as coal miners. I was half-surprised that they hadn't edited me out of the shot.

Ruts came out in November, the same month that the Joe Perry Project had its first gig. It was at the Rathskeller, the student union at Boston College. I wasn't all that surprised to see Steven before the show. He'd come by to say hello and wish me well. I appreciated that. Later I learned that he didn't stick around to hear any of the music, but Brad Whitford was there and stayed for the whole set. The crowd reaction was strong and the reviews were great. A few weeks later we played the Paradise in Boston and tore it up. We were on our way.

Writers were saying that the decline of Aerosmith left a void that was being filled by young rock bands like Van Halen. I liked Van Halen. They made a great rock record. As a guitarist, Eddie Van Halen was an obvious prodigy and an amazing technician. He led a hungry band with the goods to back up their claim as the next big thing. David Lee Roth's wit and humor were a perfect foil for Eddie's brilliant playing.

I was happy with the Joe Perry Project. I was happy digging my new sense of freedom. I was gratified that fans and critics were raving about us, and I was eager to jump in the bus and hit the clubs. I felt like I was on fire.

The fact that I didn't curb my excessive highs didn't lower the flames.

That heat burns inside me no matter what. I always knew this to be true, but in the transition period between Aerosmith and the Project, I was never more aware of my overwhelming drive to make music no matter what. The music was coming out of me in torrents. I had to start recording.

Columbia had been reading the press on the Project and was interested in giving me a solo deal. Their hesitancy, though, had to do with timing. All too aware of Aerosmith's history of taking forever to make a record, they thought I'd follow that same pattern. But I swore the opposite. I had the songs, the lyrics, the band. I was ready to rock. I could turn out a complete record in five or six weeks. Miraculously, they took me at my word, and I delivered.

I recruited Jack Douglas, who was just as ready as I was. He wanted to do it at the Hit Factory in midtown Manhattan. The contrast between the torturous ordeal of recording Aerosmith and the seamless groove that characterized the Project was remarkable. We ripped through the basic tracks in less than a week.

The songs I wrote were largely autobiographical. "Let the Music Do the Talking"—the title track—spoke for itself. It was just how I was feeling. I didn't need to talk. Didn't need to explain how much I wanted to be on my own, working on my own timetable, free to work at my own speed, which was plenty fast. "Conflict of Interest" was inspired by my feelings about the shady side of the music business. I was going straight back to my roots, as demonstrated by the R&B-heavy "Rockin' Train." Songs like "Life at a Glance" and "Ready on the Firing Line" were constructed around riffs that had been bouncing around my brain for months. I had to get them out of me, and Jack proved the perfect producer to facilitate that process. He kept saying that some of the nine tunes I wrote could have saved the Aerosmith *Ruts* record from going down the toilet. The best part of it was the certain knowledge that I was moving in an upward direction. My lyrics for "Shooting Star" say:

No one knows much time has passed
That I've returned from space at last
A lot of wounds that hurt and bleed
The scars of which you'll never see

My brand-new ship is stellar bound
To search out a place I've never found
Where I go only time will tell
There's a lot of space between heaven and hell

ROCKS

Another great thing about this "brand-new ship"—the Joe Perry Project—was that I was not only writing lyrics but singing again as well. I shared lead vocals with Ralph Morman on two songs and sang lead alone on another two. I had no illusions that I was a Steven Tyler or a Freddie Mercury. I was simply following the adage of the old bluesmen, who believed that every guitarist should sing his own songs. But I also knew that the larger point was to pour myself—all of myself—into my music. That meant my voice as well as my guitar. Both were extensions of me.

Reviews were good. Given the enthusiasm for the record, I expected it to perform better than it did. My lawyer, Bob Casper, did what he could from New York, but I was essentially managing the band. Casper was trying to free up some money from Leber-Krebs, but ultimately he came up against the same stone wall.

No matter what Columbia did or didn't do for the album, no one could suppress the fire of our live set. We were smoking, playing a mix of some of the new things we'd just recorded and also a few Aerosmith numbers, like "Walk This Way" and "Same Old Song and Dance." Yet for all my enthusiasm for my new band, it wasn't without drama. Few bands are. This first drama was especially improbable because it involved me, a guy not exactly known for sobriety, going off on Ralph Morman for being drunk. In my mind there's operative drunk and then there's fall-down, I-can't-perform drunk. When I hired Ralph, he was in control. Now he was on the verge of becoming an out-of-control drunk. One night when he showed up an hour late to a gig in a state of wild inebriation, I hauled off and decked him. That's how enraged I was. That's how determined I was to keep the Project on track. We were off to a great start and I was bound and determined to maintain a high musical standard. That meant firing Ralph and finding another singer. For a while I became that singer, and that was fine. But I needed a singer who could deliver some of the songs I loved to play. I was a guitarist more obsessed with guitars than ever. I'd go out there with two guitars—a left-handed Strat that had a left-handed Telecaster neck and a midnight-blue Travis Bean L500 with dual pickups. I felt like I was rediscovering my guitar again.

I was surely feeling free from the dysfunctional depression that had dragged down Aerosmith. I was also feeling that I had something to prove—that I could do it alone. On the road, I was feeling more than a little liberated by being away from Elyssa. The marriage continued to be a strain. My heroin snorting hadn't stopped. I was hooked on the drug. That became clear during that first Project tour when I ran out and had to go to a doctor for Darvon and Catapres, meds that helped me cope with my withdrawal.

Come the spring of 1980, I was hard-pressed in all areas. I saw the band as a success and wanted to build it up. The first tour had been all clubs. The next tour would be theaters. I also thought about hiring a keyboardist and maybe a second guitarist to give me a little relief. Up until now, it had been all on me. Then my money got funny. I wasn't earning anything close to what I'd made with Aerosmith, but I was making decent dough. However, back in Boston, Elyssa, who refused to get a driver's license, was taking limos to the supermarket. She was living it up like in the pre-Project days. I tried to tell her that this was no time buy porcelain vases and silk sheets. There was a good chance we'd have to sell our house. In no uncertain terms, I'd made it clear that we'd entered a period of austerity. But Elyssa didn't get it—or didn't want to get it. In the meantime, the IRS was sending special-delivery letters about hundreds of thousands of dollars of back taxes. By then I was broke and badly needed the fee for a weekend where we were booked at a club. Elyssa came along. She had something she wanted to tell me in person. She was pregnant.

All this was on my mind as we pulled into Austin, Texas, for one of the last gigs of the tour. Then came the call.

"Sorry, Joe," said the booking agent. "The gig fell through. The club's closing."

"The weekend of our gig?"

"The very weekend. I'm sorry."

"I thought we had a guarantee."

"We did. But when a club closes, all guarantees are off."

We were up there in the Travelodge with nothing to do and nowhere to go. When I tried to use my credit card to book us plane tickets home, the card had maxed out. So had my drugs. And so had the drugs that helped me withdraw from my drugs. If it hadn't been for my lawyer Bob Casper and his willingness to front me ten thousand dollars, I might still be in Austin.

I found another singer—J. Mala, who'd been with Revolver—who stayed with us for a short while. Mala was replaced by Charlie Farren, a world-class singer/songwriter who'd been fronting a local Boston band, Balloon. The lead-singer slot was something of a revolving door that started spinning really fast. We played the Palladium in New York and were glad to get a two-month tour as the opening act for Heart. That was enough for me to keep my head above water—barely. Things got weird, though, when my father-in-law claimed to have found a threatening note on the windshield of my car back in Boston. It was from drug dealers saying to pay up or else. I didn't know—or I had forgotten—who they were. All the more reason to stay out on the road.

The gigs kept coming, but with so many hungry dogs on my heels needing to be fed, I felt like a pauper. The Project was making decent money, but I owed so much cash that every cent was spoken for before I could get it.

I was talking to Jack Douglas about doing another Project record during the time he was working with John Lennon and Yoko Ono on *Double Fantasy* and *Milk and Honey*. It was Jack who called me to say that John had been shot and killed. I was numb. I didn't know what to do, what to say, how to react. I had met him briefly at the Record Plant, but I never knew the man. Without him and his Beatles I wouldn't have been doing what I was doing. I saw him as a searcher, a brave artist. He could have lived off those Beatles songs for the rest of his life, but at the end of his life he was still making daring and important music. He had written some of the best pop songs of all time, yet he was a true rock and roller. John was, is, and always will be, one of my great inspirations.

While I was out with the Project, Steven had replaced me with Jimmy Crespo, who was supposed to resemble me. The band was having a terrible time. Steven was collapsing onstage. The thing seemed to be falling apart. Six months after I had left Aerosmith, Brad Whitford couldn't take it anymore and quit. He joined forces with Derek St. Holmes, Ted Nugent's vocalist, to form Whitford St. Holmes. I wished Brad well and meant it. Later on Brad would come out and play occasional dates with the Project. It was always great to have him onstage with us, both for me as a friend and the fans for the rock and roll. I welcomed him. As guitarists we've always been totally compatible and instinctively know how to complement each other.

Stories kept coming in about Aerosmith's attempt to make another album, the one that would eventually be called *Rock in a Hard Place* and the only Aerosmith record on which I'm totally absent. The band recruited Jack Douglas to produce. It took them over two years and cost nearly a million and a half dollars. Jack told me that it was the same old story—months and months of Steven procrastinating about his lyrics and vocals. I can't tell you how relieved I was not to have been in the middle of that mess.

Yet I was facing a financial nightmare of my own. At the time, I blamed the old Aerosmith management, who I was convinced were withholding money that I was owed. My fear was they wanted to squeeze me until I'd rejoin the band. I thought they were acting like dicks. But, if I were to have been honest about the situation, I'd have had to see my own culpability. I certainly see it now. Back when the money was pouring in, I should have complained louder about the lack of accountability, but that's all I did—complain. I could have quit earlier. I could have hired my own independent accountant. I could have gotten my financial act together if I had asserted myself, but I didn't. I floated on the high of the band's huge success. The truth is that I didn't have any idea what I was making or spending. I never gave a second thought to taxes. All those years, I assumed Leber-Krebs were taking care of the taxes. As the son of a highly professional and well-respected cost accountant, I realized that I was sliding into financial chaos. I also realized that if I'd ever needed my dad's help and guidance, I needed it now. And he wasn't around.

But arrogance remained my middle name. Years before, when Steven started introducing me to the crowds as Joe *Fuckin'* Perry, he was referencing that arrogance. That arrogance was a cover-up for all the emotions I didn't want on display—fear, vulnerability, uncertainty, anger, and confusion.

Bob Casper, the lawyer who had helped me out in the past, was gone. In his place was Don Law, the cat who ran the Boston Tea Party and went on to become the top promoter in the city. I looked to Don to save me, money-wise. I was on the verge of losing my house. But Don could only do so much. There was a decent advance for the second Project album on Columbia. I turned all my attention to writing and producing that record. Had it not been for the prospect of another major musical effort on my part, I might have lost it.

We went to the Wherehouse to start the process. The other guys came up with strong material. David Hull wrote two songs—"Dirty Little Things" and "Buzz Buzz." Charlie Farren wrote "East Coast West Coast" and we reworked a shuffle of mine and called it "South Station Blues." I was encouraged when Bruce Botnick came on board. He had produced *L.A. Woman*, the great Doors album, and before that had worked as their engineer. I loved the way the Doors records sounded.

I decided to get the Record Plant to drive their truck up from New York and park it outside the old Boston Opera House on Washington Street in what was called the Combat Zone. We recorded on the same stage where *Aida* and *Don Giovanni* had been performed numerous times. The theater was like a gorgeous woman gone to seed. You could see and feel traces of her former glory, but the paint was peeling and the floors were cracked. I liked all that decay. The rooms were huge marble affairs harking back to a different era. The acoustics were naturally sublime.

I called the album *I've Got the Rock 'n Rolls Again* because I did. Like the first Project record, this one was made without strife or procrastination. I was hoping that my promptness might convince Columbia not only that was I still taking my band seriously, but that my band was here to stay. When the reviews came with even more praise than had been lavished on *Let the Music Do the Talking*, I began hoping that the label might give it a hefty promotional push. They didn't. I barely remember any promotion.

When I'd left, David Krebs had said that he didn't see me as critical to Aerosmith's success. He figured that without the tension between Steven and me things would straighten out. But the very opposite had happened. It gave me no small pleasure when time and again I heard stories about Aerosmith gigs with fans screaming out, "Where's Joe Fuckin' Perry?" It became a mantra. The mantra didn't make me want to return. But I did derive satisfaction when I read a Krebs quote saying that he had underestimated my value to the band. That's when he had to completely reverse himself. Rather than applaud my departure, he spent years trying to get me back. Decades later, I happened to run into Krebs's partner Steve Leber. When I asked about my suspicion that Leber-Krebs had tried to undermine my solo career so I would come back to the band, he came clean; he admitted they wanted me to fail.

These were the same years—the late seventies and early eighties—when my marriage was on its last legs. Our son, Adrian, was born on January 25, 1981. I'd always wanted a son and was overjoyed. But when it came to Elyssa, aggravation had overwhelmed happiness. We had essentially become incompatible. Certainly my quirks, compulsions, and addictions were as powerful as hers—if not more so. The time had ended, though, when we could balance our twin insanities. Those insanities had long been moving in opposing directions. Emotionally, we were opposing one another. Even the birth of my first child couldn't recommit me to my marriage. I didn't want to stay home. I wanted to cut loose. And as a working musician, I had many opportunities to do just that. But I also kept coming back home because I wanted to be a father. This was the only way possible to keep contact with my son, the child that I had longed for years earlier in our relationship.

So with one foot out the door and one foot in, my life continued. This was 1980, the year I turned thirty. The Project was working, but money was tight and my debts were high. The IRS was unrelenting. My road manager,

Doc McGrath, kept telling me I needed help. What else was new? My last manager, Don Law, was a good guy, but what more could he do for me?

"You need someone who will do more," said Doc.

"You know someone?" I asked.

"Yes," said Doc. And for the first time in my life I heard the name of a person who would change my life and spin this story in a dozen different directions: Tim Collins.

"Who is he?" I asked.

"A booking agent who wants to be a manager," said Doc. "And he's really fuckin' smart."

My first meeting with Collins was uneventful. It happened at the apartment of our lead singer, Charlie Farren, who lived in the Back Bay. Collins didn't make a big impression. He was a young guy—overweight, nerdy eyeglasses, overgrown beard, disheveled, but with a pleasant personality. He said he had once played guitar in high school and now managed Jonathan Edwards. At first I got the idea he was a wannabe, but that notion was quickly dispelled when we got to talking. He was one smart motherfucker. He was also a fan who knew a lot about Aerosmith and had only praise for the Project. He told me that he had a partner, Steve Barrasso.

There was no follow-up to that meeting, though, because we were touring. It didn't help that my singer didn't like him.

"That guy gives me the creeps," said Charlie. "I can't see him managing you."

I dropped the idea for a short while. Then I picked it up again when I realized that I couldn't make heads or tails out of my money mess. Don Law wasn't willing to bail me out. Who was? I thought back to Collins. I remembered him telling me that if there was anything he could do to help, just ask. So I did.

When he came over the first time, Elyssa didn't want to let him in. I'm not sure what her antagonism was about, but she finally relented and agreed to listen to him. I was in bad shape. I was on the verge of losing my house. I was fucked up from drinking. I thought I was at the bottom, but every day that bottom kept getting deeper and darker.

The meeting at my house was brief. He brought along some cocaine that we snorted together. Due to my lack of funds, this was a time when

I rarely saw coke. Collins was upbeat. His favorite saying was "There are no problems, only solutions"—and he spoke like he meant it. Tim was also eager and extremely bright. I liked all his metaphors. He talked about rolling up his sleeves and helping me find some answers to my financial dilemma. He talked about getting in the trenches and figuring out how to maximize the money I was making on the road. His mantra was simple and clear: *You need help. I can help. Let me help.*

I tested him out by opening up this big drawer where I threw all my mail. I never bothered to look at most of it. It was an unruly pile of bills, including IRS claims and foreclosure notices. There were even uncashed royalty checks for thousands of dollars. When Tim pointed them out, I said, "Hey, I'm not a businessman."

After he examined the pile of papers for a couple of minutes, I asked, "You willing to go through the stuff and make sense of it?"

"I am," he answered. With that, I emptied the contents of the drawer into a grocery bag and handed it to Collins. A week later he told me that he was willing to pay off a big portion of my debts.

"What are the conditions?" I asked.

"There aren't any," he said. "I figure that I need to do this to win your trust. I believe in your talent. I believe your best years are ahead of you. I want to manage you."

I didn't see what choice I had. I called Don Law and told him that Collins was taking over. I told Elyssa the same thing. No one could argue with me, because no one else was willing to put his money on the line. Collins was, and that was all I needed to know.

The Project always found work. Beyond opening for Heart, we played on bills with ZZ Top and the J. Geils Band, who were steamrolling and having great success with this new thing called videos for MTV. "Love Stinks" is still one of my favorites.

On the personal side, Elyssa kept living like I was still in Aerosmith. I kept touring, taking every gig I could get. I was living the dream of an independent artist. Though we traveled in a van and stayed in Holiday Inns, I still loved it. Anything I earned went back to pay off my heavy debts.

I could live with the idea of no longer being in a band that could headline at huge venues all over the world. I knew if I stuck to my guns I'd work my way out of the financial mess, but the impossibility of conveying that idea to Elyssa made me realize that the relationship was over. The vicious cycle had gone on for so long that I couldn't even remember what life without marital combat was like. We had gone through years of high drama and high conflict, with no resolution. We had endured years of staying high—which was what let us cover up the problems. I needed relief. I needed to leave. And that's just what I did: Like a thief in the night, I slid behind the wheel of my black Porsche and took off. I finally got the fuck out.

FURTHER OUT

When we legally separated, Elyssa and I had been married for six and a half years. It would take another three years for our divorce to become final. The breakup was an ugly one. Enraged, Elyssa did all she could to keep me from seeing Adrian, who had just turned one. Almost every visit required me to get family services to intervene. On the financial front, things were bleak. Elyssa and Adrian moved into an apartment in a luxury high-rise in Chestnut Hill, within walking distance of one of the most expensive malls in Boston. Elyssa, who still didn't have a driver's license and refused to look for a job, kept spending money that we didn't have, digging holes that I'd eventually have to climb out of. I was sending her what I could.

An old band friend whom we'd met in Detroit back in the seventies had an apartment in the same high-rise as Elyssa. When we first met him he was just another cat with a few grams of coke here and there. But he got involved in selling large quantities and was found dead hanging from a pipe by his wrists. It was rumored that he'd gotten on the wrong side of some other heavyweight dealer and been strangled. I wasn't happy that Elyssa had our son in such an environment, but my own environment was hardly Disneyland. Eventually she and Adrian changed locales. Ironically, they moved into a complex where she and I had first shared an apartment. I could never figure why, of all the buildings in Boston, she chose that one.

The only steady force in my life was Tim Collins, who kept saying just what I wanted to hear: "You've got to keep playing on the road, and you've got to make another record." I spent lots of nights on Collins's couch. Mark Parenteau, a WBCN DJ who had long championed Aerosmith, was also a loyal friend. Between Tim and Mark, who were always generous with their drugs, I found shelter and support.

Because Collins, unlike Leber-Krebs, wasn't a suit—a corporate guy with corporate connections—I trusted him. I desperately needed someone to trust. I desperately needed someone to keep me on the road and in the studio. To his credit, Collins got me out of my deal with Columbia. He got MCA interested in doing the next Project album and was able to secure a small advance. That gave me something to work for besides just touring. A new record meant new songs. Even during this time of intense debauchery, I responded to the call of the studio. My love of writing and playing never died.

Because I had to cut back salaries, I lost the original cats and changed the Project personnel. Enter Cowboy Mach Bell, another madman lead singer. I felt connected to him, not only through our common rock-and-roll madness, but because he came from Holliston, Massachusetts, the town next to Hopedale.

Out on tour, Cowboy and I were in L.A., lost in time. We had a vague notion of a gig at the Golden Bear in Huntington Beach, some thirty-five miles down the coast in Orange County. Due to our heavy drinking, we'd lost track of the other cats in the band—at that point, Danny Hargrove was on bass and Joe Pet on drums—and decided to hitchhike to the club. Given the fact that we hadn't changed clothes or showered in a couple of days, we had a tough time getting a ride. On our extremely slow-going walk, we stopped every few miles to fortify ourselves at neighborhood taverns. At the rate we were going, we wouldn't have made Huntington Beach for six months. An especially good-natured waitress took a liking to me. She may or may not have recognized me. But she believed me when I said we were working musicians on our way to a gig. Back out on the road, just when the trek was getting the best of us, the friendly waitress pulled up in an old Ford Fairlane and offered to drive us the rest of the way. Her companionship was extended from the club to my motel room.

On another tour I met a cute chick at the Keystone rock club in San Francisco. There was room in the van and she came along as we criss-crossed the country. She was young and a free spirit—no commitments, no responsibilities. When we got back to Boston, a friend of Collins sublet us an apartment in the North End, a heavily Italian section of the city near the Bay. For several months we lived on cannolis from Mike's Pastry. Eventually the thrill wore off for both of us and I sent her back to California.

It's strange, but this was the only period of my life when sexual escapades became part of my routine. It lasted for a little more than a year and it's telling that I've never been less satisfied. Maybe I felt obligated to taste the fruits of freedom. It was amusing but not the kind of life I wanted to live. I found myself with an assorted group of waitresses, strippers, stewardesses, salesgirls, and Playboy bunnies. I quickly learned I hadn't been missing anything. The one-night stands did not prove satisfying on any level. I felt that I was using and abusing these women's emotions as well as my own. One-night affairs left me lonely. As Cowboy ran the hallways stark naked, as I sought solace in the arms of women whose names I did not know and whose faces I would immediately forget, I couldn't deny that the sadness in my soul came from being far away from my son, Adrian.

At the same time, being on the road playing hard rock and roll and living like a gypsy provided a powerful energy. All I had to my name were a few guitars, a pile of amps, and a couple of suitcases of clothes. We lived hand-to-mouth. My bibles were *On the Road* and *Fear and Loathing in Las Vegas*. I was up for anything and everything.

In the Southwest I befriended a fan who was a full-blooded American Indian. He came in the van and traveled with us for a few weeks, regaling the band with Native American folklore. We played in towns and clubs I never knew existed. We ran wild for days, slept for days, and then started the cycle all over again. Despite all this excitement, I wished there was some way to see Adrian on a regular basis. When I made it back to Boston, though, Elyssa wouldn't hear of it.

Nearly four years had passed since I'd left the band. When we happened to be in the same city and I went to see the new Aerosmith, Steven, Tom, and Joey were friendly. There seemed to be no hard feelings. No harsh words were spoken. I was introduced to Jimmy Crespo and Rick Dufay, the guitarists who had replaced me and Brad. It was all very civil, but it was also very strange. The awkwardness got to me, and I didn't stay long. I also didn't go to their show. Why stick around and listen to the band? If they were great, that wouldn't make me happy. If they sucked, I'd be even unhappier. I just split.

After that, I'd occasionally call Steven, or he'd call me.

"Hey, man, how are you?" he'd ask.

"I'm all right."

"How're things going?"

"Great," I'd lie. "How about with you?"

"Great," he'd lie. "Band's sounding great. You gigging?"

"All the time."

"Yeah, man, we're working everywhere."

The bullshit flew thick and fast. I knew he was playing smaller and smaller venues; I knew he was having trouble getting through a show. And he knew I was playing clubs. I was opening for bands who, only a year or two earlier, had opened for Aerosmith. But what Steven didn't understand was that the variety of gigs we were playing, no matter the size, was giving me that rock-and-roll jolt that had been missing during those last years of Aerosmith.

"Well," he'd say after a few seconds, "just wanted to say hi."

"Glad you called."

A few months later, he showed up at the Project's show at the Bottom Line in New York. He came to my dressing room and asked, "Is that fat guy I just met your new manager?"

"Yeah. That's Tim Collins."

"You like him?"

"So far."

"He getting you work?"

"Oh yeah."

"And you got a new album deal?"

"On MCA."

"That's great. We're about to finish our record down in Miami."

"You've been working on it awhile," I said.

"You know me," said Steven. "It takes a while."

I nodded. "You gonna stick around for the show?"

"You bet your ass. Like everyone else waiting out there, I came to see Joe Fuckin' Perry, and I'm not leaving till I hear him play his guitar."

It was several months later—sometime in 1983—when I happened to be in Boston for one of my rare stays. I heard that Aerosmith was playing at the Worcester Centrum and decided to go to the show.

Steven was happy to see me. Just the two of us hung out in his dressing room. We were yukking it up and having a few shots when the assistant came in to say, "Show in ten minutes."

"Hang around," said Steven. "Cyrinda's on her way. She'll be arriving with a nice surprise."

Just about showtime, Cyrinda did arrive and, not surprisingly, the surprise was heroin. I couldn't remember the last time I'd had any and was more than willing to indulge. Steven downed two tumblers of gin before laying out the lines. After we snorted it up, he went out to perform, fifteen or twenty minutes late. I stayed behind because I wasn't sure I could stand—that's how strong the shit was. As I was reeling and trying to keep it together, I heard a couple of Aerosmith songs—and then nothing. The thunderous music went dead. The next thing I knew, they were carrying in Steven, who had passed out onstage. Tom came running in afterward, flipping out.

"It's just like the old days, Joe—you're no good for this band. Look what you did! Why don't you just stay the fuck away from us?"

I tried to explain to Tom what had happened. But all his frustrations with the band's tenuous situation came pouring out. There was nothing I could do but leave—so I did.

The Project carried on, and there were some strong musical moments. For many dates we opened for ZZ Top, whose *Eliminator*, one of the great rock records of all time, was tearing up the charts. It was always a lot of fun to play with Billy Gibbons and company. Their backstage was always a happy, mellow party—so different from Aerosmith.

The Project released *Once a Rocker, Always a Rocker*. I was a coproducer, along with Michael Golub, who understood just how raw I wanted this record to sound. We cut it at Blue Jay Recording Studio in Carlisle, outside Boston. The bulk of the lyrics for the song "Adriana" came from Cowboy and concerned our guide and road manager during our tour in Venezuela, who became my girlfriend for the trip. We recorded T. Rex's "Bang a Gong," something we'd been playing live. Another track, "Women in Chains," was something from a band in Tennessee that I heard as a women's protest song. It was an antidote to all the misogynistic songs being written by some of the heavy metal bands. I wrote another song, "Black Velvet Pants," which rearranged my reality more profoundly than anything I've ever written. You'll see why in a minute.

Before the record was released, I wrote a line on the back cover to express my attitude about the changing musical technology so pervasive in 1983: "There are no synthesizers on this album." This was my last stab at denying the fast-changing technology.

During the making of *Once a Rocker, Always a Rocker*, I was living with a woman named Glenda, who had been introduced to me by Cowboy. The idea was that I'd sleep in her spare bedroom, but by the second night I was sharing Glenda's bed. Glenda was a hairstylist who did my hair for the cover of my album. That shot is all about my hair. It's not my favorite photo, but that's what happens when your roommate-girlfriend is in the hair business and you're drinking way too much Jack Daniel's.

The label gave me a little money to do a video. They thought that "Black Velvet Pants" was the most commercial thing on the record. I liked the song and saw it as nothing more than fun. The lyrics said:

I love the way they look
I love the way they feel
Come on, babe, I'm not made out of steel....
Your black velvet pants are all I need

The main job became choosing the woman who would appear in the video in black velvet pants. Collins had a bunch of books sent over from talent agencies. I thumbed through halfheartedly until I came to a picture that stopped me in my tracks—a headshot of a beautiful blonde named Billie Montgomery. There was a look in her eyes that got to me, heart and soul. I had to meet her. Ironically, Cowboy had mentioned that Billie was a friend of his girlfriend. He'd told me she was the hottest chick in town, but at the time, I was preoccupied with the band and never pursued his suggestion to seek her out.

A few days passed. I was in Collins's office when Billie arrived. The second she walked in, I thought of the old cliché that, until this moment, had never applied to me: *Love at first sight*. I had met some good-looking women in Boston before, but most of the real knockouts were in New York or L.A. Billie was a real knockout.

For a few seconds I was speechless. When we did get to the business of talking about the video, I fell into her blue-gray eyes. She spoke with humility—not at all like someone stuck on her own beauty. She had an easygoing, down-to-earth, and caring demeanor. At the end of our brief conversation, she thanked me for my time, shook my hand, and left. It felt like the office had emptied out. She carried an aura and expressed an energy I'd never felt before. I was in a daze. I wanted more.

"She'll be really good in the video," said Collins.

"The hell with the video," I said. "I think I'm in love." I know it's a cliché, but when I said it, I was dead serious.

It took me a while to remember that this was the same Billie

Montgomery who Cowboy had been wanting me to meet. He had also told me that she was in the middle of a separation and had a young son. Right off the bat we had an important thing in common.

I came up with the self-serving idea that it'd be really important for the video if Billie came to see the Project live. She accepted my invitation to our gig in a quaint New England village in New Hampshire. After our sound check, she and I walked across the street to a small country fair. Riding the Ferris wheel and merry-go-round, we spent the afternoon together. The more I got to know Billie, the more my feelings grew.

There were hundreds of fans at the show that night, but I saw only one member of the audience. All my concentration was on Billie. And you can bet that I burned up the stage with everything I had.

Billie said she enjoyed the show. In the van on the way home we shared a few swigs from a bottle of Jack Daniel's. The mood was easy and light—lots of laughs. A song came on the radio. I asked the driver to turn it up.

"Who is this?" asked Billie

"Cheap Trick," I said. "One of my favorite bands."

"I've never heard of them," said Billie, "but I like the song."

I was surprised that Billie didn't know about Cheap Trick, who were all over the radio. She explained that she was into alternative college radio, new wave, and punk and didn't listen to much mainstream rock. I didn't say anything about my previous band. After all, that had been nearly five years ago. Besides, I didn't walk around with a big *A* on my forehead.

We talked a little more about the kind of music that Billie liked. She described her mom as a hip lady who played Elvis, Ray Charles, and Patsy Cline downstairs while her older sister blasted Motown upstairs. When Billie was old enough to buy records of her own, her first were Frank Zappa and the Mothers of Invention along with the Doors and the Beatles' White Album. She spoke about her childhood in a little town in southern Indiana. Unlike my background, Billie's family had been in America many years, on both sides, going back to the early 1670s. On her mother's side she's related to Davy Crockett. When she left, she never looked back. From a young age, she took care of herself. Billie lived with her eleven-year-old son, Aaron, of whom she had full custody. She spoke about her separation from her second husband, Willie Alexander, who, in the world of Boston bohemia, was known as the godfather of dada punk. He was fifteen years older than Billie. Although I know she loved Willie, I think he was also her mentor. He is a killer piano player, painter, and poet, and he encouraged her own pursuit of painting and poetry. For all her creative gifts, Billie was also practical. She'd finished high school and attended the Massachusetts College of Art and Design for three years but had given it up in order to support herself and Aaron. She had a talent agent—Maggie Inc., on Newbury Street—and took night classes at Emerson College and sometimes traveled to New York for acting and modeling work. In Boston she had a good job selling advertising for WBOS, the country radio station.

When the evening ended, we both felt strongly connected to each other. The spiritual attraction was there—and so was the physical allure. But sensing this was going to be a deeply serious relationship, we understood the importance, before anything else, of developing a solid friendship.

I couldn't wait to see Billie again and was excited when the day of the video shoot arrived. The premise of "Black Velvet Pants"—a straight-up rocker—was simple enough: In her black velvet pants, Billie comes to the theater where the Project is playing. She comes onstage, picks up a sax, and pretends to play as I wail away on my guitar.

We were in perfect sync. Everyone at the shoot could feel what was happening between us. But Glenda, who had been watching the whole thing, flipped out. As Billie headed back to her dressing room during a break, Glenda jumped out of a corner and attacked her. Billie didn't know what was happening. There was no way she was going to get into some fight. After all, this was just another paying gig for her. So she just dropped to the floor and covered her head. Collins and I rushed over and got Glenda off Billie, who walked to her dressing room without saying a word while Glenda was screaming, "Stay away from Joe! He's mine! I'm going to marry him!" Well, that was news to me.

The fight freaked me out. My first concern was Billie. On my way to the dressing room to make sure she was okay I thought about the bullshit that Glenda had just pulled: We were nothing more than roommates who slept together. She had her friends and I had mine. There had never been talk of any long-term relationship. Our understanding was that every time we left the apartment, we did so with no strings attached.

When I got to the dressing room, I was relieved to see Billie was calm and composed.

"What was that all about?" she asked.

"I'm not sure," I said, "but I know my days at Glenda's apartment are numbered. I'm sorry this happened."

"Don't worry about it, Joe. It wasn't your fault."

A couple of weeks later I asked her out again. All I could think about was getting her in the sack. But I knew that would be the wrong move. I also knew that she was winding down her relationship with Willie Alexander, and I wanted to give her the time and space she needed.

We spent a beautiful evening in an outdoor Japanese restaurant where we sat under colorful lanterns and, for the first time, Billie had a taste of sake. Our talk deepened. I learned that Billie, having been abandoned by her dad at an alarmingly young age, had a low tolerance for unreliable men. She was all about responsibility.

The video shoot for "Black Velvet Pants" took place in June. That summer and fall I was mostly out of town promoting my new record. My dates with Billie were few. But with each one, the attraction intensified. After six months of the hottest platonic relationship imaginable, I was more than ready to take it to the next level. And yet Billie, always reasonable and caring, remained cautious and concerned about my family. I'd been separated from Elyssa for more than two years but was not yet divorced.

"Before we commit to each other," said Billie, "I think it's important that you're a hundred percent sure about your feelings about your marriage. I think it's a good idea for you to spend Christmas with your wife and son and see what happens."

I hit the roof. *What! Are you kidding?* I was baffled by her suggestion. It was the last thing I wanted to do. Even though I understood Billie's attitude, I had no doubt that my marriage was over. Still, I called Elyssa to say that I would be there on Christmas Eve to see Adrian. It was great being with my son, but after a cold night on the edge of my side of the bed, I couldn't wait to get out of that apartment. I went from there to a party, where I nursed a bottle of Jack Daniel's and thought back over the last six months. I knew what I wanted.

At 2 A.M. on that freezing December night, I asked a friend to drive me over to Billie's apartment, on Broadway near Harvard Square in Cambridge.

I rang the buzzer.

"Who is it?" asked Billie in a sleepy voice.

"Joe. Can I come up?"

Long pause. I could tell she wasn't happy about being awoken in the middle of the night. I felt like Marlon Brando yelling "Stella!" in *A Streetcar Named Desire*. I hoped and prayed that she'd let me in.

She finally hit the buzzer. My friend and I went upstairs. Billie was alone. Her son, Aaron, was at his dad's for the Christmas break. After a while, sensing he was a third wheel, my pal split. Billie played her favorite music for me while I told her about my experience at Elyssa's the night before.

Finally, I said, "I got a couple of Quaaludes. Do you want one?"

She laughed and said, "Are you trying to drug me and get me into bed with you, Joe? No thanks. Let's just go to sleep."

We went to bed together—my dream for the past six months—but ironically, I fell fast asleep without fulfilling that dream. But as soon as the rooster crowed, that dream was realized. Words can't describe the overwhelming intensity of what I felt. I'd finally found my true soul mate. I knew that I wanted this woman—forever.

That morning I asked if I could come back that night and stay.

"Yes," said Billie.

And the night after that?

"We'll see," she said with a sparkle in her eye.

I never left.

A few weeks later, we were driving to a party in Billie's white Chevette when an Aerosmith song—I can't remember which one—came on the radio. I pulled over to the median strip and said, "That's the band I was with."

I'd mentioned Aerosmith to Billie—just in passing. The name never registered. She lived a different lifestyle, more arty, and listened to alternative music and punk rock, so the name didn't mean anything to her. Now I mentioned the name again. "We were pretty successful in the seventies," I added.

"I don't really know that group," Billie admitted.

I was secretly thrilled. It was miraculous to have found a woman who was interested in me, not a guy in a supergroup carrying the promise of money, glamour, and glory. I took it as further proof that Billie was the one and only woman I would need for the rest of my life.

One morning after making love, we were in bed when I put my thick gold chain around her neck and announced, "I'm going to marry you."

She laughed and said, "You're crazy!"

Tim Collins had been negative about my relationship with Billie from the start. He didn't like the idea of my forging an alliance with an independent, strong-minded woman and explained to Billie that she could not, under any circumstances, go on tour with me. He said that I had a record to promote and that nothing was going to stand in the way of that. I couldn't have cared less about Collins's views on my love life. This was sacred ground. Because she had a good job and a son to raise, Billie had no interest in going on tour anyway—and she told Collins that in no uncertain terms.

While I was falling in love with Billie, there were still demons at my door. The thrill of the Project was starting to wear thin. Collins was still able to hustle up gigs, but the failure of the MCA album to make a dent in the marketplace was a blow. I was still drowning in debt. My soon-to-be ex-wife and her lawyers were taking me to the cleaners. For years we had needed to sell Villa Elyssa, but Elyssa wouldn't let a real estate agent through the door. Consequently, the IRS was about to foreclose. She had sold off our furnishings and antiques, as well as my guitars, and kept the money for herself. Meanwhile, she'd gotten her driver's license and was driving around town in a brand-new VW Jetta. Her attorney made me out as a deadbeat dad to the point where a judge instructed me to get a real job—an especially humiliating moment for a musician who had been working continuously for the past fifteen years.

In contrast, I saw the harmonious relationship between Billie and Aaron's dad. For the good of their son, they went out of their way to keep their relationship civil. They were more like cousins than ex-spouses.

As badly as I needed money, I had no thoughts of returning to Aerosmith. I had heard they were having their own problems making gigs and presumed that drugs were putting the final nails in their coffin. I was still determined to make it on my own and pay my own way.

"I don't want to live here rent-free," I told Billie. "I'll pay half your rent."

"It'll be great when you can pay it all," she said. "Until then, I'm in a better financial position than you to cover the costs."

In the following months, things began to change inside my head and heart. The most important change was my relationship with Billie. I wanted to protect it at any cost. I had found a deep and luminous love that helped me see the future from a different perspective. I was no longer a single entity wandering through the world on my own. I had a partner for whom I wanted to provide.

That was the personal side of things. On the professional side, there was and would always be music. I wanted, I needed, I had no choice but to keep making music. That's all I knew. That's who I was. But now the urgent questions were right in my face:

What is the way forward?

Do I keep the Project alive?

Or do I reconsider the pledge I made when I walked away from Aerosmith, swearing never to return to that madness?

Is it that madness that is calling me?

Or, beneath the madness, is it the power of Aerosmith's blistering rock and roll that won't leave me alone?

PART 5

THE SECOND RISE AND FALL (AND RISE AGAIN)

BACK

I had put the drugs away, but there were still days when, while living with Billie, I found myself drifting out to the bars to break the boredom of a weekday afternoon. On one such afternoon Billie came home early from work to find me passed out in bed, an open gallon jug of wine on the kitchen counter.

"Look, Joe," she said. "I get up every morning at seven to make breakfast for Aaron and get him off to school. We're out the door by eight. You see that I'm basically working two jobs. If I get a call from my agency, the radio station gives me the time off from my sales gig, but that's time I have to make up. My advertising clients require constant follow-up. So to come home and see you in this condition isn't going to fly. What the hell are you doing with yourself?"

"I got up late," I said. "I took a walk and stopped in a pub for a couple of drinks."

"And then got a gallon of wine? I didn't know that they made bottles that big."

Not knowing what to say, I stayed silent.

"This isn't going to work, Joe. If you want to live your life this way, I want you to leave. Because I'm not having it. It has nothing to do with how much I love you. It has to do with my own sanity. I don't want to be around you in this condition, and I certainly don't want you to be around Aaron. So it all comes down to a simple choice on your part. You can go or you can stay. But I'm not living with a drunk."

I heard what Billie said, and I didn't hesitate in replying.

"You'll never see me like that again," I said. "I'll get it under control."

And I did.

My decision made for a happy Valentine's Day, the same day that Aerosmith was playing the Orpheum in Boston.

"Steven called and invited us down," I told Billie.

"What'd you say?" she asked.

"I said thanks but that I was busy. Then he said we should at least meet him and the guys after the show for some beers and oysters."

"Are you going to?"

"I don't think so."

"How come?"

"Just don't feel like it."

"I don't understand why you wouldn't want to go by and say hi. After all, you played with these guys for all those years. If it gets weird or uncomfortable, we can always leave."

I was conflicted. Part of me wanted to say hello to the band and introduce them to Billie, but another part of me wanted to avoid the whole scene. In the end, Billie and I went.

We showed up at the after-show hang at the Parker Hotel where Steven was seated at a long table with a few crew members and Joe Baptista, our road manager from the old days. I introduced everyone to Billie.

"Man, you look just like Linda Evans from *Dynasty*," Steven told Billie. He was on his best behavior. After a beer or two, he invited us upstairs for a quick hello to his girlfriend Teresa, who had replaced Cyrinda as the love of his life.

The band had taken over an entire floor, and a couple of the doors were wide open. It was a typical Aerosmith party—lots of fat lines of coke decorating the tops of coffee tables, quart bottles of the best booze, and all the vintage wine you could drink. Pot smoke wafted from room to room. Everyone was indulging.

"Is it always like this?" Billie whispered in my ear.

"Pretty much," I said.

I actually felt right at home. The guys were happy to meet Billie. After an hour or so, Billie was ready to leave. Although everyone seemed nice— Steven was charming and funny and she especially liked Terry and Tom Hamilton—she was a bit overwhelmed.

The next day I started some serious reflection about why I had left, what I had gone through during these Project years, and whether I could see myself going back. The answer was still no. The previous night's get-together had been nice, but I sensed that the animosity hadn't completely dissipated. Besides, Aerosmith was still being managed by Leber-Krebs, a situation I found intolerable. To extricate themselves from that situation would mean all sorts of legal complications. Just thinking about that gave me a headache. I was enjoying the freedom of being on my own and having a manager like Collins, who never pressured me to go back with Steven. Yet I couldn't deny that it was good talking with Steven and the rest of the guys and enjoying the kind of rapport we'd had in the early seventies. But no, I was not going back—at least not now.

That was February 1984. In March something else came up—a chance to work with one of my favorite singers.

I'd been pressing Collins to find new opportunities for me. I knew I wasn't working to my potential. The Project had been winding down for some time. I needed new sources of income and creativity. I really wanted to provide for Billie.

"What do you think about Alice Cooper?" asked Collins.

"I think he's great."

"I've been in touch with Shep Gordon, his manager. Alice is interested in working with you. What do you say?"

"I say yes."

It sounded like just the thing.

I went to Shep's fabulous brick mansion in upstate New York, a monster of a house out of *The Addams Family* and the perfect place for Alice to be lying low. The author of *The Amityville Horror* had recently stayed there. There were catacombs in the basement, huge walk-in fireplaces, and a ghost—said to be one Mr. Brown—who, according to Alice, wandered around at night. There were stories of objects moving on their own. And at one point a series of loud rumblings from downstairs had all of us running out of the house in the middle of the night.

When I first arrived, I was told that Alice was out playing golf. I walked around the estate for a few hours. When Alice showed up, he looked great. He'd given up drinking and said his only addiction was golf. We'd met a few times before and hit it off. This time was no different. Alice was a friendly and funny guy, but if he wanted to give you the look, even without wearing his makeup, he could scare the skeleton out of your skin. He was quick to say how the last owner had drowned in a pond right in front of the house. Alice loved telling horror tales that convinced me the house was haunted. After these stories, he suggested that we work after dinner. I was ready.

Our post-dinner session was short and pleasant. I riffed on guitar, he jotted down a few lyrics, and after an hour or so he said he was tired and called it a night.

"We'll meet up in the morning," he said.

But when morning came he was already at the golf course and gone all day. That left me lots of time to myself. Sometime that afternoon I decided to call Steven. At the time, he was staying at the Gorham Hotel in New York.

Every time we talked there was a certain amount of bullshit—him telling me how good he was doing; me telling him the same.

"I'm working all the time," he said. "Things are great. What are you up to?"

"Out here working with Alice Cooper. Things couldn't be better."

"The Aerosmith shows have all been selling out. How 'bout you?"

"I got all sorts of offers for the Project."

I knew that he knew I wasn't happy. He knew that I knew he wasn't happy either. And yet we kept up the charade. We were both basically down and out and too proud to admit it. Men playing a macho game.

For all the hype between us, talking to Steven was still like talking to a brother. I missed our camaraderie and kept hearing Billie's voice echoing in my head. *Are you really sure you don't want to play with your old band?*

At one point Steven said, "You coming to New York anytime soon?"

"Actually, Alice isn't around this week, so I could come down to the city. I could also bring my manager, Tim Collins. I'd like you to meet him. What do you say?"

"Call me when you get here," said Steven. "We'll have dinner at my hotel."

A few days later I went to the city. We were set to meet at the restaurant at the Gorham. Tim and I arrived first. When Steven walked in, Collins went to the bar. He thought Steven and I should first have some private time. After we talked for a while, I invited Tim over to the table. Immediately I sensed that Steven didn't trust Tim. But I also knew that suspicion is part of Steven's personality. At the same time, Steven responded to Collins's sense of humor and his willingness to take on the world. He reacted positively when Tim said, "There are no problems. Only solutions." The meeting went well. Collins split and I stayed around to have a few more beers with Steven. The reunion felt good.

I returned to Shep's mansion to meet back up with Alice and Billie, who had come up from Boston. It was Easter vacation and her son, Aaron, was with his dad. Alice was leaving in a few days for Spain to shoot the movie *Monster Dog*. I still hadn't done much work with him. Our abbreviated jams had not yielded any completed songs. Billie soon saw that the main entertainment lay in Alice's gift as a raconteur. He loved telling ghost stories about the invisible Mr. Brown. Once he hid and jumped out of a corner brandishing an oversize cooking knife at Billie, à la *Psycho*. It scared her out of her wits. Everyone had a good laugh.

Alice flew off to Europe and, thanks to Shep's hospitality, Billie and I stayed behind for a few days of relaxation. Strolling through the lush acreage that surrounded the mansion, we had time to talk. During our long walks in the woods she helped me assess my professional situation. I valued Billie's perspective because she was neither emotional nor calculating. She asked the right questions. She came from the right place—the heart—in trying to get me to understand what I wanted and needed.

"I like Alice a lot," she said. "Do you have a feeling that you and he can work on a permanent basis?"

"If we had more time, I'm sure we'd come up with some great things. I'm sure I could work well with his band."

"Has he asked you?"

"Not yet. But I know it's an option. It's also got me thinking about what it would mean to join another band or to put a supergroup together."

"If you're thinking about joining a band, why wouldn't you just go back to Aerosmith?" asked Billie. "I know you like those guys, and it seems like whatever happened in the past is ancient history."

"There's more to it than that. In a perfect world, what you say makes sense. But in a perfect world I never would have left Aerosmith. The whole thing turned into an emotional mess."

"No doubt. But you guys are older now—and more mature. On a musical level, it worked before. Are you sure it won't again?"

"At this point I'm really not sure of anything."

Inside my head, the arguments raged on: *All bands have their problems. But in going back with Aerosmith, at least I'd know what the problems are. At least I'd know the nature of the beast. Isn't that an advantage? Yes and no. Like Billie says, maybe age has made us wiser. Maybe after five years away I have a clearer idea of how to avoid those old conflicts. In the old Aerosmith I was with a woman who did all she could to create drama. This time around, I'm with a woman who seeks nothing but harmony. She sees the situation for what it is: a chance to rebuild on an artistic foundation that is already a proven winner. Steven can sing his ass off. Joey, Brad, and Tom can play their asses off. Together—no matter how crazy we got—we kicked serious ass. Couldn't we, shouldn't we, don't we have to do it again?*

The more I thought about it, the more I leaned toward getting back together with my old buddies. To do so, though, I knew I'd have to take it slowly. I'd need at least one more get-together—just Steven and me.

"Why don't you and Teresa come up to Cambridge?" I asked Steven on the phone. "You're both welcome to stay with us in Billie's apartment."

Steven accepted the invitation but decided to check into a nearby hotel. It was early May. A freak snowstorm hit the city. On the first night, Billie had them over for dinner, and Steven was wild for her homemade bean-and-ham soup. The freezing weather outside and the warm fire inside created a sense of intimacy. Billie and Teresa got along like sisters. While they were chatting, Steven and I started addressing the elephant in the room.

"If it's gonna happen," I said, "it can't happen with Leber-Krebs."

"So you want your man to manage us?" asked Steven.

"You should think about Collins. He's driven and he's not afraid to take on anything. He'll get in the trenches with us. That's what he did for me. I also like that he's close to our age—and that he likes to party. But he's seriously dedicated. Once he sets a goal, nothing stops him."

"We have a management contract with Leber-Krebs."

"We'll find a way out of it. Collins can deal with that. I want to put the band back together with you, Steven, but it's gotta be under new management. That's the one point I can't compromise."

"Let me think about all this," said Steven.

"Take all the time you need."

We chatted a bit more before Billie and I drove Steven and Teresa back to their hotel. The snow was still falling and the vibe between all of us still felt good. Under a fresh blanket of snow, the city looked beautiful. I felt optimistic.

"What do you think?" asked Billie after we dropped them off.

"I think it'll happen," I said. "I think Steven wants it to happen. I need to talk to all of the guys together in one room. Then, if they're into it, we all have to get together with Collins."

It took only a week before Steven called and suggested that we all meet at Tom's house. He wanted me to know that he still hadn't resolved the management issue in his mind, but he wanted to air it out with the other guys. Was I willing?

I was. We got together. Handshakes and hugs all around. We were all understandably a little nervous. I was the one who broke the ice. "Look, guys," I said, "I know there's lots to talk about—what happened before we broke up, what happened after, what's happening now. We all have feelings. But we don't even need to get into the emotional stuff if we can't get past one critical point—management. I can't, I won't go back to the old management. I say we let Tim Collins manage us. He's smart, he's driven like a motherfucker, and I think he's honest. He saved my ass when it didn't look like my ass was worth saving. He's got a worldwide vision of what we can be. He can help make it happen."

"So what you're saying," said Tyler, "is that if we don't accept your man Collins as a manager, you're not coming back."

"I'm saying if you have someone better—someone who's not Leber-Krebs—I'll look at him."

"We don't have anyone else," said Joey.

"Not that I know of," echoed Brad.

Steven wasn't happy. He had fallen into a routine with Krebs, who was paying his bills at the Gorham Hotel. Every day Steven would walk to the Leber-Krebs office, where he'd be given his dope money—twenty-five bucks. I think it was Krebs's naive way of trying to help Steven control his habit. Leber saw Aerosmith as a cash cow. But it seemed as though Krebs had some genuine concern for the band, and especially for Steven. I knew that Steven would have a hard time leaving Krebs. As much as Krebs believed in the band, he was up against a wall. He didn't have all the tools to deal with all the monsters in the house of Aerosmith that kept us apart. God knows he tried.

There was also something about Tim that Steven didn't like. There was something in Tim's approach to handling people that set off an alarm in him. That alarm proved to be right, but it would take me—and the rest of the band—years to see it. The reason it took so long was because part of my perception of Collins proved to be accurate. He did have an enormous ambition and intelligence. He was driven to rebuild our brand. And he was confident. He'd be the first one to tell you that what Brian Epstein did for the Beatles, he would do for Aerosmith. But unlike Epstein, who took a local band and helped turn them into an international phenomenon, Collins had set himself the goal of taking a dead band—a burnt-out band, a band of drunks and druggies led by the notorious Toxic Twins—and somehow making them viable again.

"I won't bring you back to where you were," Collins liked to say. "I'll make you twice as big as you ever were."

Steven was skeptical. I could see that Tom was also skeptical. I was cautious but convinced that without Collins we didn't stand a chance. Joey saw my conviction and went along with it. Brad's attitude was honest and right to the point: "Guarantee me a hundred thousand a year and I'm in." The democratic framework of the band, as fragile as it might have been, remained in place. The majority ruled. Collins was in.

When Tom and I started out in the Jam Band, we were teenagers. When Aerosmith first got off the ground, we had just turned twenty. Now we were in our thirties and facing some daunting questions—could we rekindle the fire? Could we put the old hurts and complaints behind us? Could we get the energy back? Did our fans give a shit about us, or had they switched loyalties to a younger generation of bands?

Another big question: Since Aerosmith was still legally tied to Leber-Krebs, what would it take to break those ties? We knew that nasty legal storms were brewing and had to wonder how long they'd last and whether we could survive them.

Our economic survival was also of paramount concern. I wasn't the only one drowning in red ink. Everyone but Tom was dead broke and in debt. To start the band again would require cash. We all knew that we needed to start making money right away—and that meant touring.

The band and I went to Collins's office to meet with him and his partner, Steve Barrasso. There were many issues on the table:

On the business side, Aerosmith had just fired Leber-Krebs. Columbia wanted to drop the band. That meant we'd have to pay them to get out of the contract.

On the creative—and most important—side, could the five of us regenerate the magic? The only way to find out was to get together, start rehearsing, and tour. Over the past five years, Aerosmith had burned a lot of bridges. We needed to show the world we could still deliver the goods. By touring, we could provide Collins with the money to plot a way through the morass of legal problems. Tim had been a master chess player in college, and his greatest talent had been strategy. We were counting on his genius for maneuvering to get us back on our feet.

We were eager to tour. I've always thought of Aerosmith as primarily a live band who took the music to the people. The studio was often agony. Live was usually a rush. If Aerosmith was to go through a rebirth, it would be a *live* rebirth. The record could come later. We just had to get back out there and go to work.

Rehearsals were held at a country club out in Millis, Massachusetts. Walking in that first day wasn't easy. I'd recently played with Brad and Joey, who helped fulfill my last Project obligations, but it had been years since I'd made music with Tom and Steven. Tentatively, we started playing without any set agenda. We fell back into our pattern of hitting this riff and that riff. The initial song we fooled with was "Movin' Out," the first Steven-Joe composition from our earliest Commonwealth days. Steven smiled when he heard those first notes. He didn't forget a single lyric. It felt good to play the song.

Good feelings were returning. It felt good to play "Mama Kin." It felt good to play "Walk This Way." It felt good to play songs that had taken us to the top. It also felt strange when we couldn't remember all the songs. We needed a refresher course.

That's how we wound up at the house of Mark Parenteau, the former DJ and great friend of the band whose dream was always to see us back together. Mark had the complete Aerosmith collection, including every bootleg known to man. It was one hell of a moment when he put on "You See Me Crying," a cut from *Toys in the Attic*.

"That's outta sight," said Tyler. "We should cover that tune. Whose original is this?"

"What the fuck are you talking about, Steven?" I said. "That's us."

"Is it?" he asked.

"Hell yes, it is."

"Where was I?"

"In the booth, singing."

When it came time to plan the actual tour for the summer of 1984, Collins went a little crazy. It was the one and only time we toured by bus—just the five guys and our women. We did sixty or seventy shows over the next few months. We did the entire tour by the seat of our pants. We didn't fight the craziness because, well, we were crazy. Steven started snorting blow again—that is, if he ever stopped. My no-drinking policy lasted through the whole tour but was supplemented by occasional pills. In one way or another, we were all getting fucked up a little here and there, even as the music got better. But what else was new? Aerosmith was famous for playing fucked up and playing great. We called it the Back in the Saddle tour and that's just where we were—back in the zone where our brand of rock and roll thrives.

The tour was easygoing and fun. Along with our extended families, we were getting to know each other all over again. For the most part, everyone was getting along. Everyone went out of his or her way to make it work. All the good that originally created Aerosmith came to the surface.

We also loved the loyalty of the Blue Army. They showed up everywhere—big cities, small towns—and cheered us on with passion and love. That made all the difference in the world to us. At the same time, there were tensions.

One afternoon, cruising down the highway, the five of us were huddled in the back of the bus having a few laughs when Brad pulled out an expensive pocketknife he'd just bought. He passed it around for us to admire. When Steven got hold of it, he started stabbing huge holes into the top of a metal container of potato chips. Brad saw red. He grabbed the knife back, got Steven in a headlock, put the blade to his throat, and hissed, "If you ever do that again to any of my things, I'll kill you." Brad held Steven in that position for a full minute. The minute seemed like an hour. After he let him go, there was dead silence. The only sound was the rumbling of the tires. We were in shock—especially Steven, who didn't apologize. Later on the tour, during one of the shows, Steven bit Brad on the head. The tension between the two of them was palpable. While I was out of the band, something heavy must have happened. I never learned what.

There were, of course, endless interviews with endlessly similar questions:

To Steven: "Why did the band break up?"

Steven: "Love among brothers turned to hate among brothers."

To me: "And what brought you back?"

Me: "Hate among brothers turned to love among brothers. Plus I believe our fans know that, no matter what Steven did without me or what I did without him, it was never quite as explosive as this Aerosmith thing."

"So you missed it?" I was asked.

I stayed silent for several seconds before answering honestly.

"I did miss it," I finally said.

"And you?" the reporter asked Steven.

"I missed it real bad."

JOHN KALODNER JOHN KALODNER

The renewal of the recording career of Aerosmith was realized on Geffen Records. We only met label owner David Geffen once, during a short get-together at his beach house in Malibu. This was the period in his career when he was signing big rock bands and I think by this time he was already looking to the day when he could sell his company and cash out of the business. In any event, he didn't seem all that interested in us. But one of his A&R men was passionately interested. This was John Kalodner, whose only demand was that his name be listed on the album credits twice. We were happy to oblige.

John became one of our chief musical counselors and a major figure in the history of the band. On our long and arduous journey back to the top, John was with us all the way. Because Collins was still a neophyte in the subject of the big-time record biz, he became John's student.

Before coming to Geffen, where he'd worked with Asia, Whitesnake, and Sammy Hagar, Kalodner had been an A&R guy at Atlantic, developing the careers of Yes, Foreigner, and AC/DC. A lover of arena rock, John was a hard-core fan who never professed to have technical knowledge of music. He couldn't tap his feet to the beat. But he prided himself on having the ears of a fourteen-year-old girl. I respected his opinion immensely.

John was strong-minded and a devoted believer in our resurrection. With his white suit, shoulder-length hair, and tiny John Lennon glasses, he was also a character with a style all his own.

Before Kalodner signed us to Geffen, we'd tried working with Rick Rubin, who had begun Def Jam records and made it big in the rap game. Rick was another long-bearded, hard rock–loving genius who loved our records from the seventies and wanted to help bring us back. We had met him at a Boston studio where I walked in with Xanax in one pocket and blow in another. I didn't play worth a shit that day and the Rubin connection, at least then, didn't work. That's when I knew that the old ways weren't working. I knew we had to change, but I still couldn't picture what that would look like.

Kalodner did make a complete commitment to the band. Geffen gave John tremendous freedom and ample funds to engineer our comeback. The first stage, though, was tentative. It involved an album called *Done with Mirrors*. I don't consider it among our greatest. That may be due to the fact that we were still engaged in mighty battles with our habits—and losing.

Nonetheless, we started work on this new record, first tooling up in a rehearsal space in Somerville before heading out to Berkeley, California, and Fantasy Studios, where Kalodner had arranged for Ted Templeman to produce. Known for working with Van Halen, the Doobie Brothers, Van Morrison, and Little Feat, Templeman was seen as our great savior. But in fact, his contribution was minimal. He showed up and watched us rehearse before watching us record. Unlike Jack Douglas, he had little input. The whole thing felt haphazard.

Steven and I had not yet returned to a good songwriting groove. In fact, the first song off the record was a redo of the title cut from the first Joe Perry album, "Let the Music Do the Talking." Steven felt obligated to change some of the lyrics, but the music was exactly what I had originally written. The other songs on the record just didn't realize their potential. When *Done with Mirrors* was released, sales were not spectacular. We still had a long way to go.

Billie and I had long wanted to marry. In 1985, soon after my divorce from Elyssa became final, that became possible. We had in-depth discussions about the kind of life we envisioned for ourselves, our boys, and our future family. Billie didn't want to raise children alone. She wanted a co-parent.

My own position was clear. "I'm not marrying you to be alone," I said. "I expect you to go on the road with me. I know the tours are long and tedious, but I'll try and make it as comfortable as possible. I want to be there to help raise the kids."

We both had made mistakes in the past that we did not want to repeat. With that in mind, we made certain we were on the same page morally, spiritually, and financially.

We also thought long and hard about a wedding ceremony that would mean the most to us. A small wedding? A big one with all the families together? Since neither of us had much regard for tradition, we leaned toward something intimate.

The big day came in September. When the band stopped in Hawaii on our way back from Japan for a ten-day vacation and checked into a hotel in Maui, I woke Billie early one morning and said, "We're getting married today." I grabbed the yellow pages and found a minister who would officiate at the Iao Needle, a spiritual location for Hawaiian natives. After calling our mothers on the mainland to relay the good news, I felt relieved. No agonizing decisions about who to invite, no worry about fancy preparations. We headed straight to the sacred spot, stopping only to pick up leis of fresh flowers for the bride and groom. I wore jeans and Billie wore gauzy beach pants and a flower-printed bandeau top. She looked tanned and gorgeous. Tim Collins and his friend Nick LaHage were witnesses.

The mountainside setting was awash with lush greenery. The sky was overcast. The vows were simple but moved us to tears of happiness. The music was Bryan Ferry's "Take a Chance with Me" on the boom box I had brought along. In the midst of the ceremony, the sun broke through, revealing the shimmering blue ocean in the distance—a good omen.

Later that week Collins threw a big wedding party on a catamaran sunset sail, inviting the band and the whole crew. Steven and Teresa gave us an underwater scooter, an extravagant gift. Given the fact that we were still struggling financially, I didn't feel comfortable accepting it. I thanked Steven but urged him to return it. He wouldn't hear of it, but I still didn't take it out of the box. I was going to return it and give Steven his money back. Weighing some fifty pounds, the boxed-up scooter stood in the hallway of our bungalow for days.

Meanwhile, the jeweler who had made my wedding band gave us some incredible Maui Wowie that we put on the shelf. A few days later, we heard Tom and Brad and their wives laughing and partying in their bungalow. They'd eaten mushrooms and were having a blast.

"What the fuck," I said to Billie. "Let's light up some of this."

The smoke tasted more like hash than weed.

Five minutes later, we took the scooter out of the box and carried it down to the beach together with our masks, fins, and snorkels. We played like porpoises in the warm water of the bay till dusk, laughing so hard we nearly drowned.

In 1986 a seismic shift happened without warning. In fact, I didn't know it was happening until after it was over. It began with a simple phone call from producer Rick Rubin.

"Do you like rap, Joe?" he asked.

"Sure," I said. "What I know of it."

Aaron, our son, was a rap fan and played it around the house all the time. For my part, I'd picked up the sounds on the street and liked what I heard. In fact, I saw rap as a new form of blues. Just like old blues, hip-hop can be in-your-face macho. The country bluesman might sing, "I'm a crawlin' kingsnake, baby," the same way the urban rapper might boast, "I'm the baddest motherfucker."

"I consider 'Walk This Way' proto-rap," Rick told me.

When I asked Rick what he meant by that, he explained, "It's half spoken, half sung and has the swagger of rap. I'm telling you this because I've been producing the new Run-DMC record. When I played them 'Walk

This Way,' they loved it. My first idea was to have them rap over samples of the song with a drum machine, but now I'm thinking that it'd be better to cut a brand-new cover, with Steven doing new vocals and you adding guitar parts. What do you think?"

I didn't have to think for long. It sounded like a cool musical adventure and I said so.

"You think Steven would do it?"

I did, and he did. Steven and I saw it as a double blessing—a chance to revisit one of our favorite songs and, at the same time, bring it to a new market.

A week later we showed up at a New York studio. The guys from Run-DMC arrived a little after us and immediately huddled up around their road manager, obviously preoccupied. From the bits of conversation we could overhear, it sounded like a rental car they had loaned to one of their roadies had gone missing. They were trying to figure out what to do next. This went on for half an hour or so. Meanwhile, they hadn't even acknowledged that we were in the studio. Finally, Rick intervened and introduced us all around, saying, "Later for the car, guys. Let's concentrate on the song."

But the concentration didn't come quickly. They were understandably obsessed with getting their car back.

"We can get into a lot of trouble," said Run.

"More trouble if we don't cut this track," said Rick. "Don't forget—Joe and Steve are here."

It took another few hours for things to settle down, but when the attention finally turned to music we were all surprised by how well things meshed.

"How 'bout putting on a new bass part?" Rubin suggested.

"Didn't bring a bass," I said.

"I'll run home and get you one," said one of the guys who had been watching the sessions. He and his friends turned out to be the Beastie Boys, another group that Rick was producing, who happened to be hanging out during the session.

When it was over, everyone seemed pleased. But there were no reassurances from Rick that the cut would even make it onto the final album. We all left as friends, with much respect all around.

I forgot about the session until a couple of weeks later when another call came in from Rubin. We were out on the road with Aerosmith.

"The cut is on the record," said Rick. "In fact, we wanna shoot a video with you guys in it. Are you game?"

We were. We flew to New York. I was with Billie, then pregnant with our first child, and Steven was with Teresa. The soundstage was in a sketchy part of Union City, New Jersey. When it was time to start filming, Steven and I were pretty buzzed. As soon as we'd arrived in New York, we had run off to separate dealers to cop the stimulants of our choice. The shoot itself took a while. Once we saw the concept, though, we knew the video would be special. Making it even more special was the presence of our women, who made fleeting appearances. Billie and Teresa are the two beauties seated in the background while Steven and I carry on out front.

The video is a visual metaphor for the meeting of two worlds—rock and hip-hop. In it, the wall that separates Steven and Joe rocking in one room while Run-DMC rap in the other is literally torn down. The rappers sport their laceless Adidas, black hats, and gold rope chains, while we're in our glitter scarves, fringed leather, and white boots. Ultimately the two styles mesh and match. The video is a raucous celebration, a happy marriage of two genres; in a twist of double irony, it represented a crossover moment for Run-DMC into the white pop world even as Aerosmith experienced a grand and unexpected entrance into the world of MTV videos. It was a big, big moment for the bad boys from Boston. First Run-DMC's version of "Walk This Way" became a hip-hop hit; then it became an even bigger hit on the pop chart. The video went into heavy rotation and soon earned iconic status. It turned out that, after Michael Jackson, Run-DMC were among the first black artists to appear on MTV.

And yet we were still fucked up on drugs. Our motives were always clear—to get back as a world-class rock band. But times had changed. We needed clearer heads to make things work.

Collins met with me to discuss the drug situation. He had stopped using and was attending twelve-step meetings. He thought it critical that Steven and I get sober. At this point I had quit snorting heroin and coke and, aside from social drinking, had given up booze, but I was strung out on Xanax. Tim wanted me to go into rehab at the same time as Steven. But Billie was within two weeks of giving birth to our first child. So I made a deal with Tim that I'd go in a week after Billie gave birth.

After the dismal results of the Rick Rubin sessions, I knew that something had to change. This twelve-step thing sounded a bit creepy, but doing the Back in the Saddle tour relatively straight had given me a window into what clearheaded creativity could be.

In conjunction with a high-priced New York therapist, Collins talked us into doing an intervention on Steven, who resented the fact that I wouldn't go with him. He was the front man who had fallen out onstage more than anyone wanted to recall. But no, he wasn't the only one who was fucked up. We all were. I told Steven that I'd be going into rehab shortly, but he wouldn't accept my explanation of wanting to be with Billie during the birth. I had a hard time accepting his lack of understanding. I couldn't believe this guy was literally asking me to miss the birth of my child and was pissed off about it. I was hoping that he'd see this opportunity to get clean as a blessing and proof that we cared for him; we were trying to save his life. But Steven didn't see it that way. His reasoning was, how could we urge him into rehab when we were still using? Nonetheless, he went.

As promised, I went in to deal with my Xanax habit in October 1986, after the birth of our son Tony. In their own time, the other guys also got sober. We realized that the only way this would work was for all of us to be sober.

In rehab I heard talk among the staff about Bon Jovi. *Slippery When Wet* had just come out with hit after hit. I heard snippets of the record—songs like "Livin' on a Prayer" and "You Give Love a Bad Name"—but they weren't exactly to my taste. Bon Jovi was being hailed as the new big thing. I didn't know it then, but, ironically, the team that had produced and helped Bon Jovi write their breakthrough record would soon be working with us.

Even though I took occasional note of what was happening in the wider world of rock, rehab really wasn't about music for me. It was more about quieting my mind and purging Xanax from my system. I just wanted to get clean.

I went to twelve-step meetings that, for several years, were helpful.

But because I'm not much of a joiner and tend to resist the group mentality, I lacked Steven's enthusiasm for recovery gatherings. I shared reluctantly and tended to keep to myself. Having also stopped snorting cocaine, smoking grass, and drinking liquor, Collins cast himself in the role of both manager and sobriety supervisor. He kept track of the number of meetings we attended. He assigned people to check up on us to make sure we were doing the twelve-step work he considered mandatory. This felt invasive and like an accusation of irresponsibility—and also went against the tenets of the twelve-step paradigm. But I knew we had to get straight and was willing to put up with whatever methodology worked.

For years we had used the excuse that, because we were America's party band, sobriety didn't go with our image. In fact, sobriety might ruin our image. Of course this argument was bullshit. But when you don't want to give up the stuff that has been feeding your head for many years, you rely on bullshit. You rationalize any way you can.

We also felt that we had to make our sobriety public. The band had burned so many bridges with half-played shows and no-shows that we had to let the business community know that this time we were serious. We had to prove we could gather our forces to make records that didn't cost millions and take years to complete.

It was a miracle that all of us got sober. I never thought I'd ever be able to play without something in me. Steven's sobriety was especially miraculous. Here was a guy who, back in school, used to get high by sticking the teeth of a comb into a cigarette and smoking the plastic. He was hard-core.

Our sobriety was a great thing, strengthened by the fact that we did it together. We helped one another by example. There was peer pressure, but in many ways the peer pressure was positive.

Yet this new arrangement, spearheaded by the wildly ambitious and always brilliant Tim Collins, was not without a corrosive element. Within a few years that element would undermine our progress and create new havoc for the band. In the mid-eighties, though, I didn't recognize that element. I had Billie; our new son, Tony; and Aaron. Fortunately, the visits with Adrian had smoothed out. The family I had always wanted had come together. I was reunited with Aerosmith and blind to the ways in which my bandmates and I were being manipulated.

VACATION IN VANCOUVER

My sobriety had a positive impact on much more than my music and the eventual resurgence of Aerosmith. Sobriety led to a renewal of a spirit that had long left me. I was able to renew my relationship with those essential elements—the woods, the water, the wonder of science, and the mysteries of nature—that had consumed me as a child. With clear eyes, I was now able to view these phenomena again, only this time as an adult. The wonder was still there. And my passion for music was stronger than ever.

In good faith, I can't completely decry drugs. Drugs brought me excitement and at times fueled my creativity. But when they stopped working, they destroyed my peace of mind. I looked downward, not upward, ignoring the stars at night. Once I was free of drugs, the simple pleasures returned: I was able to appreciate a day of blue sky, an afternoon walk in the woods, holding my infant son Tony in my arms, holding the hand of my beautiful wife, renewing my fascination with the sea, snorkeling, fishing, and hunting. I began thinking of things I'd wanted to do since childhood—like commanding a prop plane over a New England landscape when the leaves turn red and gold in fall. I took flying lessons and went on ski trips and diving excursions, all of which were more enjoyable with a clear mind and an open heart. Mostly, though, I was focused on two primary goals—working hard to help bring Aerosmith back to the top, and enjoying a stable and happy family life.

Aaron's dad moved down the street from us to help Billie care for their son, now a teenager. So when we traveled, Aaron stayed with his father and continued his schooling, occasionally visiting us on the road. As soon as we came home, Aaron moved in with us.

The fact that Elyssa had taken Adrian, at age six, and moved to California really messed up my relationship with my son. She seemed bound and determined to keep us apart. A clause in our divorce agreement gave me the right to make them stay in Boston. But given how we were always on the road, I knew that wouldn't stand up in court. As Adrian grew older, he'd spend a few days out of the summer and holidays with us. I'd also see him when I came to L.A. But the separation between father and son deeply hurt us both.

The band got into the touring groove. We sold out two nights at the Greek in L.A., a milestone in our comeback. It was great to see attendance increasing. The Run-DMC thing was also great, although we saw it as a side adventure. Even if it hadn't happened, we would have kept touring. But when we realized that this was the first time MTV had put rap artists in heavy rotation, we were especially gratified to be part of a positive historical change. We also didn't understand the boost it gave to our career until we got to Europe, where many fans thought this was our first single ever! Who knew that this little riff that had come to me in Hawaii would still be making noise a decade later?

The success with the reworked "Walk This Way" was tremendous, but we needed a fresh hit. Done with Mirrors just didn't have it. It sounded like we were warming up. It contained no smashes and caused no stir about a new and improved Aerosmith. We had to create that stir. So when John Kalodner suggested a new paradigm for recording and producing our new album, I listened. Given John's track record, I'd have been foolish not to give his suggestions my full attention.

It wasn't that the band didn't argue with Kalodner. We argued passionately, especially when his ideas seemed to be taking us away from the essence of who we were—hard-core rockers. But at the same time, John was connected to the marketplace in a way that we were not. He knew what was selling and which producers and studios had the magic touch. So when he suggested that we go to Vancouver and work with the team assembled by Bruce Fairbairn, who had just produced Bon Jovi's mega-selling *Slippery When Wet*, it didn't take long for us to decide to go.

I loved Vancouver. It's a world-class city surrounded by miles of forest and mountains and populated by beautiful people. As a creative hub, it had a great vibe, like a kind of Canadian L.A. Along with Billie and little Tony, I arrived two weeks early to get a sense of the studio and the people I'd be working with.

I was a little apprehensive about writing and playing completely sober. So when the riff to "Hangman Jury" came flying off an old funky Silvertone guitar I had found, I was relieved. The music was there. The music was always there. The music for "Hangman" reflected the rapport I'd always felt for Taj Mahal's deep-rooted blues. I knew we were off to a good start. I kept telling myself that, as a sober kid, I had loved music. The excitement and drive were built in, not supplied by a bottle or a drug.

Bruce Fairbairn was an odd duck. He seemed to own only two pairs of pants and one shirt, which was decorated with a pattern of flying mallards. He wore dorky shoes and seemed pretty straight—at least, that was the side of himself he revealed to us. He was a stamp and coin collector who took time off each week to either buy new stuff or organize his collections. Little Mountain Sound studio, with its SSL soundboard, was funky but comfortable. You'd start on time—1 P.M. every afternoon—with Bruce exerting a quiet but firm control over the proceedings. I saw him as a coach. We had the energy, but he had the skill to harness it. He also had no fear of standing up to anyone—including Steven.

I went over to Jim Vallance's studio to start work on new material. Jim was Bruce's childhood friend and roller-skating partner from their days of busking together. He could play virtually any instrument, but he was primarily a songwriter. Over the coming years we'd wind up writing many songs together. When Steven arrived, it was Jim who helped us find the final form to "Hangman Jury." Writing with Vallance was fun. He was one of the first guys I knew to use an Apple computer, generating all sorts of electronic sounds that kicked my creativity into high gear. With his late-model drum machine spitting out rhythm after rhythm, I found it easy to write riffs. It was a lot like when Steven would play drums in the early days.

To get the hits we were all looking for, Kalodner wanted us to work not only with Fairbairn and Vallance but with the same writer who had cowritten those smash songs I had heard in rehab—"Livin' on a Prayer" and "You Give Love a Bad Name." That was Desmond Child, a charismatic guy who had put together Desmond Child & Rouge, a pop band, in the seventies. Kalodner's idea was that Desmond could help Steven with his lyrics. Not all that willing to reduce our ownership of the songs with a third partner, we fought the idea at first but eventually decided to give Desmond a chance. Good decision. Desmond was a skilled tunesmith.

In the case of the breakout cut from this record—"Dude (Looks like a Lady)"—Desmond served primarily as song doctor. After I'd composed the AC/DC–inspired music for "Dude" with Steven, Desmond came up with the great title that triggered Tyler's cross-gendered story. For the first time, we'd been fooling around with a sampler—that's how we created the truncated sound that starts off the track.

There were long discussions about sharing ownership. Finally, Desmond's logic made sense to me: If you have a giant factory that breaks down because of one missing part, what is the worth of that part? A great deal. Desmond provided that part and wound up owning a third of the song. But the money was the least of it. Our reluctance to let an outsider dilute our sound with their influence was mostly an ego thing, especially for Steven. I had no problem coming up with riffs and music, but it just seemed to get harder for Steven to settle down and write lyrics. In the end, because "Dude" became one of the biggest in our history, we appreciated that Desmond had helped get our factory up and working again.

Up until this point Steven and I had been a two-man songwriting team. I concentrated on finding riffs that would inspire Steven. I was always there to support him until he came up with the lyrics. But after finishing "Dude," we felt more comfortable working with outside writers. That dynamic changed, though, when I walked into the rehearsal room as Steven and Desmond were finishing a song that would become "Angel." I was stunned. I would have expected Steven to have called me and said, "We're working on something. Come on over." But no. The song was completed without me, setting a new precedent that has continued until this day: *Steven and I were a songwriting team only when it was convenient for Steven.*

When Steven didn't get around to helping me finish the lyrics for a piece of music I had written, it was Desmond who stepped in to complete "Heart's Done Time," a song inspired by my love for Billie.

"Rag Doll" was born out of another collaboration. Steven, Vallance, and I had the song written except for the title. Holly Knight came in and named it. Again, we willingly shared credit evenly, not only because Holly earned it, but because the machine was humming along so efficiently. If you had something to do with the writing of the song, it was split evenly. That took the pressure off any credit disputes and let the creativity flow. And since the band would ultimately play the song, no matter how it started, it always ended up sounding like Aerosmith.

One of our most successful collaborations yielded the final track, "The Movie," an instrumental jam I initiated from a guitar synthesizer. When I was fooling with the synth, in my mind's eye I was imagining a film—a moody thriller shot in Sweden or Poland, one whose language was not my own but whose narrative had me enthralled. The resulting song was an example of what we could produce when everyone in the band—including Steven on keyboards—worked together on a single vision.

Collins was a neophyte in the music business, but he had a brilliant mind for knowing what he didn't know. He surrounded himself with people who had the knowledge he lacked. He called them his Brain Trust. Keith Garde, for example, who had begun as Tim's assistant, rose to the position of virtual co-manager. Keith was brilliant, especially when it came to videos and new technology. He also had great expertise in dealing with the press. The office staff claimed that the originality of Keith's ideas was co-opted by Collins, who, due to his insatiable ego, required all the credit. The co-opting was done subtly and without our knowledge. But then we heard Keith was doing the same with ideas from the staff under him. Already, things were getting weird on the management side. Ego, raising its ugly head. Also, Collins's original partner Steve Barrasso's name mysteriously came off the door of his office. Collins explained that the pressure of managing us was too much for him, and he decided to leave the company.

Another key member of the Brain Trust was Marty Callner, the director who made certain that the video component to *Permanent Vacation* was as strong as the music itself. If Kalodner was the main impetus for our new crop of hit songs, Marty was the man behind our new crop of hit videos. To make it back to the top, we needed both components. Before Marty, we thought we could do it all by ourselves—write, produce, and direct. But our self-styled video for "Let the Music Do the Talking" from *Done with Mirrors* was probably not shown more than twice. No doubt, we needed Marty.

Marty had experience with hair bands like Whitesnake and knew what it took to create an MTV-friendly video. The process would start with all of us sitting in a room and kicking around concepts. Marty wasn't big on specifics; he was a broad-strokes painter; no storyboards or outlines. But there was a willingness on his part to involve us in every aspect of the video. His thing was, *Let's just get out there and shoot*. And man, did he love to shoot film—rolls and rolls of film. He shot "Dude (Looks Like a Lady)," the first single, in a concert setting with dozens of takes, including one with Steven in drag. In another shot, long-bearded John Kalodner trades in his all-white suit for an all-white bridal gown. Billie once again took on the role of the saxophone-playing blonde. The theme, of course, was switched-up sex roles, narrated with humor and high-powered energy.

"Rag Doll," another high-priced Marty Callner video from *Permanent Vacation*, had us winging down to party in the bordello-happy ambience of New Orleans. We wore Mardi Gras Native American headdresses while scantily clad pretty young things ran around the French Quarter. At four in the morning, I was sent out into the middle of Bourbon Street to play my guitar. MTV played the shit out of the video, and thanks also to "Dude" and the perpetually popular Run-DMC/Aerosmith "Walk This Way," we were on TV screens all across the Western world.

These were the days when videos were starting to cost a million bucks to shoot. Neither MTV nor the label paid. *We* paid. MTV, who had no qualms about exploiting their monopoly, got free programming; the label got free ads; and, ultimately, if the video worked, we saw an increase in record sales. If we were going to compete in this new age where jewel-boxed CDs and splashy videos were all the rage, we had no choice but to absorb the costs, though it did seem that the network was ripping off the bands. What's new . . .

In the winter of 1987 we hit the road. With these new songs from *Permanent Vacation* getting strong radio and television attention, the press began talking about our rebirth as an accomplished fact. It felt great to perform in front of big crowds that included both older and newer generations of fans.

But it didn't feel so great to have Collins monitor us as if we were schoolchildren. We understood that sobriety was now part of the band's narrative. We saw that nearly every press report included the story of Aerosmith getting clean. That was fine. We recognized the importance of staying on the straight and narrow. But Collins's need to control every aspect of our lives was becoming apparent. When we played L.A., he'd book us into a hotel down in Laguna Beach. If we stayed on the Sunset Strip, he feared we'd be too close not only to the party people, but to managers whom he saw as his competition. He and his minions—especially our road manager, who acted as a Collins spy—were constantly monitoring our attendance of twelve-step meetings, cleaning out the minibars in our hotel rooms, and making sure that there were no drugs or alcohol backstage. Our every move was being watched. We didn't need to hear Collins continually say, "If you don't stay sober, you'll ruin everything."

We knew full well that we had regained our financial and creative footing. But because we didn't want to lose what had been tough to regain, we probably didn't want to recognize the fact that we were in the hands of an overly controlling manager whose machinations were slowly creeping into our private lives. Our minds were being conditioned. Without such a strict program, we feared that this sensational comeback would crumble. We saw the statistics. The odds of one person staying sober were small. But five guys? Unheard-of. We were doing something no band had ever done before. Dozens of groups had died or faded away. In this business, no one gets a second chance. Yet we were more successful than ever.

We were also back into the rhythm of the road, where things happened fast and furiously: performing before huge crowds, flying from city to city, being interviewed, applauded, and congratulated. It felt great that we were able to put the past behind us. Our focus was on our day-to-day work. The five of us had reclaimed the Aerosmith magic.

In the summer of 1988, the story took another twist when we learned through Collins that David Geffen and John Kalodner wanted Guns N' Roses to open our shows. Their first album, *Appetite for Destruction*, out on Geffen Records, had begun to sell. The video for the single "Welcome to the Jungle" was exploding on MTV. I heard the band as balls-to-the-wall rock and roll. I was blown away by their sound and flattered when they talked about our influence on their music. Slash talked about *Rocks* as the seminal album in his life. Axl praised Steven to the sky. If they represented the next generation of rock, I was gratified because that put us squarely in the continuum. Beyond that, I liked the guys and was glad to have them on the tour.

But then the bullshit started. We started hearing stories that we insisted they could have no booze or drugs. Maybe our manager made that demand, but we never did. We didn't presume to have dominion over any band other than ourselves; what they did was their business. We treated them like adults, even as our management was infantilizing us. I wasn't embarrassed or shy about my sobriety. But I also wasn't a braggart or a Bible thumper. I don't believe in trying to convert the world to my way of life. The last thing in the world that baby bands like Guns N' Roses want to hear is preaching. Besides, preaching doesn't work. Just as the addiction drama suffered by Janis Joplin or Jimi Hendrix or Keith Moon had not straightened me out, I lacked the ability to straighten out anyone else. You learn through living, not through preaching.

In short, although we were sober, we were hardly sobriety Nazis. And to see us described as such in press reports, with Collins leading the charge, really pissed me off. Guns N' Roses could get as fucked up as they wanted—and with no repercussions from us.

Billie and Tony came with me on tour. I was into a whole new way of dealing with the road. No more crazy man looking for new highs, just a crazy rock and roller passionate about music. Billie and I were also passionate about raising our son right. Because the Aerosmith plane was too small to accommodate our families, Billie and Tony had to take commercial flights to keep up with the band. It was rough traveling; Billie worked overtime to make sure that things ran smoothly at home while making the transition to life on the road with our boys.

As we stormed the country, it became clear that Guns N' Roses was the new young thing. It had been years since we had played that role. At one point *Rolling Stone* came out to do a story about our comeback but wound up writing about Guns N' Roses. I wasn't happy, but I understood. By the time the tour was over, the focus had flipped from us to them—and deservedly so. We were playing great, revitalized by a fresh slate of songs and a hot record, but here in the eighties Axl and Slash had that kind of fresh-blood energy that had characterized us in the seventies. They were in their twenties; we were in our thirties—a huge difference in rock. If anything, their heat helped us fuel our own fire. The tour ended, a tremendous overall success. The old tradition had the headliners giving gifts to the openers—and the openers letting the headliners have it. In our case, that meant a giant pie fight at the end of the last show. We gave each of the Guns N' Roses guys a set of top-of-the-line Halliburton luggage as a token of gratitude. When I see Slash these days, he says he's still using those suitcases.

DINOSAURS EATING CARS

It was funny looking at Bruce Fairbairn, noted stamp and butterfly collector, running through the open field chasing butterflies with a net. It isn't an activity usually associated with a rock producer. But there he was, in the fields of Massachusetts, chasing down some rare species while, from the porch of the rehearsal studio, Steven and I watched in amazement.

By then we had moved into houses on the suburban South Shore of Boston. We had both bought big places on large plots of land not far from each other. Steven had married Teresa and was relatively calm—that is, calm for Steven.

The studio where we worked, halfway between Steve's place and mine, belonged to our friend Rick Tinory, whose fame came from writing a hit song about the Pope visiting Boston.

Fairbairn had flown in from Vancouver along with Jim Vallance to help us get started writing songs for our new record, our third for Geffen and our second with Bruce as producer. Although we liked Jim as a songwriter, we weren't at all sure we needed to collaborate with outsider writers again. We viewed Aerosmith as a self-contained unit. We were certain we had all the necessary writing talent. But John Kalodner saw it differently. Like all record men, he had a simple attitude—repeat the winning formula. Because we were so confident in our ability to write hits, especially after we'd been doing just that for some eighteen years, we challenged that attitude.

We prevailed because Steven and I were working with greater synchronicity than ever. I came up with the riff for "Monkey on My Back" early in the rehearsal process, and Steven nailed the lyrics. We were on a creative roll. Tom inspired the music for one of Steven's most serious lyrics, "Janie's Got a Gun"—a song about physical abuse by a parent—which wound up winning a Grammy. Steven collaborated with Brad on the stirring "Voodoo Medicine Man."

To shake things up, I listened to "Rag Doll," from *Permanent Vacation*, backward and, strangely enough, began developing new chords that turned into "Don't Get Mad, Get Even." We didn't simply want to follow up our last album with something good; we were driven by the Aerosmith ethos: *Fuck whatever we did last time. This time we can do it better. 'Cuz in this biz you're only as good as your next record.*

I wrote the riff to "My Girl" out of my passion to reconnect with the raw rock of the sixties that I'd heard in the Kinks. Steven's lyrics matched the frantic pace of the music. It was a great one to play live.

"Young Lust" contained that same kind of a paradox—a throwback to the days of horny youth even as we approached our forties.

Kalodner insisted on bringing Desmond Child back into the mix. Desmond helped us write the bridge to a tune that didn't make the record. Oddly enough, another song written by Steven and me needed a bridge and the discarded one worked. Thus the Perry-Tyler-Child collaboration called "F.I.N.E.," which stands for "Fucked up . . . Insecure . . . Neurotic . . . Emotional."

"Love in an Elevator," still another expression of Steven's libido, was a pure Perry/Tyler product. In fact, of the final ten songs, Steven and I wrote six alone.

During the recording at Little Mountain Sound in Vancouver, I was after the maximum sonic boom. With Fairbairn's help, we achieved it. To borrow a phrase from Frank Zappa, it sounded like dinosaurs eating cars. To heighten the record's drama, between each track we inserted short, bizarre interludes: cries, chants, and foreign dialogues. This was done with the help of a local Vancouverite who had an astonishing collection of world instruments. Our motto was, "If it makes sound, use it."

The last piece of the puzzle was the title. As usual, deliberations went on for weeks. It was only Brad's question—"Why don't we just call the thing *Pump*?"—that sealed the deal.

We also wanted videos that matched the energy of the music. Director Marty Callner understood how to project the larger-than-life images that would show a band reclaiming its former stature. On "Love in an Elevator," our sexiest video to illustrate our sexiest song, we start out as well-mannered patrons in an art deco department store and wind up grooving on a variety of voluptuous beauties in a variety of positions. Billie is the topless woman I'm making out with in the elevator. It was Billie or no one! The theme is athleticism in the name of love. The performance segments are shot in an arena-like ambience to underscore the point: Aerosmith is back rocking huge venues.

"The Other Side" has us, as stiffs, being carried out of coffins and placed onstage—a metaphor for our rebirth. Steven is more animated than a Disney cartoon, back-flipping like some scrawny teenager.

Was that good? Was that bad? Whatever it is, it was Aerosmith—a hardworking rock band gunning for mega-success the second time around.

We did things that went against the grain of our original vision in the seventies. But this was a new era. We slipped under the wire and still looked young enough to fit in with the new baby bands on MTV. As a result, we were bigger than ever. Rather than lose old fans because of our sobriety, we gained new fans because we tried new things. We also played better than ever. All this came in the middle of the Golden Age of Arena Rock.

Adding to the allure was a third video—this one with a radically different feel—that immediately went into heavy rotation on MTV. For "Janie's Got a Gun" we hired David Fincher, the future director of *Fight Club*, who fashioned a compelling crime narrative with top production values to complement Steven's noirish lyrics. If you calculated the cost of these videos—many done by top-flight feature-length directors—on a per-minute basis, each would have the cost of a high-budget action movie.

Released in 1989, *Pump* was our farewell record to the eighties. Like *Permanent Vacation*, it sold multimillions. Even reviewers who had spent much of their careers kicking our ass had to admit this was some strong rock and roll from a band that was not about to fade away. We couldn't wait to play it live for the fans.

On the first part of our tour, a new band called Skid Row was set to open. Their lead singer, Sebastian Bach, was like a kid in a candy store, loving every minute of his new success. Before one of our shows he came to my dressing room and said, "Man, my greatest dream in the world would be to smoke some hash with you and Steven."

"That's not gonna happen," I said, laughing.

"I need to get high with you guys, just once," he insisted.

"Sorry," I said.

And that was it.

As much as I appreciated Skid Row's appeal to a younger generation, I couldn't help but bemoan the dilution of the musical tradition. I'd be shocked if anyone in most of these young bands had ever put a needle down on a John Lee Hooker record. The blues, the basis and beating heart of this art form, was slipping further into obscurity.

No matter—I loved the tour. Not only did we blast fresh music from *Vacation* and *Pump*, we also played on one of the coolest sets of our career: a stage set that replicated the rooftop of an urban apartment building. Steven and I ran up and down staircases and ramps while Joey's drums spun like a top.

We flew from city to city on a Citation II that we christened Aeroforce One. Our touring paradigm had us based in a central city like Chicago or Dallas that we used as a hub for two weeks at a time. From there we'd hit every city within an hour's flight. We'd leave the hotel about 2 P.M. and fly back to the hub that same night. Billie would travel commercially with little Tony and set up house at the various hotels. I'm glad to say that the Perry family adapted to this gypsy lifestyle. Billie homeschooled Tony on the road; when we were in Boston, he entered a Montessori school whose flexibility matched our own.

Steven had renewed his fascination with backstage groupies. After the show I'd have to stand around for hours before we left. This became a real source of friction between me and Steven. I was never one for the short-skirt room. I sometimes imagine myself standing outside the Pearly Gates with St. Peter, who asks me, "You wasted how many hours of your life waiting around for this guy?"

On the Citation II, the Aeroforce pilot let me sit in the copilot seat and at times fly the plane as we cruised to the next show. I must have logged hundreds of hours in that copilot seat. By then, I had spent a good many hours taking private lessons in a small plane. One night the pilot let me land the Aeroforce jet. When the other guys saw that I was at the controls there was dead silence. It was too late for them to do anything about it. After I executed something close to a textbook three-point landing, most of them were impressed and didn't mind. But Tom was upset. In a low voice he said, "That's the last time you'll ever do that."

The Black Crowes, another young band about to break through, opened the second leg of our American *Pump* tour. I was glad to have them aboard because their first album was one of the best rock records in recent years. There was an uncomfortable friction between the two brothers—Chris and Rich Robinson—who ran the band, but I saw that as growing pains. Chris had a big mouth and, as much as he'd admired us in the seventies, he yapped to the press that we were sellouts because we had a guy who helped with background vocals; he also said that we used tape vocals. Only the first accusation was true, but he still didn't have to go to the press. As the years went on, however, we let it go, became friends with the Crowes, and often played on the same bill.

By the end of the summer of 1990, right around my fortieth birthday, in one year alone we had played to more than two million people in America during our one hundred–plus shows. We also had a very pleasant moment doing MTV's *Unplugged*.

When we got to Europe, the pandemonium continued. In England, Jimmy Page, by then a good friend of mine, and his manager spent the weekend with us. We were set to play the Marquee club, followed by a big gig at Monsters of Rock.

Standing onstage at the Marquee during the sound check, Jimmy, Brad, and I had our favorite Les Pauls in our hands while Steven blew harp. I felt like I was seventeen years old again. My mind went back to suburban Hopedale, where I'd sit in front of the record player for countless hours, trying to absorb Page's electric mojo. I did that by letting the riff play, lifting the needle, trying to copy it on my guitar, and repeating that process for hours. Now we were colleagues. We played those Yardbirds songs—"I Ain't Got You" and "Smokestack Lightning"—that had lit up my life as a boy and changed my life as a man. When Jimmy sat in at the show, it was so intense that we blew out the power—twice. But it was during that five-hour sound check that we were living the dream, playing every Yardbirds song in the book.

The next night Jimmy rode with us on our bus out to Donington Park for the Monsters of Rock, a huge outdoor event. Jimmy sat in again during our last few songs, raising the stakes even higher. It was a night when we really rode the wave of the crowd's incredible energy. As we were walking off-stage—sky-high on the music—we heard a huge roar that drowned out the crowd. We looked up at the sky and saw the Concorde taking off just one thousand feet above our heads, the perfect punctuation point to a weekend none of us would ever forget.

For me, the start of the nineties was a good time. Billie proved to be the woman I had longed for. Her ethic and mine were the same: to live a happy and healthy creative life free of drama. We planned for our second child together. The longer my sobriety lasted, the freer I felt. I had successfully learned to fly a small prop plane solo over the rooftops of our South Shore surroundings. I had even buzzed Steven's house and wiggled the wings to say hello. With Billie in the back, I had flown over the breathtakingly beautiful New Hampshire mountains in peak fall foliage. Outside the band, life was sweet.

Inside the band, the drama would never cease—then, now, and forever. The truth is that in the beginning of this new decade, the Aerosmith drama deepened, turning crazier with each new day.

CULT

There are many definitions, but the one that hit me hardest says, "A cult is an insular sect built around the veneration of a person or belief where outside criticism cannot be tolerated."

As amazing as it might sound, this hard-core rock-and-roll band made up of five rugged individualists embraced a cult mentality. This happened for an alarmingly long period of time beginning in the late eighties and moving into the nineties. The cultlike ambience was the product of Tim Collins, the mastermind behind our spectacular comeback—one that, in the rock-and-roll business, was unprecedented. Our stunning resurgence blinded us to the ways in which we were being played. We didn't want to see it. And once we saw it, we didn't want to admit it. We just wanted to go on enjoying the enormity of our new success. We were back in the good graces of our fans. And because of all this new adulation, we were on top of the world and didn't want to reexamine the managerial mechanism that had gotten us there. Beyond that, we were playing better than ever.

By 1991, it was clear that our new professional life was not in our own hands. We were the puppets and Collins the puppeteer. For example, he never wanted any of our wives around, even if, in truth, none of them were causing problems. By this time, we were all raising families, trying to live our lives as grown men. Our wives were essential parts of those lives. But Collins insisted that they have their own separate therapy meetings with the shrink of his choice. God forbid they missed a single meeting. The same applied to the band's group therapy. Miss a meeting and there was hell to pay.

Then there were his pernicious triangulations.

Billie would ask Collins for a touring schedule and, in response, Collins would call Steven to say, "Joe and Billie are micromanaging the band. Joe is acting out."

That would hit a nerve in Steven, who would go around bad-mouthing me. Then Collins would call me and say, "Tyler is enraged. He's furious with you, but I can handle him."

The rest of the band would get word that Steven and I were fighting and, in reaction, retreat to their own corners. Finally Steven and I would get on the phone to sort out the mess—but this would be weeks later, when the emotional damage was already done. Collins thrived on messes like this. The plain truth was that we were healthy and sober. But, as I came to see it, in order to maintain control over our lives, Collins had to perpetuate the atmosphere of dysfunction. Dysfunction gave him control and, paradoxically, worsened his own psychological health. He became a junkie for control. The puzzlement went like this:

The healthier we became, the sicker he became.

His sickness took the form of trying to undermine our health.

The less stable we became, the more power he could wield.

His drug was power and, as with any addictive drug, he could never get enough.

Because Steven's personal life was spinning out of control, it didn't seem unreasonable for him, at Collins's insistence, to check into the Sierra Tucson care center for rehab. Our understanding was that his treatment was for a combination of issues, including his alleged drug use and sexual addiction. The decision as to whether he should go or not should have been made by Steven and his family. But the Brain Trust, which included John Kalodner and well-known celebrity twelve-step sobriety therapist Bob Timmins, prevailed, and Steven went into rehab for an extended stay.

Before our next tour, Steven told us the Brain Trust had the audacity to visit him at his home to say that they felt it was okay for him to get blow jobs on the road. In their view, blow jobs wouldn't be considered cheating on his wife. Apparently they were afraid that were Steven to remain monogamous, his lyrics would lose their sexual edge. Steven was right to get furious about their meddling. What a mind fuck!

Another mind fuck, this one concerning business: Collins was fighting with Geffen. Tim was talking about taking us off the label and bringing us back to Columbia/Sony, who apparently were willing to pay an incredible amount of money. The numbers made our heads swim.

Collins was pulling all the strings. Not only had he gained a reputation as the guy who ran Aerosmith, but he had also built up his own personal brand as Rehab Guru. It was as though he possessed a magic cure. If a band was strung out on drugs and didn't know what to do, their manager would call Collins. If he could save Aerosmith, he could save your band as well. Even politicians called him for sobriety advice. His reputation inflated his ego bigger than that of any rock star I had ever known—and his ego rested on his ability to keep us in line.

We never knew, for example, at some special events band members could buy extra tickets. We later learned that Collins was buyng them instead and using the tickets to invite his own sobriety buddies, outside business associates, and big shots he was looking to impress. So much was happening behind our backs, and yet, with so much success, we were looking ahead, not behind us.

In the summer of 1991, Collins called a band meeting. He had recruited a shrink, a specialist in addiction, to sit by his side and echo his position. He demanded that all of us go to Sierra Tucson for rehab.

"For what?" I asked.

"This band is in trouble," said Collins. "Your sobriety is in danger."

"It is?" I asked. None of us had had a drink or a drug in years. I didn't understand. "We're sober," I said. "We're all sober."

With support from the psychologist who would have one-on-one meetings with him before our meeting, a paradigm that Collins used with all the therapists, Collins went on to describe how the band had turned dysfunctional all over again. I didn't buy it.

"How?" asked Brad.

"Not everyone is working their program to the best of their ability," said Collins. "You're all too dependent on your wives. You're involved in unhealthy codependent relationships."

"What the fuck does that mean?" I asked.

Collins's minion rattled off some psychobabble. We were mystified. No one was happy about this. No one could understand it.

"I still don't see the point," said Tom.

"The point is that I can't manage a band that's addicted to anything," said Collins.

"And codependency," the shrink chimed in, "is as big an addiction as alcohol. Codependency is as destructive as cocaine."

I wanted to get up and say *Fuck you.* But I was also operating under the psychology that said, *With the band surging, don't rock the boat.*

But I couldn't buy this codependency business. I loved Billie. I valued her opinion. I was closer to her than I had been to anyone. But Billie didn't tell me what music to play or how to conduct my professional life. She didn't have anything to do with my songwriting or my performing except to encourage and support my progress as an artist. I had to break out the dictionary and read the definition of codependency: "Pertaining to a relationship in which one person is physically or psychologically addicted and the other person is psychologically dependent on the first in an unhealthy way." The love I had for my wife had nothing to do with codependency. We had an unconventional lifestyle, we had children, and we were doing the best we could to keep our family together in the crazy world of rock and roll. And then there was the fact that my marriage was no one's business but my own.

But the more the band argued with Collins and his shrink, the more blowback we got.

Why are you being so defensive?

Your defensiveness indicates how threatened you must feel.

Defensiveness and denial go hand in hand.

The platitudes were driving us crazy. "If we disagree, does that mean we're being defensive?" I asked. "Maybe it just means we disagree."

That's when Collins laid out his trump card.

"Look, Joe," he said. "I can't manage a band that I feel is this unhealthy. I can't manage a band about to fall off the wagon. In good conscience, I can't go to Sony and say, 'The band's in fine shape. We'll take your millions.' No, I can't say that when I know that the band is falling apart."

Falling apart? Everyone in the room was stunned. The band had never been tighter or stronger.

But, in essence, and literally, Collins was saying, *Go to Sierra Tucson or I'll kill the Sony deal.* And since Sony saw him as the Svengali who kept the band together, his threat carried weight. Needing time to examine our options, we decided to think over his threat.

I thought back to the beginning of our sobriety. That was when our weekly band meetings had begun. They included Tim and a therapist of his choice. All fine and good. We were all aware of the significance of our accomplishment: Getting one person sober is a miracle. Getting five rockers sober is impossible. Yet it had happened. These meetings were a good place to air our fears. We had feared that in our new state of sobriety we'd lose fans, that our playing would lose its fire, that our funky mojo would go missing—none of which proved true. But as these meetings continued, we learned that behind our backs Tim was coercing certain therapists. If they didn't back him in whatever plans he had for the band—whether personal or professional—he'd threaten to get their licenses revoked. The thing got insidious.

The meetings had begun with the idea that we were all there to help one another. Everyone had a chance to express his concerns. Everyone spoke about the tensions in his life. When we had an issue with a fellow band member, we confronted him. When that member needed support, we supported him. The meetings were set up as a safe place to share.

But when it came time for Collins to share and tell us what was happening in his life, he skimmed over the question or shut down entirely. For example, one of his chief issues was rage. Any small matter could send him into a fit of crazed anger. For those who worked for him, he was an emotional tyrant. The staff feared his moods and would often complain to us. When we brought up the subject, Collins either claimed it had no relevance to the welfare of the band or, enraged, simply got up and left the room.

When it became obvious that our sobriety was holding, Tim faced a dilemma: how to keep us dependent on him. His method was to keep lighting ground fires while casting himself in the role as the only one capable of putting them out.

In short, this amazing and inspiring story of a crazy rock band embracing sobriety had somehow morphed into a twisted psychodrama. And at this point in the story, Collins, who saw himself as the playwright, was threatening to write us out of the plot.

The wheels to move to Sony were already in motion. We had already shaken hands with the big Sony boss. John Kalodner was moving over to Sony as our ongoing A&R guy. I'm a very pragmatic person. When it comes to shit like this, I'm bottom-line. My mind immediately imagined Collins walking into Sony and saying, "The band is falling apart again. The guys are using."

If we retaliated by saying, "That's a lie," who would Sony believe—the rock-and-roll pirates with their infamous history of bad behavior? Or Collins and his staff of therapists backing up his every claim?

It wasn't close.

We decided to go to rehab.

"That's outrageous," said Billie, then pregnant with our second son, Roman. "Collins is using rehab as a way exert his power over you guys."

"I know," I said. "But he has that power. Sony is listening to Collins. Not to us. Sony is going to do what our manager says."

"But your manager is not simply managing the band, he wants to manage your entire life. So now he's saying you have to go to rehab, when, in fact, there's no palpable need."

"If we don't go," I said, "he'll scare off Sony."

"No, he won't," Billie insisted. "He wants the commission."

"Look, Bill, maybe we should just go."

"I don't like this, Joe."

"I don't either, baby, but I don't want to risk it. I know what it's like to be broke, and I don't want to go through that again. I don't even want to think about another financial meltdown. Collins is holding all the cards, and if going to rehab can resolve this crisis, I say we should go."

On issues like this, I usually deferred to Billie's judgment, relying on her uncanny clarity. But being the provider, and remembering how hard we had worked for our success in the seventies only to lose it all, I had to be cautious. I had to remind myself that this comeback, although spectacular, was tenuous. This comeback required constant maintenance. Like my other bandmates, I wasn't about to risk throwing it away. Man, this was a tough one, especially with Billie eight months pregnant. I hated capitulating to Collins's irrational demand, but I bit the bullet and went to rehab—kicking and screaming.

Karen Whitford, on the verge of giving birth, couldn't fly. But a very pregnant Billie flew out for family week. My sister, Anne, and my mother also came to lend support. When the therapists met with Billie and me for a single session, their conclusion was that there weren't any issues to address.

In fact, after a few days in the facility, all the therapists who worked with the band members said what we already knew: There was no reason for us to be there. Fearing that very thing—that there was nothing wrong with us—Collins proudly announced he had met with the staff in advance to orchestrate "a custom program" for us.

When I explained to my therapist that I was not thrilled at having to spend my forty-first birthday in rehab, she said, "You could have just as well spent it at home. Even if there were a need for therapy, it easily could have been facilitated in outpatient mode back in Boston. I have no idea why you're here."

Well, I knew why. We'd been coerced. Collins had even coerced our producer, Bruce Fairbairn, to check into rehab with us. It was like a sick joke. Except I wasn't fuckin' laughing. The entire enterprise accomplished only one thing: Collins reestablished his control. That control, though, came at a heavy cost. Deep resentments were growing deeper.

By far the best thing that happened in 1991 was the birth, on October 20, of our son Roman. I loved this child, as I loved all my children, with heart and soul. Billie insisted on natural childbirth. Man, watching her go through that was the most incredible experience of my life. She knew it would be our last child and was determined. My respect and love for her reached a peak even I couldn't have foreseen. Filled with gratitude for the arrival of new life, Billie and I recommitted ourselves to putting family first, although, given the demands of the Aerosmith family, that would never be easy.

The week before Roman's birth, Aerosmith performed for the MTV *10th Anniversary Special,* taped at the Wang Center in Boston. I remember carrying a beeper with me in case Billie went into labor. With a huge orchestra behind us, Steven sang "Dream On." This was the first time we'd done a live show in many months. The hometown fans, always amazingly loyal, showed up with lots of love. It was a great gig.

In the history of Aerosmith, we've been blessed with a countless number of great gigs. Our brand of rock is essentially upbeat. But after the shows were over and the fans went home, our happiness was never long lasting, especially during these bizarre years when the five of us were still struggling to break free of a cultlike mentality.

TRYING TO GET A GRIP

At the start of 1992 we went off to work on our fourth and final Geffen record. We loved Vancouver. *Vacation* and *Pump* were great records, Little Mountain Sound was a great facility, but enough was enough. Except for our first album, we had always left Boston to record elsewhere. The conventional thinking was that there was no world-class studio in Boston. Personally, I think great records can be made in the living room. But try telling that to four other band members and the band's managers and label execs. In any event, we compromised. Rather than record in Vancouver, this time—as usual—we brought our families but went to L.A. We rented apartments in West Hollywood, where Sam Kinison, may he rest in peace, lived below us. It was a riot bumping into him.

During a six-month period, four baby boys joined the Aerosmith family. The Whitfords had Graham; we had Roman; Teresa and Steven had Taj; and the Hamiltons had Julian. It was a lot of fun watching the boys grow up as a group, both on and off the road. Eventually Aerosmith would have a multigenerational consortium of children totaling seventeen.

During our time in L.A. we worked in A&M's famous Studio A with its huge glass *Star Wars* door that automatically opened as you approached. Because the door was usually on the blink, everyone wound up walking into the glass at least once, always reminding us of the Three Stooges. Down from Vancouver, Bruce Fairbairn was geared up to produce a classic Aerosmith record. Being in the heart of the L.A. music scene helped upgrade our sonics. Cats constantly dropped by the studio, offering old amps, new amps, and custom-made guitars. Shelly Yakus, an old friend from the Record Plant, opened the door to his astonishing collection of antique gear and said, "Help yourself." We dug in and rocked out harder than ever, resulting in a batch of hot tracks.

When John Kalodner came to review the tracks, though, he reacted with the line no artist ever wants to hear, especially after having worked diligently for three months: "I don't hear a single."

Admittedly, there were some raunchy songs—"Black Cherry" and "Your Momma Wants to Do Me and Your Daddy Wants to Do Me In"—but I liked them and thought they fit into the Aerosmith aesthetic. Kalodner's judgment pissed us off and we reacted in predictable ways: Steven went off the deep end and I smoldered. Steven called John every name in the book while I sank into silence.

After discussing the dilemma among ourselves, Steven and I decided to head up to Vancouver, where, working with Bruce on his home turf, maybe we could come up with a couple of singles. Although we would soon be on Sony, contractually we had no choice but to complete this last record for Geffen. We called it *Get a Grip*.

While we went to Canada, Billie took the kids to Florida and the Tyler family headed home. In Vancouver, Steven and I faced the double agony of finding a way to write new songs—plus the triple agony that came with getting lyrics out of Steven, who had transferred his animosity toward John Kalodner to Bruce Fairbairn.

Like Kalodner, Bruce wouldn't mince words. "Go to Studio D," he'd tell Steven, "and write your lyrics."

"I'm listening to guitar parts in Studio A," Steven shot back.

"You don't need to listen to guitar parts," Bruce retorted. "You need to write your goddamn lyrics."

"I'm not a machine."

"I don't need you to be a machine. I need you to be a writer. Write!"

I could sympathize with Steven, who hated not being in the room when the tracks were cut. After all, he and I had nurtured these songs from nothing. But he would procrastinate until Bruce, backed up by the rest of us, drew the line. It seemed like the more success Steven achieved, the less he would focus on writing lyrics. One way or the other, though, he had to get the lyrics written. Sometimes I'd go to Studio D and repeatedly play my guitar over the parts he was working on. Sometimes I'd throw in a word or two, and sometimes I'd sit there just to keep him company.

He and Bruce had a series of brutal verbal fights. Steven made his usual vow regarding anyone who produced us—"I'll never work with him again!" But as a pragmatist, I recognized the huge success we had enjoyed with Bruce, a producer who always got the best out of us. When he died some seven years after we recorded *Grip*, he was only forty-nine. I mourned his passing. He was a good man who helped us enormously.

During this two-week trip to Vancouver, though, nothing much helped. Nothing much was accomplished. It was summertime, and Steven and I figured we needed a break.

I took off for Florida and joined my family on vacation. Steven took off and joined up with his family. It felt so good to swim in the warm waters of the Gulf of Mexico and not have to think about gigs or writing or recording or the business or Collins. It was a chance to get back in touch with the things that mattered.

That summer we continued work on *Grip* in the Boneyard, a full-blown studio in the basement of my house. The name had originally been ascribed to my gym, which stood in the space now occupied by the studio. No matter how hard I worked out, I was always going to be skin and bones—thus the Boneyard. At first I just wanted a place to lay down my ideas on equipment good enough to capture great guitar sounds. But with the help of Billie, who acted as general contractor and oversaw the construction, Michael Blackmer, who forged the sonic design, and Perry Margouleff, who put together the equipment, and brought in the world-famous sound engineer George Augsberger, the Boneyard became a world-class studio capable of hosting full-band recording sessions.

At this point, working with outside writers had become standard operating procedure. When Desmond Child worked on *Permanent Vacation*, he had helped complete songs that were already in progress. But after writing "Angel," Steven saw the advantage of having someone help him with lyrics. I also came to like the stimulation of collaborating with a new writer who brought fresh ideas to the table, especially lyrics. But it also gave me an insight into Steven's outlook on our so-called writing partnership. At this point it was just a glimpse, but I had a feeling things weren't going to get better as far as my trusting him to be a true partner.

The process was simple: Steven and I would get the ball rolling before inviting someone in. We'd give each writer a couple of days, and if it felt like magic was in the air, we'd ask him to stay longer. In this period of *Grip*, we had the DeLeo brothers, Dean and Robert, from Stone Temple Pilots; Tommy Shaw from Styx; and Jack Blades from Night Ranger. We had a relaxed schedule, kicking off in the Boneyard in the afternoon, breaking for one of Billie's incredible dinners, and then going back to work at night.

Lenny Kravitz made his way to the Boneyard. At the time, he was living in New York, didn't like flying, and showed up in an RV. Lenny's a great guy and a true artist. We came up with "Line Up," a song that, in addition to appearing on *Grip*, was used in Jim Carrey's *Ace Ventura: Pet Detective.*

Kalodner also suggested we meet with Mark Hudson, a unique character who became close to Steven. Mark had gotten his start on a Saturday morning TV show, *The Hudson Brothers Razzle Dazzle Show*, and later worked as Joan Rivers's musical director. He went on to become a freelance songwriter and producer.

Slowly, the record came together. Jim Vallance helped us complete the title song and "Eat the Rich"; Desmond Child helped with "Flesh" and "Crazy"; I wrote one song alone—"Walk on Down"; and Mark Hudson helped out on one of the two tunes that Steven and I had started—"Gotta Love It"—and brought "Livin' on the Edge," my favorite song that he put on the table. Jack Blades and Tommy Shaw contributed to "Shut Up and Dance."

With Bruce Fairbairn back in the producer's chair, we returned to

Vancouver and laid down the tracks and vocals with few problems. At this point, I thought the drama was behind us.

But when John Kalodner came up to hear the mixes, he wasn't happy. "Something's wrong," he said. "It's not the songs. It's the sound."

"Can you be more specific?" I asked.

He couldn't. Despite John's gift for possessing the ears of the average rock fan, he couldn't verbalize the problem. This was frustrating as hell. We sat around scratching our heads. We asked our engineer to try another mix. John took it home to L.A. to listen on his own speakers. While we were waiting up in Vancouver, Kalodner called and said, "I know what's wrong. The songs are great. It's not recorded right."

By then I figured I was too close to the material and decided to go along with John's suggestion. We decided to have it remixed by someone with fresh ears—Brendan O'Brien, who'd been with the Georgia Satellites and had produced Stone Temple Pilots.

Steven, Teresa, Billie, and I flew to L.A., where we watched Brendan operate fast and furiously. He was easy to work with and responsive to our ideas. He had the thing mixed down in a few short weeks. It sounded great. *Get a Grip* was finally—and I mean *finally*—complete. The fans loved the album and it sold millions. This was our goodbye to Geffen.

Three years earlier, David Geffen himself had, in his own way, said goodbye by selling his label to MCA. That maneuver ultimately resulted in Geffen becoming a billionaire, largely on the huge success of Guns N' Roses, Whitesnake, and Aerosmith. It's always a kick in the butt for artists to watch label owners get rich beyond reason on creative work that those owners were lucky enough to market. If you think they'd give bonuses to the people who helped make them so rich, think again.

With the release of *Grip* in the spring of 1993, we would support the marketing of the Aerosmith brand in our tried-and-true manner—by touring constantly. We'd play all over the country and all over the world. We'd sell the record—and ourselves—city by city, market by market, concert by concert.

But even as the tour wound its way from continent to continent, even as the crowds got bigger and the cheers got louder, a corrosive force was also gathering strength—a force negative enough to do us all in.

The first lineup of the Joe Perry Project in 1979. First gig at Boston College's Rathskeller. Left to right: David Hull, Ralph Morman, me, and Ronnie Stewart.

On the road with the second Joe Perry Project. Left to right: Charlie Farren, me, Ron Stewart, and David Hull.

Early shot of me and Collins.

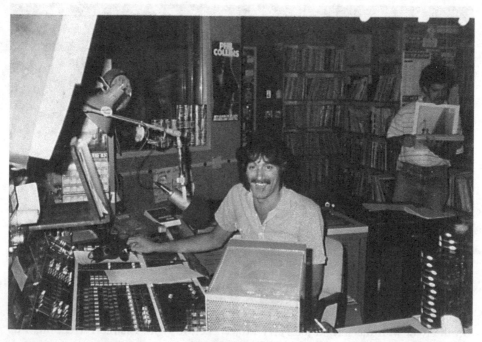

Mark Parenteau, the top DJ at WBCN, in the early '80s.

The third lineup of the Joe Perry Project, 1983. Left to right: Joe Pet, me, Cowboy Mach Bell, and Danny Hargrove. Without a doubt the wildest and most fun bunch of guys I have ever played with. It was rocking as close to the edge as I will ever get. Truly a band of pirates.

Mixing tracks for the third solo CD at Blue Jay Studios in Carlisle, Massachusetts. Zunk convinced me that Jack Daniel's tasted better out of the pint bottles. I think he was right.

Above: The girl who still rocks my world. One of the photos I saw in Billie's modeling portfolio while I was still with the Joe Perry Project. *Right:* Billie and me at the very first reunion gig of Aerosmith in Concord, New Hampshire. She had no idea what she was in for. Right from the start I loved her with all of my heart.

Tom and me at one of the first gigs during the Back in the Saddle tour.

Steven and me in the hotel room before the Lynn Bowl, our first local Boston gig after we got back together.

Billie and me right after our wedding vows at the Iao Needle on spiritual ground in Maui, Hawaii, September 21, 1985.

Aaron, Billie (seven months along with Tony), me, and Adrian on the way to Sullivan Stadium to play a festival with Aerosmith, while Adrian plays with the limo gadgets, 1986.

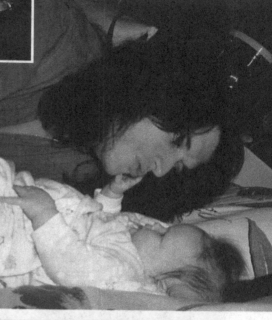

Me and baby Tony, November 1986.

Collins and me.

In Chicago, Buddy Guy came to our show and sat in with us. I went down to his club, The Checkerboard, and sat in with him. Left to right: me, Buddy, Tom, and Brad.

Dr. J. Jones and the Interns, the nom de guerre we would use when we would play clubs in the '70s, and a few times in the '80s.

Billie and me at Les Paul's birthday party that Gibson threw for him at the Hard Rock in Manhattan.

Me and Billie on October 4, 1991, just sixteen days before she gave natural childbirth to Roman.

A band dinner with Collins at the head of the table in Nashville, after one of Collins's vision meetings.

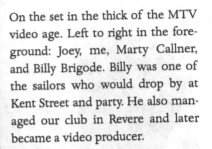

On the set in the thick of the MTV video age. Left to right in the foreground: Joey, me, Marty Callner, and Billy Brigode. Billy was one of the sailors who would drop by at Kent Street and party. He also managed our club in Revere and later became a video producer.

Aerosmith doing some sightseeing.

The Tylers and the Perrys on one of our many family outings in costumes at the Renaissance Faire.

Me and Cheap Trick at my fiftieth birthday. From left to right: Rick Nielsen, Bun E. Carlos, Robin Zander, me on guitar, and Tom Petersson.

Steven and me getting ready for one of the shots in the "Pink" video.

Perry Marguleff and me. Perry is the most knowledgeable guy I know when it comes to guitars and classic studio gear.

I thought I would let the fans have a go at the peak of one of my solos. It sounded a bit rough, but we had a good time.

After a fund-raiser at my and Steven's restaurant Mount Blue in Norwell, Massachusetts. Left to right: my sister Anne, Billie, me, and my mom.

After a show at one of my birthdays in the mid-late '90s.

Filming a video for the indie movie *This Thing of Ours*. Left to right: me, director Danny Provenzano, and Frank Vincent. Danny used the music from the band the Porch Ghouls in the movie.

Paul Shaffer and me talking, the week I sat in with David Letterman's band. The other stringbender in the picture is Sid McGinnis.

In the desert outside of Vegas getting ready to perform on rapper Nelly's video for the song "Number 1." Left to right, front row: me; Trudy Green, Aerosmith's manager and my dear friend; and Roman Perry. In the back, left to right: Tony Perry; bodyguard; and John Bionelli.

Steven and me after taking a dive in the New England Aquarium in Boston, watched by some of our children. Left to right: Chelsea and Taj Tyler, and Roman Perry.

Skiing the slalom course on Lake Sunapee.

Jimmy Page, James Brown, me, and Slash at the House of Blues in Los Angeles.

A day off on the way back from the pool in front of our connecting villas. Me, Billie, and Steven in Bangalore, India.

Our beloved and devoted German Shepherd, Grant.

Our first time playing in India. The first time in Aerosmith history the elephant in the room was real.

Beating my guitar with my shirt.　　　　Now I feel better!

In Dubai on a shoot with Ross Halfin.

HOW IT WORKED

While the two-hundred-plus-date tour for *Get a Grip* was being planned, Billie and I called Tim Collins to ask for a detailed calendar.

We'd later learn that he, in turn, called Steven to say, "We have a problem. Billie and Joe are micromanaging the band again."

When Steven got pissed off, Collins said, "Don't worry. I can handle them."

A few weeks later Collins called us and the other band members to say, "Steven's sex addiction is out of control again. He's on the verge of a breakdown. The whole tour might have to be canceled."

Naturally Billie and I were alarmed. That is, until we got another call from Collins, saying, "Don't worry. I was able to get Steven some help. I have him under control. The tour is on."

Then Collins called Steven and said, "*Billboard* is doing a story and they only want to talk to Joe, but I'll get them to talk to you."

Then he called me and said, "*Billboard*'s talking to Steven, who doesn't want them to talk to you, but I'll make sure they do. I'll handle it."

Understandably, Billie lost all patience.

"This man is controlling our lives," she said. "I can't take it anymore. I can't stand living under a microscope. I'm fed up with these wives' meetings where his therapist is acting as a spy. I'm fed up with watching him manipulate you and Steven. I can't stand how he turns everyone against everyone else. I've had it. I'm thinking about taking the kids and just renting a loft in Boston. It's not that I want to leave you, Joe. I don't. But I have to leave Tim Collins."

I knew that Billie's pain was real and her convictions right. This was soul-damaging stuff. We discussed Collins for weeks on end. Yet I couldn't see myself galvanizing my bandmates to fire him. We were about to go out on a huge world tour and this was no time to overturn the apparatus, all in Collins's control. Ultimately, for the sake of our young children and the sake of my own sanity, Billie decided to stay. I was greatly relieved. I couldn't see living my life without her. I promised her that things would change.

As Billie predicted, Collins's campaign for power only intensified. If Johnny Appleseed went around planting apple seeds, Tim Collins went around planting bullshit seeds. By asking insidious questions and spreading half-true rumors among the band members, he cultivated instability. Then he'd argue that if we wanted stability, he was our only hope for achieving it. He wanted us to believe that without him the operation would collapse, our deals would disappear, and it would all fall apart.

The final straw came when we went to the Sony offices to sign our new $30 million contract, a huge milestone for the band. Photographers were brought in. The big execs were all there—Tommy Mottola, Don Ienner, and Michele Anthony. We were ecstatic about being back at our original label home. Everyone was in a great mood. But five minutes before the actual signing took place, Collins said he needed a few minutes alone with his band. That caught us by surprise. We excused ourselves and filed into a nearby conference room. Then another surprise: Collins was accompanied by his lawyer. While the attorney spoke, Tim couldn't look any of us in the eye.

"As soon as the contract is signed," said the lawyer, "Tim wants to be paid his commission on your advances immediately."

We were stunned. Our policy was that advances be held in escrow until we delivered on the terms. This applied to all our deals, whether merchandise or records. But now Collins was demanding all his commissions up front. If, God forbid, something happened and we couldn't fulfill our side on the contract, we'd be responsible for paying back millions of his commission out of our own pockets. It was outrageous, especially given the timing—minutes before the contract signing. We acquiesced because, for all practical purposes, we had to. Otherwise Collins could still kill the Sony deal. But this manipulation opened our eyes. This man, who had once railed against the slimy practices of music business managers, had pulled the slimiest move of all.

My own psychology was driven by one strong motive—to keep the band together. If it fell apart, I wasn't sure I had the strength or the means to put it back together. Remembering what happened last time—the confusion and anger, the whole goddamn mess—I desperately didn't want to repeat that fucked-up scenario. And if the world had taken a number of unexpected turns that had put Collins at the center of Aerosmith power, I'd have to deal with that reality.

The reality was that Collins continued to cultivate his reputation as both someone who had tamed his own cocaine addiction and the genius who'd gotten Aerosmith sober. This was especially disturbing in light of Tim's still untreated food addiction. Not only was he dangerously overweight, but after the shows he'd hang around the food platters and slip handfuls of chocolate chip cookies into his pockets.

These were the psychological subtexts, the eroding forces under the surface. As far as the public went, Aerosmith was still soaring. Thanks to Marty Callner, our presence on MTV was stronger than ever. His videos for the songs on *Get a Grip* were among his best.

"Livin' on the Edge" opens with a naked Steven Tyler, his hand covering his dick, a green demon oozing out of his side. Flying on Rollerblades, schoolgirls destroy cars. Playing my solo on a train track, I'm nearly run over by a speeding locomotive. There's additional teen rebellion and, in the end, a young man puts on a woman's wig, smears on lipstick, and is ready to rock.

The videos for "Crazy" and "Amazing" continue the rebellion theme with strong female characters. We were catering to the young demographics. In "Crazy" two high school girls go crazy and act out a series of go-for-broke romantic/sexual fantasies. "Amazing" is amazing in its extravagant production value, as it focuses on computer projections of far-out fantasies and spacey visual trips. The videos accomplished the goals—they kept us on TV.

The Grip tour went on for much of 1993 and 1994, and the album sold some twelve million copies. That was satisfying because, as always, critics, arguing that Aerosmith had peaked long ago, had predicted a downslide. The emergence of grunge was supposed to have made our sound obsolete. In my mind, I thought we'd always been grunge guys. Besides, the Pearl Jam guys, the Soundgarden guys, and the Nirvana guys all talked about being Aerosmith fans. Even Kurt Cobain, the real deal in this new wave, came to our show in Seattle. He and I made small talk in the food room. When he went off to chat with someone else, his wife, Courtney Love, breathlessly told me, "He doesn't like anyone but he really likes you guys!"

We tried to get Stone Temple Pilots to open for us but were told they thought it would hurt their alt rocker image to be associated with an eighties hair band. Later, though, the Pilots' DeLeo brothers told me that they would have played with us in a heartbeat had they known about the offer. It had been a few biased managers who decided we were passé, not the cats themselves. From then on, we found it nearly impossible to get an up-and-coming band to play with us. Most would rather headline clubs that held eight hundred people than open for us at a fifteen-thousand-seat arena. Go figure.

At the same time, the new bands said they'd been raised on groups like us, Cheap Trick, and Led Zeppelin. We didn't have to adjust to any changes in music because, in my view, our sound was classic. That doesn't mean we didn't have to keep getting better—writing better, playing better, performing better—but only that our brand of blues-rooted rock wasn't outmoded. I don't believe it ever will be.

Although for the most part we enjoyed an easy and respectful relationship with other rock bands—both older and younger than Aerosmith—at the start of the Grip tour, when Megadeth was opening for us, there was a nasty moment. Megadeth leader Dave Mustaine went onstage and badmouthed us as being over-the-hill. Not cool. We dropped them from the tour.

We ran off to Europe, where we added new countries to our schedule—Spain, Finland, and Austria. We were back home to do our traditional Boston Garden New Year's show, our last time at this beautiful funky old arena slated for demolition, originally built for boxing and filled with old memories and dreams of our youth—that same Garden where, before we made it, Steven and I stretched out on the stage floor and said to the empty arena, "One day . . ."

We kicked off '94 with our first tour of Latin America. Stadium-size crowds everywhere we went—Chile, Brazil, Argentina. In Buenos Aires, Jimmy Page hung out backstage. Unbeknownst to us, he met his future wife, Jimena, at our show. The next day Billie and I went to lunch with Jimmy, who asked a question that knocked me out. Would I induct Led Zeppelin into the Rock and Roll Hall of Fame? As much as I hate giving speeches, this was an honor I couldn't refuse. Apparently Robert Plant asked Steven as well.

We made it back to the U.S. in time for Grammy week. That year we got one for "Livin' on the Edge." When we did *The Late Show with David Letterman*, it felt so good to be in New York that I stayed around all week. I was glad to accept an invitation to sit in with Paul Shaffer's great band every night.

In early summer, we were out to L.A. for the grand opening of the House of Blues. Aerosmith had a small piece of equity in the club, and we were glad to see it get off the ground. From there we were flying to Japan, where the Grip tour would continue. All was well. Too well. Time for Collins to start stirring the pot.

Wanting to upgrade the Boneyard, the basement studio I'd built in my home on the South Shore, I decided to buy a Neve recording board. My friend and technical adviser Perry Margouleff found a great one for fifty thousand dollars.

But when Tim Collins learned of my plans he called and said, "You can't do that, Joe."

"Why not?"

"Because having that kind of professional-level recording equipment will tip the balance of the band."

"What are you talking about?"

"When it's time to record," said Tim, "you need to go to Vancouver or New York or L.A. You'll be tempted to do it at home. We can't have it. That's the job of professional producers and engineers. That's their role, not yours."

"That's crazy," I argued. "You don't know what the fuck you're talking about."

"What you're proposing is disruptive."

I disrupted the phone call by hanging up. *I'll do as I damn well please.* But Collins didn't leave it there. He gathered the troops together for a band meeting that turned into an intervention on the afternoon of our House of Blues gig. The point of the intervention was to prevent me from buying the board. Collins pulled out all the guns. He brought the band's accountant and his therapist du jour, who argued that spending money was our new addiction. The other guys, probably worried that the last car they bought might land them in rehab, didn't say anything. I argued that this shouldn't even be a band issue. But for the moment, I let it go. We had a big gig that night and then were off for Japan.

It was only a few days later that I had time to deal with the board. But by the time I got in touch with Perry to tell him to pull the trigger, he said, "Too late, it's been sold for sixty-five thousand dollars."

"Then let's look for another Neve," I said.

That entailed a worldwide search. There was one in Australia but, ironically, an even better one in Boston owned by PBS Studios and once used to record the Boston Symphony. A great find, a great deal, and a great addition to the Boneyard.

All this was happening in the margins of our extensive tours to Asia and Europe. Billie and the kids were with me all the way. For the majority of the tour, so were the wives and families of the other guys. We played the

Budokan in Tokyo, a huge rush, before headlining festivals in cities we had never seen before: Budapest, Warsaw, and Prague.

In August we were back in the States to close the big Saturday night show at Woodstock '94, the twenty-fifth anniversary of the original Woodstock, which both Steven and Joey had attended. The location, Winston Farm in Saugerties, New York, was just down the road from where the first festival had been held. Just like in 1969, it rained like hell.

There was unbelievable hype around this gig. I resisted the comparisons to the original Woodstock, an event that could never be duplicated. But I was excited nonetheless. I loved playing the traditional European festivals and hoped that this new Woodstock might be the start of an American tradition.

We started out on Saturday watching it live on TV at home. Late that afternoon Billie and I were driven to the airport some forty minutes from our house, where we met the rest of the band and their wives. We loaded up onto Aeroforce One for the short flight to upstate New York. From the local airport, a fleet of vans took us to a boat landing on the Hudson. A small passenger steamer made the forty-five-minute trek up the river. By now it was dusk. A haze hovered above the water. A dense and mysterious forest hugged the shore. Above the sounds of the water lapping on the sides of the boat we began to hear the rumbling of subwoofers and occasional cheers. But those sounds were faint. As the sky darkened we saw a dim glow ahead. A very *Apocalypse Now* moment. All was hushed around us, but just beyond the reach of our senses we could detect an energy force that felt out of control. It was only when we drew up to the landing dock that we began to make out actual songs. We began to see barefooted people walking with backpacks. Once off the boat, we loaded up into a fleet of vans that took us down dirt roads. The drive through the forest, filled with pup tents, port-a-potties, and an army of stoner fans, took another forty-five minutes. We finally arrived at the backstage area.

I noticed a huge presence of product placement, on everything from billboards to buttons to remote-control balloons. The happy sight, though—the overwhelming sight—was that expansive sea of people looking to re-create the original Woodstock. As far as I could tell, they had succeeded. Steven wanted to take his shirt off and dive into the mud to relive his past but bailed at the last minute, wisely saving himself for our show. The backstage chaos was such that it was impossible to find the other performers to say hello.

When we heard the roar of the crowd that greeted Metallica, we knew we had our work cut out for us as closing act. Metallica went well into overtime. By then it had begun to rain. With the rain came technical problems with the power. The delay had us on edge. But when we finally walked out on the slippery stage in front of this muddy ocean of humanity, we were greeted with a thunderous welcome. We blasted through our set. It felt like it was the power of our playing that stopped the rain. With the sky clearing and the stars shining down, we played our hearts out. It was a dreamlike set. As we walked off the stage, a fireworks display exploded above our heads. Strong winds blew and fireworks debris flew everywhere. On our area backstage, the sky was raining fire.

We made it back to our waiting van and navigated the reverse journey home—through the forest, down the river, and onto the plane for the bumpy flight back to Boston. We stumbled out of the limo at six in the morning. We went inside, turned on the TV, and fell asleep to the next day's coverage of Woodstock '94, when Bob Dylan, the Red Hot Chili Peppers, Peter Gabriel, and Santana were set to play.

Before the year's end, the Tylers and the Perrys spent another family vacation together—this time on the enchanted Caribbean island of Anguilla. It was a beautiful moment of calm that, at least for those few weeks in paradise, lulled us into thinking that the rough weather was behind us.

It wasn't. The weather was about to turn into a shit storm.

THE MELTDOWN

"**Y**ou gotta go to L.A. for the TV show to promote the record," said Collins.

"I gotta rest," I said. "We all gotta rest. If we had taken a rest at the end of the seventies, when we were so burned out, we probably wouldn't have broken up."

"This isn't the seventies. This is the nineties, and you need to promote the new record."

"We've already promoted the hell out of the record. We just did a huge tour."

"That was overseas, Joe. America has a short memory."

"If anything, we're probably overexposed."

"The old videos are stale."

"They're becoming classics."

"We need a new slate of songs—right now—and a new slate of videos."

"The band's health trumps anything else. Don't forget, Tim—I've seen this movie before."

"All I can tell you is that the label's nervous."

"Let them be nervous. We've been dealing with nervous labels for the past twenty-five years. We've never delivered an album on time. So why worry about that now? " I laughed.

I hung up on Collins only to get calls an hour or two later from Steven, Tom, and Joey. Collins was telling them I was undermining the band's enthusiasm. I assured everyone that I was not. I was fine. We were all fine. We had sold a shitload of records and tickets off of *Grip*. It was time to chill.

But Tim worked off fear. He knew that practically every rock artist has a fear of being obsolete. And yet at the start of 1995, I wasn't feeling fearful.

Adrian had learned bass and started playing on some of the demos we were cutting in the Boneyard. He had grown up into an exemplary student and talented musician. During the summers, he'd come in from California to spend time with Billie, his brothers, and me. Nothing made me happier than seeing all our sons together. As the years went on, the boys grew closer and eventually formed a band—called Dead Boots—of their own.

As Aerosmith approached our first album for Sony, the initial work was done at the Boneyard. Though Geffen was out, John Kalodner was still in—and so were a host of outside writers who came through to help us facilitate the process. Glen Ballard, who had written hits for Michael Jackson, began working with us. Mark Hudson was also there, as was Robert DeLeo of Stone Temple Pilots—all of us looking for the lost chord.

It turned out, though, that the person most lost was Tim Collins. He wasn't happy when Steven and I took off Easter vacation to continue our writing down in Florida. We brought our families along, got houses on the beach, and even did a little boar hunting. Even though songs for the new album were not complete, we needed time off to renew our spirits. That's when Tim fell into a deep depression. It's also when he started to lose it.

His manipulations had always been handled with a certain subtlety. Now they became blatant and even desperate.

"Your relationship with Billie has reached a new level of neuroticism," he told me. "If we don't intervene, it could ruin the entire band."

Of course, we'd heard this song and dance before. This was the same type of bogus argument that had taken us to Sierra Tucson. This time, though, I ignored Tim and let him rant. When he made his case to the other band members—that my marriage to Billie was a threat to everyone—the guys ignored him. That only made Collins angrier. He felt himself losing power and, in turn, began scrambling for ways to hold on.

It was strange, for example, that at a big Aerosmith family gathering—a baby shower for Brad's pregnant wife, Karen, given by Terry Hamilton, Tom's wife—Collins didn't show up.

But he did show up that same summer at a band meeting that included the wives. He called these get-togethers the "Vision Meetings," yearly events to discuss big ideas. It was his chance to express his vision for the band's future. The meeting went along as per usual, with Tim and the therapist du jour pontificating to the group, always letting the band and wives give enough input, so we wouldn't feel manipulated or controlled.

After the break, instead of pointing to the future, though, he began by saying what was wrong in the present. In front of everyone, he pointed to Billie and me as examples of what had gone wrong. Having whispered these accusations to the other band members and their wives in private, he now delivered them in public, thinking that would win him even greater favor. He leveled the same tired old argument that we'd been hearing for years, using the same tired old phrase.

"You two are undermining the health of the band," he said, "by trying to micromanage our every move."

To stay grounded, Billie had been going through individual therapy of her own for the past six years. Professional outside opinions helped her understand how the band was caught up in Collins's cultlike culture games.

"Give us an example of how we micromanage," she said.

Collins was shocked. He wasn't used to being challenged and didn't like it. He had no answer.

Billie went on. "If we ask for a schedule three months in advance, that's because our kids travel with us and we have to consider their educational needs. That's not micromanaging. That's simply being good parents. You've been throwing around that term for years. Not only is totally inaccurate, it's insulting."

At this point Tim was white as a sheet. By now it was late in the day. Everyone had been sitting in a circle for hours. Tim saw his big moment to get Billie and me, when everyone, including us, were worn down by the meeting. It hadn't worked. All he had to say at this point was, "This meeting is over," before getting up and leaving the room.

I was wrong to think that all this madness might soon pass, but nonetheless, that's how I was thinking. I couldn't face the prospect of attempting to disassemble the management team. Besides, Steven and I needed to write new songs; the huge new Sony deal was in place, and we needed to move forward. We needed to keep working.

In 1995, once again our drama was heightened by our inability to fashion a new record in a reasonable amount of time. The writing process was as slow-moving as ever. So we decided to shake things up. Since it had been eleven or twelve months since the band had played together, we performed at a Boston club in which the band members were investors—Mama Kin. The gig was great, but it didn't help us finish the record. For that, Steven and I hit the road to work with other outside writers.

In Minneapolis, Jimmy Jam and Terry Lewis were warm hosts and good collaborators, but nothing really jelled. We went to Nashville and started a song with Taylor Rhodes that eventually wound up as "Full Circle." Kalodner also brought Marti Frederiksen into the mix—another major character in the annals of Aerosmith writers.

Marti and I became fast friends. He was a whiz. In addition to being a great bass player and drummer, he had mastered the Linn drum machine, the magical technological tool at the heart of Michael Jackson's *Thriller*. In the music business, producers and musicians grow enamored of certain sounds and the new machines that make them, convinced that those innovations hold the key to commercial success. The Linn was one such innovation. There was a cult around it. But Marti was more than a good technician; he was a real hard rocker, a brilliant cat with whom I loved to jam. When he came to the Boneyard, we'd have a blast building up a large catalogue of riffs.

In the beginning, Steven didn't want to work with Marti, who was just starting out. He didn't see his talent the way I did. He also hadn't yet realized that Marti could write lyrics. But I kept insisting that Marti come back, and ultimately I prevailed. The three of us wrote "Something's Gotta Give," which appeared on the album we eventually called *Nine Lives*. The completion of that record, though, was still in the far-off future. At that point we didn't even have a producer.

That's when Kalodner brought up Glen Ballard's name again. Initially, Glen had worked with us as a writer. Now John was saying that he should produce the entire project. Ballard was coming off the success of his work with Alanis Morissette and her *Jagged Little Pill* project. The story was that Glen did it all with a drum machine, Alanis and himself on guitar. The record sold more than twenty-five million copies—so naturally Kalodner was impressed. Steven was even more impressed with the Ballard-Morissette story. He kept saying how we'd be working with the hottest producer in the world.

With the world beating down his door, Ballard came off humbly, but you could tell his enormous ego was bubbling under the surface. Capitol was building him his own studio. He was forming a production company that would not only make records but movies as well. All this was happening when Steven and I went to Miami to write for two months, living at the Marlin Hotel. We'd work all week and then I'd fly home to Billie and the family on weekends. Tyler stayed in South Beach, whose bikini-clad skaters inspired his lyrics. Mark Hudson, Desmond Child, and Richie Supa were also around, helping us put together our material.

South Beach was a cesspool of rumors. The gossip rags ran a photo of Steven at a party surrounded by three or four girls, implying the worst. But the truth was that we were just writing—or trying to write. Other than Steven's occasional walk on the beach, our trip was all about work. The scene was a composers' free-for-all, all the writers wanting Steven to sing their songs and add to their royalties.

The longer we labored, the crazier Collins became. He had spies who went to the twelve-step meetings that Steven attended. Our attendance was monitored closely. For my part, I stopped going to meetings. As far as I was concerned, Collins had perverted the process. If his spies reported me absent, I no longer gave a shit.

At this point, Collins had turned over the day-to-day management to our accountant, Burt Goldstein, who was also Brad's brother-in-law, and our publicist, Wendy Laister. It seemed like Collins was spending all his time fighting with Steven and furiously resolving crises that he—Tim—had created. For example, convinced that Steven was drinking and drugging, he had his guys search Steven's room for evidence. When no evidence was found, Collins remained adamant. In his mind, Steven was about to go off the deep end. Only Tim could save him and, by extension, once again save the band.

At the same time, we were hearing alarming news from up north: Joey was having serious problems. It had always been hard for Joey to gear up to go to the studio with Steven. A drummer himself, Steven was unrelenting in his critiques of Joey's playing. The pattern of verbal assault had been going on for years. Eventually Joey wrote a book, *Hit Hard*, in which he spoke openly about the abuse he took from Steven.

Early on, I told Steven, "Lay off this guy. He's doing the best he can. He busts his ass and practices more than anyone in the band. No amount of yelling is going to make him play like you. You have your style and Joey has his. His style works for the band. Just leave him alone."

When Steven hemmed and hawed, I said, "Look, either we fire him or accept the fact that he's our drummer."

I didn't want to fire him; I just wanted Steven to stop badgering him and let him do his thing. But Steven's harping never stopped. More than anyone, Joey took the brunt of Tyler's moods. Whenever we would gear up for a tour or a recording session, Joey would fall into a depression. He knew it meant getting back in the ring with Steven. Over the years, the emotional beatings got worse.

The passing of Joey's father a few years earlier had been another blow. The loss was heavy on his heart. A guy who loved to zip around in his sports cars, Joey locked himself up in his home. When Tom, Brad, and a few of Joey's friends showed up, they came to the obvious conclusion: Joey was suffering a breakdown.

Joey's friends helped facilitate his admission to Steps, a rehab north of Malibu, California, run by therapist Steve Chatoff. He'd be there for a while and unable to work on our new record. Joey's well-being came first. I was glad he was getting help, but we were also facing a deadline for this first

Sony record. Our options were to stop everything and wait for Joey or to carry on without him. We didn't know how long his treatment would continue or, once he completed it, whether he'd come back at all. That's when we decided to bring in session drummer Steve Ferrone. If Joey returned in a reasonable amount of time, he could redo the tracks laid down by Ferrone. If not, we'd keep Ferrone's work, which, by virtue of his experience with Average White Band, we knew to be superb. Style-wise, Ferrone could play anything. At the same time, without Joey's distinct style, the tracks didn't have the usual Aerosmith fire.

During the sessions Collins made himself scarce. This was not his way. In the past, he'd been hands-on with practically every project. He'd come to the studio, go on press junkets, and accompany us on tour. It was odd that he showed up in Miami only once. Something strange was afoot.

Steven took off one day to fly to Washington, D.C., where he met his wife, Wendy Laister, and Tim Collins at the White House Correspondents' Association dinner. Later, Wendy asked me why Billie and I hadn't attended.

"I didn't know we were invited," I said.

"The invitation came to the office," she said. "Collins didn't tell you?"

"No."

"Well, it was a rough evening. Steven and Teresa kept going off on how you and Billie are codependent on each other to the point that you need to go into rehab."

"I'm sure Collins loved hearing that," I said. "I'm sure he agreed with every word."

"He did."

I began to see that both Steven and Collins were going crazy in different ways. Many of the problems we blamed Collins for were really caused by Tyler. By carrying out Steven's crazy schemes, Collins was able to stay in Tyler's good graces.

Still certain that we all needed professional help, Tim sent a female psychologist to evaluate the band members and our wives. Tim hoped that she would concur with him and send us back into rehab. But she concluded the opposite. After meeting Billie, the therapist, said, "Why, there's nothing at all wrong with you and nothing neurotic about your relationship with Joe. You're as sweet as can be. I wish there were more marriages like this."

That wasn't what Tim wanted to hear. He wanted the psychologist to report that we were sick and needed immediate treatment. When she undercut his theory, he threw a fit. He sent a nasty fax saying that he was firing her and that she could no longer have any contact with anyone associated with Aerosmith or he'd take legal action against her. We learned that because, by accident, Collins sent the fax to our house. Further proof that his crazy control mania was out of control.

The musical part of the puzzle was equally complicated. We'd demoed up a group of songs and gotten Brad and Tom down to Miami to record with me and Steven—all under the auspices of Glen Ballard, who had become obsessed with the Alesis Digital Audio Tape, known as ADAT, a format that enabled the simultaneous recording of multiple tracks onto a Super VHS tape. At first Glen used three ADAT machines, but he soon expanded to eight. By the time it was over, we were recording on 170 tracks. Not only was Ballard running a ridiculous number of tracks, he wouldn't make a decision about which take to use. If we wanted a rhythm part, he'd record eight versions and keep them all. "We'll decide in the mix," he'd say. In the past, our track sheets—showing what music was on which track—were a couple of pages long. In this instance, our track sheets for each song formed a binder a hundred pages thick. In the past we'd always gone home with rough mixes of what we'd done that day. But with no decisions made on which tracks to use, it was confusing. Without any basic mix, we were lost. We couldn't get a handle on what the fuckin' songs were sounding like.

The recording process left me feeling disassociated from the music. Too much tech, too little blood and guts. There was also the fact that Glen was preparing to produce Van Halen. He was always on the phone and never fully present. Steven gave him a hard time, antagonizing him by claiming that Bruce Fairbairn's production methods were far superior to Ballard's. In spite of these nasty fights, the record somehow got done. It was time for the Sony execs to hear it.

The suits flew down to Miami for a listening party. We played them the album from start to finish. After the last song, dead silence. The silence lasted an uncomfortable thirty seconds. Then one of the suits said the very words that were on my mind: "I don't like it."

"Why not?" asked Ballard.

"It doesn't sound like an Aerosmith record."

"Why not?" Glen repeated.

"Because I don't hear the band. I'm missing the band."

Ballard argued but, ironically enough, it was Steven who flipped out in defense of the record. I could understand that, because Steven had sung his ass off on these songs. He had labored long and hard.

"It just needs a different mix," said Steven. "It'll be fine."

"You need to start over," said the exec. "You need to scrap this and start over."

The aftermath was ugly. The attempt to salvage Glen's production by having Joey—out of rehab and back in shape—replace Steve Ferrone's drum parts didn't work. Sony took Ballard off the project. When they gave it to someone else to mix, the man couldn't make heads or tails out of the tracks. So the only option was to recut the songs.

Steven was enraged. His wig-out reached unreasonable proportions. Once again, his logical and useful ideas were buried under the uncontrolled anger that he took out on everyone. I sympathized with him. I didn't want to go through the whole fuckin' process again either. But what choice did we have? Sony had turned down the tracks. They had a contractual right to demand another record.

Because I didn't like the sound of the Ballard record anyway, my attitude was, *Let's give them something different. Let's move on.*

Steven's attitude was, *I'm not budging.*

Collins's attitude was, *This is the worst crisis we've ever had. Steven's tantrums are about to break up the band.*

No matter the differences in attitude, there was nothing left to do but leave this Miami nightmare behind and go back to Boston and face the next crisis—the final crisis with our manager.

That breakdown took an especially pernicious turn because it coincided with Steven's emotional unraveling. The dynamic between Collins and Tyler was complex enough to fill a library on psychology. The essence of it, however, was this: Collins saw that the way to control the band was to control Steven. And for Tim, the best way to control Steven was to stick him in rehab. Or agree with him. There were times some of the things Collins said sounded suspiciously like the things Steven would complain about most: my relationship with Billie and its effect on the band.

Back in Boston, Collins called a band meeting without Steven. There were therapists in the room. It was a goddamn circus. Emotions were flying high. Tim's management style of mixing fear and peer pressure had reached a point of no return. He began with a pseudo-psychological rap about how Steven was out of control. He wasn't sober. He was acting out sexually. He was raging to the point where Collins could not reason with him. Collins pressed our buttons as only he could.

I took a counter-position, arguing that I'd been with Steven practically 24/7 during our months in Miami and hadn't seen him using or acting out. I agreed that he had been raging uncontrollably. But that was about redoing the record. That was a separate matter. Collins said that rage was rage. No one could communicate with Steven. We needed a plan of action. What should we do? Ideas flew around the room. People were getting up and shouting. People were coming and going. It was chaotic. It was hard to tell who heard what. Basically, we were sick of this meeting stuff. Collins was grasping at straws.

After a break, Collins said, "Something has to happen. We have to do something concrete. So I've written a letter that I want each of you to sign."

The letter, addressed to Steven, said that he was out of control; that he was in a constant state of rage; that he was a detriment to the well-being of the band; that his volatility prevented us from getting any work done; and that, unless he addressed these issues and sought immediate help or changed his attitude, we could no longer work with him.

We were all hesitant to sign. It seemed too confrontational, too harsh. But there was a thread of truth to it. We all were tired of bearing the brunt of Steven flying off the handle. Maybe the letter would help him take another look at himself.

"It's the only thing that will work," said the therapist.

"Not to send it is to risk losing everything," yelped Collins.

In my gut I felt like it was overreaching and wrong, but I signed it anyway. So did Joey, Brad, and Tom.

Steven had been going off the deep end for a long while. But I also knew that Collins was also an emotional wreck, something that became painfully clear when he dropped another bomb.

"I just called Teresa," said Collins. "I felt like I had to tell her."

"Tell her what?" I asked.

"That Steven has been not only been using, but cheating on her."

"You what!" I exploded. "You called the man's wife to say he's been fucking around without having any fuckin' proof?"

"You've seen the pictures from South Beach with him and those bimbos."

"That's not proof. You can't take a picture in South Beach without a fuckin' bimbo in it."

"You and I both know that he's been acting out."

"I *don't* know that—and even if I did, I wouldn't run behind his back and tell his wife. I can't believe you did this, Tim. You've been meddling in our lives ever since we met you, man, but this shit is too much. You've gone too far."

The others were as aghast as I was. We stormed out of his office and could only imagine the impact on Steven when he was hit with this double whammy—our letter and Teresa's reaction to Collins's call.

I should have called Steven to explain, but we were told that if the letter was to work we shouldn't contact him. Besides, there was some truth to what we had written. We could no longer reason with Steven or deal with his raging tantrums.

In a wider sense, this was all part of Collins's method of dividing and conquering that he'd established long ago. By now, no one in the band ever called each other or addressed issues outside of business meetings. That had long been the Aerosmith style—*together* on the road, constantly touring and recording; and *apart* off the road, everyone retreating to his home and family. Our distance from each other—our reluctance to face each other directly with our concerns—was what gave Collins much of his power.

A month went by with no word from Steven. To give him time to absorb the letter, we decided to leave him alone. This gave us all a chance to look objectively at the state of our band, painful as it was.

Ironically, for all his bellyaching about my so-called codependent marriage, Tim often called Billie for advice during times of stress. He respected her intelligence and insight.

After a month of Steven's silence, Tim panicked. Billie and I saw him in Boston at the Four Seasons Hotel, where he called us to his room. He looked terrible, his eyes filled with fear.

"I really fucked up by calling Teresa, didn't I?" asked Collins.

Billie and I both said, "You did."

"I need to call and apologize to him and Teresa, but there's no getting through to him."

Collins was a man falling apart. The master manipulator had manipulated the situation to a point of madness.

These were difficult weeks. The *Nine Lives* album, the much-anticipated debut project of our massive new Sony deal, had been rejected by our new label. Artistically, we were at a standstill. We couldn't tour until the album was complete, and, even if we could, we didn't have a band. Our lead singer was MIA, and Collins was useless. Steven called a lawyer to talk over his options. He was through with Collins. On that he and I agreed. I wanted to run over to Steven's house, grab him by the shoulders, and say, "Hey, man, let's just talk!" but by then the rift was too deep.

We hit a stalemate. The situation was fucked up from the inside out. Finally, Tom, Brad, Joey, and I got together with Collins in a hotel room on the South Shore of Boston. We said the obvious: We need to have a band meeting with both Steven and Collins present. We need to sort this shit out. We also need to do it in a neutral place with a neutral therapist. Joey suggested the man who helped him out of his depression, Steve Chatoff. We decided to go to his facility, Steps, outside Malibu. It would be a place where we could put all complaints, misunderstandings, resentments, and expectations on the table. It would be a chance to bring the band back together. Collins agreed. He would attend. He was enthusiastic about the idea. The get-together was even given a name: Conflict and Resolution Week. But what if Steven refused to attend?

Tim stretched out on the couch and, with some arrogance, said, "I'll get Steven's therapist to convince him to show up. If the therapist doesn't agree to help us out, I'll threaten to have his license removed. I can do that." Collins said this with an alarming sense of calm, as though such a maneuver was the most natural thing on earth. It seemed to be a clear window into what he'd been doing for years. Walking out of that meeting, I thought, *Man, this is one week I'm looking forward to. Collins is gonna have to face some pretty intense music.*

We were all relieved when Steven agreed to meet us in California. He was just as eager as us to iron things out. When he showed up at Steps, it was great to see him. The feeling was warm.

Steve Chatoff had a professional demeanor. He wore a suit and tie and didn't try to look like a rock star. He was a New Yorker, a man who announced that he himself was in recovery. He gave the impression of being a sensible and sensitive therapist. The first thing he said was that he wanted to meet with the band alone. Collins would wait in a nearby hotel until we were ready for him.

It didn't take Chatoff long to see what was happening. Even before this first meeting, Collins had been calling him, trying to plan the agenda and manipulate the outcome. Chatoff had told him that he wanted no contact with him before speaking with the band and would accept none of his calls. This was critical: Collins could not manipulate Chatoff.

At this point Chatoff extended the initial band-only meeting to a second day. He wanted us to vent all the feelings and facts without Collins's involvement. Chatoff was a good listener, and we had a lot to say. Steven was the most vocal. But we all had a go at it. Our view was that Collins had polluted our relationships, that he lacked any reasonable boundaries, and that his managerial style had wreaked havoc. In the course of the meeting, the dialogue went like this:

Tom to Brad: "Collins said *that* about me to you? I can't believe it."

Brad to Joey: "Collins said *that* about me to you? I can't believe it."

Joey to me: "Collins said *that* about me to you? I can't believe it."

Me to Steven: "Collins said *that* about me to you? I can't believe it."

The revelation of half-truths and innuendos came spilling out. All of us had stories that we hadn't shared with each other. We put our petty complaints aside. This was the five of us against an outsider. Finally, the band had pulled together. At the end of that day, Chatoff said what we had already known. "You guys are fine. You're at a good point in your recovery. You just have to figure out what you want in a manager—and what you don't want."

After a few days of being alone with Chatoff, we had some clarity. We were grateful to Collins, who had been there when no one else was. He'd helped bring us back from the dead. But he had gone too far by entangling himself in our private lives. The new paradigm would be simpler: Take care of our business. Period. No more interfering in our personal stuff. No more triangulation. No more psychobabble bullshit.

"I think you're ready to meet with your manager now," said Chatoff.

But Collins refused. He said he felt like he was being set up. He would not subject himself to any of our questions. This was not a setting in which he felt safe. Although he was in a hotel down the street, he would not—under any circumstances—come to meet us. In short, Collins boycotted Conflict and Resolution Week.

To Chatoff, Collins's boycott was not the critical point. "The critical point," he said, "is that you guys are not using. You're not acting out. You've stuck with your sobriety and simply want to get back to making music. My overview is that you've lost your power as a band and need to take it back."

Chatoff added, "Steven's going to be the way he is. You can't change him. If Steven wants to change, that's going to have come from Steven. Collins can't fix him. Collins can only fix Collins. Joey can only fix Joey. We are who we are. And if we don't accept each other as we are, we'll be spending all our time angling for control. Ultimately, that's an exercise in futility."

With those few sentences, Chatoff turned on the lights. At that moment, it all seemed so clear. Collins couldn't face us. He couldn't face the truth. He had to go.

Finally, in heart and soul, we were back together as a band and ready to move on. It was decided that we would call a meeting back in Boston and invite the entire management team. Since I had brought Tim on, it was also decided that I'd be the one to dismiss him. We'd keep Burt Goldstein and Wendy Laister as managers until things settled down. After all, for the past couple of years they'd been acting as our day-to-day managers. That would assure our label and promoters that business would continue as usual.

I felt as though an enormous weight had been lifted off my shoulders. The thought of the band taking back its power was thrilling.

I went to the suite we had reserved at the Four Seasons, the battleground for so many of these monumental meetings. We knew that Collins was running around like a madman, trying like Humpty Dumpty to put the pieces together. But it was too late. Conflict and Resolution Week had proven to be an apt name. We had to resolve this thing. We had to rid ourselves of a manager who had co-opted our autonomy. Billie had made the point to me for years, but for years I didn't want to realize she was right: The man screaming loudest about the pitfalls of codependency had made us all pitifully codependent on him.

Now all that would change.

With the full management staff in attendance, the mood was somber. Collins knew what was coming.

I led off. I said, "We appreciate all your hard work. We appreciate all that you've done for us in these past twelve years, but we're moving on. We don't need your services as a manager anymore."

We went around the room and everyone—Tom, Brad, Joey, and Steven—addressed Tim directly. No one was accusatory or caustic. We all simply thanked him for his service and let him know, in no uncertain terms, that his services were no longer required.

We took back our band.

The coda to our dismissal of Tim Collins was especially painful. Maybe we should have seen it coming, but we didn't. After we let him go, he took one last shot at us. He called a gossip journalist to say that band members were still using. The item was reported in several national magazines. It was a deliberate lie to make us look bad. He painted himself as the clear-eyed, sober manager that only a band of drunks would be foolish enough to fire. We decided not to dignify or prolong the attack with a response. We just wanted this long and torturous chapter in our lives to end.

BROTHERS

After the big meeting in Boston, I took off a few weeks and went to Lake Sunapee with Billie and the kids. I needed the water and the woods to help center me. We called this "the Endless Summer." It was unusually hot. We were on the boat from morning till dusk, and one night we watched a huge meteor shower. Another night we saw the northern lights.

It was strange and wonderful being at Sunapee—strange because it was the place where, a hundred years ago, the seeds of Aerosmith had been sowed; and wonderful because the place gave me the same peace as an adult it had given me as a child. The peace of a startling purple-pink sunset; the peace of a starlit night; the peace of the placid lake, the warm afternoon sun, boats bobbing in the harbor, our boys playing by the shore, me waterskiing through the slalom course, trying to improve my speed.

It was in Sunapee where I reconnected with my brother Steven.

There are many kinds of brothers, from Cain and Abel, to the Marx Brothers, to Orville and Wilbur Wright. There's good and bad blood among brothers, love and jealousy, compassion and resentment, and every other emotion in between. I have no doubt that, in a deep and abiding way, Steven Tyler is my brother. Together we have forged and maintained a great band; together we have changed each other's lives. Our stories are intertwined. For that I'm grateful.

In the long and agonizing drama in which Tim Collins wound his way into the center of our lives, my relationship with Steven was injured, as was my relationship with Billie. It was difficult for my wife, a strong woman, to see me in a weak position. The whole experience with Tim damaged my relationship with Billie the most. It took several years, but our love proved to be resilient, although the scars were deep for both of us, especially Billie. Our relationship was eventually repaired. Steven was another matter. If our partnership was going to continue, we needed to take stock of what had happened. The damage was considerable.

Because Steven loves the water and the woods as much as I do, it was there in Sunapee—during that same "Endless Summer"—that we walked and talked about where we'd been and where we were going. One afternoon, we took a break from our families and walked through the woods together.

We talked about what had happened in the most general terms. Steven knew that I knew that he had, to a large degree, been right about Collins. I also knew that Steven knew that Collins's contributions had been critical to our comeback. Little more needed to be said. It was just good to be walking through the woods with an old friend.

A month or so later we were walking through horn-honking crowded midtown Manhattan, going from the Sutton Place apartments we had rented to the West Side, where work on *Nine Lives* had reconvened. We had reached out to John Kalodner to recommend a producer to replace Glen Ballard. John had suggested Kevin Shirley, a tough South African who had been raised in Australia. His nickname was Caveman. Built like a linebacker, Shirley had the look of a Viking—long dark blond hair and a no-horseshit attitude. His thing was straight-up rock-hard rock and roll. I liked Kevin, though he could be brusque, not a useful quality when trying to communicate with Steven.

As calm as Steven had been walking through the woods, walking through the concrete canyons of Manhattan had him unhinged. When we went back to work on *Nine Lives*, his old resentments returned. He kept harping on all the time we had spent on the Glen Ballard version down in Florida. I kept saying, "The past is the past, let's just move on." We both needed to vent, and vent we did. Walking to the studio gave us a chance to plan the day and have a few laughs. Taking different side streets, we soaked up the energy of the city, stopping to talk to shopkeepers and street sweepers, some of whom we got to know on a first-name basis. By the time we reached the studio, Steven had calmed down—then his arguments with Kevin Shirley began.

I respected Kevin. His primitive approach was in stark contrast to the over-the-top high tech of Glen Ballard. Kevin wanted uncut rock and roll. He wanted all five of us playing together live in the studio, recording on a good old-fashioned 24-track tape. That should have been simple, but Steven gave him fits. They argued over everything, especially which vocal part was more suitable than another. In the studio Steven is meticulous to a fault. He'll obsess over the smallest musical detail. Kevin was the opposite. He was going for a raw sound. I was with Kevin, but mostly I kept quiet and let the two of them work it out. Keep in mind—the songs hadn't changed. They were the same basic tunes we had written with Ballard, Hudson, Frederiksen, Supa, and Child in Florida. Now they were stripped of their multiple overdubs and rendered with greater grit. It took a long time to do that strip-down. Weeks of walking from the East Side of New York to the West-Side studio, me trying to chill out Steven on the way. Weeks of running down the songs to where Steven would finally sign off on the final version. Weeks of verbal confrontations between Steven and Shirley to the point where Steven swore he'd never work with Caveman again—which was the same thing he'd said about every producer we'd ever worked with, starting with Jack Douglas.

In the end, *Nine Lives* probably should have been called *Nine Hundred Lives*, because that's how many lives I felt we had lived to its completion. I thought it came out great—and so did Sony, eager to finally put this sucker out. The overall sound was intense. The album graphics pushed the envelope: A cat in an Aerosmith T-shirt is plastered to a dartboard with knives coming at him. Hints of Hindu symbolism surround the artwork.

Our love of hot Indian cuisine fueled "A Taste of India," one of the hotter songs on the record. "Falling in Love (Is Hard on the Knees)" was the initial single and video, the story rendered in a series of images of men trapped in containers and cages being lorded over by voluptuous women. At one point Steven sings in a straitjacket. In the next video, for "Hole in My Soul," the power ballad that we wrote with Desmond Child, Steven is singing in an electric chair as we follow an abstract narrative tapestry of male romantic fantasies.

The album took off, and so did we. The 1997 *Nine Lives* tour, like practically every Aerosmith tour before and after, was wildly ambitious. We'd cover the world. We'd conquer the world. We were back together as brothers in arms. Wendy Laister, who effortlessly made the transition to manager, was handling the operation. She had been a superb publicist and knew us as well as anyone. Together with Burt Goldstein, she could tend to all the critical details of our business—or at least we thought so.

After all we'd gone through with the making of *Nine Lives* and the unmaking of Tim Collins, it was an enormous relief when the album took off. The demand for our personal appearances was greater than ever. Once again, the seemingly indestructible Aerosmith machine hit high gear. We played *Saturday Night Live* in March before flying off to England in May. All that summer we played Europe. The highlight was selling out two big shows at Wembley Stadium, where Jimmy Page and Brian May from Queen turned up to say hello.

Artistically, I felt more alive than ever. For the foreign edition of *Nine Lives* we included "Falling Off," where I got to stretch out and sing one of my own songs. It became one of the encores of our European shows and a source of great satisfaction, especially when fans kept telling me how it reminded them of the Joe Perry Project.

When the tour was over and we were back home, we faced a new opportunity. We were asked to record a song, "I Don't Want to Miss a Thing," for the Jerry Bruckheimer blockbuster movie *Armageddon*. It wasn't just any song, but one written by the lovely and eccentric Diane Warren, famous for her long string of number-one hits.

The band met at the Sunset Marquis and listened to the tune. It was a slam dunk. No doubt Steven could sing the hell out of it and we could put the Aerosmith stamp on it musically. Maybe it didn't have the masculine edge of our other ballads, but it was a beautiful song.

There was the added inducement that Jerry was going to include several songs from the Aerosmith catalogue in the film. Additionally, "I Don't Want to Miss a Thing" would be turned into a video featuring footage from the movie along with that of Aerosmith performing the song. Yet we still weren't completely sold. We wanted to see the film itself.

Jerry took us to his editing room and ran some footage with Aerosmith songs dubbed in the background. That blew us away. Our music sounded great over the explosive images. We were also proud that Liv Tyler, Steven's beautiful daughter, was featured in the film along with Bruce Willis.

When Jerry Bruckheimer throws a premiere, he pulls out all the stops. This one happened at NASA in Florida, where we got a VIP tour of the entire facility. We saw the holding room where the rockets are housed before launching; we saw the space shuttle itself; and we took turns landing the shuttle in the trainer. One point of paternal pride: According to the instructor, my six-year-old son Roman executed the smoothest landing of anyone.

Since Diane had written the song for the film, it was eligible for an Academy Award. When it was nominated, we were invited to play it during the ceremony. We'd been to a thousand award shows, but, man, Oscar night was a whole 'nother animal. We were pumped. Then a snag: Seconds before we took the stage we were told that the monitors were down, and we had no choice but to go on. This was being broadcast live to the world. In spite of the breakdown, the band performed the song flawlessly. No one in the audience knew anything was wrong.

The tent in which the elegantly appointed gourmet dinner was held afterward was decorated like a movie set. With gossamer fabrics floating down from the tent's high top, it was a dreamlike evening.

A few weeks later Steven and I were back at Sunapee trying out a few pieces of new hardware. The two of us were walking through the fields of Trow Hill. It was another one of those good times when we could relieve the pressures of the practical world by simply escaping to the woods. It was also an opportunity to shoot off a little steam—literally.

In his new six-wheeler amphibious hunting vehicle, Steven drove us to a safe place, the side of a remote hill, for some target practice. That's when his phone rang. The smile of his face said it was good news.

" 'I Don't Want to Miss a Thing' just went to number one," he told me after hanging up. "They're saying it's our first number-one pop hit."

"In all these years," I said, "we've never had a real number-one pop hit?"

"I guess not."

Surprised, we were happy as hell and, in celebration, ripped through a couple of magazines.

But the celebration didn't last long.

That spring of 1998 we took the *Nine Lives* tour to Alaska, where we'd never played before. The cool air was exhilarating, the landscape wild and inviting. It felt like another country.

The Anchorage fans were so excited that both concerts were sold out. On our day off, Steven and I planned a fishing trip with our tour manager, Jimmy Eyers, an expert outdoorsman. We left our hotel at 6 A.M.—late by Alaskan fishing standards—for the three-hour drive down to Seward, where the boats were moored. Just that drive down would have been adventure enough: the pristine snow-covered mountains, moose by the score, flocks of bald eagles. Halfway to Seward, we stopped at an old house with a sign advertising handmade knives. Steven and I, both collectors, marveled at the display. The most striking one was crafted from a motorcycle chain and pounded down to a perfectly precise edge.

We got to the boat a little before ten and found our captain. Because we had arrived so late, there wasn't enough daylight left for us to make it to Jurassic Park, so named because the halibut are as big as barn doors. Less fertile areas would have to do. We got on board and began the ride down to the ocean. The wind was blowing, and Jimmy, Steven, and I were freezing, even in three layers of clothing. But there was the captain, commanding the boat in nothing but shorts and a T-shirt. A few hours later we dropped anchor, dropped lines, and starting pulling in some of the biggest fish that any of us had ever caught. We threw them all back until the captain advised us to keep one—a four-foot beauty of a halibut. We ate it that night in a restaurant in the harbor where they prepared your fresh catch. It was a great meal and satisfying to know we'd caught the fish ourselves.

The concerts were a blast and the crowds at Anchorage's Sullivan Arena were delirious. The second night's show was about over when we broke into our last encore—"Mama Kin." Steven was doing his thing with his scarf-covered mic stand—whirling it around—when he accidentally smashed it into his left knee, crushing the ACL, the ligament that holds the joint together. We rushed him to an ambulance. The doctors said he'd be out of operation for months. We had to cancel the rest of the tour. We also thought we'd have to cancel the video shoot for "I Don't Want to Miss a Thing," but Tyler insisted we keep the plans intact. Still in excruciating pain, he showed up wearing a brace. For the umpteenth time he proved his professionalism by turning in a stellar performance. Because he couldn't really move, they shot him from the waist up. Having torn up my ACL twelve years before, I could relate to the excruciating pain.

Come summer Steven had healed up and was ready to go back out. The tour was just about to reconvene when another near-tragedy struck: While Joey was getting his Ferrari filled up at a Boston gas station, a negligent attendant didn't notice that the nozzle had fallen to the ground with gas pouring out. The result was a hellish explosion in which Joey, running through the fire, suffered third-degree burns and barely escaped with his life.

Months later, with Joey recovered, we finally completed the Nine Lives/I Don't Want to Miss a Thing tour.

On the business side, the majority of us were not completely satisfied with the way things were going with Burt Goldstein and Wendy Laister. We were convinced we needed a real manager. Howard Kaufman was our first choice. Howard had managed the biggest acts in the business. He was a former accountant who knew the ins and outs of the money game. He understood recording contracts and had vast knowledge of the finances of touring. He was tough and fair. Moreover, he was mellow. He didn't care about going on the road or involving himself in personal areas. His main concern was our career. One of Howard's partners, Trudy Green, who would be involved with our day-to-day operation, also had a levelheaded attitude that assured us boundaries would be established and honored.

We played Tokyo Dome at the end of 1999. This was the year of Y2K. Many people fearing a worldwide computer collapse stayed home New Year's Eve. Slips of paper were placed under the doors of our hotel room telling us to stay off the elevators an hour before and after midnight. Even though Japan is one of the world's safest countries, we had extra security. Everyone was on edge. No one knew what might happen. In the end, nothing happened—except for Aerosmith putting on an end-of-the-century New Year's show for some of our favorite fans in the world.

Taking stock at the end of the twentieth century, we had much to be grateful for. We had survived every kind of personal and professional storm imaginable. Our hope was that it would be smooth sailing ahead. We were entering a new millennium with renewed hope.

I would love to tell you that, for the next decade, harmony was the theme. But the truth is that the Aerosmith way of life would never change.

ROCKIN' IN THE TWENTY-FIRST CENTURY

PUSH

It was 2000 and we needed to get started on a new record. After discussing the long and checkered history of Aerosmith producers, Steven and I thought we should produce it ourselves. I suggested that Marti Frederiksen work as our engineer. Steven wanted to bring in Mark Hudson as well. I wasn't thrilled, but Steven always felt he needed someone he could rely on to back him up. We had worked successfully with both these guys in the past, and they were enthusiastic about coming aboard. There weren't any discussions about studios. It was just presumed that we'd get the ball rolling in the Boneyard, by now a world-class facility with just the right mix of vintage gear to offset the cutting-edge computers.

After we laid down the basic tracks over the next few months, we decided to turn our guesthouse, just a few hundred feet from the main house, into the mixing room. That way we could keep working on tracks and still check on the mix. Marti set up a Pro Tools rig in the family room of our main house so we wouldn't have to stop recording to edit the Pro

Tool files. Perry Margouleff brought in experts to tune the rooms. Paul Caruso, my friend and main engineer, not only helped record the CD but was instrumental in connecting these three studios that were equipped with black-and-white TV monitors and speakers, enabling instant communication. To get a natural reverb sound, we even recorded guitars and vocals in our private steam shower.

In the beginning, the teams broke down to Joe/Marti and Steven/Mark. Before long, on a record we'd eventually call *Just Push Play*, Mark and Marti became coproducers. Marti and I clicked on all the hard rock items. We ran off riffs with amazing consistency. Steven and Mark had their own collaborative methodology. Mark was a Beatles freak. Every composition had to be measured in relation to a Beatles song. That could be maddening, but that was Mark's motivation. Because both he and Steven were hyper-extroverts, they often fought each other for attention. I remember them riding down the driveway of my house in Steven's car. You could hear the two of them shouting at each other, both trying to be heard above Steven's blasting stereo.

The screaming drove me crazy. But if that's how they wanted to deal with each other, so be it. More importantly, I was excited because, after all the records we had made in Miami and Vancouver and New York and L.A., this one was being done at home.

For the next ten years, the Boneyard was where the creative process usually started. Steven and I always referred to it as the Net—the place where we caught ideas. It was also where *Just Push Play* began.

Here's how it worked: Marti, Mark, Steven, and I wrote the songs and played the demos. Then Brad, Tom, and Joey would come in to cut their parts—one player at a time instead of the band playing together. That bothered me, but that's just how it evolved. That's also when, in my view, things began to break down. I started feeling disconnected from the other guys in the band and thought they should have more of a chance to be involved. There was also limited spontaneity and virtually no room for variation. Tom, for example, had to learn the parts that Marti had written.

I argued that Tom should be given the freedom to play what he felt, but the other three producers wanted it done their way. It was beginning to not sound like an Aerosmith album—and I didn't like that feeling. The more we worked, the more controlling my coproducers became.

Up until now, with the exception of Ballard, none of our producers had been interested in songwriting. But in this case, Marti and Mark wanted a hand in the songwriting as well as the producing. That moved the focus from a collaborative Aerosmith record to one that was self-serving for Marti and Mark. Steven had no objections because he knew that these two producer-writers would help him with lyrics.

Joey was unhappy because he didn't think he could get the drum sound that he needed in the Boneyard. I disagreed but had to yield. Joey had domain over his own sonics. That meant going to still another studio to record the drums. The result was even more disconnection because a good part of the drum sounds were samples anyway.

A band like Aerosmith is about energy. It was ridiculous that all five of us were never in the same room at the same time—a point I should have insisted upon. I take my share of the blame but, looking back, I realize that I was fighting a losing battle. Most of the arguments were three to one, and I was the one.

The writing process was also marred. Marti and his wife and kids had been living in the guest wing of our compound for months. Because he was a coproducer, cowriter, and friend, I wanted him to be as comfortable as possible. With only four or five songs without lyrics, he and Steven decided to go up to Lake Sunapee for the weekend. They said they would focus on completing the lyrics.

"If you guys start writing something new," I told Marti and Steven, "call me and I'll run up there." It's only a two-hour drive from my house to Sunapee.

"Sure thing," they said.

When they returned, they had written "Jaded." The song was undoubtedly commercial. I heard it as a hit and saw it as the first single off the album. But what had happened to Marti and Steven's promise to call me if they'd begun to write?

Steven gave his usual excuses.

"I thought you said you wanted to have a weekend alone with Billie," he said.

"You know I never said that, Steven. I said call me if you start writing something new. You guys were supposed to be going up to finish lyrics."

"That's not what I heard."

"You heard what you wanted to hear. You make up your own truths to suit yourself. But what else is new?"

Marti's attitude also puzzled me. In just a few short weeks he'd moved from working with me to excluding me from his work with Steven. When I confronted him, he said, "I would have called you, man, but Steven didn't want to. He said it wasn't necessary."

That hurt. And yet it had been become a pattern. Steven had displayed a cavalier attitude that undermined our partnership. Strong partners—like Lennon and McCartney or Jagger and Richards—have each other's backs. Once in a great while they may wander off and compose alone or with another writer, but the understanding is clear: When it comes to their band's material, their partnership is paramount. They're a team. Steven only viewed us as a team when it suited him.

Meanwhile, Steven had thrown Mark Hudson out of his house. Evidently the vicious Steven-Mark arguments got to be too much. Until now Mark had always been Steven's friend, but during the course of this production it became clear that Steven was co-opting Marti, the guy he initially never wanted to work with. In essence, both Marti and Mark were writing songs for Steven. That's why, after all was said and done, I viewed *Push* as an album that lost its focus. Instead of concentrating on an Aerosmith record, the process turned into a competition among coproducers angling for songwriting credits, with Steven leading the charge. The band became incidental. After months of good feeling between Steven and me, the positive vibe was slipping away. By now I knew enough to realize that when push came to shove, he couldn't be trusted.

Certain songs—like "Trip Hoppin'"—seemed a desperate and ridiculous attempt by Steven to be hip. "It's a phrase that all the kids are using," he said, always enamored of street jargon. "I don't care," I said. "For an Aerosmith record, the song sucks." But Steven and Mark were certain that this phrase would resonate with young listeners; they wouldn't hear of eliminating it from the record. Marti agreed with me, but I could never get him to back me up in a room with the others. Marti's main weakness was his inability to stand up for himself. His main drive was to be a songwriter, and he knew that the best way to achieve that was by getting close to the singer.

The final product reflected the differences between Steven and me that had been there since the beginning: He's more pop; I'm more rock. Yet we both wanted quality singles. Still, I believe that starting from the place of let's-write-a-hit is the death of creativity. And that's the place from which Steven, Marti, and Mark were starting. If we had recorded it together—the five of us in a room—it would have sounded like an Aerosmith record. In spite of how it came together, there were a few good Aerosmith songs on *Push*.

I didn't like the cover art that showed a female robot wearing a fifties dress, a chauvinistic rip-off of the famous photo of Marilyn Monroe standing over a subway grate, her white dress billowing. You don't fuck with perfection. When the publicists decided to have females dressed as robots parade around our press conferences, I hated the idea. I thought it was a waste of money. But the band outvoted me and the robots had their day. As a press event, it was a flop. To me, the whole event felt cheesy. It was symbolic of what I felt was the most disconnected album we put our name on.

In September 2000, Billie threw me the party of parties for my fiftieth birthday. She put it together at Mount Blue, a restaurant in Marshfield, Massachusetts, in which Steven and I were part owners. With the help of my first lieutenant, John Bionelli, Billie was able to recruit one of my favorite bands, Cheap Trick. I'd always wanted to play a full set with them and began woodshedding. As a bonus birthday gift, they let me pick out my favorite songs. Come the night of the party, I was ready.

Billie went all out. Outside the restaurant there was a small circus for the kids with a big rock-climbing wall. Inside was Laurie Cabot, the famous Salem witch, telling fortunes, as well as a palm reader and an astrologer. Elvis and Marilyn Monroe impersonators walked around while a master barbecue chef served a huge smoked pig, apple and all. Family and friends came from everywhere—including musicians from my early bands and the Joe Perry Project.

I figured that the highlight of the evening would be my set with Cheap Trick. But at its conclusion there was something even better, a presentation that blew my mind. Here's the backstory:

Back in 1980 when I needed money, I did something I came to regret: I sold my 1959 Gibson, one of my most cherished guitars. The 1959 Les Paul Gibson is to guitars what the 1957 Chevrolet is to cars—a classic of classics. In 1959, Gibson made only two in the color they called tobacco burst. Mine happened to be one of those two. In spite of their reputation, not all '59s sound great, but this one was a true gem. I hated parting with it.

A few years later when the band got back together, I got a call from Eric Johnson, a blues guitarist from Austin. He said he had bought this legendary Gibson and that when he learned that it had been mine, it hadn't set easy with him. He realized the sacredness of the instrument and was willing to sell it back to me. Given the value of the guitar, the price he was asking— eight thousand dollars—was not unreasonable, but because I was still struggling financially, I had to pass. That killed me all over again.

As the years went by, I lost track of the guitar. But with the rebirth of Aerosmith in the late eighties, I found myself with more than enough dough to buy it back—if only I could find it. Eric Johnson had sold it long before and lost track of the instrument. Brad Whitford, whose passion for guitars is as great as mine, knew the story of my lost '59 Gibson as well as anyone. So when he happened to see a photo spread in *Guitar Player* magazine with Slash in front of all his guitars, he immediately spotted mine. He brought me the picture.

"That's your '59 Gibson, isn't it?" Brad asked.

"Sure as hell is," I said.

By then Slash had become a friend, so I immediately called him.

"I'd been hoping you'd never call," he said when I asked about the guitar. Naturally he knew it was mine. "When it came up for sale, that's what made it so special. That's why I had to have it."

"I appreciate that, brother," I said, "so you can really understand why I want it back so badly."

"I was hoping you wouldn't ask, Joe."

"I have to. It's not about the money. You can name the price."

"It's never been about the money," said Slash. "Just like the *Mona Lisa* isn't about the money. It's priceless."

"So you'll sell it back to me?"

"I gotta think about it, Joe. Give me a little time."

I couldn't argue. But in the course of time, Slash and I lost touch. He was out doing his thing while I was out doing mine. I tried to reach him a couple of times but didn't hear back.

The next time I saw him was in 1992 at a huge venue outside Paris. Guns N' Roses asked Steven, me, Lenny Kravitz, and Jeff Beck to perform with them as special guests. They sent us tickets to fly over on the Concorde.

This was Slash's heavy drinking period. Both before and after the concert I tried to talk to him, but it wasn't easy. Finally I sat him down and said, "Look, man, this '59 Gibson is fucking up our friendship. I'm not going to ask you about it anymore. If you decide to sell it to me, fine. If not, that's okay."

"Just give me some more time, Joe. I need some more time."

"Take all the time you need."

I forgot about it, but other guitarists didn't. The story of my '59 Les Paul took on a life of its own. I heard that Jimmy Page had given Slash a hard time about selling it back to its rightful owner. Other guitarists weighed in as well. But I considered it a lost cause. I understood how Slash felt. It was a beauty, it was history, and it felt so fuckin' good to hold and play.

So you can imagine my surprise when in the middle of the set with Cheap Trick, my guitar tech walked up to me and handed me my sacred Les Paul '59 tobacco-burst Gibson. With no price tag attached, with nothing but love and respect, Slash was giving it back—an amazing end to the most amazing birthday party I'd ever had.

The *Just Push Play* tour began that summer. On many of those gigs, Run-DMC opened. This was also the summer when we tried something new—working with two stages. The first—stage A—was the regular huge setup used for large outdoor venues.

But the second—stage B—was set up with small amps, as if we were playing in a club, and placed out on the lawn to give the fans an up-close and personal feeling. Our manager Howard Kaufman didn't like the additional expense of a second stage, but I argued that word would spread and ticket sales would increase. Fortunately that proved to be the case. It paid for itself.

Logistically, though, we had to work out a problem: How to get from stage A to stage B? And how to utilize the time it took to make the journey? I suggested that we make the three-minute trip part of the show. Walk right through the crowd, with cameras following us to capture the trip on the giant screens. It would be a few minutes of chaos but I thought the crowd would love it. Steven thought otherwise. Justifiably, he was a little worried about being manhandled by the fans. Finally, though, I prevailed and the experiment was on. I prayed no one would be hurt.

After a good hour on stage A, we put on black satin robes and started the march to stage B. We were surrounded by security but were still able to return the fans' high-fives and avoid most of the zealots looking to pull our hair and grab our clothes. The trek took what seemed like an eternity, but when we got to the club-like Stage B and played that second set, it was magic. It was great playing face-to-face for fans who were used to watching the video screen.

On the way back to the main stage, we took a shorter route but were not able to avoid more mayhem. When it was all over, I thought the guys would kill me for coming up with this potentially dangerous walk from A to B and B to A. But they actually loved it. They got as big a kick out of it as the fans and voted to keep it a permanent part of the tour. The stage transition turned into a highlight of every concert. When we brought the show indoors, we entered from the back of the building and opened on the B stage, a big surprise for the fans.

All in all, the *Push* tour was going great. Dual stages added to the excitement. The band was playing as a solid unit and, show by show, the crowds were growing larger and larger.

But then came that morning when the world seemed to stop turning, the morning that threw our country into a state of tragedy, panic, and fear.

9/11

Something September 10, 2001, was my fifty-first birthday. This was the first summer that our family had rented a bus to accommodate us on tour. We had a gig in Virginia Beach and happened to notice a startling number of naval ships leaving port. For reasons Billie can't explain, she felt it best for our family to sleep on the bus that night. It made us feel more secure. We were having breakfast the next morning with our boys when John Bionelli knocked on the bus door. We could tell by the look on his face something was wrong. He took us aside and quietly explained that the twin towers in New York had just been brought down by two planes flown by terrorists. Like the rest of the country, we went into shock.

Obviously our show that night was canceled and all gigs postponed until further notice. Being on a naval base, the whole area was on lockdown. The Perry family had transportation out of Virginia Beach—our bus—and we were ready to give the guys a ride. Fortunately, our crew was able to secure a takeoff time for the band's plane. We stayed until we knew everyone was safely on the way home before heading to our condo on a key in Sarasota, Florida. We were unable to tear ourselves from the television news. We awoke on the morning of the twelfth to the sounds of a thundering hurricane, something that the newscasts, preoccupied with the catastrophe at the World Trade Center, had not reported. Someone suggested that the storm was the perfect symbol—nature reflecting the emotional turmoil of our souls.

A few days later, we began discussing when to reconvene the tour. After juggling our feelings of sorrow, grief, and anger over the terrorist attacks, we had no choice but to face reality. The America we grew up in would never be the same. Our kids would grow up in an entirely different world.

We wanted to get out and play, knowing that we might be able to lift some spirits. But on the other hand, how wise would it be to gather ten or twenty thousand people in one arena? The word *terror* was on everyone's mind. Where and when would we be safe? This was when our manager Howard Kaufman suggested that we follow baseball, a sport that had been the backbone of American culture through two world wars. When the baseball games started up again, so would our tour.

In the aftermath of 9/11, Billie and I went into full-on survival mode. There was talk everywhere about other attacks, including assaults using anthrax. Because we were traveling as a family with our boys, we felt obligated to provide as much protection as possible. We bought our own custom bus and hired a driver, Mark Langley. A former police officer and military man who had his finger on the button of the Pershing missile during the Cold War, Mark became our constant companion for the next twelve years.

Our bus became a survival camp on wheels. We had everything from gas masks to cases of dried foods to a supply of antibiotics. Even before 9/11, Billie and I had strong feelings about the precarious nature of life in America in this new century—and how to prepare for the worst.

When the tour got under way again, the other guys were blasé about new security precautions, but I insisted. I interviewed security consultants who were quick to point out the vulnerabilities of the major venues we were playing. In one arena, for example, the ventilation air intake could easily be accessed by grills right along the street. All you'd have to do is park a chlorine truck next to the grills, blow it up, and some twenty thousand people would be dead. Knowing this, I followed the advice of the consultant who said, "Station an engineer in the machine room. That way he can cut off the air-conditioning system in the case of an emergency." We also reconfigured our backstage operation. The location of the dressing rooms, catering rooms, and tour manager rooms in relation to the exits is always a maze. I had directional tape with clear arrows put on the floor so, if need be, we could all find our way out in an orderly fashion—and in a hurry. We also made sure that our vehicles parked in the back-of-venue bays were all aimed out in the direction of the nearest exit.

In some ways, the threats posed by an unpredictable and violent world brought us closer together. This was certainly true of my family. The bus became our cocoon and comfort. In a fundamental way, our kids were educated on the road. We traveled with a private tutor. We closely supervised their schooling and made certain that their lessons were never ignored. But beyond the books, we also made time to stop at points of interest all over the world—museums, art galleries, battlefields, monuments, and historic sites of every stripe. We went down to caves in Georgia and out to the UFO crash site in Roswell, New Mexico; we toured Monet's garden in France, the Tower of London, and temples all over Japan. On those rare occasions when my family wasn't with me, the bus also allowed me to make a quick escape from the stage to the road. In the past, I'd have to hang around for hours and wait for the other guys.

The bus also afforded me a privacy that I cherished. I'd often ask Mark to go off the interstate and roll onto the blue highways where the America I grew up in was preserved. I loved seeing the farms and funky antique shops, the little stores selling homemade jam or jewelry made of old copper wires.

John Bionelli, who traveled with us on the bus and was by now practically a family member and virtual co–road manager of the band, did everything from assembling our set lists to running the teleprompters with our song lyrics. John also helped me discover out-of-the-way barbecue joints. Barbecue and hot sauce became a passion. I loved meeting the characters who ran these establishments. Every barbecue pit boss has his own little secret, and it was great using the *A*-word to get back to where the action was:

the kitchen. I was also inspired to start my own food company, Joe Perry's Rock Your World, run by our son Aaron.

We once stopped in a farming community, a one-horse town, that had a shop set up in a converted 1880s train station/hotel. They sold everything from crystals to scarves to dream catchers made by Native Americans. The elderly woman who owned the store did the canning herself. When I asked about the process, she went to great lengths to describe everything she did. Patience, she said, was the key. Listening to her, I had the feeling she could have been living in the nineteenth rather than the twenty-first century. I liked that feeling.

"Before you leave," she said, "I'd like you to meet my husband. Let me fetch him. He's right upstairs."

I waited a few minutes. I heard footsteps coming down the stairs, and when I looked up I saw a man who, like his wife, was in his seventies. Unlike his wife, though, he was wearing a vintage Aerosmith *Toys in the Attic* T-shirt. When he saw me, he turned around and went back upstairs, only to reappear with a complete set of vintage vinyl Aerosmith LPs.

With a sweet smile, he said to me, "We're fans."

The bus also gave me time to read. A few years earlier I had begun to read the classics, from Homer to Faulkner—stuff I had missed by not going to college. I developed a deep appreciation for Hemingway, whose clipped, muscular prose affected me deeply. His troubled notions of manhood were riveting: what it meant to hunt and gather, what it meant to love and lose and face one's fears. I also read Twain and Steinbeck. Rolling through America reading American authors was a beautiful thing. The sixty-mile-an-hour rhythm of the road was exactly right for me. It was also a joy to avoid airports.

I had flown over the Grand Canyon a thousand times but had never walked to its edge. The bus freed me from the band's unwieldy travel schedule, giving me time to walk the cities and towns and talk to fans. It got me feeling like an ancient troubadour, wandering the back roads of a lost America.

In this post-9/11 period, through a friend of the band's who worked for the Secret Service, the Joe Perry and Brad Whitford families were allowed to go to the Pentagon and view some of the damage. It was an opportunity for us to thank the workers.

We appreciated the incredible devotion of the men and women who were sweating profusely in their hazmat suits as they followed dogs through the rubble, never knowing what they might find. Dump trucks were hauling off debris. The air stank of jet fuel. Workers were still pulling plane parts out of the building. We shook every hand we could. It was a sad and sobering sight.

We had long made a habit of visiting Walter Reed National Military Medical Center in D.C. to visit wounded soldiers, just to say thanks and help lift their spirits. When the war started in Afghanistan—and then Iraq—we redoubled our efforts. These were inspiring human beings, and it was an honor to be able to hear their stories. Being a rock-and-roll warrior is one thing; being a real warrior quite another.

On the rock-and-roll front, I got an idea from the nose art on the fighter planes from World War II. I loved how they put sexy drawings of their wives or girlfriends or pinup girls like Betty Grable on the noses of their planes. The images took a little sting out of the danger they faced, while adding to the energy that drove them to fight. Sexy women give men energy. Billie, the pinup girl of my dreams, was also the love of my life, and I wanted to see her in a Vargas-style painting on the body of a Gibson guitar. Without telling her why, I took photos of her in an alluring red dress and then sent them to John Douglas, the drum tech for ZZ Top who had done a series of similar paintings for sets of drums. He did a great job and my Billie guitar, with my wife looking especially voluptuous, came to life.

After the artwork was done, the guitar went to Gibson in Nashville for final production. As luck would have it, we had a gig there, giving us an excuse to take the kids on a tour of the Gibson factory. At the end of the afternoon, they brought out the just-completed Billie guitar. Billie's face turned as red as the dress she wore on the body of the guitar. She was embarrassed for months but finally got over it. I loved the instrument, not only because it bore an image of my woman, but because it turned out to be one of my best-sounding guitars, no doubt due to Billie's mystical mojo.

When the band saw it, Brad thought it was cool, but the others gave me some shit. Considering my bandmates' attitudes toward wives and girlfriends, though, their reaction wasn't unexpected. I figured that Steven would complain. He got used to it, however, to the point where he would occasionally bend over and kiss her face during a show. Sometimes women in the audience would point to the guitar and scream out, "Who is it?" I'd point to my wedding ring and the girls would cheer.

In 2002, Sony and Geffen got together and decided to issue a two-CD ultimate Aerosmith hits collection called *O, Yeah!* To increase the set's value, they asked us to write a couple of new original songs. Steven and I thought it was a good idea. Our plan was to go to Maui after some dates in Japan and work there. That was a dream Steven and I had shared for years. But Steven changed his plans without telling me. He was about to leave early and write with Marti Frederiksen, leaving me in the lurch. It reminded me of what happened with "Jaded." This time, though, I caught him.

"Look," I said, "if you want to write songs alone with Marti, you can't do it on the band's dime. And if you guys are going to be working on Aerosmith songs, I should be there."

Marti and Steven stayed in a house where they set up a small Pro Tools system. I stayed down the street in a hotel with Billie and the kids. We'd work on music from early afternoon through early evening till friends of Steven's would start showing up, people I didn't know. As the focus turned from the recording rig to the hot tub, I took it as my cue to leave.

Nonetheless, we came up with a few cool riffs and pulled together a song or two. Marti and Steven became enamored of something called "Girls of Summer." I put guitar on it. But a few overdubs don't really change the guts of a song. I thought it was a waste of time and wrong for an Aerosmith record. I suggested that Steven save it for a solo album. The rest of the band agreed. But Steven prevailed and the song was recorded. Tom, Brad, Joey, and I thought so little of it that we refused to be in the video. Both the song and video faded fast.

Some of that tension dissipated when Steven and I went on a dive off the coast of Maui. It was a good way to let off steam. It was the first shipwreck dive that either of us had participated in. It also showed we were able to put our musical differences aside, still get along like brothers, and have a good time together.

Back on the mainland, the *Just Push Play* tour gained new momentum when Kid Rock and Run-DMC opened for us.

We'd met Kid Rock when he inducted us into the Rock and Roll Hall of Fame and invited us to his party, which took up an entire floor at the Plaza hotel in New York. Another time when we played Detroit, Kid came to see us and threw another party, this one in his home studio. After the show, he and his then girlfriend, Pamela Anderson, got on our bus and rode to his house—me and Rock jamming on guitars. More jamming in his studio with his band while Pamela planted herself on the lap of our son Tony, then fourteen. She began feeding him pizza bite by bite. We were a little taken aback but didn't have the heart to interrupt a teenage fantasy come true.

When the tour rolled into Massachusetts, we returned the favor and invited Kid Rock and Pamela to our house for lunch and a tour of the Boneyard. Later that day we all rode on my bus to the show in Mansfield.

The road led to Louisiana, where, being on the bus, I could go out beyond the levees into the backwoods. Aerosmith had been playing New Orleans off and on for thirty years. I always loved the city and was fascinated not only by its complex cultural and musical history but by the voodoo mystique.

Just to do something different with the kids, we—along with Brad and his family—met a "white witch" who gave us a legal midnight tour of some of the city's most historic sights. Beneath a full moon, we used flashlights to make our way through a graveyard filled with ancient tombs, mystical ley lines, Masonic symbols, and a scaled-down obelisk. Not spotting any ghosts, the kids returned to the bus. Billie and I spent another hour or two taking in the history of the area.

I had read books on the subject before actually meeting a voodoo priestess who had a little shop in the funky Ninth Ward of the city. I mentioned to her that I was interested in getting a tattoo with voodoo symbols for good luck.

"That's fine," she said, "but you need to have a ceremony *before* you get tattooed. The ceremony must happen at the crossroads."

"My tattoo artist," I said, "is in Atlanta."

"You can find crossroads anywhere. I'll give you instructions."

I took the instructions and, next time I was in Atlanta, made the arrangements. Billie, by the way, was not happy about any of this. She had bad vibes about my interest in voodoo.

Nonetheless, Billie, my trusty sidekick John Bionelli, driver Mark Langley, and I set out to find a crossroads. When I found the one that felt right, I was supposed to put some pennies on the ground and pour rum over them, a ritual that acknowledged one of the great paternal voodoo icons. Once this was accomplished, I'd head back to the hotel and get tattooed with the voodoo symbol.

I performed the ceremony, and within a second of finishing it we heard a screech of tires. We turned to see two cars plowing into each other, only a few feet from where we were standing. The collision was horrific. The ensuing explosion prevented us from approaching the vehicles. Ambulances arrived quickly. Thank God no one was seriously injured.

Everyone was stunned. Back at the hotel, I told my tattoo guy that I was going to change the design. No voodoo symbolism today! Instead I put the ancient equal-sided cross, as opposed to a Christian one, to represent the crossroads. Then I added an image of my eye, for when my eyes were opened at the crossroads. Billie's name was integrated into the tattoo along with appropriate astrological signs for each of our sons' birthdays, plus Billie's and mine. I got the tattoo and said goodbye to voodoo with a deep respect for its power. Like Billie says—"Don't open doors when you're not ready to deal with what's on the other side."

One day in Memphis, Billie, John Bionelli, and the boys and I were touring Sun Studios. The tour guide was a tall skinny guy with muttonchops, thick black-rimmed glasses, and a scruffy skateboarder look. He gave me his CD, and when Billie and I listened to it, we were enthralled. "Holy shit," I said, "this is fuckin' brilliant." They were a band called the Porch Ghouls.

The lineup was classic porch stomp. One cat played Danelectro guitar on his lap. The front man, Eldorado Del Rey, played guitar standing up and sang. The third guy played harp and shakers and the fourth played suitcase drums. Their sound was raw and their songs were deep. I immediately signed them to my fledgling label, Roman Records, with distribution through Sony. They went in and recut their material using better recording equipment. I got them a van and had them perform on that summer's Aerosmith tour, playing the B stages at various venues. The record came out, got good reviews, and left me feeling proud that I helped introduce the Ghouls to the world.

There's a video by the Porch Ghouls on YouTube with music from the independent film *This Thing of Ours*, directed by Danny Provenzano. At the top, Billie, Steven, and I play bit parts in a parody of *The Godfather*, with Eddie Lynch, and Frank Vincent of *The Sopranos* in the lead role. Unfortunately, the Ghouls broke up not long after.

Far and wide, home and abroad, in indoor arenas and outdoor festivals, we pushed *Just Push Play* as far as we could push it. Despite my reservations about its quality, the record did well. The tour pushed the new songs out there and helped preserve the classics. We persevered in the major and minor rock capitals of the world. Our new relationship with our old label Columbia was off to a good start. But then came the old challenge that was always a new challenge and never an easy challenge.

A new record.

New songs.

The cycle of touring-recording-touring-recording had not changed at all. My fervent hope was that, for all the aggravations in the past, the present would be different. It was different, but in ways I could have never predicted.

HONKIN'

There were the good times—
even the great times—when Steven and I walked the world as brothers: In
Salt Lake City, we spent a day paragliding off a four-thousand-foot mountain cliff. It was fun hanging together without the stress of the band. On
another trip, the rapper Nelly asked me to play a solo in the desert outside
Vegas for a video shoot for his hit song "Number One." Afterward, Steven
met Billie and me for an afternoon of paragliding over an enormous lake
bed, another over-the-edge experience.

The Perrys and Tylers have a treasure chest of shared memories.
There were big cookouts at Lake Sunapee, where we'd watch our kids play
in the same lake where we had played as kids; day trips with our families to
the Medieval Faire; Thanksgiving and Christmas Eve dinners, Easter egg
hunts, mountain climbing, rock hunting, fishing. Not to mention water-
skiing. Steven and I spent a lifetime of summers skiing at Sunapee. We'd ski
in an air chair that lifts you over the lake, we'd ski on banana peels (which
are skis without fins), I even skied without skis, just the soles of my feet

keeping me aloft. Throughout the years the Tylers and the Perrys have been able to go on many family vacations together. All beautiful memories, and yet . . .

As we moved deeper into the twenty-first century, my hope was that the collaboration between Steven and me as composers and producers would finally find the right rhythm. It had long been obvious to the rock-and-roll world—especially as we entered our fourth decade—that we were meant to work together.

Back in 1986 we were performing in Dallas when my worn-out boot heel slipped out from under me. I fell some four feet off a riser and tore the ligament in my right knee. I finished the tour using a knee brace and had my first surgery when I got home. For the first few years everything was fine, but as the touring went on, the knee wore down. At this point I'd been living in considerable pain and was told I required surgery. The doctor predicted that it would only be a matter of scoping and repairing a torn tendon. He didn't think the ACL required replacement. In the end, though, he had to replace that ACL with a cadaver's. Rehab was rough, but I managed to make it back for the "Girls of Summer" tour of 2002. A month into it, I was walking down a staircase to the stage when I heard something pop and knew my knee was still fucked. My plan was to grin and bear it. My work ethic wouldn't let me miss a single show. So for the next few years, I dealt with it. Elastic braces helped a little, but I still had to figure out how to move onstage without falling on my face. In the bus after the show, Billie would be waiting with a bag of crushed ice and I'd gulp down a bunch of painkillers. As time went on, the pain got worse.

The pain of writing and producing with Steven had also increased. No progress had been made on a new record. This would be the project that would fulfill Sony's contract and make us free agents. I wanted us to be in that advantageous position. I wanted this record to happen.

The business had changed radically. Every six months new technology would come along and encroach on the labels' ability to retain power. Napster and other Internet paradigms had made it easy for people to bootleg or steal music. The record companies were doing little about it, simply hoping the thievery would stop. Record industry people were losing their jobs left and right while the suits were desperately trying to hold on to their seven-figure salaries or find a way to jump ship and cash out. Everyone saw the changes coming but no one knew what to do about it—especially the over-paid suits occupying the executive suites.

I didn't like how Sony had absolute musical control over everything we did. Granted, we had one of the best royalty deals out there. But the contract that we had signed ten years earlier was woefully behind the times. Sony still got the lion's share of our money and exerted total control over how our music was exploited. After all these years in the business, we felt stuck with a label that was failing to protect our interests. They were far too proprietary. For example, when Steven was asked to play drums and sing background on a Ringo Starr solo record—a huge honor—he ran into the studio and had a ball jamming with one of his idols. But when Sony got word, they nixed it, contending that Steven playing with Ringo would hurt Aerosmith sales. Sony made certain that Steven's background vocals were stripped off the tracks. This was embarrassing for Steven and a fuckin' ridiculous argument to boot.

At the same time, we had to make a new record and were getting nowhere fast. This disturbed me because I was eager to get back in the studio and do something great—something that represented our rock core with new vitality. My eagerness, though, was met by Steven's reluctance. Once again we were back to the old pattern that had plagued us from the start: Steven was distracted from his job of writing. He wanted hit pop songs. My attitude was that every time you sit down to consciously try to write a hit single you edit yourself to death. I loved having a hit single as much as anyone—but I hated sounding like we were trying too hard. Steven and I were at opposite ends: He was obsessed with making the best pop record ever, while my top priority was getting out of our antiquated Sony deal. I was ready to follow the Rolling Stones formula, where they'd gotten out of their Decca deal by doing "Cocksucker Blues"—just cut a bunch of unplayable funk with outrageous lyrics and let the label dump you.

Meanwhile, we had to get back on the road. Our new tour was titled Rocksimus Maximus, and it would take us across America from July to

December of 2003. Aerosmith was co-headlining with Kiss. Even without material for a new record, we could—and we would—always tour.

Like us, Kiss is a band that takes it to their people. Gene Simmons and crew never stop working. Their work ethic is every bit as strong as ours. Decade after decade, they go out and satisfy their core fans. Beginning in the seventies, we also had a shared history. They'd gone through their shit; we'd gone through ours. They had managed to prevail and so had we. I admired their survival skills and they admired ours. They had also skillfully matched an original theatrical performance with great party rock and roll.

The only issue was Steven's attitude. Because he wasn't a Kiss fan and was unhappy about the pairing, he refused to do any press or promotion for the tour. Fortunately, we didn't need much press. The crowds were huge.

During the tour I was intrigued when John Bionelli, a rabid Kiss fan, mentioned that no musician had ever jammed with the band. They also have a strict rule—no one's allowed in their dressing room for an hour while they become Kiss. I didn't know this and, a half hour before their show in Oklahoma, I went into their dressing room.

"Hey, Gene," I said. "Great tour. I'm really digging it."

Surprised but glad to see me, Gene said, "We are too, Joe."

Paul said, "Joe, what would you think of jamming with us one night?"

"I think that'd be great," I said. "But I need to wear the boots. Gotta wear the boots! You have a spare pair? You must have a few spare pairs for the cats who come up and jam."

"No one has ever jammed with us before," said Gene, reconfirming what Bionelli had said.

"Then this is a double honor," I said.

Paul handed me a pair of boots and said, "See if they fit."

I tried them on. "They're going take some getting used to. Mind if I borrow 'em for a few days?"

For two days I stumbled into furniture and knocked over lamps until I steadied myself in the boots. I also practiced "Strutter," my favorite Kiss song. When it came time, I was ready. I took the stage and rocked out with Kiss, a definite rush. Plus, we made a little rock-and-roll history.

We still couldn't ignore the need for a new record. To push things ahead, Steven and I recruited Jack Douglas, our main man from the seventies, to coproduce with us. We had three months, plenty of time for us to record an album of original music.

As the five of us started discussing the project at the Boneyard, Steven's heart wasn't in it. He either came in late or not at all. Nothing was getting done. That's when I remembered that Sony exec Don Ienner had suggested years before that our first Sony album should be a blues record. Well, why not now?

I called Steven and said, "Look, when it comes to this new record, why don't we just simplify things?"

"How?" he asked.

"By making a blues record. We can do it in two months. We can cover the blues songs we love the most, the ones we've been listening to our whole lives. It's a way of getting back to our roots and having some fun."

Silence. I could hear Steven thinking.

"What do you say?" I asked.

"Sounds okay."

Steven's tone told me that he was doing it only to appease me. He really wanted a hit record. So did I. But I also clung to my conviction that the best music does not come from a place of "let's write hits."

Whatever Steven's hesitations might have been, we moved ahead with the project. The band built a new rehearsal room with a recording studio at our old warehouse in Hanover, Massachusetts. Our intention was to cut the album right there. In the meantime, we could rehearse in the Boneyard. The rehearsals were relaxed. It was summertime, so in between takes we'd walk outside and have a cigar in our lush garden, a semi-secluded spot perfect for chilling. During the *Just Push Play* sessions, Mark Hudson had even painted a purple wooden heart with the words *Avant Garden* to mark the spot. I had a couple of dirt bikes and four-wheelers for tooling around the grounds. Without the pressure of having to write new material, we could simply dig each other's company and focus on hot-rodding some of our old favorites. For me it was probably the most fun of any Aerosmith recording project.

It was also fun working again with Jack Douglas, who knew that Aerosmith had to be Aerosmith—five guys meshing in one room. And for us to bang out the blues was, as the Beatles put it, to get back to where we once belonged. Jack had been hoping for all-new material, but he realized that wasn't gonna happen. He saw the blues record as a necessary step in that direction.

Other than Sony exec Don Ienner, the other label bosses weren't thrilled about the direction. They argued that a blues album, as opposed to one filled with hit singles, lacked mass-market appeal. They were right, but when I told them that something was better than nothing—especially with our tour looming ahead—they had to agree. We could turn out an album in a hurry—something hot, genuine, and true to our souls—and give our fans a treat. In the end, Sony had little choice but to go along with our plan. Because it was not a studio album of originals, it did not fulfill our contractual obligation. The album was treated as a side deal with Sony, separate from our original contract. Even after this record, we'd still owe the company another album.

Picking out the songs and laying down the tracks was a blast. We covered classic numbers by Willie Dixon ("I'm Ready"), Sonny Boy Williamson ("Eyesight to the Blind"), a couple by Fred McDowell ("You Gotta Move" and "Back Back Train"), Big Joe Williams ("Baby, Please Don't Go") and Peter Green of Fleetwood Mac ("Stop Messin' Around"). We also slipped in some vintage soul—"I've Never Loved a Man," Aretha Franklin's first hit on Atlantic from 1967.

I knew the project was blessed by the delta gods when, one day, while having my first cup of coffee, I glanced at the local paper and saw that Johnnie Johnson was playing at the House of Blues in Cambridge. Johnnie, who'd been inducted into the Rock and Roll Hall of Fame on the same day as us, had been Chuck Berry's original piano man and co-architect of the Chuck Berry sound. Before this, I had been determined to make this a guestless album, and the rest of the band had agreed. So many people had asked to sit in, but I felt it should just be the band. But Johnson was too good to pass up. He was among the greatest blues-based boogie-centric keyboard cats of all time. I asked John Bionelli to see if he was willing to come out to the Boneyard.

Two hours later a limo pulled up to my house with the great Johnnie Johnson aboard. He came to play.

"I'm a jazzman," he told us. "I do that for love, but they pay me to play rock and roll."

"No problem," I said. "Just pick any keyboard you want. We have a Steinway upright if that suits you."

"Give me anything electric and I'll be fine."

That's just what we did. Johnnie tore up two tunes—Smiley Lewis's "Shame, Shame, Shame" and "Temperature," a song that harp genius Little Walter, Muddy Waters's favorite harmonica player, had recorded back in the fifties. Within ninety minutes, Johnnie had the job done. For the rest of the afternoon, we sat around and listened to his great war stories. Because I knew he liked cigars, before he got into his limo to head back to Boston I slipped a thousand dollars into a five-hundred-dollar box full of Montecristo Cubans and handed him the package with my thanks. Holy shit, Johnnie Johnson had recorded in my house!

Johnnie's fabulous playing started to get Steven in the mood. Although we weren't writing, he was still having problems coming to work. In fact, I recorded placeholder vocals on practically all the songs until Steven finally decided to show up consistently. Once he got into it, however, he jumped in with both feet. He brought Bo Diddley's "Road Runner" to the party and cut loose. For Tyler, when he's into it, the blues is rare red meat.

Our approach was to show our appreciation of the blues by attacking the genre with everything at our disposal. The album is the blues filtered through our ears and our lives. Early in our lives, we had heard Them covering Big Joe Williams's "Baby Please Don't Go." The Porch Ghouls happened to be in town and were in the studio when we cut it. It was a magical live take. It was also us covering a cover. You can't get any more perfect than that.

I first heard the blues through the Englishmen who were reinterpreting the genre themselves. As a teen, I started looking at the writers' credits and searching back to hear the real thing. This project was a continuation of the tradition. We called it *Honkin' on Bobo*, a title I loved, suggested by

Steven, because, well, it just sounded like the right title for a blues album. It was our version of Lennon's *Rock and Roll* album.

There was only one original, "The Grind," which grew out of a riff that Tyler and I had worked up with Marti Frederiksen. Everything else belonged to another time and place.

*H*onkin' *on Bobo* got us back on the road with fresh product. During the tour that followed we played "Baby Please Don't Go" in classic blues fashion. It never came out the same way twice and was always a highlight. Cheap Trick, an inspirational presence, opened in many of the venues. Winding our way around the country I was able to stop off at South by Southwest in Austin and catch Little Richard in concert. After the show, I went backstage to pay my respects. It's always humbling to stand before one of our immortal pioneers. He lived and breathed the gospel of rock and roll. He looked ageless. Richard walked me back out to my bus and, in formal fashion, proceeded to bless it. No blessing has ever been more appreciated.

Making this blues-intense period even more special was the release of Antoine Fuqua's documentary *Lightning in a Bottle*, in which Steven and I appeared along with heavyweights like Hubert Sumlin, B. B. King, and Buddy Guy. We play Slim Harpo's "I'm a King Bee" before breaking into "Stop Messin' Around," with me on vocals and Steven on harp.

On another break during the Canadian leg of the tour, Steven joined my family and we took an excursion on our bus to Drumheller, a town in the badlands northeast of Calgary, Alberta, where we spent the day digging for dinosaur bones.

Then, in September 2004, Steven's battle with hepatitis C took him out of commission. He could no longer perform, and the Aerosmith operation suddenly ground to a halt.

Looking back on the process of recording *Honkin'*, I realized that Steven's lack of interest probably had much to do with his health problems. He already knew that he had contracted hep C and had to be worried about the upcoming treatments. That would take the wind out of anyone.

While Steven was out, I went down to the Boneyard and kept

working. It had been years since I'd cut an album of my own and figured it was time. The record that emerged, called simply *Joe Perry*, was coproduced by me and my engineer Paul Caruso, who understood my musical mind and soul as well as anyone. Except for a cover of Woody Guthrie's "Vigilante Man" and the Doors' "Crystal Ship," a composition I had long loved, I wrote all the songs. With Paul on drums, I sang and played bass, guitar, synth guitar, and keys. My muse was Billie, who, hearing the music drifting upstairs from the studio, was taking care of the business end of things.

When the record came out there was time for only two promotional concerts—one at Webster Hall in New York and another at Harpers Ferry in Boston, where, in a display of camaraderie that I deeply appreciated, my Aerosmith bandmates came to support me. Later that year one of the tracks, "Mercy," was nominated for a Grammy in the category of Best Rock Instrumental. I lost to Les Paul. I called him in the hospital, where he was fighting pneumonia, and told him that, if I could, I would have voted for him.

The mid-2000s was a time of intense health concerns. Steven, whose mood volatility was always off the charts, was going through a divorce. He had serious foot and throat problems. In March 2006, for example, our national tour was curtailed for another medical emergency—Steven required throat surgery.

This issue of Steven's throat was one that had been bothering us for years. He used to say, "You can change guitar strings, Joe, but I can't change vocal cords."

"That's true," I'd reply. "So why are you shouting and screaming on your off days? Why aren't you resting your voice?"

Time and again, he brushed me off, saying that wasn't the issue. But I knew it was. The problem only got worse when Steven refused to rest his voice. You could never keep him quiet.

When he went to the hospital to have a blister on his vocal cords removed, Billie and I were with him the morning of the operation. His doctor said that Steven had a million-in-one voice, a uniquely large voice box. But even after the successful operation, the pattern didn't stop. His solution was that we'd play fewer gigs, to rest his voice. We were quick to agree. But then he refused to stay quiet on his off days. On top of that, he rarely took advantage of ear monitors that both reduce the volume of the band behind him while enabling him to sing with more dynamics and less strain. This is one of the many tools today's singers have at their disposal to preserve their voices. As we musicians get older, we need to make adjustments.

But Steven is stubborn. Steven is a shouter. During our off days he's always shouting—shouting on the phone, shouting at the road crew, shouting at the top of his lungs about anything and everything. He claims his talking voice is different than his singing voice. But his form of talking is often just shouting. My concern is much more than the reduced number of gigs we play during a tour. At this point, it's limited to two shows a week. My concern, as a brother, is that one day Steven will wake up with laryngitis that will not go away. And it'll be too late.

Back then I was hurting as well.

Since my ACL replacement, my knee had gotten considerably worse. It was painful to walk, let alone move onstage. But I had this bullheaded attitude, common to the human male, that I would simply ignore the pain and keep on keepin' on. Responsible physicians wrote responsible prescriptions for responsible pain medicine. For the most part I administered the medicine responsibly. My only interest was in managing the pain to the point where I could play and perform. But once an addict always an addict. In slow but certain ways I could see myself enjoying the pain pills a little too much and, once in a while, ingesting more than was needed. I still had no interest in hard drugs like coke or heroin, nor did I go back to booze. But I did lean on Percodan. Percodan worked. Its mixture of aspirin and oxycodone is powerful medicine. I was grateful for the relief and I liked the high. I tried to forget the fact that Percodan is habit-forming.

In late June the band was in our rehearsal studio getting ready for the Root of All Evil tour with Mötley Crüe scheduled for later that summer. During a break, Steven came into my office.

"I got something good," was all he said.

I wasn't sure what he meant until he locked the door. He quickly took out two pills and crushed them up. They looked like oxycodone. I knew he'd been taking pain pills for his feet and he knew I'd been taking pills for my knee, but we hadn't discussed the issue or exchanged our prescription drugs.

Now I looked at the crushed line and said, "Oh, man, I don't want to start this shit. If Billie finds out she'll kill me. Even worse, she'll leave me."

"Okay," said Steven, "I can dig it. But just this once."

I hesitated. And then I hesitated again. But then my addictive mind took over. My addictive thought was *I don't want to see it go to waste.* So we snorted the stuff up and went back to rehearsal.

A week later on the Fourth of July we had a big concert with the Boston Pops at Hatch Shell by the Charles River. It was a huge honor. More than a hundred thousand people would be there. There would be fireworks and cannons set off by the National Guard. I remembered seeing such a show at the Shell back in the seventies and being blown away. I was really up for it.

I arrived with Billie and the boys and was ready to play. Before the show I went to Steven's trailer. He was in the back bedroom with his girl-friend Erin Brady, the woman he began dating after the end of his marriage to Teresa. Erin worked for the promoter Live Nation in their accounting department, where, among other things, she collected the ticket money for our shows.

"I got something to show you," he said. He locked the door and laid out two lines.

"I asked you not to do this, Steven," I said.

I wasn't worried that it would affect my playing. I'd played many shows on painkillers. I just didn't want it in front of me. And yet . . .

I snorted it up.

Seconds later, Billie walked into Steven's trailer looking for me. This was unusual. Billie always gave Steven and me our time alone before the show. She obviously had picked up a vibe. She began pounding on the locked bedroom door as we were cleaning things up.

"What's going on here?" she asked when we finally opened the door. "Why is the door locked?"

"We were just talking about what to give the crew for Christmas," said Erin. "We're thinking of giving them engraved knives."

Looking around the room, Billie said, "Isn't it a little early to be talking about Christmas?" It was July, after all.

With that, Billie turned her back and walked out to my dressing room, where she packed up her stuff and called for the car to take her home. She knew damn well what I had done. She knew I'd been taking medication for my knee, but she'd made it clear that if I ever took it further she would split. Now she had caught me red-handed. She was leaving and I was freaking out. I'd let down my wife, who was also my best friend. I felt like shit. I felt like I couldn't go on. But it was time for the show. A long line of policemen were waiting to accompany me to the stage.

"If you leave," I told Billie, "I won't go on."

"Yes, you will," she said. "You'll go on. I'm outta here."

I stood my ground. I refused to go onstage.

Seeing that I was serious, she said, "Okay, I'll stay. But just for the show. After that, I'm leaving you."

An emotional wreck, I managed to get through the show. On the ride home with the kids in the car, Billie remained quiet. But that night, for the first time in twenty-three years, she took her pillow from the bed and slept in another room, where she stayed for five days. I apologized profusely. But she wasn't having it. I was unable to sleep in our bed alone, so I moved a chaise lounge to the bathroom, where I tried to sleep. Seeing that I had vacated our bedroom, days later Billie moved back in—but kept me out. It was hell.

As the days went by, we didn't fight, but the silence between us was deafening. Finally she called my manager, who agreed that I needed to go to rehab. Then there was a conference call with two of my doctors. One said, "I think Joe can stop on his own. Forcing rehab on someone who is capable of quitting on his own can cause even greater trauma. I wouldn't recommend that."

Billie didn't agree and was still furious. "The only reason I'm not leaving you and moving to Florida," she said, "is because of Roman. Tony's off at college in New York, but Roman is looking forward to making the transition from homeschooling to high school here. Now more than ever, he needs his family intact. His well-being is more important than anything. If I have to fake it, I will."

Billie's words were devastating. This was the most critical challenge our marriage had faced. I was relieved that she wasn't leaving, but I also knew that I couldn't continue living under the same roof with my wife and not share a bed. That's the first step to breaking up. I wanted to save our marriage. Deep down I sensed that Billie felt the same. It was obvious our relationship required concentrated repair. It would either collapse or, as a result of this crisis, it would grow stronger.

Thank God it grew stronger. We recommitted to one another. I committed to having a knee replacement as soon as the band schedule permitted. Until then, I would manage the painkillers and watch out for Steven. His issues were his and mine were mine. The fact that we had snorted together had knocked some sense into me. I could only hope that it did the same for him.

Steven has a side that can be evil and cruel. He knew what he was doing that night. He was always jealous of my relationships with women. He saw my weak spot and took advantage of it. It's easy for Steven to manipulate people. I, of all people, should have known that. I also should have known that, given the wrong circumstances, the addictive side of my personality could take over. Ironically—and almost tragically—my attempt to relieve my pain only caused more pain: pain suffered by me, and pain suffered by my wife.

In between the pain there was the pleasure of knowing that our band was still going strong. We had been in Elmore Leonard's *Be Cool*, which starred John Travolta and Uma Thurman. Even cooler than that was an invitation to hang out with Chuck Berry.

I had met Chuck, my guitar idol, only once—on an airplane ride in 1976. We spent that time comparing our Pulsar watches. Thirty years later, in October 2006, the band was in Chuck's hometown of St. Louis when I was invited to his eightieth birthday party at his nightclub. At the same time, former vice president Al Gore invited us to dinner at his home. After Billie and I had watched Gore's film *An Inconvenient Truth*, we urged Steven to see it. We thought it would be cool to get an edited version to show the fans as they were entering our concerts. We had begun to do just that.

Gore was kind enough to invite Steven and me to dinner the same night as Chuck's party.

What to do: the politician or the guitarist?

Not a close call.

Before the party, Chuck and I had met for lunch, where we shot the shit about guitars. Apparently Chuck's son Butch had showed him my tribute to him in *Rolling Stone*, where I called him "the Hemingway of rock and roll."

The night of the party I got to the club early and couldn't wait to jam. Chuck was cordial but also a little prickly. He brought me onstage and called for an unfamiliar tune in a Chuck Berry key. Anyone who has played with Chuck will find this story familiar. Even the keyboardist, who'd been with him for years, was confused. All I could do was play a little rhythm. I guess I passed the acid test, because the next song was "Round and Round," a familiar song for which I got to play some lead and afterward hear a few words of praise from the master. That was enough to make my day—and my year.

The next time Aerosmith came through St. Louis, Chuck and his family showed up at my dressing room before the show. I was floored. His son Butch said this was the first rock-and-roll show Chuck had ever wanted to attend. He just wanted to talk, and talk we did. Naturally it was all guitar talk—about Chuck's affinity for the Gibson and all his many early influences, including country music. It was just picker to picker. He sat there sipping on a Virgil's root beer. When he got up and left, I was careful to keep the empty bottle. Since then, that bottle has become a permanent part of my dressing room decor, a talisman from the man who, along with Bo Diddley and Little Richard, first rolled the rock that changed the world.

Another happy coincidence: That winter I was with my family during a snowy week in Vermont when we invited Steven to come up and spend a couple of nights with us. It was a magical time when the chaos of the noisy world was becalmed by a blanket of freshly fallen snow. We were driving through the quaint town of Woodstock when Billie noticed that the town hall movie theater was showing a film about a reggae band, Sierra Leone's Refugee All Stars. It turned out that the director lived nearby and this movie was his labor of love. As we sat down, we didn't know what to expect. Within seconds we were drawn into a story that blew our minds. The narrative involved the struggle to lead a great mass of refugees back to Sierra Leone, a country that had been traumatized by the slaughter of innocent citizens. The central story focused on a band that was trying to cut a record. These were the All Stars, who had heartbreaking tales of their own. Their music was magic. When the film was over, we talked to the director and exchanged numbers.

Billie and I helped bring the All Stars themselves to Woodstock's Pentangle Arts and Music Festival in Vermont the following summer. They were touring America on the strength of the film, and while Woodstock wasn't nearly large enough to justify a stopover, we helped make it happen anyway. The band members were not only the nicest human beings you'd ever want to meet—ranging in age from sixteen to fifty-six—but superb musicians. The first half of their set was reggae-based and the second traditional African. Amazing, when you consider that this was a band put together in the abject conditions of a refugee camp. I was honored when they asked me to jam. Their traditional instruments were works of art, but their electric stuff wasn't in good shape. I rallied my instrument manufacturer friends to donate new gear. Everyone came through. The youngest All Star was a teenager who was into rap and wanted to go to college. When we put a new Mac PowerBook complete with Pro Tools recording programs under his arm, he had stars in his eyes. The All Stars spread joy wherever they went, proof of the power of music to help people overcome the most horrific circumstances.

That same summer, with both Steven and me working with broken-down knees, we took our tour to Europe, the Middle East, and India.

A few months earlier Billie, John Bionelli, and I, longtime fans of Tom Jones, had gone to his show his Vegas and hung out with him afterward. He and I had a warm chat and agreed to go into the studio together someday soon. Then came this worldwide tour that had Aerosmith in England the same time that the sons of Princess Diana threw a huge charity show at Wembley Stadium to honor what would have been their mother's forty-sixth birthday. Tom Jones—who was headlining along with Elton John, Duran Duran, Rod Stewart, and Kanye West—called and asked me to accompany him. As luck would have it, I was off that day. *Hell, yes, I'll play with Tom Jones.* I went out there, standing next to Tom, for a two-song set. As eighty thousand Brits cheered, he hit every note like a kid in his prime. That was one guy who took care of his voice.

Steven had been invited and turned it down. But he remained unhappy about my playing with Tom Jones without him and wasn't shy about letting me know. He blasted our manager Trudy Green with a jealous e-mail about my appearance at Wembley.

The tour took us to exotic locales and introduced us to new worlds of fans. I was especially happy because Billie and I had invited my mother to come along. There were huge crowds in Dubai, and, most spectacular of all, there was India. We were driven through the streets of Bangalore in crazy traffic. The air was clouded with heavy exhaust smoke. Minibike riders seemed intent on committing suicide. Suddenly we turned into a walled compound where a huge ornate gate opened before us. The elaborate structure was left over from the days of British rule. We climbed out of our cars and looked around at a lavish botanical garden. It was dusk. The air smelled of burning incense. Torches were lit. Moments later, the peace was broken as a parade came our way, complete with traditionally garbed men and women dancing alongside an Indian-style marching band. Blessing us with incense smoke, women draped exquisite silk scarves around our necks. We were given an exotic blend of fruit juice that tasted divine. Like royalty, we were escorted to our private bungalows.

As a surprise for Billie I had arranged in advance to have hundreds of night-blooming tuberose flowers hung above our canopy bed. When we opened the room, the sight of the roses—the same beautiful flowers that had been used in our wedding leis in Hawaii—brought Billie to tears.

A few days later a large, painted elephant appeared for a photo session, marking the first time in Aerosmith history that the elephant in the room was a real elephant.

When it came time for the show, the moon was full and the crowd ecstatic. I worried whether the fans would actually know our music. I had no reason to worry. They sang along to the words of all our songs.

That night in ancient India, time stood still.

When we got home, more good news awaited us. The Aerosmith edition of Guitar Hero was out of development and would soon be in stores. It was great knowing that we were making our way into the world of high-tech video games. We were the first band to have a game of our own. It wound up selling more than any music game ever. As of April 2010, it had sold 3.2 million copies. In fact, it far outsold our last album, *Honkin' on Bobo*, and exposed Aerosmith to a whole new generation of fans. Guitar Hero had the same impact on our career as having a hit album.

Steven wanted more money than the rest of us because of his lip-synching. But his argument didn't hold water. The game was called Guitar Hero, not Vocal Hero. The guys who developed it even told him, "We don't need you to do that extra work. We have pros who can handle it." But Steven insisted. His ego was getting more and more out there. In the end, we ignored his demands for a bigger share and split the money five ways.

Our success with the new format should have had us jumping for joy. But Steven turned it into a nut bust for everyone involved—the band, our management, and the game's producers.

Triumph turned to exasperation—the Aerosmith paradigm continued.

CONFUSION AND PAIN

After a series of arthroscopic surgeries, in March 2008 I had a total knee replacement. I'll spare you the bloody details. But I will tell you that nine months later, my knee was not looking good and I was not feeling well. The pain hadn't diminished. I thought it was because I'd gone back on the road too early without giving my knee a chance to heal. Because it was swelling, I had the knee drained. When the results came in, the doctor put me in the hospital the very next day for emergency surgery. The knee had become infected and at any moment the infection could have spread through my body. We caught it just in time. But that meant going through the whole damn replacement thing and months of painful rehab all over again.

On the Aerosmith front, the band was reeling from more internal conflicts. The battle with Steven had entered a new and perilous stage. He was pissed about Guitar Hero. Even more pointedly, his relationship with Erin Brady radically changed the band dynamic.

I had first gotten to know Erin when she and Steven went out on a double date with Billie and me in Vegas. I was impressed. She seemed easygoing and good for Steven. We were happy for them. Then, while still working for Live Nation, Erin moved in with Steven. It was during that period that Steven called me and said he wanted to have a meeting with Erin, Billie, and me. Could he and Erin come over? Sure.

Still on crutches from his foot surgery, Steven arrived alone.

"Where's Erin?" I asked. "Is everything okay?"

"No, everything's not okay," he said. "I've gotta get her outta here. I've gotta get her on a plane tonight. She's fuckin' unbelievable, Joe. She's worse than Elyssa and Cyrinda put together."

I was shocked to hear that. Several days later, though, Erin was still at his house. At that point I knew the relationship was going to be a hell of a ride for Steven, but I never expected that the band would go on the ride with them.

The more involved Steven became with Erin, the more she became involved with his career. She got deep into Steven's ear and deep into our business. She became a divisive factor, reminding me of those disruptive influences that had injured the band back in the seventies. But even Elyssa never got into band business. She caused trouble, but she knew not to cross the line. In contrast, Steven gave Erin the run of his end of the business. He also reversed our policy of excluding wives and girlfriends from our meetings so that he could include Erin. She had much to say, especially about cost-saving measures that turned out to be inconsequential. After the initial one, Billie refused to attend any more band meetings that included girlfriends and wives. She thought the band meetings should be just that—band meetings.

Steven considered Erin an insider when it came to sales and marketing. It didn't matter to him that we had our own insider—our manager Howard Kaufman, who had more experience and expertise in the field than anyone.

Erin had Steven convinced that we were being cheated left and right by forces both known and unknown. She fed Steven's paranoia to the point where he separated himself from Howard and the band. He insisted on his own representation. He was drawn to Erin, not only for what he considered her superior business acumen, but also because she had a wild side. She liked to party. So it became Steven and Erin versus the world. Erin excited his ego and his already elevated sense of entitlement. She convinced Steven that now, more than ever, the band needed him far more than he needed the band. That made him almost impossible to work with.

In April 2009, I went to Cleveland to play with Jimmy Page and Jeff Beck at Beck's induction into the Rock and Roll Hall of Fame. We also jammed with new inductee Metallica. We decided to play "Train Kept a-Rollin'." Because it was a classic blues that had been handed down from generation to generation, I was surprised that Metallica didn't know it. We spent most of the sound check showing them the song. Even so, Metallica earned their spot in the Hall of Fame. I could see, though, that with Jimmy, Jeff, and me representing the old school, rock and roll was getting farther away from its roots.

Late that summer, I was itching to start work on a new Aerosmith album—that final record we owed Sony. I called Steven on a Sunday and said, "It's been too many years since we've written together. And when we have, the room's been too crowded. Let's get back to basics—you and me. You play drums, I'll play guitar. Let's try it for a couple of weeks and see what happens."

"You're right," he said after thinking about it for a few seconds. "I'll come over to the Boneyard tomorrow."

The next day he called at 3 P.M. "Sorry, Joe, I got involved in some phone calls. We'll start fresh tomorrow."

Tuesday came and went. No Steven. Finally he called and said, "I forgot I had a dentist's appointment."

He also blew me off on Wednesday and Thursday. When he finally showed up on Friday, we hit a good groove for three or four hours, putting some solid ideas down on tape. The new Aerosmith album was off to a good start.

"That was fun," said Steven with a happy gleam in his eye.

I agreed. "If we keep this up, in a few weeks we'll have a batch of stuff to work on," I said. "Can you come back Monday? I'll be down here working all weekend."

"All right," said Steven. "I'll call you tomorrow to confirm."

Saturday, no call.

On Sunday I left messages on all his phones but never heard back. Monday and Tuesday—no sign of Steven.

Then late Tuesday night came the news: I learned that over the weekend he had flown to England, where he was auditioning for Led Zeppelin. *What the fuck?*

Two weeks passed before I heard from him again. But I did hear from others and read in the papers that his Led Zep audition had been, according to Jimmy Page, "shambolic." Apparently his voice was in rough shape. What's more, he hadn't learned the lyrics to the songs. By all accounts it was a disaster.

By now, being treated this way by Steven was nothing new—just another window into our "partnership." But I wondered about Jimmy Page's side of the story. When Steven finally did mention it, he said, "Jimmy didn't have any material I liked. Besides, it would have been just for a few gigs." Yet several months later when I saw Jimmy and asked him about it, he said, "My first question to Steven was, 'What about Joe?' Steven's answer was, 'Joe doesn't want to work right now.'" Jimmy also said he hadn't even wanted to audition Steven but did so because he'd been hounded by his manager as well as his old roadie Henry Smith. When I spoke with Henry, he in turn said that it was Steven who had hounded him to get Jimmy to agree to the audition. Henry wasn't happy about being put in the middle. He also wasn't happy that Steven had missed the first day of the audition or that, when he finally did show, he had been embarrassingly unprepared.

You'd think that by now I'd have been used to Steven's lying. But I guess you never get used to being disrespected by someone who has been your bandmate for four decades.

I was pissed, not only because Steven was trying out for another band, but because he'd done it behind my back. If he had come to me and said, "Hey, Joe, I'm burned out on Aerosmith. I think I'm gonna try and sing with Zep. What do you think?" I wouldn't have been happy, but I would have given him credit for being up-front. Steven had pulled stunts like this before, yet this was a new low. The incredibly defensive version of the audition that he gave to the press was laughable.

The Zep fiasco had taken place in September. There were gigs that fall. We went on the road, where, in Aerosmith tradition, we buried the resentments. We brought in Brendan O'Brien to help kick-start our new album, but we never got very far. Steven wasn't really willing to work. Five years had passed since *Honkin' on Bobo*. Five years is a long time without a record.

Brendan started coming in every few weeks to help get the ball rolling. We began working up some of the rough riffs that would form the backbone of the new record. Steven either showed up late or not at all. He just wasn't into it. That was surprising because, like me, he was a big fan of Brendan's and loved how he had mixed *Get a Grip*. Despite everyone else's enthusiasm, though, Steven was emotionally distant. He was getting higher and higher, while I was suffering with knee and painkiller problems. Nonetheless, we moved ahead. The material was getting strong. I felt like I had a tank of high-test gas in a sixties muscle car. I was ready to rock. Plans were made to record in New York. The studio was booked, a schedule blocked out. But a week before we were due to start, Steven withdrew. He said he had pneumonia, which would require three weeks of rest. Scratch New York. Nothing could be done until the following summer.

Well, I had all this creative energy inside me. I had to bust loose. It had been four years since my *Joe Perry* album. So I did what I've always done. Rather than drive myself crazy waiting on Steven, I started making new music.

I had a ton of original material—music and lyrics—ready to go. Plus Billie had happened to catch a German vocalist named Hagen on You-Tube singing the hell out of "Dream On." The guy had a killer voice and I thought he might be just what I needed for my solo record and possible tour.

Billie and I went down to Atlanta to check out Brendan's studio. He and I cut some tracks with his session drummer and also played the clip of Hagen. "The kid has pipes," said Brendan. I asked Brendan if he could produce the record, but he had other commitments, so he did the next best thing—he let me borrow his great engineer Tom Tapely to cut the tracks back at the Boneyard for what would be my fifth solo record.

We weren't the only ones who were enthusiastic about Hagen's powerful voice. Howard Kaufman also liked the idea. He pointed out that, were I to tour behind the record, I'd need a vocalist to sing the heavyweight Aerosmith songs. So we flew Hagen in from Germany and, from day one, he was perfect for the Joe Perry Project.

I worked closely with my engineer Paul Santo, who's also an accomplished drummer and keyboard and guitar player. It was Paul who helped me put together one of my favorite tracks, "Wooden Ships," an instrumental dedicated to the memory of Les Paul, the great guitar master. Beyond his ability to play beautifully in any number of genres, he was the inventor of an archetypal guitar model that changed the nature of popular music—and certainly changed my own life.

I brought in my old friend and founding Project player David Hull as well as Ben Tileston, a drummer in my sons' band and a student of percussion at Boston University. We even had Boston's godfather of dada punk, Willie Alexander, playing killer keyboards. Hagen and I shared the vocals. In the past, I tended to write in keys that suited Steven. But now, in addition to writing for Hagen, I was also writing in keys that suited my voice.

Certain songs—like "Slingshot"—took me back to the very beginning, my boyhood love of rock and roll. It's a song, by the way, that I had to sing myself. It was that close to the heart. The entire record, *Have Guitar, Will Travel*, was close to my heart, a reconfirmation of my commitment to keep rocking and rolling as in days of old.

In what was largely a dark period for Aerosmith, a bright light came shining through my own life. I was asked to participate in the Rock Stars of Science project. The underwriter was the Geoffrey Beene Foundation, which donated 100 percent of the proceeds to cancer and Alzheimer's disease research. I was drawn to the project primarily because of my own father's struggles with cancer.

I was both impressed and humbled to meet with Drs. Francis Collins and Rudy Tanzi. Collins, an internationally respected geneticist, served as director of the National Institutes of Health, while Tanzi, a professor of neurology at Harvard, directs Massachusetts General Hospital's Genetics and Aging Research Unit. In addition to discovering the Alzheimer's gene,

Tanzi coauthored *Super Brain* with Deepak Chopra. Both physicians are true rock stars of science.

Beyond raising money for cancer research, the idea was to generate a media campaign that inspired kids to work in the sciences. The liberal arts have always been glamorous. As a musician, I've lived my life devoted to the arts. But I've always had a great passion for science. The fact that America is turning out scientists at an alarmingly slow rate does not bode well for our future. I was happy to join this effort to stress the creative joy of scientific research.

It turned out that Dr. Collins played guitar and Dr. Tanzi played keyboard. So during the period of my *Have Guitar, Will Travel* album, we jammed together and made a Rock Stars of Science video. We met up in Washington, D.C., where the three of us testified at a joint meeting of congressmen and senators on the need to fund research into cancer and Alzheimer's. At a post-hearing jam, we were asked to play unplugged. The keepers of the House were afraid that the loud rock buzz might smash the crystals in the chandeliers.

The campaign continued in New York two years later, when I was honored by the Memorial Sloan Kettering Cancer Center labs. I spent the day with doctors, scientists, and researchers, looking and learning. We did interviews that were posted on YouTube and created a Rock Stars of Science poster—"Rock Gods Don't Follow Orders"—that showed me and the scientists looking like we were about to take the stage. The New York Yankees got behind the effort and plastered the poster all over their stadium. Within a few weeks, the poster was all over the country.

Despite the lack of headway on a new album, Aerosmith forged ahead. Another summer meant another tour. This one, though, would be short-lived. It was also the tour that brought up the question that had never quite gone away: *How long can this band stay together?*

FALLING

Steven's moods grew increasingly erratic. He was either flying high or falling low. When we finally got it together to go on the Guitar Hero tour during the summer of 2009 with ZZ Top, he was increasingly out of it. Then, on a cloudy night in August in Sturgis, South Dakota, as we were about to break into "Love in an Elevator," the power went out. While the technicians worked to fix the problem, out of the corner of my eye I saw Steven lose his footing on a ramp and stumble off the stage. The bodyguards down there began to lift him up. I moved in to see if he was okay but he was already mobbed by security and stagehands hustling him backstage. None of us knew what was going on. Then he was put in an ambulance that roared off into the night.

What followed was a long and difficult separation between Steven and the band. We were extremely worried about him but also furious that he had played in such a fucked-up state. We had to end the tour. Even more worrisome was the thought that Steven could have fallen differently and wound up killing himself. He claimed that before the show he had only snorted Lunesta, a sleeping aid, which would have explained his wooziness.

Man, were we pissed! Steven had cost us a summer tour with one of the best bands in the country. We were all ZZ Top fans and had been working to get this lineup together for years. It was the big sold-out tour of the summer. Its cancellation meant that thousands of rock fans wouldn't get to see the show, not to mention the money it would cost both bands and their crews.

More importantly, we were concerned about Steven. I tried to call him but couldn't get through. A few days later his manager sent an e-mail to us and our management. He stated that Steven was being bombarded with phone calls and did not wish to speak to anyone. If we had any questions, we could address them to Steven's manager. Steven made it clear that he had spoken to everyone he wanted to speak to.

Well, he had not spoken to us, his bandmates. The silence continued for months. That was fucked because Steven made it impossible for us to check on his well-being and, more importantly, how his condition would affect the band's future, and our finances. He made it hard to have any sympathy for him. Later he'd bitterly complain that we had ignored him. That was only because he had insisted we stay away.

Later that year he did show up for a few gigs that we had to make up as a result of the cancellation. Mark Hudson came along as his companion/assistant. But Steven never spoke a word to any of us, and as soon as the shows were over, he disappeared.

In early November 2009, after a concert at the Abu Dhabi Grand Prix, I flew to England, where, on behalf of the band, I received an award for our classic album *Rocks*. Ironically, it was in *Classic Rock* magazine that I read an article headlined "Is Aerosmith Headed for a Permanent Vacation?" In a postshow interview back in Abu Dhabi, Tyler had discussed the future of Aerosmith: "I don't know what I'm doing yet," he said, "but it's definitely going to be something Steven Tyler, working on the brand of myself: Brand Tyler." He also spoke about taking two years off from Aerosmith.

He hadn't said a word to us. This was the first we learned that he intended to go out on his own. It reminded me of how he had handled the Zep auditions: a unilateral move done on the sly.

I figured I had two choices: I could wait with the other guys until Steven's "Brand Tyler" operation was over and hope he'd rejoin the band, or I could keep making music. I chose the latter. Fortunately, I had a new album, *Have Guitar, Will Travel*, which allowed me do some traveling and promotion. It was a way to stay creative and positive.

We received a letter from Steven's manager confirming that Steven was taking off two years to develop "Brand Tyler." Then came another letter from Steven, restating his decision to leave. He claimed that Brad, Tom, Joey, and I had been auditioning other singers to take his place. This wasn't true. On the other hand, if Steven had really decided to jump ship we'd be justified in coming up with a Plan B. So when the press approached me on the issue, I said that we were exploring our options. In fact, no other vocalist ever rehearsed with us or tried out for the gig. But then the press did what the press loves to do—they distorted the story and said Aerosmith was looking to replace Tyler. None of this was true.

I could tour behind *Have Guitar, Will Travel* because Aerosmith's slate was empty. There were great moments that year: When Johnny B. and I were on a promo trip on my bus, we were in Chicago for the weekend. By coincidence, Lollapalooza was happening Saturday, and Jimmy Buffett was playing Sunday. At Lollapalooza, before sixty thousand screaming fans, I sat in with Perry Farrell and Jane's Addiction on "Jane Says," and the next night I found myself jamming with Jimmy Buffett on "Margaritaville" in front of sixty thousand Parrotheads.

Howard Kaufman got behind the CD, released on my Roman Records and distributed by Mailboat, Buffett's label. We headlined at large rock clubs and at several arenas opened for Mötley Crüe. The experience of playing with my own band again felt great. No backstage drama or yelling. In its place were good vibes and lots of laughs. Just play and give it all you got. There were no politics, no backstage tension, no wondering if there was going to be a freak-out because the toilet paper was the wrong color. Granted, I was the boss. But top of my list was finding guys who could really tear it up, get along, and have fun making music together. Whether playing before a hundred or a hundred thousand, it was a blast, reminding me of the bands I had formed in the sixties before Aerosmith.

The highlight was opening for Paul Rodgers and Bad Company during their reunion tour of the UK. I'd met Paul over the years and knew that, like Aerosmith, his band had gone through heavy changes. On this tour, though, there were no problems. Paul had taken great care of his voice, treating it like the precious instrument that it is. He belted out those great songs with more power than ever. All the fans—including me—were thrilled to be seeing Bad Company in its original glory.

As the Project prepared to leave for the UK, we played Irving Plaza in New York. During the encore break, much to my surprise, Billie came into the dressing room and said, "Steven's here," just as Steven, Mark Hudson, and entourage walked through the door. Tyler had timed it so he'd arrive backstage during the break. Having just completed a steamroller set, we were exhausted.

"I want to sing 'Walk This Way,'" said Steven coldly. I could see that he was not in good shape. He made it plain that he had not come to discuss reconciliation. He simply demanded to sing the song as my encore.

"Fine," I said, "but you'll have to sing it as a duet with Hagen."

He kept saying he wanted to sing alone, but when I made it clear that wasn't going to happen, he agreed. Onstage, he sang over Hagen's lines anyway. Making matters more confusing, he also announced to the audience that rumors of his quitting Aerosmith were bullshit. He said that he was not leaving the band. All fine and good, but I knew the truth. Over and again he'd made it clear that he *was* leaving. At the same time, at the end of this great show I wasn't about to comment. Let Steven say whatever he wants to say. After he had his say, he walked offstage and left the building— no goodbye, no thanks for letting him sit in, no anything.

After the show, I saw a clip on YouTube of Tyler and his crew leaving the club. Mark Hudson was shouting at reporters and cameramen on the street, "Did you hear what went on in there? Does that sound like Steven is leaving the band?"

Mark had worked himself up into a frenzy over an announcement that apparently he and Steven had planned.

This was a dark period for Steven. He was back on heavy drugs. Fortunately, at the start of 2010 he checked into the Betty Ford Center for rehab, where he remained for three months. When he got out, still another uneasy peace between Steven and the band was forged. He was angry with us for supposedly looking for a new lead singer. Although he had his own management separate from the band, he wanted back in. Fine. But at this point we couldn't trust him. We decided that he'd have to sign a contract to do forty gigs a year for the next three years. He agreed.

The tour, known as Cocked, Locked and Ready to Rock, was tense. Once again, we traveled the world. Our fans embraced us just as our fans always have. But the underlying discord—the friction between Steven and the band—was palpable.

In Wantaugh, New York, as Steven was swinging his mic stand around, it caught the side of my head. I knew it was an accident, but it was a clear example of how Steven, disregarding everyone else, feels that it's his stage. I've certainly bumped him by accident enough times over the years, but never with the potential damage that can come from a twenty-pound metal mic stand crashing into your head.

In Toronto, I was standing at the edge of the stage. The spotlight was in my eyes, blinding me to the boxes and wires below. Since time immemorial, Steven has had the habit of cozying up to Tom, Brad, and me as we're playing. Sometimes he'll put his arm around us or bump into us. Since we're concentrating on our instruments, this can catch us off guard. But because we know the audience thinks that Steven is acting out of exuberance or spontaneous affection, we give him a lot of leeway. For my part, I don't like it, especially when I'm at the edge of the stage. So when he bumped into me in Toronto, nearly knocking me down into the pit, I got pissed.

I was furious, my heart pounding in my chest. I'd asked him innumerable times not to bump into me from my blind side—whether he thought it was cool or not. As I walked back from the edge of the stage, I gave him a slight hip check, never thinking it would throw him off-balance. I just wanted to give him a taste of his own medicine. He wavered a little, then tipped over the side of the stage, into the waiting arms of a security guard. As I reached down to help him back up, he tried to pull me into the audience. I resisted. When he was finally back onstage, I said, "Sorry you fell, but don't bump me from behind—ever again." After that, the tour wound its way around the world without further incident.

When we returned to L.A., it was time to finally start the much-postponed Aerosmith album that we owed Sony. In a perfect world, that should have been be no problem. But in the world of Aerosmith, there are nothing *but* problems. And this new one turned out to be a motherfucker.

 # IDOL

We were in L.A. when the Sony execs came out to meet with Steven and me about the long-delayed new album. First they met with Steven, then with me. The enthusiasm was high. Our commitment was absolute. With the approval of Joey, Brad, and Tom, Steven and I asked Jack Douglas—the greatest of all Aerosmith producers—to come on board.

"I can't wait to get started," said Steven. "It's gonna be the bomb, and not only that, this one's gonna be delivered on time."

We were all grateful that Steven was into it 100 percent.

A day or so later I saw Randy Jackson at our gig. That wasn't unusual since celebrities are often at our shows in L.A. and Vegas. But that same night there were rumors that Steven has been chosen as a judge on *American Idol*. It was hard for me to believe this would happen without his saying something to the band. I dismissed the rumors—until the story went viral on the Internet.

Up until then the band had been playing great and all of us getting along. There were the usual ups and downs, but things were generally smooth.

The next day we played Vegas. I went to Steven's dressing room and asked his entourage to clear out. He knew that meant I needed to talk heart-to-heart. When we were alone and seated on the couch, I asked about the *Idol* business. What was the story?

"I couldn't turn down the offer," he said. "If I had told you guys about it, the band would have tried to talk me out of it."

"That's not true. It's an opportunity for you. But this was obviously something you had been planning for a while. Yet not one fuckin' word to us. No thought on your part how this might impact the band."

"I knew that the band would be jealous."

"Nobody's jealous. It's not about jealousy. It's about trust. Between your talk of Brand Tyler and taking off two years and now this *Idol* thing, how the hell can we trust you?"

He had no good answer.

"We see this is a once-in-a-lifetime deal for you," I said. "And that's great. But what's not great is how you went about doing it without the least respect for us. You didn't respect the fact that what you do impacts our lives and the lives of our families. Every time I've done anything on the side that could affect the band, I've let everyone know way ahead of time. I expect the same of you."

"It just came up. It was sudden."

"Don't bullshit me, Steven, I know goddamn well that something like this has been in the planning stages for weeks. That's when you could have let us known what you were considering. Instead you cut us out and we learn about it the same time as the rest of the country. Man, that's not only disrespectful, that's fuckin' insulting."

There was more I wanted to say. I wanted to say that it took all these long years of hard work on the part of the band to help Steven get to the point where he could attract such an offer. I wanted to say that, rather than disregard us, he ought to show us some gratitude. But I'd said enough. I stayed silent and just shook my head in disbelief. I knew by now my feelings and sense of propriety would have been met by more bullshit.

I thought to myself: *This is Steven. This has always been Steven.* Steve

Chatoff's words were ringing in my ears: "Steven will never change." But after forty years, I saw he was getting worse.

At this point we had no idea how many years Steven would be away from the band—or whether he wanted to be with the band at all.

Beyond that, there were the Sony execs who had learned about *Idol* the same time as the rest of us. They had just been to L.A., where Steven acted like his first priority was the new record. Now this. They were disheartened and understandably vexed.

One of the execs asked me, "How can we trust this guy?"

I didn't have a good answer.

Months passed before we knew what was happening. As usual, Steven kept us in the dark. But when talks finally did begin, it was clear that he did not want to leave the band. He also agreed to start work on the long-postponed album.

Once again, in spite of everything, Aerosmith, the band that could survive anything, was still intact, a major miracle in the history of embattled bands playing this thing called rock and roll.

ANOTHER DIMENSION

Before we started the new album, I realized that something else was long overdue: I had to address my dependence on pain pills. I still had not reverted to hard drugs or alcohol. My behavior wasn't unruly or out of control. But I knew I was indulging. The series of operations over the past five years had allowed me legitimate access to prescription drugs that I took for legitimate reasons. As time went on, though, the line between legitimate and indulgent continued to blur. For a long time, Billie and I had been talking about my going into rehab. Now I knew it was time.

Steven gave Billie the number of his contact at the Betty Ford Center in Rancho Mirage, California. I called and we spoke about my entering their program. I made arrangements to fly there from our farmhouse in Vermont. My plan was to go alone. I didn't feel the need to have my hand held.

"Don't fly commercially," said Steven when he learned what I was doing. "I'll rent a private plane and I'll take you there myself."

"Thanks, man," I said, "but there's no need for that kind of extravagance."

Steven was insistent. He wanted to accompany me to the center and introduce me to his therapist friends who had helped him some months before. He said he'd call me with the details. When I didn't hear from him that weekend, I figured he'd changed his mind. Just as well. As I was confirming my commercial flight, he called to say that he had rented a plane. He couldn't wait, in his words, "to hook up my brother with my people at Betty Ford." It seemed like he had turned my decision to go to rehab into a personal crusade, as though it were his idea. It started feeling like another opportunity for him to take credit for something he hadn't done. The bottom line, though, was that I just wanted to get healthy. When he kept insisting on flying me out in a private plane, I took him up on his offer.

We arrived in Rancho Mirage and were driven to the center, where Steven said goodbye, hugged me, and wished me luck. I knew that he took pride in walking his brother through the door, but I sensed another agenda. Later I learned that he was chairing a big meeting that night at Betty Ford to celebrate his months of sobriety—something he had never mentioned to me. Even his lawyer and agent came out to hear him speak that night. He had led me to believe that he was making the trip for me and me alone.

The kicker was that, while I was out there, my accountant called and said she'd just received a bill for the private jet—sixty thousand dollars. I hit the ceiling. I was the one who'd been perfectly happy to travel commercially; it was Steven who had insisted on flying me out on a private plane. Of all the screwed-up things Steven had done, this was among the screwiest. I told the accountant to send Steven the bill. The bill came back to me a few more times until Steven got the idea that I was not paying it under any circumstances.

During the South America tour of 2011, Aerosmith was at an all-time high, the bandmates getting along as we sold out huge arenas. Yet even in the midst of this period of goodwill, the underlying tensions came out.

Steven was heard telling the promoter that the only reason he was touring was because the band—not he—needed the money. He said that he made his from *American Idol*. On the road he had to split his money five ways, and he didn't like it.

His insatiable ego was even more evident when *60 Minutes* came to call. In his interview, Steven implied that he alone had carried the band to greatness, complaining that the rest of us were riding on his coattails. When I heard that statement, I thought, *That ungrateful fuck. God may have blessed him with a million-dollar voice, but when I think of the thirty-five years that the five of us worked together—and this is what he's got to say?—my respect for him as a human being drops to almost nothing.*

There also were insightful statements from my bandmates, who said that my opinion of Steven was far more important to him than his opinion of Joe Perry was to me. Surprising me, Tom Hamilton said, "Joe defines cool. Joe is the rock star of the band." This, though, was one of the various interviews that the show placed on their website, leaving the juicier bits in the segments that were aired.

The band watched Steven's bullshit, knowing he had spoken his truth and we had spoken ours. For good or bad, the *60 Minutes* piece showed the true band dynamic.

Home from the tour, I was asked to play and sing on Amnesty International's fiftieth-anniversary CD dedicated to the songs of Bob Dylan. I was honored to sing "Man of Peace" and pleased when they made a video of my performance and asked me to sing the song on *The Tonight Show with Jay Leno*. I was also honored to sing the song at Muhammad Ali's televised seventieth birthday party in Vegas, a charity event for the Cleveland Clinic. I was thrilled to shake the champ's hand. Even in a wheelchair he appeared larger than life. When we locked eyes, I saw a powerful gleam that spoke of great determination and indomitable strength. His mobility may have been crippled by Parkinson's, but nothing could stop that fighting spirit.

At long last the band settled down to turn our attention to our next record, *Music from Another Dimension!*, a much-belabored album with an infinite number of stops and starts. You could say we'd been working on it off and on since the aftermath of *Just Push Play*. Given that Steven was taping *Idol* in Hollywood, we decided to finish the tracks we had recorded at our Vindaloo studio the summer before the Japan, South America, and Australia tour. Jack Douglas was amenable and, as always, proceeded according to his first rule in producing Aerosmith—get the boys playing together. That did my heart good and gave me hope that we'd be able to turn out an exciting record even in our sixties.

One of the most meaningful songs I wrote was "Freedom Fighter," which I wound up singing on the record. When I got ready to cut the track, I'd just gotten off the road and didn't have all my studio guitars. Around this time I met Johnny Depp. He'd known Jack Douglas for years. Jack had invited Johnny and his buddy Bruce Witkin down to the studio and, fortunately for us, he was an Aerosmith fan. Later on, Johnny invited me to his studio, where he lent me a guitar. Rooted in our common love of guitar rock and blues, we became fast friends. You can hear Johnny and Bruce singing background on "Freedom Fighter."

In 2012, Los Angeles, as always, turned out to be a hot spot for musical creativity. Great guitarists, innovative guitar makers, and edgy new equipment were everywhere. I used an Epiphone, a semi-hollow-body guitar with a short-scale neck that gave the strings a tighter, more percussive sound. You hear that sound on "Legendary Child," a track Steven and I worked up with our friend Jim Vallance from Vancouver. Combining the old with the new, I played into a '50s Fender Bandmaster, an old three-speaker amp that's one of my studio basics. I'm also partial to going back to the by-now ancient technique of avoiding an amp altogether by plugging the guitar directly into the board. Many of the new amps diminish the sound of the foot pedals. Plug in directly and you get a fuller sonic feel.

Another song I wrote alone, "Oh Yeah," was a riff that had been kicking around my head for years. It was on my B list. But Steven loved the lyrics and kept pushing it to the A list. I really wanted to sing it, but Billie had an idea.

"If Steven likes it so much, why not let him sing it?" she said. "Or at least do it as a duet."

She was right. With Steven's vocals, "Oh Yeah" turned into an Aerosmith song strong enough to be included in our live show.

"Oasis in the Night" was my Valentine's Day present to Billie. "Too many talking heads," I wrote, "what was it that they said / When we're apart my days are dark / When I'm with you I'm in the light / You're my oasis in the night."

"Something" was another song I composed and sang alone. "There's something that tells me that you got everything you need," I wrote, "but all you want is more." It's a slow, bluesy rock tongue-in-cheek lament about my deep dissatisfaction about our past managers. I urged Steven to play drums on it, and he played it perfectly ragged, giving the song an edge unique to his percussive instincts. Every measure felt like it was going to collapse, only to be brought back with twice the power.

There are two strong Steven-Joe songs—"Luv XXX" and "Out Go the Lights"—and two superb songs for which Tom Hamilton wrote both music and lyrics: "Tell Me" and "Up on the Mountain." Brad nailed some rockers, the feel of which hadn't been there since "Kings and Queens" from *Draw the Line* back in the seventies. I thought the ballads were weak, with the exception of Diane Warren's "We All Fall Down." But those were the songs that Steven wanted out there and, in the spirit of the record, we put them on. You never know.

For his part, Steven busted his ass on this project. He'd come to the studio after a full day at *Idol* and spend another eight hours recording. Whether tracking, overdubbing, or mixing, he didn't miss a single session.

There were videos—my favorite a live concert performance at the Hollywood Bowl of "Train Kept a-Rollin'" with Johnny Depp rocking out on guitar—and cool features in the CD package itself, the best being a sketch made by Slash when he was in high school study hall: his pen-and-ink drawing of Aerosmith in 1982.

Our fans received *Music from Another Dimension!* enthusiastically, sensing that we had struck the right balance between hard-core rock and beautiful ballads. I also loved the fact that everyone in the band threw in his own ideas. *Dimension* came as close to a classic Aerosmith album as we had made in years.

The thinking was that because Steven was a high-profile presence in the pop landscape on *Idol*, the band would benefit. That might have happened during the first season, when he was wacky, funny, and unpredictable. He was on. But unfortunately fame on a show like *Idol* doesn't translate into ticket sales or turn songs into hits.

During the second season, things got tired and went flat. There were rumors he was not invited back for a third season. That was fine with me. His presence on the show, though, did dramatically widen Aerosmith's reach while giving Steven more of what he really craves: fame. From the start, Steven made no bones about it. More than money, more than being the best songwriter—a skill at which he's no slouch—fame is his driving force.

Analyzing the relationship between *Idol* and overall Aerosmith income, we saw an uptick of a couple hundred percent on two Aerosmith songs for a very short period of time. We were all hoping this exposure would give us another bump—like *Armageddon* or Guitar Hero—but it didn't work out that way. I felt that most of the *American Idol* watchers weren't the kind of Aerosmith fans who would come to our shows and buy our records. At the same time, hard-core Aerosmith fans might have seen our brand as somewhat tarnished by Steven's association with the show.

At least Steven had a great time on the show and some of his dreams came true. We were all happy for him because we knew how much it meant to him to have been a judge on *American Idol*. But his excitement and willingness to do a Burger King commercial only confirmed what I thought was the truth. Fame, not an allegiance to writing music or the tradition of carrying on the blues, was and is his driving force.

When the Songwriters Hall of Fame inducted both Steven and me in a formal ceremony in New York in 2013, it was an unexpected thrill. It was great seeing nonperforming songwriters get a turn in the spotlight. It was also great to be honored with writer/performers like Elton John, Bernie Taupin, Mick Jones, Lou Gramm, and J. D. Souther.

But even though Steven and I were inducted as partners, I felt that a piece was missing. While it's true that the majority of Aerosmith hits were written by me and him (and an occasional third party), those hits would not have been hits had they not been played by Tom, Brad, and Joey, who also toured tirelessly to promote them.

Unlike the legendary team of Jerry Leiber and Mike Stoller, who conscientiously guarded their partnership and almost never wrote with others, when it came to Aerosmith material, Steven wrote with whomever he liked whenever he liked. He was never a partner I could count on. As much as he wanted our writing relationship to mirror Mick and Keith's, he seems to have missed the trust part.

I continued to push ahead. I did sound track work for movies, including *G.I. Joe: Retaliation* with Bruce Willis. Thanks to Phil Conserva, I wrote some music for *CSI: Crime Scene Investigation* and, thanks to Randy Spendlove and John Debney, contributed to Tyler Perry's *Madea's Witness Protection*. I also did a cameo playing myself in *Glory Days*, a film shot while we were in Singapore.

Meanwhile, Aerosmith played on. We continued to tour the world. Few other bands of our era had their original members—alive, kicking, and still together. Few other bands enjoyed the kind of fan loyalty of our always faithful Blue Army—not to mention a whole new generation of teenagers. Scarred and damaged, angry and resentful, issues misunderstood and issues unresolved, we kept working—for the music, for the fans, for the money. We did it out of habit, we did it with ambivalence, but mainly we did it because our passion for the music drove us. Today that passion still makes us feel like eighteen-year-olds.

But mostly it's seeing a fan wrap his or her arms around one of us and hearing words like *Your music got me through rehab. . . . Your music kept me afloat. . . . Your music saved my life.* That's strong stuff. Steven's antics, my arrogance, all the stuff that went on with the other guys—it all pales against the knowledge that long ago this band became something bigger than all of us.

And then there are those moments that surprise even us. A huge example was Japan.

In March 2011, a few weeks before we arrived, the country was hit by one of the worst natural disasters in its history: a massive earthquake and tsunami that resulted in a catastrophic nuclear meltdown. For reasons of safety, we were told to cancel our tour. For reasons of obstinacy—and plain devotion to our Japanese audience—we refused. We went over and played a series of sold-out concerts that were among the most emotional of our career. Fortunately, our video director, Casey Patrick Tebo, filmed the concerts and interviewed many of the fans in attendance. With tears streaming from their faces, they spoke about what it meant for us to have shown up for them at a time when strength was desperately needed.

The DVD documentary, *Rock for the Rising Sun*, includes an interview with Nobu San, one of our most dedicated and generous fans. He has been to some two hundred Aerosmith concerts the world over, sometimes bringing his whole family. When he heard we were coming back in 2013 to promote the DVD in Japan, he offered us three hundred thousand dollars to do five songs he had never heard us play live. In the past, we'd taken suggestions from fans about songs to add to our playlist, yet this was an entirely different request. We quickly decided to honor Nobu San's request but donate the money to the Japanese Red Cross tsunami relief fund—a great result for everyone.

When terrorists bombed Boston in 2013, two of our sons lived within miles of the explosion and manhunt. That really brought it home. And when Aerosmith played the Boston Strong concert to benefit the victims, once again I felt how rock and roll, born in the blues and rooted in rebellion, can comfort, strengthen, and inspire people to embrace hope over fear. In the face of a violent world, trepidation is understandable. Yet rock and roll—at least Aerosmith's brand of rock and roll—stares trepidation in the face and says, "Fuck fear. We came to play!"

VERMONT IN THE SUMMER

Vermont winters are under-rated. They can be so brutal that when Nobel Prize winner Aleksandr Solzhenitsyn was expelled from the Soviet Union he came to live in Cavendish because it made him feel at home. Cavendish is only twenty-five miles down the road from our farmhouse, a refuge from the world. Winter, fall, spring, or summer, I always feel at home in Vermont. It brings me back to the elements I love best. With its many lakes and mountains, it brings me back to the water and woods and the beginnings of my life on this troubled planet. Living in Vermont is like living in a country apart from time.

A year ago I was sitting on a hillside with hundreds of acres of wilderness behind me. Before me I saw the quaint farmhouses and huge barns built centuries ago that belonged to my neighbors. As I looked over the landscape, my black-powder Kentucky long rifle rested on my lap, I heard the chugging of an old car engine far in the distance. All I could see was a black dot making its way up the dirt road. As it came into view, I realized it was a friend driving his rebuilt Model T Ford. He noticed me on the hill and we waved to each other. It dawned on me that this was a scene that could have taken place a century ago. I got goose bumps. I thought to myself, *I love this setting. I love this moment. I was born in the wrong time.*

Now another year has passed and I'm back in Vermont for another summer, another chance to step away from the noise of modern existence and look inside my mind and life. I take a deep breath and feel grateful for the fact that, here in Vermont, I am with my entire family. All my sons are here with their wives, girlfriends, and children. Billie is here. Both our mothers are here. And so is my sister, Anne. These are the people I love and care for most deeply. To see the various generations smiling, laughing, and loving with such ease makes all the struggles worth it.

I leave the family at the farmhouse to take a late-afternoon walk into the wilderness. This is the time of day when the animals start coming out. Maybe I'll be lucky enough to see a bobcat. The fragrance of the pine forest is overwhelming. The smell is pungent, fresh, and strong. The air is crisp and exhilarating. An early-morning rain has washed the sky clean. The sky is cloudless, a bright and luminous blue. I spot deer behind the ancient trees. I keep walking, moving up a hill, moving through what feels like an eternal moment.

There are philosophers who claim that we are always in an eternal moment. The past, they say, is regret, and the future is fear. Now is eternal. Yet even in the now we look back with wonder. And one of the most amazing things I'm now remembering is something that happened not long ago when, in spite of a lifetime of conflicts, Aerosmith stood tall and united in front of 1325 Commonwealth, the Boston apartment building where, forty-two years earlier, five scruffy kids came together to form a rock-and-roll band. What were the chances of us making it? A hundred to one? Millions to one?

The area around Commonwealth had been closed off to traffic. Forty thousand fans had come to hear us give a street concert and see the unveiling of a plaque that acknowledged the historical significance of this spot. High-ranking politicians were in attendance as well as celebrities like Tom Brady. The New England Patriots cheerleaders were cheerleading. It was a mad celebration for a mad band that had, despite it all, survived. It was a once-in-a-lifetime moment.

I looked at the crowd and then turned to look at the second-floor bedroom that had been my room forty years ago. What the hell would I have thought if, at age twenty, I had been in that window looking at the sixty-two-year-old Joe Perry? Would that young kid—so full of fire—even recognize the rock and roller who had been to hell and back?

Those heady thoughts of Commonwealth recede as I walk deeper into the woods. I think of Steven and our struggles. I think of the countless times we were furious with each other. I also think of the times we have walked through the woods together like brothers. I think of his great volatility and his even greater talent. I think of him as one of the world's greatest rock-and-roll singers. I think of the time when he was on *American Idol* and I surprised him by coming on and playing "Happy Birthday" for him. Afterward, I went over to the judges' podium and gave him a hug. It wasn't planned. It came from the heart. He is my brother. Even though we've drifted apart, there's that guy in there that I still love. I have great love for Tom, Joey, and Brad—brothers all. I am deeply grateful to all of them.

Recently we played Australia for the first time in twenty-two years. We put on shows in places where we've never appeared before—Singapore, the Philippines, and New Zealand. At this late date, it's great to still be expanding our audience. To be touching music fans the world over in a positive way continues to be—along with the love of my family—the great blessing in my life.

I've been walking for a good hour. When I reach the top of this hill, I stop to look at the mountains and the green valley below. It stretches for miles. It's absolutely breathtaking. I think back on a lifetime in rock. Have the struggles been worth it? The music has made it all worth it. And I know there's still music to come. As long as there is breath inside me, I will make music. Music is the ongoing miracle that gives my life meaning. Music inspired me as a child; music changed me, directed me, and set me on the path that has led me to this moment.

I have no idea what the coming years might hold, but for now everything is calm. The sky is turning pink. The distant mountains are bathed in a mystical purple glow.

The sun will soon set.

Night will come.

And tomorrow, a new day.

Suited up in action-capture gear for the Guitar Hero game.

Chuck Berry and me backstage at an Aerosmith concert in St. Louis. I wouldn't be playing guitar if it wasn't for this man.

Billie had our bus painted with Guitar Hero artwork as a surprise for me before a tour. I guess she got me back for me putting her picture on my guitar.

Joe Perry Project on tour in Edmonton, Canada, playing songs from my fifth solo album, *Have Guitar, Will Travel*. Left to right: David Hull on bass, Hagen Grohe sharing vocals, drummer Marty Richards, and me.

Standing next to our bus driver of twelve years, Mark Langley. Some Virginia State Troopers helped us on the way to a gig in a traffic jam.

In the Boneyard Studio at my house in Massachusetts, listening to playbacks for *Just Push Play*. John Kalodner is known for only dressing in white. We thought he would get a kick out of us dressing like him.

Steven and me relaxing after shooting an ESPN video outside of the Boneyard.

The Joe Perry Project band I put together to promote my fourth solo album, *Joe Perry*. The song "Mercy" from that album was nominated for a Grammy. Left to right: Charlie Drayton, Paul Caruso, Audley Freed, and me.

Ross Halfin trying to get us to settle down to get the next picture.

And he got it!

Me and my road manager, as well as best friend, coadventurer, and hockey freak, John Bionelli.

The band on a break, hanging in the Avant Garden during the recording of *Just Push Play* in the Boneyard.

On stage with my favorite guitar.

Billie and me taking part in Project Aware's cleanup of the Gulf of Mexico on the Sun Coast of Florida.

This was when my knee was in such bad shape I could not bend it and caused me constant pain during the shows. I had to change how I moved on and off stage to accommodate it.

Right: Dr. Francis Collins, the Director of National Health and one of the "Rock Stars of Science," talking with me about the video we were making to play in front of Congress as a fund-raiser for cancer and Alzheimer's research. *Below:* First Rock Stars of Science campaign poster in JFK in NYC, with Dr. Rudi Tanzi to the left, me, and Dr. Francis Collins, Director of National Health.

Me with the Sierra Leone's Refugee All Stars at the Woodstock Vermont Arts Festival.

At the Rock and Roll Hall of Fame induction ceremony for Metallica, among others. One of the others is sitting at the table with me and the great Jimmy Page—the mighty Jeff Beck. A night I will never forget.

Me asking Chuck's keyboard player what key we're in.

Boys' day out at Gillette Stadium to cheer on the home team, the New England Patriots. Left to right: Roman, Aaron, Jonathan Kraft, me, Robert Kraft, Tony, and Adrian.

John Bionelli is friends with one of the Bruins players who brought the Stanley Cup they won in the 2010–11 season to the band's studio.

The famous Johnny Johnson layin' it down during the *Honkin' on Bobo* sessions while Jack Douglas and I soak it up.

Brad and me having a laugh at a show.

Warming up the Theramin at sound check with Trace Foster, my guitar technician.

Aerosmith in South America. Steven on the left and me on the right.

Practicing throwing rock shapes while wearing seven-inch heels. Broken lamps, chairs, and black and blue marks attest that it ain't as easy as it looks.

Rock and roll history in the making. I am the only person to have jammed with Kiss. I had a great time.

On the set of *Sons of Guns*. We are getting ready to test-fire my cannon, which they had just refurbished.

It only took three shots to nail the sailboat, thanks to *Sons of Guns'* Will Hayden, Stephanie, Chris Ford, and crew. It was another great day.

Dr. Rudi Tanzi and me at a rehearsal for the Jay Leno show, where we performed "Man of Peace" off the Amnesty International CD.

Me and Trace working on a demo for "Freedom Fighter" in a villa at the Sunset Marquis.

Alice and me backstage at a festival in Kristiansand, Norway.

A great day visiting the Sea Shepherds'
home base in Australia.

In the backyard in Vermont, cutting loose. Left to right in back: Aaron, Tony, my sister Anne, Roman, and Adrian. Left to right in front: Austin, Billie, me, Mamaw Hobson, Genevieve, and Anne. My mother was with us in spirit; she was too ill to make the sitting.

Johnny Winter and me on his bus. I'm holding the guitar
I saw him play back in 1969.

Hanging out in my dressing room with my buddies. In the front, left to right: me, Bruce Witkin, and Johnny Depp. In the back, Caroline Kaufman, Billie, and Aerosmith's manager Howard Kaufman, the smartest man in the business, my really good friend, and mentor.

Johnny jamming with Aerosmith onstage at the Staples Center in LA. We played "Train Kept A-Rollin'" and it sounded great. The man can play.

Where Aerosmith began. Forty years later, I still can't believe it.

Taken the day 1325 was made a Boston landmark.

ACKNOWLEDGMENTS

When I was eight or nine I had a brother named David who died when he was a couple days old. I've always had this feeling I was supposed to have a brother. I remember much sadness at the time, but after that, nothing was really said about it. I can't help but wonder if that loss doesn't play a part in my relationship with Steven Tyler. We'll never know, but it's these kinds of memories that spring up when you write a book like this. If the book was going to be worth doing, it meant digging down, a lot deeper than I thought I would have to. When Billie suggested that maybe it was time to think about writing it, I said yeah . . . it just felt like the right time.

Much thanks goes to David Vigliano, our agent, whom we met during the writing of *Walk This Way*. He and Billie remained friends all these years, and he was invaluable from the start with advice, helping us get our deal with Simon & Schuster, and finding David Ritz, who turned out to not only be a great partner in writing the book but also became a great friend and fellow musicologist.

I want to thank Billie, my wife, lover, and soul mate, for her help with my book—organizing, following up, and the patience it took, and for having lived hand-in-hand with me over these last thirty years. Without the fates bringing us together, I probably wouldn't be here to tell this story, or gotten back with Aerosmith.

ACKNOWLEDGMENTS

Thanks to everyone at Simon & Schuster: Jonathan Karp, Cary Gold-stein, Erin Reback, Richard Rhorer, Anne Tate Pearce, Dana Trocker, Ed Winstead, and the rest of the team there were great to work with, and they pretty much gave me the run of the joint. And a very special thanks to my editor, Jofie Ferrari-Adler, whose advice, experience, and guidance proved to be invaluable in helping me through the final process of delivering my book which was, up until now, foreign to me.

I've got to thank all the friends who helped me on the journey this book is about, especially my four comrades, bonded together through thick and thin, spanning a forty-year-plus journey none of us counted on, by the power of the music on this undefinable but inevitable leap of faith: Tom Hamilton, Joey Kramer, Brad Whitford, and Steven Tyler. And, on the other side of the footlights, the fans, our Blue Army, who were incredible when it came to supporting the band. I count myself one of you, and have all these years.

Thank you to Howard Kaufman and Trudy Green for doing such a great job managing Aerosmith all these years, and for helping me with my side projects. I only wish I had met the two of you years earlier. Thanks so much.

Thanks to John Bionelli, my true friend who has helped watch out for me and my family's well-being all these years. Also for all of the work in assembling the appendix in *Rocks*. I can't say enough to thank you, my man.

And much thanks to Johnny Depp. We became friends three years ago, but it's not the length of time you know a person, it's the experiences you share in that time. It started over our mutual love of the blues and guitars, and when you heard I was looking for a place to focus on this project in L.A., you generously gave us the use of a space, an incredibly calm and neutral space, where Billie and I could focus with Mr. Ritz. And thanks to Bruce Witkin, your longtime buddy and now my close friend as well, for the support, and for engineering my reading of the audiobook in your studio. Both you guys gave a lot of support, sometimes in ways you'll never know.

But the people who I want to thank the most for their love, support, and understanding are our sons Aaron, Adrian, Tony, and Roman. Alongside your mom, bringing you guys up was an experience second to none.

I love all of you. You make it all worth it. This book is the background, as close as I can get it, to the adventure of that experience.

And to Anne, my loving sister from the earliest days playing on Lake Sunapee to being by our mother's side when she passed last autumn and I couldn't be there. You have done more to help me indirectly on this journey than you will ever know. Thanks for being my "first" fan, Annie! I love you.

When I decided to write this book, I had no idea what it would take out of me. Yeah, it was cathartic, and I learned a lot more about myself, human nature, and life in general, but mostly I got a chance to get down on paper, as close as I could, what turned out to be an adventure I absolutely had no idea was in store for me.

Billie, again, thanks so much. David, it was incredible working with you. All best from the depths of my heart and soul to you all.

APPENDIX

GUITAR TECH INSIDE INFO
by John Bionelli

Back in 1975, when Aerosmith went out on their first big tours, arena rock was in its infancy. Sure, there were British groups like the Beatles, the Rolling Stones, the Who, and Led Zeppelin all doing it, but for American bands coming out of the clubs and playing these massive venues it was still pretty new. To accomplish this mighty task, you had to assemble a crew of loyal soldiers who took pride in what they were doing and could endure the daily rigors of an entire tour, sharing a beat-up van with nine other fellow road soldiers, traveling from city to city, night after night. These crew guys had names like Rabbit, Nitebob, Henry the Horse, and Mad Dog. Since this is Joe's book, I thought it would be cool to visit with the guys who helped make Joe's sound a reality. After talking to his guitar techs I discovered a common thread, which was how loyal they were to Joe and how loyal Joe was and is to them.

I spoke to Rabbit first. Rabbit (real name: Dick Hansen) got his nickname from another crew member who found out Dick was a vegetarian. He came aboard in 1975 and started out working for Aerosmith's sound company. He took care of the band's monitors at first and then switched over to being Joe's guitar tech, a position he would hold for two years, traveling the globe with the band. Rabbit's job was pretty straightforward back then. He had to uncase Joe's thirteen guitars and set up his back line (amps and speakers). While this sounds like a fairly simple job, wiring the rig to Joe's exact specifications could take hours. Guitar techs weren't required to know how to play guitar as 99 percent of them do today; they just had to make sure the guitarist's rig was set up the exact way he wanted it every night. Joe was constantly changing his rig (he still does this), sometimes on a nightly basis, so you had to be ahead of the curve or you weren't going to survive. To accomplish this, the crew was constantly trying to simplify the setup of the rig while staying true to Joe's vision for his sound. Joe was always experimenting with sounds. To keep things from getting chaotic onstage, Rabbit, Henry, and crew chief Nick Spiegel made this change to the band's back line. I'll let Rabbit explain it:

Rabbit and me at a soundcheck.

Rabbit

Joe's amp stack was four custom-built 4 x 12" cabinets mounted in two aluminum welded frames. The frames allowed the speakers to be tilted up and down. Between the speaker cabinets were custom-modified Music Man HD-130 amps. The front had black anodized plates with the Aerosmith logo engraved in silver. In addition, the front panel also had red LED level meters in a horizontal line. The amp had direct outs added to the back so we could feed the PA system and slave the amps. Next to the amp racks toward stage left was what we called the "toy rack," which was an aluminum frame that held a Crown DC-300A with a custom Aerosmith logo. Half of the Crown was used for a wedge, through which Joe could listen to himself, which we would place in different

This is the finished amp line in the late '70s.

Homemade air bag that I've had since 1974.

Using my pedal board to activate the "air bag" during "Sweet Emotion" in the late '70s.

At a soundcheck in the mid-'70s.

positions. The other half of the Crown was used as a wedge through which Joe could listen to Brad; this way Joe did not have to rely on the monitor mixer. On the floor set into the toy rack was a Music Man 212-HD 2 x 12" amp. It was used to power the "voice bag," which was an Electro-Voice driver with a plastic tube attached to it. Designed by Walter Lenk with input from Nick Spiegel, at the top of the rack sat the "toy box," which contained all of Joe's effects pedals. It also had a custom Aerosmith black anodized front plate. The toy box had a custom triple preset MXR digital delay and also contained a Colorsound overdrive, MXR graphic EQ, MXR phaser, and an MXR flanger. There were on/off switches with LED indicators on the front panel. Out of the toy box to the front of the stage was a multi-pin cable connected to the custom V-shaped mic stand. On the mic stand were eight on/off foot switches with small lightbulb indicators. On the same stand, we mounted a small black anodized box with the Aerosmith logo that had LED indicators. Also out on the mic stand was another multi-pin extension, which led to a straight-bar foot pedal; this was placed in the exact area where Joe took his solos. This also had a small lightbulb indicator. There were three places onstage from which the pedal effects could be controlled. I also had a foot switch to kill the feed to the amps so we could repatch the guitars without making noise during the guitar changes. I worked for Joe until spring of 1978, and he was always using a guitar cable. At one point, we checked out the Schaffer-Vega wireless system but decided not to use it. In the tuning room we used a Music Man 212-HD. We modified it by taking one *of the speakers out so we could put tuners in the cabinet. We started with the Conn strobe tuner, and then used a Telesis LED tuner and finally, a Yamaha tuner. The wood cover where the foot pedal for the tuner was stored had a small mirror glued to the inside.*

Back in those days, the band would tune all their own guitars before the show; most of the time the guitars would be out of tune by the time they were used. Joe's collection of guitars grew steadily to twenty-six. One night close to Christmas, Joe asked Rabbit what he wanted for a holiday gift and he replied, "Someone to tune guitars." Enter Neil Thompson.

Neil Thompson and me around 1978 or '79.

Neil Thompson worked in a guitar shop (owned by legendary guitar player Danny Gatton) in Maryland. One night in 1976 he got a call asking if he could come down to an Aerosmith show in Landover, Maryland, to fix some guitars. He came down and helped out. Neil maintained a relationship with Rabbit, and then came George Shack, who by 1978 had taken over for his vegan friend.

Neil was asked to come out on the road for the Live Bootleg tour. He stayed for five years, setting up a tuning room in every venue the band played. His job included tuning, restringing, and polishing every instrument the guys had. By then, Aerosmith was traveling with almost thirty guitars. Neil's days were spent making sure the band members' guitars were in perfect running condition. According to Neil, his tuning room became a safe haven for Elyssa, Joe's wife, who had trouble finding a comfortable place to hang when the guys were sound checking.

Joe had two guitars for every song and then a few more. It was during this time that he started playing his B.C. Rich Mockingbird and then later, the B.C. Rich Bitch. Neil would take the set list and start tuning guitars according to the order in which Joe used them. He would also

The B.C. Rich Bitch 10 String. One of the first off the line.

tune the backup guitars and send them out to the stage, via a runner, to George. In the seventies, the band didn't have the guitar coffins they now use. Every guitar had its own case and had to be accounted for, uncased and cased. Neil would spend all day in this room with a practice amp. If the door didn't have a lock, he would have his meals brought in so nobody

would fuck with the guitars. After the show, all the guitars would be cased up, put in the truck, and moved on to the next city. This was a real burn, as the crew, along with the band, had begun to break down.

Neil was also an accomplished musician and can be heard on the song "Mia" from the album *Night in the Ruts*. By 1983, Joe was gone, and Neil didn't like the direction the band was going in, which was downward. After a canceled tour, he packed it in and moved on. Neil was an innovator and kept the Aerosmith guitar machine running through all the mayhem and chaos.

Three-pickup Black Beauty Les Paul; judging by the outfit, this was taken at Boston Garden.

A Note from Joe

After years of touring with Aerosmith and then a few years on the road with the Project, my custom backline of amplifiers was starting to fall

apart. Right around this time, Peavey Amplifiers, who had a huge following in the country end of the business, was trying to make a mark with the rock and rollers and they offered to supply me a free backline of new amps. I was very thankful for their generosity and used them every night. But not being able to afford road cases, they quickly suffered from the rigors of the road and I used them until they literally fell apart. I'd like to give a big thankful shout-out to Peavey. They were a big help in keeping the Project on the road.

My first Les Paul in the early 1970s.

Elwood Francis

I came on board in the last year and a half of the Joe Perry Project. My brother, Toby Francis, was mixing front-of-house position and I would visit from time to time. I got to know Joe and we'd always talk guitars. Eventually he just asked me to handle his guitars on the road. It really was that simple. Once Aerosmith re-formed, the Joe Perry Project crew was absorbed into the Aerosmith crew along with a few of the old staples: FOH soundman Nitebob, lighting director John Broderick, production manager Joe Baptista, and Joey Kramer's tech, Patrick O'Neil.

Elwood and me.

Most of the guitars had doubles, which were spares for live use. When I list new touring guitars, they are added to the list of previous touring guitars. So the number of guitars grew from year to year (as I'm sure you've noticed). Sometimes a touring guitar is retired for a while. For example, Joe retired the Tele-Rat by 1987, but I read recently that he brought it back out to use. When I started working with the band in 1983, Joe was still using the Aerosmith rack and "A" pedal board. All amps were Andy Topeka–modified Music Man 130 amps paired through 4 x 12"s, four heads and four cabs on Joe's side, with another head and cab on stage right for his cross-stage delay. A Music Man 130 head was also used to power the "air bag" and two Leslie 147s.

"Modified" version of the first generation custom-built amp line, as of late 1978.

The Joe Perry Project touring guitars included:

The Tele-Rat: Left-handed Stratocaster body with left-handed maple Telecaster neck. The body was finished in solid black with the top sanded to natural. It had a black pick guard loaded with three Bill Lawrence pickups originally but those were swapped for Barcus Berry pickups around the Back in the Saddle tour.

Telecaster: Natural with black pick guard and Bill Lawrence pickups, one humbucker in the neck position. This Tele and the Tele-Rat were the main guitars Joe used at the time.

Me and my basement studio in my first house with a custom-made solid rosewood B.C. Rich Mockingbird they built to replace the one that was stolen.

The original Dan Armstrong that I use for open tuning on songs like "Draw the Line" and "Let the Music Do the Talking."

Gibson Firebird. Custom Shop–built. I didn't want to take the original on the road.

This guitar was the second B.C. Rich Mockingbird built. I got it through Nite Bob. He got the first one. This one was stolen within months of me getting it.

A one-off (as far as I know) double-neck B.C. Rich.

One of my first Strats, probably new. The shot was taken at our first sold-out Orpheum show in Boston.

Bill Lawrence prototype: Ash, neck through body.

B.C. Rich Mockingbird: Solid rosewood.

B.C. Rich 10-string Bich: Red.

2 Travis Bean guitars: One black, one silver.

2 Dan Armstrong clear-bodies: One with a Bill Lawrence pickup and the other stock.

Gibson Firebird 7: Sunburst.

I'm also aware of these, but they were not used for Joe Perry Project tours during my tenure with the group:

Fender Bass 6: Sunburst.

Gibson Les Paul Jr.: Refinished in black with custom vine/skull inlay.

Gibson EB-6: Cherry red.

Gibson ES-6: Tobacco burst.

B.C. Rich 6/12 double-neck.

Boogie Body Stratocaster.

Rickenbacker lap steel/amplifier, with motorized tremolo.

Music Man Sabre: Natural finish.

1956 Fender Stratocaster: Black with maple neck. This guitar pops back up in a couple of years. At this point in time it had three Bill Lawrence pickups, but otherwise it was stock.

2 Fender Telecasters: Each with Bill Lawrence pickups, humbucker, and Tele bridge. Dark red and silver, respectively.

Back in the Saddle tour:
The amp line consisted of a row of Marshall 4 x 12" cabs powered by various Marshall heads (JTM45, 1959, JCM800) and the Aero Music Man 130 amps.

The original six-string bass I wrote "Back in the Saddle" with. Very rare with the four switches.

The Strat I used until I left the band in 1979. I used it to record "Walk this Way," and it has gone missing.

My first Tele in the mid '70s.

My 6-string bass for "Back in the Saddle."

On the road with the Mary Kay replica.

Playing one of my first Strats in the mid-'70s.

The "A" pedal board/rack was still being used along with the JPP touring guitars expect for the Firebird and 10-string Bich.

The Fender Bass 6 was brought out for the song "Back in the Saddle."

New guitars included:

Bob Meltz–made lefty Stratocaster: Camo finish, maple Strat neck, Kahler tremolo, single humbucker in the bridge.

2 ESPs: Black, Stratocaster style, two humbuckers. One with rosewood neck, one with maple.

Hendrick Generator: Gumby green. It had an unusual shape, with a humbucker in the bridge and a Telecaster-style neck pickup.

Kramer with a locking tail piece, captured here in 1985.

Done with Mirrors tour:

The amp line was a single row of 4 x 12" cabs powered by various Marshalls (JTM45, 1959, JCM800), and Bedrock (1200, 1400) amps. The "A" pedal board and rack were gone. In their place were amp signal splitters, to send Joe's signal to as many as twelve amps.

Effects: Boss DSD-2 delay/sampler, Boss SD-1 overdrive.

The 1956 Fender Stratocaster was restored to original condition and brought out on tour.

New guitars:

An ESP Stratocaster-style guitar assembled by Nitebob, named "the Spoon," started making an appearance. It had an ash body with flamed maple top, cream binding, and no finish, with three single-coil pickups and a Kahler tremolo. The pick guard was cut down to cover only the control cavity. I modified it to house a bridge humbucker and eventually installed a Floyd Rose tremolo. While I was changing pickups, I took the soldering iron and burned a small skull into the back of the headstock. Joe saw that and liked it, and requested I decorate the entire guitar in that style. It took a long time. This guitar was used in the "Angel" video.

Guild guitars also started showing up, and he used these models:
Aviator: Stratocaster shape but with symmetrical cutaways in black.

Blade Runner: Black. This is the guitar he used in the Run-DMC "Walk This Way" video.

Songbird: Electric/acoustic.

T-250: Black Telecaster style with EMG active pickups and Hipshot B-bender.

Permanent Vacation tour:
Amps were the usual variation of different Marshalls (JTM45, 1959, JCM800, 2550) and a couple of Bedrocks (1200, 1400). The amp line was three stacks of Bedrock 4 x 12"s.

Effects: TC Electronic TC 2290 for delays and chorus, a TC Electronic booster/line driver, and a Marshall Guv'nor overdrive.

New guitars:
1955 Les Paul: Gold finish.

Rickenbacker lap steel.

Fender Champion lap steel.

Gibson SG-1: White, used in the "Rag Doll" video.

Gibson Howard Roberts Fusion: Upgraded with DiMarzio pickups.

Gibson Les Paul Custom Lite: Black with DiMarzio DLX-1 pickups.

3 custom Spector guitars made by Chris Hofschneider: Joe's Travis Bean was traced for the body shape of the first one. The guitar was blue with three Seymour Duncan Hot Rails. The next two guitars were shaped closely

to a double-cut Les Paul Jr. with added contours; one is green and the other a dark-red rubbed finish. Each guitar was equipped with a bridge humbucker and two single coils. They arrived during the tour and the red one was used quite a bit.

"The Donkey." It is kind of ugly.

I also put together a couple of Stratocaster-style rat rods. The first one was blue with left-handed maple neck, three Seymour Duncan Hot Rail pickups, and a pick guard, which covered only the control cavity. The second guitar was a natural wood Stratocaster body with three DiMarzio DLX-1 pickups and a Danelectro neck. Joe referred to this one as the "Donkey" and used it quite a bit (and I don't know why, because I thought it was ugly and odd looking).

Gretsch Silver Jet: 100 percent stock. The guitar was bought from producer Bob Rock and used for the recording and video of "Dude (Looks Like a Lady)."

Pump tour:

Amplifiers of various makes: Marshall (2555, JTM45, 1959, JCM800, Studio 20, & Lead 12), Bedrock (1200 and1400), Aero Music Man 130, Fender Twin, Roland JC-120H, Leslie 147.

Cabinets of various makes: Fender 2 x 12"s, Fender 2 x 15"s, Marshall 4 x 12"s, Bedrock 4 x 12"s.

Effects: TC Electronic booster and Marshall Guv'nor overdrive.

New guitars:

Gibson Les Paul Standard: Black, with Bill Lawrence pickups.

Gibson Les Paul Custom: Wine red, with DiMarzio pickups.

Steinberger TransTrem: Used on the song "Young Lust."

Fender Stratocaster: Black, with Lace Sensor pickups.

Supro Ozark: I picked this up for Joe in Louisville, Kentucky, and sent it to him while they were writing for Pump. *I knew he'd love this one!*

Gibson Chet Atkins SST steel-string solid-body acoustic: Chris Hofschneider installed a Seymour Duncan humbucker wired to a switch to blast through Joe's touring amps for the solo in "Janie's Got a Gun."

Elwood saw Aerosmith rise up and take back their position as the baddest band in the land back between 1984 and 1990, flying high off the success of the *Permanent Vacation* and *Pump* albums.

The next two years, 1991–92, saw Joe and the band take a hiatus from touring. The guys entered the studio in Vancouver to finish *Get a Grip*, Aerosmith's most successful studio album to date and the last album they recorded for Geffen Records.

In need of a guitar tech for the project, Joe tapped Jim Survis, who lives in Vancouver and had just finished work for Jimmy Page. Jim proved to be Joe's longest-tenured guitar tech, staying until 2009.

Jim Survis:

One of the guitars that that really stood out for me at that time was a Supro Ozark guitar on which he played slide with an open tuning. It was the same make guitar that Jimi Hendrix's father bought him as his first guitar. Elwood told me he used it for "Monkey on My Back" from the Pump *album. He used it in open-A tuning. Joe is also into vintage amps and one of his favorites is a 1970 50-watt Marshall. He has many vintage amps, including Marshall, Supro, and Magnatone. He's got all kinds of gear and I learned a lot from him. Joe has a great pedal selection, too, including a whammy pedal that I brought over from my time spent working with Jimmy Page; Joe ended up using that whammy pedal on "Livin' on the Edge."*

That first tour in 1993 was very difficult. We worked many days a week and Joe had a very complex rig. The brain of the rig was a Bob Bradshaw–designed switching system, and that was the crux of it. We had multiple amplifiers; these included a 1962 Vox AC30, an old Matchless head and cabinet, and an old Fender. We also had some Marshalls, and we would switch amps and pedals all night long.

Joe was interested in trying to build a replica of his Tele-Rat guitar from the late seventies, so I found a cheap used left-handed tobacco-burst Strat from Mexico and bought it. Then I went out shopping for a neck and found one with a reverse headstock and I bought that too. I ordered custom-wound pickups from Joe Barden and took all the pieces up to Long View Farm in western Massachusetts, where the guys were recording. After the sessions—I thought we were done for the day and Joe had split—I retreated to my room in the loft and sparked up a bowl of Mother Nature's finest and got baked. Joe ended up staying and we just started putting the guitar together, but we fucked it up good before we did. Joe threw it in the fire and I put it in the deep freezer for a night and really made it look mean. That guitar turned out really good. It's still one of Joe's favorite guitars. He uses it mainly on "Sweet Emotion." It had a whammy bar on it and stayed in tune even with Joe torturing it.

With Jim Survis in the Boneyard, trying to decide on which guitar to use.

Some of the pedals I used for recording *Honkin' on Bobo*.

Another more recent amp line, around 2006.

Jim also took Joe's vision of having a guitar with his wife, Billie, on the front of it.

First, I asked him what kind of guitar and pickups he wanted. Then I told him I knew the perfect guy to draw Billie. His name was John Douglas and he was a great artist and also a drum tech. The guitar itself is a Gibson 335 B. B. King Lucille with no f-holes. It's basically a modified Lucille. He hasn't put it down since he got it. He mainly uses it on "Cryin'," but sometimes uses it on other songs in the set.

Jim Survis's workstation.

After Jim left in 2009, Joe hired Trace Foster. He came in at the tail end of the first leg of Joe's Have Guitar Will Travel tour. Trace was hired to help Joe's interim guitar tech, who was in a little over his head. Joe and Trace immediately hit it off, and Trace has been with Joe ever since. Trace grew up idolizing Joe, so getting to tune his guitars and setting up his amp line was a dream come true. It also proved to be the hardest job he ever had in his life but he's always been more than up for a challenge. Trace had just come off a Melissa Etheridge tour, where he'd tune three or four guitars a night. With Aerosmith, he was thrown into the fire, tuning upward of thirty guitars a night.

Trace

The hardest part of coming in is inheriting somebody's gig. You don't have three or four days in the middle of the week to rebuild a whole rig in the middle of a tour.

The first guitar I pulled out of the rack was the Billie guitar. I had heard all the stories about it and knew it was Joe's most photographed guitar and thought, Wow, this is great but the nut is worn down—I gotta put a new one on it. Also, he had the '59 Les Paul on the road with him. I thought, Geez, I gotta keep my eye on this thing especially in a club, someone could just walk away with it. Thank God Joe usually kept it with him on the bus and brought it out for the sound check. The 1959 Les Paul is the Holy Grail of guitars. With only six hundred made that year, there aren't a whole lot of them around. I had been familiar with those guitars because I was on the road with Cheap Trick, and Rick Nielsen used one. That's the kind of guitar where you don't fix anything on it. You let it go as is, because if you fix something or change something you could knock twenty or thirty thousand dollars off the value of the guitar.

The real '59 after a few takes for my last solo CD, *Have Guitar, Will Travel.*

This is the infamous '59 Tobacco Burst Les Paul.

Reproduction of the '59 Tobacco Burst. You can tell by the smile on my face they did a great job.

Custom Shop–built Tele with Parsons/ White B-Bender.

Plexi B.C. Rich, custom made. Sounds great, looks great.

"The White Rose" that Echopark Guitars made for me in 2012.

A small part of my pedal collection in the Boneyard.

Thanks to Pat Foley at Gibson's custom shop, there is a 1959 reissue model of the exact guitar. Pat took the '59, measured it, and weighed it, so the new one is exactly like the original. Pat and I brought the guitar out to Joe several times and he would say, "The color is off or it doesn't feel quite right; it needs to sound more like this or that." It was a lot of work, but with the finished product you're getting something as close to the '59 as humanly possible.

Joe also uses a thin-line Gibson Les Paul that is a one-off. It was a guitar that Joe had an idea for. It's way thinner and lighter than a normal guitar, and there's only one of them. It has all the extra wood shaved off and only has one volume knob and one pickup. It also has a whammy bar on it, which is also very, very rare. It's black and may be one of my favorite guitars that he plays.

Every night after the set list is approved, I go into Joe's dressing room and run down the set and find out what guitars he feels like playing that night. I'll give him some input and tell him the Strats are sounding really good in this venue. He usually takes my word for it. For some songs he changes guitars, but for "Cryin'" and "Dream On" he always uses the Billie. For "Sweet Emotion" Joe always uses the guitar he and Jim Survis made.

For "Back in the Saddle" he uses a six-string baritone bass guitar. Joe originally used a Fender six-string bass in the seventies, which was stolen. He now uses a Music Man and he has two of them. On the song "Draw the Line" he uses a Dan Armstrong Plexi model.

I used to bring fifty guitars out on the road but I'm now down to thirty; I'm trying to keep our footprint a little smaller.

He has been getting into these new Echopark guitars handmade by Gabriel Currie in L.A. Gabriel came down while they were recording the new album and he and Joe hit it off. Joe gives him input on what needs to be changed, and he has been really happy with the results.

What a lot of people don't realize is that Joe is hands-on with the way his guitars are built and sound and he's not afraid to get in the trenches when it comes to getting the sound and feel he wants.

I have worked for guitar players who are completely clueless when it comes to what they are using. With Joe I wouldn't doubt him if I were you.

Pedal-wise I inherited his pedal board and with his help I completely overhauled it. Every pedal board is made for a specific tour, with specific lengths and cables for specific stage specs. The one I inherited was perfect for the 2010 tour, but for the next tour we redesigned it with the help of a company called Trailer Trash. It's a Plexi see-through pedal board and I also made it a little smaller. There are eight to ten pedals on at any given minute. There's also a siren pedal made by Rob Lohr from Allstonamps for "Livin' on the Edge." His Klon distortion pedal is a mainstay. They're really hard to find now and are worth thousands of dollars. That's his main pedal. Also there is a Duesenberg, which is a 30-db clean-boost pedal, and that one has been regularly used for a few years.

Joe also has two delay pedals. One is a TC Electronic delay pedal, which he programs himself before the tour. We have a TC flanger that he uses on "Sweet Emotion." Another mainstay is an Electro-Harmonix POG. The POG is a guitar synthesizer effect that was upgraded by Rob Lohr. There's a DigiTech whammy *pedal for his lower octaves, and a custom-built wah pedal by Dunlop, which is perfect and one of a kind. He has a Pigtronix distortion pedal and when he hits that one, all hell breaks loose. If he walks away from it I have to run out there and shut it off. We pretty much have doubles for all the pedals but some of them are getting harder and harder to find. I'm always looking for backups.*

On this tour for amps we have two Marshall JCM100 amps, a Morris head from Canada that Jack Douglas turned me on to called an Egnater. It's a small 12-watt amp that's great for grit and growl. A couple of late-sixties Marshall Plexis that are the Holy Grail of amplifiers. Joe has a great relationship with Marshall. They're awesome and will help Joe get any Marshall amps from any year he wants. One of the highlights of my career was getting to tour the Marshall plant with Joe and Paul Marshall. There are tons of other amps, but none can really compare with the Marshall amp. From Hendrix on down, they can't be beat.

A different line-up of amps, around 2010, with the Wandre' guitar.

One of my more recent amp lines.

We just finished a South American tour, and Joe continues to amaze audiences in every country the band visits. Joe Perry is always at the top of the lists when guitar and music magazines have their yearly polls, and he will continue to have that high ranking until the day he decides to keep his axes in their cases, which I don't see happening anytime soon.

SELECTED DISCOGRAPHY

by John Bionelli

Aerosmith Studio Albums (with release dates)

Columbia Records:

Aerosmith (January 5, 1973)

Get Your Wings (March 1, 1974)

Toys in the Attic (April 8, 1975)

Rocks (May 3, 1976)

Draw the Line (December 1, 1977)

Night in the Ruts (November 1, 1979)

Rock in a Hard Place (August 1, 1982)

Geffen Records:

Done with Mirrors (October 21, 1985)

Permanent Vacation (August 18, 1987)

Pump (September 12, 1989)

Get a Grip (April 20, 1993)

Columbia Records:

Nine Lives (March 18, 1997)

Just Push Play (March 6, 2001)

Honkin' on Bobo (March 30, 2004)

Music from Another Dimension! (November 6, 2012)

Aerosmith Live Albums (with release dates)

Columbia Records:

Live! Bootleg (October 1978)

Classics Live I (April 1986)

Classics Live II (June 1987)

Geffen Records:

A Little South of Sanity (October 20, 1998)

Columbia Records:

Rockin' the Joint (October 25, 2005)

Aerosmith Compilation Albums/Box Sets

Columbia Records:

Greatest Hits (October 1980)

Gems (November 1988)

Pandora's Box (November 1991)

Geffen Records:

Big Ones (November 1, 1994)

Columbia Records:

Box of Fire (November 22, 1994)

Geffen Records:

Young Lust (November 20, 2001)

Columbia/Geffen:

Oh Yeah (July 2, 2002)

Columbia/Sony:

Devils's Got a New Disguise (October 17, 2006)

Geffen Records:

Tough Love Ballads (May 10, 2011)

Columbia/Legacy

The Essential Aerosmith (September 13, 2011)

Aerosmith Videography (with release dates)

Aerosmith Video Scrapbook (1987)

Permanent Vacation 3x5 (1988)

Live Texas Jam '78 (April 25, 1989)

Things That Go "Pump" in the Night (1989)

The Making of "Pump" (1990)

Big Ones You Can Look At (1994)

You Gotta Move (November 23, 2004)

Rock for the Rising Sun (July 23, 2013)

Joe Perry Solo Albums (with release dates)

Columbia Records:

The Joe Perry Project, Let the Music Do the Talking (March 1980)

The Joe Perry Project, I've Got the Rock and Rolls Again (1981)

MCA Records:

The Joe Perry Project, Once a Rocker, Always a Rocker (September 1983)

Sony/BMG:

Joe Perry (May 3, 2005)

Roman Records:

Joe Perry, Have Guitar, Will Travel (October 6, 2009)

Notable Aerosmith Bootlegs

New York City, 1975 (Central Park) (http://aerosmithsetlists.com/setlist.php?d=197508290)

Houston, 1977 (http://aerosmithsetlists.com/setlist.php?d=197706240)

Landover, MD, 1980 (http://aerosmithsetlists.com/setlist.php?d=198001250)

Boston, 1984 (http://aerosmithsetlists.com/setlist.php?d=198412310)

Philadelphia, 1990 (http://aerosmithsetlists.com/setlist.php?d=199001210)

London, 1990 (Marquee Club) (http://aerosmithsetlists.com/setlist.php?d=199008200)

Boston, 1994 (Mama Kin) (http://aerosmithsetlists.com/setlist.php?d=199412190)

Osaka, Japan, 1999 (New Millennium) (http://aerosmithsetlists.com/setlist.php?d=199912310)

Joe Perry Bootlegs

Boston, 1979 (http://www.youtube.com/watch?v=WGYVhVkq5PE)

Michigan, 1980 (http://www.youtube.com/watch?v=LHEQg0Vu7KI)

New York City, 2009 (Fillmore show) (http://www.youtube.com/watch?v=8bG29mvuwpk)

Index

PHOTO CREDITS

Photos in the inserts are courtesy of the Perry Collection unless otherwise noted below:

Insert 1

pg. 2 bottom: Bill Wright

pg. 3 bottom left: Bill Wright

pg. 4 bottom: Chris Smith Collection

pg. 6 top: Ed Malhoit

pg. 8 top: Connelly Family Collection; bottom: Ron Pownall

pg. 10 top: Ron Pownall

pg. 11 top: Ron Pownall

pg. 12 top: Ron Pownall; bottom: Dick Hansen, aka Rabbit

pg. 13 top and bottom: Ron Pownall

pg. 15 top: Nite Bob; bottom: Dick Hansen, aka Rabbit

pg. 16 top: Dick Hanson, aka Rabbit

Insert 2

pg. 1 top: Ron Pownall; bottom: Mark Weiss

pg. 4 bottom: Ron Pownall

pg. 5 top: Billie Perry

pg. 6 middle: Billie Perry

pg. 7 top: Billie Perry; bottom: Ron Pownall

pg. 8 top right: Elsa Dorfman

pg. 9 top: Gene Kirkland; bottom: John Bionelli

pg. 10 top: Gene Kirkland; middle: Perry Marguleff Collection; bottom: Robert Knight pg. 11 bottom: Billie Perry

pg. 12 top: Danny Provenzano Collection; bottom: Billie Perry

pg. 14 top: John Quakenbos; bottom: Ross Halfin

pg. 15 top left: Ross Halfin; bottom: Billie Perry

pg. 16 top photos: Paul Lyden; bottom: Billie Perry

Insert 3

pg. 1 top and bottom: John Bionelli; middle: Billie Perry

pg. 2 top: Jessica Squire; bottom: John Bionelli

pg. 3 bottom: Billie Perry

pgs. 4 and 5: Ross Halfin

pg. 6 top and bottom: Ross Halfin

pg. 7 top and bottom: Billie Perry; middle: Adrian Perry

pg. 8 top: Ross Halfin; middle and bottom: John Bionelli

pg. 9 top: John Bionelli; bottom: Michael Coleman

pg. 10 top: Robert Knight; middle: Billie Perry; bottom: Casey Tebo

pg. 11 top: John Bionelli; bottom: Ross Halfin

pg. 12: Sons of Guns

pg. 13: Billie Perry

pg. 14 top: Zak Whitford; bottom: Courtesy of the Sea Shepherds Australia

pg. 15 top: Roman Perry; bottom: John Bionelli

pg. 16 top two photos: Gene Kirkland; bottom two photos: Melissa Mahoney

Appendix

pg. 374: top: Ron Pownall; bottom: Walter Lenk

pg. 375: top: Billie Perry; middle: Walter Lenk; bottom: Ron Pownall

pg. 376: top and bottom: Ron Pownall

pg. 377: top and bottom: Ron Pownall

pg. 378: top: Elwood Francis Collection; bottom: Nite Bob

pg. 379: top left: Karen Whitford; top center: George Chin; top right: Annamaria DiSanto; bottom left: Ron Pownall; bottom center: Billie Perry; bottom right: Ron Pownall

pg. 381: all photos Ron Pownall except: bottom left: Billie Perry

pg. 382: Ron Pownall

pg. 384: Ross Halfin

pg. 386: top left: John Bionelli Collection; center left and center right: Billie Perry; bottom right: Billie Perry

pg. 387: bottom left: Billie Perry; bottom right: Ron Pownall

pg. 388: top left: Zack Whitford; top center: Todd Kaplan; top right: Ross Halfin; bottom left: Perry Collection; bottom right: Billie Perry

pg. 390: left and right: Trace Foster